MW00608434

# MASTERING
## THE ART OF
# COMMAND

# MASTERING
## THE ART OF
# COMMAND

★ ★ ★ ★

## ADMIRAL
## CHESTER W. NIMITZ
## AND VICTORY
## IN THE PACIFIC

★ ★ ★ ★

## TRENT HONE

Naval Institute Press
Annapolis, Maryland

Naval Institute Press
291 Wood Road
Annapolis, MD 21402

© 2022 by the U.S. Naval Institute

All rights reserved. No part of this book may be reproduced or utilized in any form or by any means, electronic or mechanical, including photocopying and recording, or by any information storage and retrieval system, without permission in writing from the publisher.

Library of Congress Cataloging-in-Publication Data

Names: Hone, Trent, author.

Title: Mastering the art of command : Admiral Chester W. Nimitz and victory in the Pacific / Trent Hone.

Other titles: Admiral Chester W. Nimitz and victory in the Pacific war

Description: Annapolis, MD : Naval Institute Press, [2022] | Includes bibliographical references and index.

Identifiers: LCCN 2022009999 (print) | LCCN 2022010000 (ebook) | ISBN 9781682475959 (hardcover) | ISBN 9781682475966 (ebook)

Subjects: LCSH: Nimitz, Chester W. (Chester William), 1885–1966. | World War, 1939–1945—Pacific Ocean. | United States. Pacific Command—Biography. | World War, 1939–1945—Naval operations, American. | Leadership. | Admirals—United States—Biography.

Classification: LCC D767.N56 H66 2022 (print) | LCC D767.N56 (ebook) | DDC 940.54/5973092 [B]—dc23/eng/20220301

LC record available at https://lccn.loc.gov/2022009999

LC ebook record available at https://lccn.loc.gov/2022010000

♾ Print editions meet the requirements of ANSI/NISO z39.48-1992 (Permanence of Paper).

Printed in the United States of America.

30 29 28 27 26 25 24 23 22    9 8 7 6 5 4 3 2 1
First printing

All maps and figures by Jim Caiella

*For Roger Jackson, who reminded me to balance wisdom with compassion.*

# Contents

# Illustrations

**TABLES**

# Acknowledgments

In producing this study, I have been fortunate to benefit from the insight, suggestions, and assistance of many friends and collaborators. Alicia Juarrero and Robert Artigiani have been extremely generous and supportive. They provided feedback on drafts and helped refine my thoughts. A collaborative group of friends—Marc Burgauer, Chris Matts, Sue Borchardt, Greg Brougham, and Jabe Bloom—inspired me to explore new ways to express the challenge of leadership. Fellow historians Frank Blazich, Randy Papadopoulos, Michael Whitby, Jonathan Parshall, Richard B. Frank, Craig Symonds, and John Lundstrom offered feedback and helped me solidify my ideas. My colleague Mathias Eifert recommended some valuable edits. Lauren Hillman, my wife and best friend, read drafts, made suggestions, and was very patient with my research and writing efforts. Without her support, it would not have been possible for me to finish this work.

Stacie Parillo and Elizabeth Delmage of the Naval War College Archives, Barry Zerby, Rick Peuser, Mark Mollan, and Charles W. Johnson of the National Archives, and Chris McDougal of the Nimitz Education and Research Center at the National Museum of the Pacific War provided invaluable assistance locating records, photographs, and other material. Jim Caiella did the maps and diagrams. The editorial team at the Naval Institute Press was a pleasure to work with and helped improve the final product.

Without the assistance of these individuals and many others over the years, this work would have been impossible. I am grateful for them all. Of course, all errors and mistakes are my own.

# Abbreviations

| | |
|---|---|
| ACNB | Australian Commonwealth Naval Board |
| AIC | Advanced Intelligence Center |
| ASF | Army Service Forces |
| BatDiv | battleship division |
| BuAer | Bureau of Aeronautics |
| BuNav | Bureau of Navigation |
| BuOrd | Bureau of Ordnance |
| BuPers | Bureau of Personnel |
| CCS | Combined Chiefs of Staff |
| CENTPAC | Central Pacific |
| CIC | Combat Information Center |
| CINC | Commander in Chief |
| CINCAFPAC | Commander in Chief, U.S. Army Forces, Pacific |
| CINCPAC | Commander in Chief, Pacific Fleet |
| CINCPOA | Commander in Chief, Pacific Ocean Areas |
| CNO | Chief of Naval Operations |
| COMAIRPAC | Commander, Aircraft, Pacific Fleet |
| COMAIRSOPAC | Commander, Aircraft, South Pacific |
| COMANZAC | Commander, Anzac Area |
| COMINCH | Commander in Chief |
| COMSOPAC | Commander, South Pacific |
| COMSUBPAC | Commander, Submarines, Pacific Fleet |
| COMSWPAC | Commander, Southwest Pacific |
| FECB | Far East Combined Bureau |
| FILBAS | Philippine basing |
| GHQ | General Headquarters |

ICPOA   Intelligence Center, Pacific Ocean Areas
IGHQ   Imperial General Headquarters
IJA   Imperial Japanese Army
IJN   Imperial Japanese Navy
JCS   Joint Chiefs of Staff
JICPOA   Joint Intelligence Center, Pacific Ocean Areas
NORPAC   North Pacific
OODA   observe, orient, decide, act
OPNAV   Office of the Chief of Naval Operations
PACFLT   Pacific Fleet
POA   Pacific Ocean Areas
RN   Royal Navy
SevRon   service squadron
SOPAC   South Pacific
SWPAC   Southwest Pacific
TF   task force
TG   task group
USN   United States Navy
VCNO   Vice Chief of Naval Operations

# Selected Code Names of World War II Pacific Operations

| Code Name | Objective Area | Outcome |
| --- | --- | --- |
| Catchpole | Eniwetok Atoll | Executed February 1944 |
| Causeway | Formosa | Deferred |
| Coronet | Honshu, Japan | Deferred |
| Cottage | Kiska, Aleutian Islands | Executed August 1943 |
| Desecrate | Carrier strike on Palau, Yap, and Woleai | Executed March 1944 |
| Detachment | Nanpo Shoto/Bonin and Volcano Islands (Iwo Jima) | Executed February 1945 |
| Flintlock | Marshall Islands | Executed January 1944 |
| Forager | Mariana Islands | Executed June 1944 |
| Galvanic | Gilbert Islands | Executed November 1943 |
| Gymkhana | Mortlock, Caroline Islands | Deferred |
| Hailstone | Carrier strike on Truk Atoll | Executed February 1944 |
| Hotfoot | Carrier strike on Japan | Deferred |
| Iceberg | Nansei Shoto/Ryukyu Islands (Okinawa) | Executed April 1945 |
| Induction | Fast Carrier Support for Operation Mike | Executed January 1945 |
| Insurgent | Fast Carrier support for Operation King II | Executed October 1944 |
| Jamboree | Carrier strike on Japan | Executed February 1945 |

| | | |
|---|---|---|
| King I | Mindanao, Philippine Islands | Deferred |
| King II | Leyte, Philippine Islands | Executed October 1944 |
| Longtom | Chusan Archipelago and Ningpo Peninsula, China | Deferred |
| Love | Mindoro, Philippine Islands | Executed December 1944 |
| Mike | Luzon, Philippine Islands | Executed January 1945 |
| Olympic | Kyushu, Japan | Deferred |
| Reckless | Hollandia, New Guinea | Executed April 1944 |
| Roadmaker | Truk, Caroline Islands | Deferred |
| Stalemate | Palau, Caroline Islands | Executed September 1944 |
| Starvation | Aerial Mining of Japanese Waters | Executed March 1945 |
| Toenails | New Georgia, Solomon Islands | Executed June 1943 |
| Watchtower | Lower Solomon Islands (Guadalcanal and Tulagi) | Executed August 1942 |

# INTRODUCTION

*Of all the activities in which mankind engages, it is the
conduct of war that envelopes it with the greatest
degree of uncertainty, ambiguity, and friction.*

—Williamson Murray[1]

In *Learning War*, published 2018, I explored the U.S. Navy as a complex adaptive system. I used that frame to demonstrate that the Navy developed a learning system in the early years of the twentieth century and then used its capacity for learning to accelerate victory in World War II. In his *New York Times* review of *Learning War,* journalist Thomas E. Ricks pointed out that the "hero" of my narrative was "not an individual but a large, complex organization."[2] Ricks' assessment was correct, and it hints at an underlying conundrum. Viewing organizations as complex adaptive systems has the potential to diminish the importance of individual action. If our organizations are systems and their evolution can be explained through the influence of past experience, broad trends, and emerging constraints, what role do individuals play?

This work builds on *Learning War* and seeks to answer that question by examining the potential and promise of leadership in complex adaptive systems. In such systems, individuals are considered "agents," because they have agency and can act to achieve desirable outcomes. Individual action can be extremely influential, especially if it comes at an opportune moment, but collective action is where the promise of organization lies. Collective action allows organizations to achieve outcomes that are beyond the reach—potentially beyond the conception—of any single individual. Leadership has two parts to play in this process. It translates individual agency into collective action and harnesses it to achieve organizational goals. It also "structures and enables conditions" that allow "creative problem solving." Through these two dynamics, leaders simultaneously set direction, defining the challenge or opportunity, and shape the process within which solutions emerge. To understand the full potential of individuals in complex adaptive systems, it is essential to explore how leadership emerges and how leaders exert their influence.[3]

Emergence is a dynamic event. It occurs when interactions between elements of a system spawn a new entity with properties that none of the individual elements possess. Many examples of emergence occur in nature. The most widely cited is the Bénard cell, a macroscopic structure that spontaneously appears in a liquid when it is heated from below. Before the heat is applied, the temperature of the liquid is broadly uniform, but as the heat increases, temperature gradients appear. When these gradients reach a certain threshold, the dynamics of the fluid change. Previously random movements of fluid molecules become constrained by the gradients. Eventually, convection cells emerge and within each of them billions of molecules "rotate in a coherent manner along a hexagonal path, either clockwise or anticlockwise, and always in the opposite direction from that of its immediate neighbors."[4] Bénard cells are an emergent phenomenon, and once in place, they exert a powerful influence on the molecules of the fluid, perpetuating themselves by reinforcing the pattern of interaction so long as there is available energy—the external heat—to do so. Tornadoes and typhoons are similar examples of emergent natural phenomena.

Leadership is also emergent, but arises from human systems, triggered by the energy people bring to their relationships. As management professor Mary Uhl-Bien has explained, leadership is "a complex interactive dynamic" that results from patterns of interactions between individuals. The existence of hierarchy—the relationship between superior and subordinate—implies leadership but does not guarantee it. Complexity requires a narrower and more precise definition. Superiors offer direction and guidance because of their positional authority; leaders, in contrast, inspire collective action through the relationships they maintain with those they lead. As part of this process, leaders continually earn the right to lead from others. The interactive dynamic of the relationship is the source of leadership. A leader's positional authority may or may not correspond to the degree of leadership they exercise. When there is a close correspondence, and an effective leader is also in a position of high authority, their potential for influence is greater because their positional authority can reinforce their leadership efforts. That increases their opportunity to spur collective action and rapidly move an organization toward its goals.[5]

That movement can be greatly assisted by leadership's second dynamic, which involves creating an "environment in which knowledge accumulates and is shared at low cost." Leaders foster "new learning, innovation, and new patterns of behavior" by enabling the "informal network dynamics" that allow knowledge to be more rapidly acquired. Leaders broker connections and interactions that allow varied alternatives to be explored through an organization's informal social network. This "network-based problem solving" scans options more quickly than centralized approaches and maximizes the potential of individual agency for collective benefit. When coupled to a means of filtering and refining solutions based on suitability, the result is increased "capacity for learning, creativity, and adaptability" at the organizational level.[6]

Viewing organizations as complex adaptive systems requires confronting these interrelated dynamics. Leaders exist within systems; separating them from their context is impossible. Assuming that they are independent actors who exert their influence on people or organizations that are somehow "separate" or "distinct" is inherently flawed. This forces a reassessment of prevailing assumptions surrounding military "genius." Victory or defeat has been frequently attributed to the inspired action of specific individuals, gifted commanders who possess the skill and experience to triumph over their enemies. Napoleon Bonaparte, Horatio Nelson, Ulysses S. Grant, Helmuth von Moltke, Ferdinand Foch, Georgy Zhukov, and Võ Nguyên Giáp are all worthy examples of this tendency, but as historian Cathal J. Nolan has pointed out, "[C]laims to genius distance our understanding from war's immense complexity and contingency, which are its greater truths."[7] Recognizing leadership as an emergent property of complex interactions allows us to access these truths more readily.

This work attempts to do that by investigating the leadership of Adm. Chester W. Nimitz as commander in chief of the Pacific Fleet (CINCPAC) and commander in chief of the Pacific Ocean Areas (CINCPOA) during World War II. It argues that Nimitz emerged as an extremely effective leader because he demonstrated a practical understanding of the two fundamental dynamics described above. He fostered collective action through effective collaboration among talented individuals and stimulated rapid learning and evolution to take advantage of new opportunities. This allowed Nimitz and his staff to create and explore new options—alternative means of fighting the war—and employ a disciplined approach to risk that balanced tactical decisions with strategic objectives. The result was an organization that blunted Imperial Japanese offensives, seized the initiative in the Pacific, and rapidly brought war to the shores of Japan.

## PREDISPOSITIONS

Leadership emerges from context. In complex adaptive systems, the importance of context is explained by the fact that systems are path dependent; their history constrains their future potential. Historian Williamson Murray alluded to this fact by emphasizing the value of history to the formulation of strategy: "A perceptive understanding of the present based on historical knowledge is the essential first step for thinking about the future."[8] History orients a system toward a particular set of futures, making some outcomes more likely than others. That orientation of a system—the greater likelihood of certain future states—is called its dispositionality.

Before assessing Nimitz's leadership as CINCPAC and CINCPOA, it is essential to place him in context and explore his dispositions. In the years before World War II, the Navy developed and refined a particular culture of command that deliberately created leadership opportunities. Outwardly, this culture emphasized decentralized authority; it relied on clear, mission-based orders that provided direction and fostered the initiative of subordinates. An informal network of connections—personal relationships between officers—supported these formal structures. Intimate familiarity, developed through years of shared experiences and collaborative relationships, was the medium through which the Navy's officer corps exercised command and encouraged leadership to emerge.

Nimitz demonstrated his skills at navigating the Navy's leadership culture as commanding officer of cruiser *Augusta* in the early 1930s. At the time, *Augusta* was flagship of the Asiatic Fleet and Nimitz was committed to ensuring that his ship excelled in all manner of competition. Her crew won gunnery exercises, individual marksmanship competitions, and athletic sports. Nimitz encouraged these achievements, but indirectly. He made his officers responsible for the performance of the crew in these competitions and delegated authority to his officers. At the same time, Nimitz set the expectation that they should strive to excel. To encourage them, Nimitz modeled the kind of behavior he desired, serving as a supportive example of effective leadership. Consistently, Nimitz's subordinates responded to the opportunity by demonstrating their initiative, creativity, and skill in a relentless pursuit of perfection.[9]

Lloyd M. Mustin, who eventually rose to the rank of vice admiral, was a junior officer on board *Augusta* during that time and remarked on Nimitz's methods: "That approach was, in very simple terms—here's the job to be done, here are the conditions under which it is prescribed to be done. We're going to go out, and not only are we going to do it, but we're going to do it better than anybody else. We're going to do it as close to perfection as human limitations permit. And we're never going to be content with anything short of that." Nimitz applied this approach to all the ship's operations. Officers who failed to embrace it or hesitated to work toward it—those who chose not to lead—were quietly removed from the ship. "Nimitz was very direct and completely ruthless, and he very speedily weeded out three or four of the officers. . . . Someone else was given their jobs."[10]

Mustin also fondly recalled how Nimitz arranged a series of lectures for *Augusta*'s officers to give them a broader appreciation of the situation in the Far East and the importance of China to U.S. foreign policy. Numerous influential individuals presented their views, including the Chinese finance minister, the Chinese minister of education, Julean Herbert Arnold, the U.S.

commercial attaché in China, and Nelson T. Johnson, the U.S. minister to China. The lectures were deliberate efforts to foster connections and grow knowledge. Mustin believed one of Nimitz's "great strengths" was the personal accumulation of knowledge from direct observation and broad experience. He encouraged ongoing education and created learning opportunities for himself and his subordinates.[11]

In the years immediately before the war, Nimitz built on his experience commanding *Augusta* and employed his skills ashore. His capacity for identifying and developing talent led to work at the Bureau of Navigation (BuNav), first as the assistant chief in 1935, and then, in June 1939, as its chief. At the time, BuNav was responsible for personnel matters. Nimitz decided which officers would be assigned to which billets and became very familiar with their service histories and leadership potential. He was still serving as chief of BuNav when the attack on Pearl Harbor brought the United States into the war.

This history gave Nimitz a specific set of dispositions, traits he would continue to emphasize as CINCPAC and CINCPOA. First, he stressed excellence, performance "as close to perfection as human limitations permit." However, he balanced that against a second trait, a habit of working through his fellow officers and inspiring them to take an interest in the growth of their subordinates. Nimitz emphasized leadership as a collective pursuit, not an individual activity. His third disposition was a focus on education; he encouraged his colleagues to learn and expand their knowledge to give them a broader base of experience to inform their decisions. Finally, Nimitz had extensive familiarity with the challenge of placing the right officer in the right role at the right time; as chief of BuNav, this was his major focus. He shifted officers into positions intended to maximize individual potential for collective benefit. These dispositions would influence Nimitz's approach throughout the war.

## FOSTERING EVOLUTIONARY CHANGE

Viewing organizations as complex adaptive systems helps explain how they evolve, adapt, and change. Leadership plays an important part in this, not only by fostering learning and innovation, but also by anchoring it to established organizational goals and missions. Historian Arthur Schlesinger, in his essay

"Democracy and Leadership," explained the challenge leaders face in a way that complements Uhl-Bien: "[There] is a perennial gap between inherited institutions and beliefs and an environment forever in motion. The mission of democratic statecraft is to keep institutions and values sufficiently abreast of the accelerating velocity of history to give society a chance of controlling the energies let loose by science and technology. Democratic leadership is the art of fostering and managing innovation in the service of a free community."[12]

This perspective can be generalized to organizations of all kinds and is especially applicable to military institutions like the U.S. Navy. As the world and our understanding of it changes, the inertia of human organizations and their governing policies lag, creating a gap. Leadership can help to close the gap by fostering the continual refresh of the perspectives that inform organizational behavior. This is a specific form of organizational learning and, in the early twentieth century—a period of substantial technological change—the Navy proved adept at it. While Nimitz was honing his leadership skills in the Asiatic Fleet, the Navy was exploring new tactics and technologies, identifying the most promising of them, and exploiting those for future use. The most visible aspect of this learning system was the regular cycle of contested exercises, the Fleet Problems, which led to a series of innovative approaches in the fields of naval aviation and surface warfare tactics. This learning system was well established by the time war broke out in December 1941.[13]

However, during the interwar period (1919–39), many of the Navy's fundamental assumptions about a potential war in the Pacific remained unchallenged, even as tactics and technology changed rapidly. The gap between "beliefs and an environment forever in motion" grew unseen until it was starkly revealed by Imperial Japanese offensives in the opening weeks of World War II. When he assumed command of the Pacific Fleet at the end of December 1941, Nimitz had to move beyond the limits of the Navy's interwar learning system and foster a broader reorientation to close this gap and refresh the perspective of his officers.

This is the process that Col. John Boyd, USAF, described as "orientation," arguably the most important and least understood component of his *observe, orient, decide, act* (OODA) loop. According to Frans P. B. Osinga of the Netherlands Defence Academy, "developing, maintaining, and reshaping one's orientation" was an "essential feature" of Boyd's theory. He recognized that organizations exist in "an environment forever in motion." For Boyd, proper orientation—a valid assessment of currently prevailing circumstances—was a prerequisite for effective observation, decision-making, and action. He urged the development of "a repertoire of orientation patterns" and the ability to rapidly switch between them to "select the correct one according to the situation at hand." The ability to reorient in this way would grant an organization "the capability to evolve, to adapt, [and] to learn."[14]

Leadership is an essential part of this process. Leaders can make the need for reorientation more apparent by highlighting the gap that exists between current beliefs and prevailing circumstances; they can encourage the acquisition of new knowledge to help close the gap; and they can foster collective action that adjusts the environment and makes future circumstances more likely to align with current beliefs. Because of the complex dynamics surrounding leadership, the actions of a leader can serve one or more of these ends simultaneously, and the impact of those actions will vary based on the established organizational context. Four specific factors are most important when considering a leader's ability to influence evolutionary change: resonance, adaptive capacity, psychological safety, and the organization's ability to process information.

If a leader's actions reflect and reinforce organizational predispositions, then those actions resonate, and their impact is amplified. Resonant actions *feel* correct. Even if they trigger substantial change, the change will be welcomed because it reflects an existing dispositionality, a leaning toward a possible future that members of the organization have already felt or recognized. As the resonance builds, others will embrace the promised future and cohere with it. Coherence is an emergent property that reflects increased shared understanding, prompts unity of effort, and obscures the original source of resonant action.

The process is analogous to jazz improvisation; psychologist Keith Sawyer described it in his study of group creativity: "My years of playing piano in jazz ensembles convinced me that what happened in any one person's mind could never explain what made one night's performance shine and another a dud. At any second during a performance, an almost invisible musical exchange could take the piece in a new direction; later no one could remember who was responsible for what. In jazz, the group has the ideas, not the individual musicians."[15] For Sawyer, the resonant medium that provided coherence was the music; for Nimitz as CINCPAC and CINCPOA, the resonant medium was the unfolding conflict. For both, the emerging coherence fostered collective action and resulted in an outcome that was far more than the aggregated sum of individual efforts.[16]

Nimitz created more space for resonant action by increasing the adaptive capacity of his organization. Adaptive capacity is a term used by David Woods, the codirector of Ohio State University's Cognitive Systems Engineering Laboratory, to describe the boundaries of performance in social-technical systems, like nuclear power plants, commercial aircraft, and operating rooms. These boundaries are conceptually similar to the limits of belief that constrain institutional organizations. As unanticipated outcomes arise in these systems, they call on their adaptive capacity—their "potential for modifying what worked in the past to meet challenges in the future"—to absorb these surprises and continue functioning. As Woods points out, adaptive capacity can be exhausted unless proactive steps are taken to extend and increase it. Either sufficient adaptive capacity is there to be called upon when the moment comes, or it is not; if not, the system will fail, often catastrophically. To avoid this, Nimitz deliberately increased the adaptive capacity of his organization to allow it to overcome unanticipated and surprising challenges.[17]

One of the ways Nimitz increased adaptive capacity was by fostering psychological safety. Like leadership, psychological safety is an emergent property of relationships; it arises from a pattern of interaction. Harvard professor Amy C. Edmondson defines it as "the belief that the work environment is safe for interpersonal risk taking." In psychologically safe environments, individuals feel comfortable sharing their thoughts and ideas; they take the initiative to move the organization toward its goals. Edmondson suggests leaders can build psychological safety in three primary ways: by establishing shared expectations and common meaning; by inviting others to participate and acknowledging their contributions; and by establishing norms that reward continual learning and sanction undesirable behavior. Doing this, Edmondson argues, will maximize organizational performance, a stance that applies equally well to today's "knowledge intensive world" and Nimitz's challenge in the Pacific.[18]

Finally, Nimitz enhanced his command's ability to keep pace with the unfolding conflict by modifying organizational structures to enhance his command's ability to process information. As historian Ryan Grauer has noted, "[T]he inherently uncertain nature of combat very often renders military power a function of armed forces' capacity to collect, transmit, process, and act on information about emergent opportunities and challenges on the battlefield." Nimitz actively sought to increase his abilities in these areas because he recognized that "an edge gained through institutional mechanisms permitting swift and accurate perception of battlefield developments can be decisive" and that "effective information management" plays "an outsized role in determining which side achieves its objectives."[19] Nimitz's efforts in this area aligned with his predisposition to learning and the leadership dynamic encouraging the discovery of new information.

Nimitz used these approaches to prompt more rapid and more effective sensemaking, so that his command could regularly and consistently reorient and keep pace with the war in the Pacific. He recognized that conflict is a struggle for understanding, and that by increasing his organization's capacity to assess, analyze, and interpret the emergent nature of the fighting, he could gain an advantage. At the same time, Nimitz recognized that organizational learning was only one aspect of a successful strategy.

## THE ART OF STRATEGY

If leadership is an emergent phenomenon that enhances an organization's ability to evolve and change, it becomes a useful lens for examining how best to formulate and execute strategy. As described above, change was central to Boyd's concept of orientation, but orientation involves more than "individual and organizational learning." For Boyd, the ability to reorient is half the battle; the other half necessitates preventing the enemy from doing the same. OODA is as much a theory of combat as organizational learning. The strategic objective, as Boyd argued in his "Patterns of Conflict," is "to diminish [the] adversary's capacity to adapt while improving our capacity to adapt ... so that our adversary cannot cope while we can ... as [events] ... unfold."[20]

What Boyd recognized is that conflict is a struggle of mindsets. The side that can better align its conceptual understanding with the unfolding nature of war will see more clearly, react faster, and act more decisively. Prussian military theorist Carl von Clausewitz understood this when he emphasized that war is "not a contest between individuals" but a struggle of wholes in which the "will is directed at an animate object which *reacts.*"[21] Bending the enemy to our will means imposing our conceptualization onto the arena of combat and making it more dominant—and thereby more accurate—than our opponent's. Strategy, then, is how an organization achieves, shapes, and sustains "fitness" for its operating context.[22]

Leadership is essential to this process. The most successful approaches to defining, developing, and executing strategy use the concepts of leadership introduced above. Leaders emerge, spur actions that resonate with established organizational dispositions, prompt collective action, and foster the emergence of coherent approaches that enhance an organization's fitness for the unfolding future. This process requires continual refinement, adjustment, and adaptation. As historian Jon Sumida explained in his detailed study of the works of Alfred Thayer Mahan, U.S. Navy officers recognized the artistic nature of this challenge. There were no linear prescriptions that could be mechanically followed that would lead to success:

Naval officers require an artistic sensibility because in war they are confronted by problems that are difficult, complex, and unpredictable. In conflicts at sea, decisions must be made quickly in the face of incomplete or misleading information, physically arduous surroundings, manifold and unanticipatable error by subordinates, personal danger, and awareness of an awesome responsibility for the lives of others and military outcomes. Like musicians, who must have a nearly simultaneous sense of not only their own expression but the response of the audience, with adjustments in performance made if required, naval commanders must be capable of judging situations in terms of both their action and the reaction of their opponent and choose their course from "a flowing series of possibilities" rather than a static menu of certain formulae.[23]

Boyd, Mahan, and Clausewitz all touched on various aspects of this challenge. Boyd believed strategy required "constant adaptation to shifting conditions and circumstances in a world where chance, uncertainty, and ambiguity dominate."[24] Clausewitz emphasized the continual revision of approaches and posited theory as a means to drive questioning that would "prevent bad intellectual habits . . . from determining strategic courses of action."[25] For all three, success in war could not be delivered by precise prescription. It required, to use Sumida's analogy, a "performance" informed by an artist's touch.

In the Navy of Nimitz's time, this performance was not an individual exercise. Like Sawyer's jazz ensembles, it was a collaborative effort, and much like Sawyer's experience, it was difficult to determine who was ultimately responsible for what. The writer Fletcher Pratt elegantly described the emergent nature of the process. There were "too many questions" for senior officers to work through all the details of crucial decisions. Instead, that work was done by "juniors, especially the staff officers." Attribution for specific ideas was nearly impossible because naval officers tended to resolve their disagreements behind closed doors in "wardroom conversations." It was "rarely possible to assign any development to an individual, or to say what an individual" had done. Accomplishments were an outcome of collaborative partnerships. In Pratt's view, individual officers were "a signpost indicating direction" and little more. This is exactly what Rear Adm. Bradley A. Fiske had in mind when, in 1916, he suggested the Navy would operate as a "vast and efficient organism" held together "by a common understanding and a common purpose." Both Pratt and Fiske ably described how leadership prompted the emergence of coherent action in the Navy's complex system.[26]

This was Nimitz's challenge, to navigate the uncertainty of war in a way that allowed him to build upon the Navy's existing predispositions, foster rapid learning, inspire the members of his organization to coherent action, and maintain the fitness of his organization for the war's unfolding context. Simultaneously, he had to work to deny the same opportunities to the enemy. Nimitz sought to fold the Japanese back upon themselves, restricting their ability to conceptualize and pursue desirable futures. Nimitz's effort to perform "as close to perfection as human limitations permit" led to a strategic orientation that maximized the potential of his organization and continually challenged his enemy. His approach to leadership demonstrated the importance of the concepts introduced above—accelerated learning, resonant action, adaptive capacity, psychological safety, collaborative decision-making, and improved structures for information processing—and showed how they can increase organizational effectiveness. As CINCPAC and CINCPOA, Nimitz led in an artistic way that recognized the inherent complexity of this challenge.

The chapters that follow explain how he did this. They are divided into three main sections. The first three chapters examine the period from December 1941 to June 1942. During this time, Nimitz developed a coherent way forward in the aftermath of Pearl Harbor, earning the confidence of his superiors and subordinates, and proving that the Pacific Fleet could defeat the Japanese in battle. The next three chapters explore July 1942 to October 1943 and the challenge Nimitz faced building a team that could execute his vision. That team first seized the initiative in the Pacific by winning victory at Guadalcanal, and then prepared for the Central Pacific offensive. The last four chapters follow the course of that offensive from November 1943 to August 1945. They focus on the flows that made it so rapid and successful; to achieve victory, Nimitz had to improve the flow of information, the flow of logistical supplies and material, and the flow of combat forces across the Pacific. Together, these chapters recount how Nimitz helped the United States and its Allies achieve victory.

# PROLOGUE

*I only hope I can live up to the high expectations*
*of you and the President and the Department.*

—Adm. Chester W. Nimitz[1]

On the evening of Saturday, 20 December 1941, the *Super Chief*, flag-ship passenger train of the Atchison, Topeka, and Santa Fe Railway, pulled out of Chicago's Dearborn Station. The train moved west across the plains, its diesel locomotives decorated in the railroad's unique "warbonnet" scheme—a stylized mix of red, yellow, and silver evocative of the American southwest. "Mr. Freeman," a silver-haired gentleman in his mid-fifties, penned a note to his wife. He described the "lovely rolling country, nice farms . . . wide vistas and far-off horizons." His secretary, a young man named "Mr. Wainwright," chose this opportunity to burden Freeman with details of his new assignment. He opened a canvas bag and pulled out a report. Wainwright recalled years later, "We opened up this thing and it was simply ghastly. I mean it was full of photographs of all the battleships turned upside down, the complete havoc that was at Pearl Harbor."[2]

The report was a detailed description of the Japanese attack. In the report, the commander in chief of the United States Pacific Fleet, Adm. Husband E. Kimmel, enumerated the damage. He began with the battleships. *Arizona*'s forward magazines had exploded, and the ship was "a total wreck." *California* had been struck by torpedoes and bombs; she was resting on the harbor bottom. *Nevada*'s crew, after freeing her from her moorings and getting under way, beached her in the harbor at hospital point. *Oklahoma* capsized from a rapid succession of torpedo hits. *Pennsylvania*, relatively unscathed in her drydock, was "ready for service." *Maryland*, although damaged, would be "fully ready" soon. *Tennessee* was wedged into her berth by the sunken *West Virginia*; the "Mountain State" battleship had been hit by at least four torpedoes and heavily damaged by fire, but at least she was upright. Three cruisers, three destroyers, and four auxiliaries had also been damaged. Losses in personnel and planes were commensurate with the extensive damage to the ships of the fleet.[3]

As the *Super Chief* made its 2,200-mile journey to Los Angeles, Freeman contemplated the challenge of his new role. He was on his way to Pearl Harbor to command the entire Pacific Fleet (PACFLT). "Freeman" was an alias; he had borrowed his wife's maiden name to travel incognito. Adm. Chester W. Nimitz watched the countryside stream past and tried to absorb the full implications of the fact that he had been asked to win a war being fought across the world's largest ocean. "I am sure," he wrote, "that by the time I reach Pearl Harbor, I will be able to meet the requirements of the situation."[4] The situation would be far more taxing than he anticipated.

When the train arrived at Los Angeles, Nimitz left his secretary—who was also traveling incognito; his true identity was Lt. (jg) H. Arthur Lamar— behind and continued on to San Diego. There, he boarded a PB2Y Coronado for the flight to Pearl Harbor. The first attempt to take off on 23 December failed; a powerful gust of wind caught the seaplane's wing and swamped the engines. The next day, Christmas Eve, 1941, they tried again. Nimitz wrote in a quick note to his wife, "I greatly regret taking these pilots away—and the crews—on Christmas Eve but I see no choice on my part." He personally apologized to them before the plane took off at 1600 that afternoon.[5] The next day, he arrived at Pearl Harbor.

# ASSUMING COMMAND

*It is an experiment, as all life is an experiment.*
—Oliver Wendell Holmes Jr.[1]

**W**hen Nimitz's plane landed in Pearl Harbor on Christmas morning, the physical aftermath of the attack—tangible and malodorous—dominated the scene. Nimitz observed "black oil, charred wood, blistered paint, and burned and rotting bodies" floating in the water. The psychological impact was arguably even more palpable. The once-proud PACFLT was wounded and reeling. Nimitz was met upon his arrival by its interim commander, Vice Adm. William S. Pye, commander, Battle Force; Rear Adm. Patrick N. L. Bellinger, commander of Patrol Wing Two; Capt. William W. "Poco" Smith, Kimmel's former chief of staff, and other staff officers.[2]

Nimitz quickly realized that he would face two challenges. First, he had to rebuild the morale of the Pacific Fleet's officers and men. The attack had shattered their confidence. They were indecisive and uncertain. Second, Nimitz had to establish a foundation for future success; he had to bring these men together and create a cohesive team that could fight and win. So far, the war had been dominated by a string of impressive Japanese victories. Nimitz had to counter this narrative. The two goals were inextricably linked; rebuilding morale would create more opportunities and achieving a victory would help restore confidence. The goals were also crucial for Nimitz. To achieve his other military objectives—the orders he would soon receive to defend the Hawaiian Islands and communications between the West Coast and Australia—he would have to restore the Pacific Fleet's faith in its leadership and in itself.

It would not be easy. The Japanese attack had been a devastating blow. It was intentionally designed to break the will of the U.S. Navy and convince its officers, its sailors, and the American people that a long war to thwart Japanese war aims in the western Pacific was not worthwhile. The attack failed to accomplish these objectives, in large part because the Navy, under Nimitz's guidance, rapidly recovered and the American public, angered by the surprise attack, overwhelmingly called for vengeful retribution. However, the psychological impact of the strike, and the extremely negative influence it had on the Navy's morale, should not be overlooked. When Nimitz assumed command and became commander in chief, Pacific Fleet (CINCPAC) on New Year's Eve, 1941, that negative influence, and the fractious atmosphere it created among senior officers, dominated Pearl Harbor. The Navy's rapid recovery was not guaranteed; it occurred because of the decisive steps Nimitz took to harness existing predispositions and create the potential for future success.

## EXISTING PREDISPOSITIONS

The Navy entered World War II with a set of well-established decision-making heuristics that had been developed and refined during the interwar period (1919–39). In the early 1920s, the second Chief of Naval Operations (CNO), Adm. Robert E. Coontz, had invested in a "learning system" built around an annual planning cycle. The most visible elements of this system were the large exercises, the Fleet Problems. The Fleet Problems and other supporting exercises trained the fleet for war and explored the challenges of a campaign in the Pacific against the Empire of Japan. They fostered the emergence of new approaches and led to the development of a particular mindset.[3]

The Fleet Problems were open-ended, contested exercises. They were intended to provide officers an environment where they could explore the potential of new technologies, like aviation, and new tactics, such as carrier operations. Through these exercises, the Navy developed new tactical doctrines, integrated new technologies, and refined its operational planning for the anticipated war in the Pacific. Officers realized that a rapid advance to the Philippines, an approach often described as the "through ticket," was a "failed strategy." Instead, they would have to advance more methodically and seize a series of advanced bases.[4]

Three tactical heuristics—subconscious mental guides for problem-solving—emerged during this period and exerted an outsized influence on the Navy's approach to battle. The first of these was an emphasis on aggressive, offensive action. Officers were conditioned to seize the initiative, control the pace of battle, and keep the enemy off balance by forcing him to react. The best way to do this formed the basis of the second heuristic—attacking effectively first. This is a modern term, coined by naval tactician Capt. Wayne P. Hughes Jr., but it accurately describes how the Navy trained its officers and men. Every weaponry exercise rewarded getting on target early and securing hits as soon as possible.[5]

The third heuristic was a logical corollary of the other two. To attack effectively first in the uncertain environment of battle, officers were trained to exercise their individual initiative. Opportunities for decisive action were expected to be momentary and fleeting. To seize them, officers had to be free to use their best judgment and not wait for permission or detailed instructions from their superiors. The Navy recognized this need early in the twentieth century and, during the interwar period, actively sought to enhance the ability of officers to think independently and act on their own initiative. This approach was augmented by an educational system that emphasized crafting orders and instructions designed to exploit the initiative of subordinates. The resulting method, called the *Estimate of the Situation*, was intended to present subordinates with a "problem" that they had to solve, a mission that they could use their creative energies to accomplish.[6]

The rapid expansion of the Navy in the last few years of peace forced career officers and senior enlisted personnel to focus their energies on more basic forms of training. Nevertheless, the three tactical heuristics—using aggressive action, attacking effectively first, and employing decentralized command and control—were core elements of the Navy's doctrine and embedded in officers' mental models. The heuristics informed their self-image. Navy officers were comfortable playing the role of the aggressor. Pearl Harbor disrupted this image. Although the Navy's war plans had long anticipated that the Japanese would initiate hostilities through a surprise attack, it was assumed that the blow would be against the Philippines and the bulk of the Navy would execute its deliberate strategy—moving across the Pacific, seizing advanced bases, and taking the war to Japanese shores. The raid on Pearl Harbor demolished those preconceptions, undermined Kimmel's plans for war, and struck at the foundations of the officer corps' identity.

## KIMMEL'S AGGRESSIVE PLANS

Admiral Kimmel had been appointed CINCPAC on 1 February 1941 because President Franklin D. Roosevelt wanted an aggressive commander willing to implement his concept of strategic deterrence. Roosevelt had deployed the fleet to Pearl Harbor in 1940 as a check to Japanese ambitions. He wanted to deter them from taking advantage of the war in Europe to seize European colonies in Southeast Asia. Adm. James O. Richardson, commander in chief of the U.S. Fleet when Roosevelt decided to base the fleet at Pearl Harbor, opposed the strategy. He complained directly to Roosevelt about Pearl Harbor's inadequacy as a base and wanted to keep the fleet on the West Coast. However, the Navy's planners in Washington, including CNO Adm. Harold R. Stark and head of the War Plans Division Rear Adm. Richmond Kelly Turner, were convinced that their aggressive posture had "persuaded the Japanese to keep their Combined Fleet at home."[7] Roosevelt agreed. He removed Richardson and replaced him with Kimmel. Kimmel immediately looked for ways to thwart Japanese plans if they decided to attack south.

A "warrior full of fight," Kimmel was aware that his predecessor had been relieved for opposing Roosevelt's strategic vision. He looked for guidance; Kimmel asked Stark how aggressively he could threaten the flank of a Japanese attack on the oil-rich Dutch East Indies. The CNO responded "that he could risk severe losses." Kimmel accordingly worked with his war plans officer, Capt. Charles H. McMorris, to devise an aggressive plan that would draw out the Imperial Japanese Navy's (IJN's) Combined Fleet.

Nicknamed "Soc" because of the Socratic wisdom and piercing intelligence he brought to his work, McMorris translated Kimmel's "instinctive ferocity" into "vivid plans of maneuver." The result was Navy Plan O-1, also known as WPPac-46. McMorris had a draft ready in March 1941 and refined it over the next several months; Stark approved a formal version on 9 September. The plan was designed to trigger a major fleet action with the Japanese in the central Pacific between the islands of Wake and Midway.[8]

Kimmel expected to use his three carriers—*Lexington, Saratoga*, and *Enterprise*—in a single raiding force commanded by Vice Adm. William F. Halsey Jr., commander, Aircraft, Battle Force. The plan expected Halsey to "reconnoiter and raid" Japanese positions in the Marshall Islands for up to four days, destroying ships, aircraft, and installations. Afterward, Halsey would retire and fall back on Kimmel's main body, with all nine of the Pacific Fleet's battleships. After a brief rendezvous, Halsey would leave the battleships behind and return to the Marshalls. This time, he would strike any Japanese ships that had been drawn to the Marshalls by his first sortie.[9]

In his study of prewar Navy operational planning, Edward S. Miller called this dual sortie into the Marshalls "a bizarre stratagem." The first raid would have alerted Japanese defenses and drawn aerial reinforcements. The second "would have courted disaster." Stark offered criticisms while chart maneuvers in PACFLT revealed the "probability of high losses," but McMorris refused to revise the basic outline of the plan. Miller has argued the plan was a deliberate effort to draw out the Combined Fleet; Halsey's carriers were bait for the Japanese battle line. Kimmel expected Admiral Yamamoto Isoroku, commander in chief of the Combined Fleet, to "put in at Truk for fuel and then approach the Marshalls from the west-southwest." If Yamamoto pursued Halsey, the Combined Fleet would encounter Kimmel's battleships, concentrated and waiting somewhere between Wake and Midway. PACFLT patrol planes operating in "maximum practicable" strength from those islands were expected to locate and strike the Japanese carriers to offset their numerical superiority. If Yamamoto followed Halsey, a decisive battle line engagement was expected to ensue, and Kimmel hoped to win it with guile, subterfuge, and aggressive tactical maneuvers.[10]

## THE SHATTERING BLOW

The Japanese attack on Pearl Harbor left Kimmel's plan in tatters and shattered his fleet's sense of superiority. The attack was a surprise in multiple, interwoven ways. It was a tactical surprise; the defenses of the naval base and surrounding airfields were caught unprepared that Sunday morning. It was also a "technological and doctrinal surprise" because the raid was delivered by an unprecedented force, the IJN's First Air Fleet, or *Kido Butai*.[11] The *Kido Butai* concentrated naval airpower in strength that was wholly unanticipated by the U.S. Navy. Finally, the raid on Pearl Harbor was a form of "model surprise" that shook deep assumptions American naval officers held about themselves and their place in the world. The combination of these factors explains why the attack was so disruptive and Nimitz's efforts to overcome the associated shock so important.[12]

The way the surprise attack unfolded has been thoroughly and repeatedly documented. In the early morning hours of 7 December, planes from six Japanese carriers struck Pearl Harbor. "By ten o'clock that morning, as the second wave departed . . . the American battle line at Ford Island had been shattered, and the aircraft at Hickam, Wheeler, and Bellows airfields and those at Kaneohe Naval Air Station lay in shambles." The military success enjoyed by the Japanese was, to a significant degree, enabled by the fact that they achieved complete tactical surprise.[13]

But that success was guaranteed by the new strategic capability inherent in the First Air Fleet. The *Kido Butai* was a new concept in naval warfare. Formed in April 1941, under the command of Vice Admiral Nagumo Chuichi, it brought together three carrier divisions into "the single most powerful agglomeration of naval air power in the world." There was no comparable equivalent in any other navy. Although the U.S. Navy had invested heavily in naval aviation, developed a sophisticated carrier doctrine, and even performed mock attacks on Pearl Harbor during the Fleet Problems, it had failed to conceive of the potential of integrating all its major carriers together into a single cohesive striking force. When the *Kido Butai* struck Oahu, it exposed a significant and unanticipated American vulnerability; there was no effective response to "six carriers and some four hundred aircraft that could appear and disappear at will."[14]

The IJN used the attack to undermine the preconceptions of the American people and their naval officers. Writing long after Pearl Harbor, Col. John Boyd, USAF, articulated a view of strategy as the effort to "dissolve" the enemy's "moral fiber, disorient his mental images, disrupt his operations, and overload his system."[15] Boyd's point was that an effective strategy will undermine an opponent's view of the world and his place in it. Implemented effectively, such a strategy would knock the enemy off balance, physically, mentally, and morally. The attack on Pearl Harbor struck all three of these levels.

The attack on Pearl Harbor was more than a military operation. It was an attempt to undermine what the Japanese had come to see as an "Anglo-Saxon supremacist ideology" that allowed Americans to self-identify as "the chosen people" and "saviors of the world." The attack was designed to crush these illusions; the destruction of the Pacific Fleet would break American will by sweeping away the pillars upon which the American sense of moral and racial superiority rested. The strike combined the IJN's long-standing faith in the power of decisive battle with a spiritual and moral blow designed to expose the fallacies in America's chauvinistic world view. As Cathal J. Nolan put it, "Americans would quail before Japan's demonstrated *seishin* (national spirit)." The IJN hoped to create a psychological state of incapacitation—known to eighteenth-century armies as *panique-terreur*—and thereby force the United States "to accede to Japan's regional dominance."[16]

Rapid advances in the western Pacific would augment the psychological blow and further cripple American resolve. The Philippines would be isolated and captured. The Dutch East Indies would be occupied. British possessions would be seized. The Royal Navy would be driven from the Pacific. Together, these triumphs would create "a great transformation in American public opinion," allow Japan "to establish a durable self-sufficient economic position," and deliver a quick victory over the United States. If the United States did not agree to an armistice, then the occupied territories—the Greater East Asia Co-prosperity Sphere—would provide the raw material to allow Japan to emerge victorious from the ensuing attritional struggle.[17]

On these merits, the attack must be judged a failure. Rather than convincing the American people that their assumptions of racial superiority were unfounded, the raid on Pearl Harbor was seen as further evidence of the deceitful underhandedness of the Japanese. American resolve was strengthened, and a newly unified nation quickly prepared for war with unprecedented resolve. However, the impact on the senior officers of the Pacific Fleet was quite different. For a force that considered aggressive action and exploitation of the initiative as core aspects of its approach to war, being caught off guard by such a powerful attack was devastating. The Japanese assessment—that a sufficiently powerful strike would undermine American morale at the outset of war—was remarkably prescient, if not for the American people, then certainly for PACFLT. Before Admiral Nimitz assumed command, "despair filled Pacific Fleet headquarters" as Admiral Kimmel and his staff desperately tried to recover from their shock.[18]

## DESPERATE DEFENSE AT WAKE

Before Pearl Harbor, Kimmel prepared Wake Island for his Plan O-1 and sent a marine defense battalion, a squadron of fighter planes, and twelve hundred civilian workers to the island. After Pearl Harbor, he resolved to defend the island and moved quickly to augment its defenses.[19] Unfortunately, the effort to reinforce Wake Island failed to keep the Japanese from capturing it and the loss of Wake became symbolic of PACFLT's impotence in the immediate aftermath of Pearl Harbor.

Kimmel issued initial orders for the reinforcement of Wake on 10 December; they called for Vice Adm. Wilson Brown, commander of the Scouting Force and Task Force (TF) 12, to escort seaplane tender *Tangier* to the island. *Tangier* would bring additional troops and supplies and withdraw the civilian contractors. McMorris examined the plan and noted that Japanese land-based bombers in the Marshalls could attack Brown while he approached and *Tangier* while she anchored off the island. McMorris proposed a raid against Jaluit Atoll, timed to occur the day before the relief force arrived off Wake, to suppress Japanese forces and ensure the relief got through. Brown's orders were revised. He would raid Jaluit with his newly designated TF 11 built around carrier *Lexington*. Rear Adm. Frank J. Fletcher's TF 14, with carrier *Saratoga*, would escort *Tangier* to Wake. Destroyer *Drayton* was sent three hundred miles south of Pearl Harbor to transmit messages and attempt to deceive the Japanese as to the location of Kimmel's striking forces.[20]

In the meantime, Secretary of the Navy Frank Knox arrived at Pearl Harbor. On his own initiative, he had left Washington two days after the Pearl Harbor raid. Knox wanted to assess the damage and observe Kimmel and his officers firsthand, to see how they were handling the war in the aftermath of the attack. After Knox returned to Washington on 14 December, he hosted a lengthy meeting at the Navy Department with CNO Stark and other senior officers. Two important, but independent, decisions were made the next day. First, Knox met with Roosevelt and convinced the president that Kimmel had to be relieved. Second, Stark authorized Kimmel to reinforce both Wake and Midway.[21]

Kimmel responded to Stark's authorization with a detailed message that presented various options for Wake. The island could be either evacuated or reinforced. A third option, "abandoning the garrison and defense workers" was never seriously entertained. Kimmel argued vehemently for reinforcement and pointed out that it would require *Tangier* to be on station "at least two days." Brown's diversion was designed to keep Japanese land-based air suppressed or distracted during that time. Stark responded that he "heartily concurred" with the plan.[22]

The operation was under way, but Kimmel would not see it through. On 17 December, he was removed as CINCPAC and ordered home. Vice Admiral Pye, commander, Battle Force, became interim CINCPAC. Pye was a former head of the Office of the Chief of Naval Operations (OPNAV) War Plans Division and a master of the art of crafting thorough and detailed plans. As a younger officer he had distinguished himself with his intellectual capacity and literally written the book on fleet scouting operations. He was also visibly shaken from the Pearl Harbor attack and hesitant to take major risks.[23]

Pye brought his staff with him to CINCPAC Headquarters, including Rear Adm. Milo F. Draemel, commander Destroyers, Battle Force, who became CINCPAC chief of staff for operations. Pye sought to put his own stamp on the relief expedition. Within a few days, he had produced an estimate emphasizing increased enemy activity in the Marshalls and his own ignorance of Japanese plans and capabilities. Pye noted that Brown would "probably" not be able to achieve surprise, might sustain "serious losses," and, therefore, his diversionary raid was too risky. Pye cancelled it on 20 December. Instead, he arranged PACFLT's three carrier task forces—Brown's TF 11, Fletcher's TF 14, and Vice Adm. William F. Halsey's TF 8—in a defensive line east of the Marshalls outside of Japanese search range. They were too far apart to immediately support each other and not arranged to quickly take the offensive.[24]

That same day, Wake reported an attack by carrier aircraft, reinforcing intelligence that a Japanese carrier division was in the vicinity. On 22 December (23 December west of the international date line at Wake), Japanese assault forces arrived. When word of the attack reached Pearl Harbor, Pye, Draemel, and McMorris discussed options, but could not agree what to do. Pye had them write their arguments down. Pye's estimate began with the claim that the "relief of Wake" by the "present expedition [is] now impossible." The only question was whether "to attack enemy forces in vicinity of Wake." Although Pye acknowledged that there was a "possibility of doing extensive damage to the enemy," he felt it was contingent on achieving tactical surprise. There were significant risks; the loss of PACFLT carriers would allow the Japanese to mount a "major operation against the Hawaiian Islands." Although Pye did not provide a specific conclusion in his estimate, he favored withdrawing all three carrier task forces without attempting to strike the Japanese.[25]

McMorris' estimate, in contrast, was characteristically aggressive. He noted that there was "no direct evidence of more than one" enemy carrier in the vicinity and that they had a favorable opportunity. McMorris acknowledged that the relief expedition could not continue as planned but that was of "secondary importance." What mattered now was striking the enemy. McMorris assumed the Japanese carrier attacking Wake was relatively small. Fletcher's *Saratoga* therefore had the "odds strongly in her favor." McMorris urged that they take advantage of the opportunity and attack "as soon as possible with TF 14" while TF 8 and 11 closed in support. This last point revealed the flaw in Pye's dispositions. Ignorant of enemy intentions, Pye had placed the carrier TFs too far apart for mutual support; if they were to strike, Fletcher would have to begin the battle alone.[26]

Draemel agreed that the important question was whether to strike the Japanese, but he thought it likely that the Japanese had anticipated the relief expedition and would therefore be "fully prepared" to meet it. Rather than a favorable opportunity, Draemel felt Wake was a trap. The Japanese might seek "a major engagement" and he asked whether PACFLT was willing to accept one so far from its base and with such a small potential margin of superiority. Draemel highlighted the risks: "[T]here are no reserves—*all* our forces are in the area of possible operations" and concluded that the situation dictated "extreme caution." He favored the abandonment of Wake.[27]

Dire news from Wake—Cdr. Winfield Scott Cunningham sent his famous message, "The enemy is on the island. The issue is in doubt"—hung over the conference as Pye and his staff discussed their options. Pye ultimately felt the risk was too great and decided that the relief expedition would turn back. Rear Adm. Herbert F. Leary and Draemel agreed with the decision. Capt. Poco Smith and McMorris, imbued with the former CINCPAC's sense of aggressiveness, were incensed at the lost opportunity and abandonment of Wake's defenders; they "barely contained their fury and contempt." Fletcher, when he received the order to withdraw, threw his hat to the deck in disgust. Wake's defenders surrendered the following day. Two days later, Nimitz arrived at Pearl Harbor.[28]

## ROOSEVELT CHOOSES A NEW TEAM

After Knox and Roosevelt decided to remove Kimmel, the president asked his Navy secretary to recommend a successor. Knox, referring to a list submitted to Roosevelt containing potential candidates to succeed Admiral Richardson, replied that he would be "satisfied with the second name on the list."[29] That name was Chester W. Nimitz. Roosevelt was familiar with Nimitz from the admiral's work in the Bureau of Navigation (BuNav); Nimitz had been assistant chief of the bureau from August 1935 until September 1938 and had been serving as its head since June 1939. As chief of the bureau, Nimitz was responsible for personnel, and he had been working diligently to secure billets for his fellow officers that matched their experience and skill. He had earned a reputation as an honest broker who could be trusted to handle such decisions professionally and fairly.

Roosevelt also looked upon him favorably, and earlier in the year, when Admiral Richardson had been removed, the president had offered command of PACFLT to Nimitz. He had "qualifications that made him a suitable relief for Richardson. He had shown himself a gifted administrator and was noted for making do with next to nothing." However, Nimitz had turned down the opportunity; he would have been promoted ahead of many other more senior officers and was apprehensive of the negative impact it would have on men he would have to work with so closely.[30] Now, Roosevelt turned to him again.

Nimitz's ability to resolve personal conflicts fairly and honestly was a key factor in Roosevelt's decision. Blame would be sought for the defeat at Pearl Harbor; there was a risk that the Navy would be torn apart by bitter recriminations and criticism. Roosevelt had witnessed such disputes firsthand. As assistant secretary of the Navy under Josephus Daniels, he had been embroiled in the disputes that erupted between Daniels and Adm. William S. Sims in the aftermath of World War I. As a young man, Roosevelt had followed the controversy that ensued after the Spanish-American War, when Rear Adm. William T. Sampson, Commo. Winfield Scott Schley, and their respective supporters spent years refighting the Battle of Santiago.[31] If American naval officers were this contentious after their victories, how would they handle a shocking defeat? A steady, firm, and capable hand was necessary to revive PACFLT and harness its energies toward war.

Roosevelt was confident that Nimitz would be that capable hand and dissolve potential disagreements before they erupted into public controversies. Not only had Nimitz developed a sterling reputation for his performance at BuNav, but he was also vehemently opposed to any public airing of the Navy's internal disputes. E. B. Potter's biography, which Nimitz helped shape, emphasizes Nimitz's negative reaction to the Sampson-Schley controversy. Nimitz resolved to never make such disputes public. Roosevelt was aware of this conviction. He also knew Nimitz was "acquainted with every senior officer in the Navy" and suspected he could forge those officers into an aggressive, coherent team that could execute the nation's strategy.[32]

Nimitz foreshadowed how he might do this in his 1923 Naval War College thesis. In it, he enumerated four "main and unchanging principles of warfare":

1. To employ all the forces which can be made available with the utmost energy.
2. To concentrate superior forces against the enemy at the point of contact or where the decisive blow is to be struck.
3. To avoid loss of time.
4. To follow up every advantage gained with utmost energy.

Nimitz also listed several minor principles; the first of them would prove most important: "Attempt to surprise and deceive the enemy as to the plan of battle, and method and point of attack." As Nimitz grappled with the challenges facing the Pacific Fleet, these principles informed his actions.[33]

Nimitz was not the only new member of the Navy's high command. On 30 December, Adm. Ernest J. King was named the new commander in chief, which he abbreviated COMINCH. The new post was to be in Washington, where, in collaboration with the president and other senior military leaders, King could formulate the Navy's strategy for global war. King was an officer of superlative competency. He had served on the staff of Atlantic Fleet commander Adm. Henry T. Mayo during World War I, in destroyers, and in submarines, and had earned his wings at the age of forty-eight. As an aviator, he had commanded patrol planes and carriers, and had headed the Bureau of Aeronautics (BuAer). In December 1940, he had become commander of the Patrol Force, later redesignated the Atlantic Fleet. King brought to his commands a firm, irascible disposition, demanding from his subordinates the same kind of competency that he himself displayed. He wasted no time impressing on the operating forces how he planned to exercise command: "It is my intention that command shall be exercised by the issue of general operating plans and/or directives and that pertinent discretion and responsibility shall be vested in appropriate principal subordinates in chain of command."[34]

King emphasized decentralized control. He wanted to foster the initiative of his subordinates and gave clear direction to Pye and Nimitz: "Consider tasks assigned to you summarize into two primary tasks in order of priority: first, covering and holding line Hawaii–Midway and maintaining its communications with West Coast; second, and only in small degree, less important, maintenance of communication West Coast–Australia, chiefly by covering, securing, and holding line Hawaii–Samoa which should be extended to include Fiji at earliest practicable date."[35]

The security of the Hawaiian Islands was in doubt. Less than two weeks before, Stark had told Pye that "Knox is not yet satisfied that Hawaiian Islands are safe from capture" and that if the Japanese struck again, any planes they destroyed "cannot be replaced except after a long period." Pye assumed a defensive posture designed to preserve his naval forces and ensure the security of Hawaii. This contributed to his decision to cancel Brown's raid and abandon Wake. Pye and Stark both feared another raid.[36] In order to ensure a coherent defense, all Army forces in the Hawaiian Coastal Frontier were placed under CINCPAC on 18 December. This positive step abolished the divided command structure that had contributed to the disaster at Pearl Harbor. However, more assertive steps were necessary, and it soon became clear to Nimitz that Pye's defensive attitude was hindering the fleet's ability to meet King's objectives.

## THE PREREQUISITE: ESTABLISHING SAFETY

Before assuming command, Nimitz worked diligently to assess the developing situation in the Pacific. He learned the details of the failed Wake expedition, the threat to Pearl Harbor, and the psychological damage the attack had wrought. To his wife, he wrote, "It seems like I am in a treadmill whirling around actively but not getting anywhere very fast."[37] That may have been so, but Nimitz quickly sensed the friction triggered by Pye's decision to abandon Wake, the divergent perspectives among the staff, and their lack of confidence. Although their sense of risk varied, it was clear that they hungered for an opportunity to strike back against the Japanese but could not agree how to do so. After assuming command of PACFLT on 31 December, Nimitz immediately set about solving this problem.

In 1961, Nimitz told Rear Adm. Henry E. Eccles of the Naval War College that his first challenge was to "restore the morale and confidence of the [staff] officers," many of whom were in a "state of shock." Capt. Elphege Alfred M. Gendreau, the fleet surgeon, was explicit with Nimitz about the condition of the officers; they were stunned, and something had to be done to reinvigorate them. Nimitz wanted to give them a clear and immediate sense of purpose so that they could be useful in the developing conflict. As Eccles recalled, "Nimitz said to me that 'my job was to save about fifty good officers for the Navy.'"[38]

When he assumed command, Nimitz departed from tradition and took a unique and compelling approach to "saving" those officers. Rather than bringing in his own staff—a team that reflected his own predilections— Nimitz retained the entire CINCPAC team. This was very deliberate; it was also unusual. All the staff members, associated in one way or another with the debacle of Pearl Harbor, expected to follow Kimmel and to be relieved.[39] Nimitz implicitly, by retaining them, and explicitly, in personal conversations with them, expressed his faith in their skills and abilities, and their usefulness to the coming conflict. He believed this was more important than bringing in his own team.

William W. Drake, Kimmel's public relations officer, recalled how Nimitz communicated his intention to the staff:

> In a very few minutes [after calling the staff together], speaking softly and slowly, he convinced all hands of his ability to lead us out of the wilderness. He began by describing the meetings in Washington which led to his selection. He emphasized that he had urged the appointment of Admiral Pye, "but such," he said, "was not to be," with Admiral Pye sitting alongside of him. As to the fleet staff, he said, there were going to be no changes. "I know most of you here, and I have complete confidence in your ability and your judgment. We've taken a whale of a wallop but I have no doubt of the ultimate outcome."[40]

This expression of confidence was an essential first step in rebuilding morale. Nimitz retained McMorris and his team as his War Plans Section. Draemel became Nimitz's chief of staff and head of the Operations Section. His responsibilities as commander, Destroyers, Battle Force were transferred to Rear Adm. Robert A. Theobald. Pye stayed on as a senior adviser. Lt. Cdr. Edwin T. Layton, the staff intelligence officer, asked to be reassigned. He wanted command of a destroyer; Nimitz kept him on, confidently assuring him he could be of more value on the PACFLT staff. Capt. Poco Smith was due to be promoted to rear admiral; Nimitz sent him to sea as commander of the cruisers in Vice Admiral Brown's TF 11. Rear Adm. William L. Calhoun remained commander of the Fleet's Base Force.

Smith's transfer to sea command was part of Nimitz's developing strategy. In addition to retaining staff members, he wanted to give his officers opportunities to lead and to strike back. Nimitz also wanted to increase the resiliency of his carrier task forces. He ordered each carrier task force commander to command from the carrier and assigned a rear admiral to each task force to command the cruiser screen and "lead surface attack groups." Smith took this role for TF 11 on 6 January. Rear Adm. Raymond A. Spruance, who had been commander of Cruiser Division Five, became Vice Admiral Halsey's cruiser commander in TF 8; Rear Adm. Thomas C. Kinkaid became Rear Adm. Herbert F. Leary's cruiser commander in TF 14. Rear Admiral Fletcher, now commanding TF 17 with carrier *Yorktown*, lacked a flag officer for his cruiser group; command fell to Capt. Elliott B. Nixon of cruiser *Louisville*.[41]

Nimitz's decision to retain and give opportunities to the members of Pye's and Kimmel's staff was important, but it was the way he brought them together to use their collective intelligence that was decisive. Nimitz established a regular routine of conferences and briefings; these worked on two levels. The first was an early-morning briefing with select members of the staff at 0800. Often, this was Layton's opportunity to present the latest intelligence; the intent of the session was to bring Nimitz up to speed on emerging opportunities. At 0900, an open conference was held. These were designed to allow the entire command—initially PACFLT and later Pacific Ocean Areas (POA)—to orient to the current situation. "Key members of the CINCPAC Staff, visiting fleet and task force commanders, and senior participants in forthcoming operations" were all expected to attend. Other senior commanders were welcome, including Lt. Gen. Delos C. Emmons, who replaced Lt. Gen. Walter C. Short as the Army's commander of the Hawaiian Department, and Rear Adm. Claude C. Bloch, commander of the Fourteenth Naval District, which included the Hawaiian Islands.[42]

The morning conferences fostered open dialog; Nimitz used them to draw out and exploit the collective intelligence of the assembled officers. Collective intelligence is the ability of a group to utilize the diverse knowledge and skill of the individuals within it. Collective intelligence is "an emergent property" that depends on how the group operates and works together. "Group structures, norms, and routines that regulate collective behavior" can enhance "coordination and collaboration" or work against it. One of the most important factors in collective intelligence is the average "social perceptiveness" of group members, how well they sense others' emotions and respond to them.[43]

Nimitz's regular morning conference was not a briefing or a one-way transfer of information. It was a collaborative session where the entire team made sense of the war unfolding in front of them. It was a structured norming mechanism that fostered the growth of collective intelligence. Nimitz intentionally welcomed conversation and debate; he believed that "an idea is more likely to generate, a decision is more likely to be reached, in informal conferences" where individuals were free to express their opinions.[44] The collaborative discussions that took place during these conferences were an essential aspect of Nimitz's approach. They allowed him to draw out ideas, make sense of emerging opportunities, and create common understanding with his staff and subordinates.

The way Nimitz hosted and facilitated these sessions was also extremely important; Nimitz was extremely socially perceptive and very effective at creating an environment of what Harvard professor Amy Edmondson has called "psychological safety." Psychological safety is "a shared belief that the team is safe for interpersonal risk taking." It is an essential ingredient for organizational learning and collective intelligence. For a team to "discover gaps in its plans and make changes accordingly, team members must test assumptions and discuss differences of opinion openly rather than privately or outside the group." Nimitz's conferences created this ability. The psychological safety he fostered within his staff allowed differences of opinion to emerge and alternative perspectives to be entertained. It gave him more options, and it gave his staff a sense that their opinions were valuable and would be useful. It created an atmosphere of effective collaboration.[45]

Meir Finkel, in his study on the importance of doctrinal flexibility, has stressed the value of these kinds of environments: "There is no alternative to an approach that encourages critical debate, initiative, and independent thinking and creates the kind of openness that enables commanders to adapt impromptu to unexpected circumstances." This is exactly what Nimitz worked to achieve with his conference routine. His initial decision to retain the PACFLT staff expressed his confidence in them and was a vital step toward creating an environment that encouraged ideas and opinions to be shared, contested, and discussed. It was an essential prerequisite to developing effective solutions to overcome the new and surprising military capability represented by the *Kido Butai*.[46]

## THE EXECUTION: HALSEY STRIKES BACK

In the first few weeks of his command, Nimitz "made every effort to convince his staff and his force commanders that an offensive strategy was the only way to win in the Pacific." Shortage of weapons and vast distances were no obstacle; the Japanese faced them too.[47] This approach dovetailed with that of Admiral King. On 1 January, Nimitz's first full day as CINCPAC, King urged him to "thoroughly consider" a raid "against enemy bases in Gilbert Islands . . . and/or in Ellice and Phoenix Groups . . . preferably coordinated with Samoa reinforcement expedition in order to, first, cover latter, second, check increasing enemy threat to Samoa–Fiji area, [and] third, *undertake some aggressive action for effect on general morale* [emphasis added]."[48] That third point especially resonated with Nimitz; in the CINCPAC files, the final phrase in King's message was underlined, potentially by Nimitz himself. He recognized that an offensive strike could address the enduring "state of shock" and be the salve his staff and senior officers needed.

The aggressive Captain McMorris satisfied Nimitz's desire for a plan to strike back. Ever since the attack on Pearl Harbor, McMorris and his assistants had been formulating a series of estimates for offensive moves. On Christmas Day, he devised a plan to strike the Japanese-held islands of Mili and Makin with TF 11 and thereby cover King's Samoa reinforcement convoy. On 2 January, McMorris followed up with a more detailed plan. In it, Brown's TF 11 would attack Wotje and Maloelap in the Marshalls in mid-January. Halsey's TF 8 would attack positions in the Gilbert Islands a few days later, covering the Samoan reinforcement effort and distracting the Japanese. Rear Admiral Fletcher's TF 17 would escort the convoy itself.

Nimitz's last carrier task force, Leary's TF 14, would offer distant support and cover the Oahu–Midway line.[49]

The next day, Brown's TF 11 entered Pearl Harbor. Although Nimitz never acknowledged that Brown was his first choice for the attack into the Marshalls, the evidence suggests that he was. Brown was the senior carrier task force commander, McMorris planned Brown's TF 11 would make the first strikes, and Nimitz recalled that "his first choice for command was very unhappy and said that it was too dangerous."[50] Nimitz approached the situation carefully. Although Brown declined to lead the offensive, Nimitz refused to relieve him or let the conversation tarnish his record. Nimitz recognized that many officers had been shocked by the strength of the initial Japanese offensives, but he had faith that skillful leadership would allow them to recover. For Nimitz, officers like Brown were redeemable.

If Brown would not attack into the Marshalls, Nimitz would have to find someone else. On the afternoon of 7 January, Halsey's TF 8 entered Pearl Harbor. Nimitz presented him with the opportunity. Halsey "jumped at the chance" and said "he would go anywhere." Nimitz had found his man. Pye refined McMorris' plan and made it more conservative by switching the targets to Mili and the Gilbert Islands of Tarawa and Makin. Pye also recommended that the strikes wait until after the reinforcement convoy was safely at Samoa; that would allow Halsey's TF 8 and Fletcher's TF 17 to concentrate and make simultaneous strikes against all three objectives.[51]

Nimitz agreed with this basic concept; the task forces would strike after the convoy arrived. However, he kept his options open, instructing Halsey and Fletcher that "[b]ecause of the time that will elapse between issuance of this plan and probable date of attacks, conditions may materially change; consequently specific positions to be attacked are not prescribed." Halsey was empowered to "choose the points of attack and the manner of conducting it." Nimitz would share details of emerging intelligence to help Halsey pick his targets.[52] The plan was not without risk; the Japanese positions were mutually supporting and could muster "considerable over-all strength." They also had an active submarine force. The same day that Halsey departed Pearl Harbor, 11 January, carrier *Saratoga* was torpedoed by submarine *I-6*. The Japanese believed they had sunk her; she survived, but was seriously damaged, eliminating Leary's TF 14 as a carrier striking force and reducing Nimitz's strength.

In the meantime, the urgency of striking into the Marshalls increased. The Australian Commonwealth Naval Board (ACNB) informed Nimitz on 9 January that their intelligence suggested the Japanese were concentrating in the Marshalls and Carolines for an attack on the islands that formed the line of communication to Australia. Fiji appeared to be "the most probable objective." From radio intercepts, Nimitz knew that the Japanese Sixth Fleet, with a variety of light forces, was based at Jaluit, and from submarines and Allied aerial reconnaissance he knew that there were bombers, fighters, and auxiliaries among the islands. King asked about the date the reinforcement convoy would arrive, and Nimitz responded that it would be 20 January. TFs 8 and 17 would "cover arrival and unloading" and then "make simultaneous air attacks [on] Gilberts and eastern Marshalls."[53] He was already considering a more aggressive plan than Pye's concept.

While the convoy headed to Samoa, Nimitz kept Halsey and Fletcher apprised. The Japanese appeared to be preparing for a campaign of interdiction to the east. Wake was becoming an "air base" and a unit described as the "19th Air Corps" was moving to the island; an estimated eighteen submarines were operating east of the Marshalls, with some basing at Jaluit. Unusual Japanese radio traffic suggested "a certain apprehension" about lines of communication, but there was "no concentration of any surface forces" that could threaten Halsey in the Marshalls. There were, however, planes and auxiliaries. Submarine *Dolphin* observed bombers, transports, and "five large ships" at Kwajalein Atoll in mid-January. Other ships were at Jaluit. These were perfect targets for Halsey.[54]

On 20 January, King urged Nimitz to accelerate the raid, as the "time factor appears paramount." To the west, the Japanese were advancing rapidly through Allied colonial possessions. King also suggested a raid on Wake "two or three days after [the] attacks" to augment Halsey's strikes and increase the damage to Japanese installations. Nimitz discussed alternatives with his staff, and they agreed to send Brown's TF 11 to "conduct [a] raid on Wake" because of the "morale factor and the indicated desires of COMINCH." These plans were cancelled on 23 January when oiler *Neches*, operating in support of

TF 11, was torpedoed and sunk. In the meantime, the large natural harbor of Rabaul on the island of New Britain fell to the Japanese.[55]

Intelligence available to Nimitz suggested Japanese attention was focused to the south, creating the opportunity for a more aggressive raid; he ordered Halsey to "expedite" his planned operation, to reduce the time spent covering the convoy, and if Halsey considered it prudent, to extend the objectives to include the western Marshall Islands of Jaluit and Kwajalein. Prompted by these messages, Halsey issued a plan that reflected Nimitz's instructions and shared it from Samoa on 23 January. Halsey would depart Samoa on "F Day" and fuel during his approach three days later. Three days after that, on "F+6," TF 8 would make "coordinated air attacks on Jaluit, Makin, and Mili at dawn." Fletcher's TF 17 would operate at a distance, in tactical support and ready to strike any force that threatened TF 8.[56]

By the evening of 24 January, the reinforcement convoy had safely arrived. TFs 8 and 17 were soon heading to the northwest. Halsey planned F+6 to be 1 February. Because he was west of the international date line, Nimitz and his staff expected the strikes on 31 January. Additional radio intelligence and submarine reconnaissance revealed more information about Japanese activities in the Marshalls; most of their forces appeared to be supporting the southward advance. The time was ripe for a strike from the flank. King pressured Nimitz: "Assume you are aware of serious enemy threat to communications with Australia . . . and have recognized that while it is inadvisable to divert part of Halsey expedition in that direction it is essential that planned attack in Marshalls be driven home."[57]

Nimitz was aware; the ACNB requested "a diversion from Japanese southward advance" and he acted decisively. He urged Halsey and Fletcher to strike aggressively: "Estimate enemy forces Marshalls have been considerably reduced in order to support operations to southwestward. Now is opportunity to destroy enemy forces and installations [in] Gilberts [and] Marshalls, and it is essential that attacks be driven home. Exploit this situation by expanding operations utilizing both task forces in such repeated air attacks and ship bombardments as developments and logistics make feasible." After receiving Nimitz's fresh instructions, Halsey and his staff adjusted their plans. TF 8 would divide into three task groups and strike Japanese bases in the heart of the Marshalls. Wotje, Maloelap, and Kwajalein would be hit simultaneously; air strikes would be coordinated with bombardments by surface ships. Fletcher's TF 17 would strike the objectives of Halsey's earlier plan: Jaluit, Mili, and Makin.[58]

The aggressiveness of Halsey and Nimitz was rewarded. The attacks came as a complete surprise to the Japanese. The first strike on Kwajalein killed Rear Admiral Yashiro Yukichi, who would have coordinated a response as commander of the Sixth Base Force.[59] The Japanese command structure was thrown into confusion. After nine hours in the middle of the Japanese defensive network—his planes bombing and strafing, his cruisers bombarding installations—Halsey and his task force withdrew. Fletcher's supporting attacks struck Jaluit, Makin, and Mili as planned, doing additional damage.

These initial strikes had their intended effect. Although the material damage to Japanese forces and installations was slight, Halsey and Fletcher demonstrated that the Japanese were mortal. The Pacific Fleet had fought back. Morale soared. Through his decisive commitment to offensive action, his willingness to keep his options open, and his aggressive instructions to Halsey, Nimitz had shown his subordinates and his staff that he would chart a new course.

Nimitz had also shown he could influence Japanese plans. Confident that *I-6* had sunk *Lexington* (sister ship to *Saratoga*) on 11 January, the Japanese unleashed their carriers to the south; in late January, the First and Fifth Carrier Divisions aided the capture of Rabaul and Kavieng while the Second Carrier Division ensured the seizure of Ambon. Although most analyses suggest Halsey's strikes caused no significant interruption to Japanese offensive plans, they prompted a strong reaction. Powerful forces were diverted to pursue Halsey and, apprehensive about future U.S. strikes, Admiral Yamamoto redeployed the Fifth Carrier Division—a third of the *Kido Butai*—to home waters.[60] Nimitz was not immediately aware of this, but he did learn about it a few days later, when the Pacific Fleet's intelligence unit noted that the Fifth Carrier Division had become part of a "defensive screen for [the Japanese] eastern frontier."[61]

In the aftermath of the raids, Nimitz also demonstrated magnanimity and a willingness to allow his subordinates to take credit for the Pacific Fleet's successes. Although he had exerted a substantial influence on the nature and conduct of the attacks, Nimitz saw to it that Halsey received the accolades. The Navy Department released details of the raids on 13 February; the *New York Times* ran ten articles about them over the following three days, giving Vice Admiral Halsey credit for the successful expedition that had "fairly well repaid" Pearl Harbor. Other newspapers replicated these accounts or offered similar ones, advancing Halsey's standing in the public eye. Nimitz was content to remain in the background, confident that his team knew what he had done.[62]

## A NEW WAY FORWARD

The weeks immediately following Pearl Harbor were a period of great instability, a notable "bifurcation point" when many potential outcomes were possible.[63] The Japanese hoped to reinforce their initial success and capitalize on a string of rapid victories to reshape the future in the western Pacific. That future was undermined by Nimitz's quick and decisive action. He had immediately acted to create a cohesive team—a CINCPAC staff that could collaborate and leverage its collective intelligence to rapidly make sense of emerging opportunities—and worked with that team to win an important victory by striking Japanese installations in the Gilberts and Marshalls. Nimitz reinvigorated the PACFLT staff and its senior leadership. He expressed his confidence in them, brought them together, and demonstrated how they could leverage their collective skill and knowledge to win. He had established the foundation for future success.

Confident that he would be able to hold his advanced positions at Midway and in the Hawaiian Islands, in January, while Halsey was preparing his strikes, Nimitz issued a new operation plan for the Pacific Fleet.[64] Operation Plan No. R5-1 built off the campaign plans Kimmel had previously issued and the Navy's current war plan, WPL-46. In it, Nimitz introduced a new, much more aggressive set of instructions. Unlike an earlier draft of Kimmel's, composed in December but never issued, Nimitz wanted to be sure PACFLT understood they would be the aggressor whenever and wherever possible. He framed their objectives this way:

A. Raid enemy communications and forces.
B. Protect the territory of the Associated Powers east of Longitude 180°
   by covering, by destroying enemy forces, and by containing [them]
   through offensive operations.
C. Escort shipping, and cover and patrol lines of communication as
   circumstances require.[65]

Even though the Japanese held the initiative, Nimitz would now begin to employ his forces to put the Japanese off balance, create opportunities, and seize them when they arose. His concept for long-term success complements the modern theories of organizational behaviorist Herminia Ibarra. Ibarra's research suggests that exploring options—continually testing out new theories—is the most effective way to discover the best way forward. This continual sensemaking has been summarized effectively as: "Instead of working back from a goal, work forward from promising situations . . . look at the options available now and choose those that will give you the most promising range of options afterward."[66] This description reflects the essence of Nimitz's mindset during this time; it was how Nimitz would explore and develop options in the early months of 1942 as he used the talents of his staff to begin to thwart Japanese offensive operations.

Nimitz was able to move forward this way because the Navy's established predispositions—its core heuristics of aggressive action, the desire to seize the initiative, and the effective use of empowered subordinates—shaped the perception and meaning of Nimitz's initial decisions as CINCPAC. He took actions that resonated with these predispositions and allowed his officers to "see" themselves in the success of the Navy's early offensive operations. Nimitz's initial decisions recast the developing narrative of the Pacific War from one dominated by Japanese victories to one that the United States and its allies could win. Nimitz's first two decisive steps—retaining and reinvigorating the staff and achieving an initial offensive success—allowed the Pacific Fleet to recover, reorient itself to the emerging nature of the conflict, and begin to prepare for the long campaign ahead.

Without Nimitz's initial decisions, it is unlikely that the Pacific Fleet would have been able to emerge from the shadow of Pearl Harbor so quickly. His decisive actions set a new course and established the conditions for future success. The way ahead would not be easy. Nimitz acknowledged as much to his wife: "While I know I am facing a difficult task—I am not discouraged and will do my best—but everyone must be very, very patient because we are confronted with a most difficult period."[67] The Japanese still held the initiative and the overbearing influence of Admiral King threatened to curtail Nimitz's initiative, but Nimitz's initial display of leadership sustained American obligations in the western and southern Pacific.

# CREATING
# OPPORTUNITIES

*Ever so many people were enthusiastic for me at the start but*
*when things do not move fast enough, they sour on me.*

—Adm. Chester W. Nimitz[1]

**B**y striking against the Japanese in the Marshalls, Nimitz had taken
the first significant step to establishing a coherent way forward for
PACFLT and U.S. strategy in the Pacific. He had reinvigorated his
command's morale. However, he still faced significant challenges. The two
most important were interwoven. First, he had to find ways to pressure the
Japanese and undermine their offensive operations. He did this by relentlessly
seeking opportunities to ambush Japanese striking forces and seize the initiative. Success against the Japanese would allow Nimitz to overcome his second
challenge, gaining the confidence of his superiors in Washington. Nimitz had
to demonstrate to Admiral King and Navy Secretary Knox that he would use
his forces aggressively and could be trusted as a theater commander. To make
it easier to gain that trust, Nimitz reconfigured the Pacific Fleet and his staff
to rapidly identify lessons from combat and incorporate them into improved
processes and procedures. He also adroitly managed Admiral King. Together,
these steps gave Nimitz the opportunity to take advantage of newly emerging
intelligence and thwart Japanese designs in the South Pacific.

## ALLIED AND AMERICAN STRATEGIC LEADERSHIP

In late December 1941, British prime minister Winston Churchill and his service chiefs came to Washington for the Arcadia Conference. Churchill, President Roosevelt, and their military leaders held a series of meetings to discuss how to collaboratively wage the war. Admiral King and CNO Stark participated along with other members of the U.S. high command, including Gen. George C. Marshall, chief of staff of the U.S. Army, and Lt. Gen. Henry H. Arnold, chief of the Army Air Forces. The conference led to the Declaration of the United Nations and several important decisions that governed how the Allies developed strategy during the war.

Arcadia codified two important principles that shaped Allied strategy. The first was that Germany was the greatest threat and, therefore, the European theater was the highest priority; the war in the Pacific would be secondary. The second principle was "unified theater command." Each of the globe's major combat regions would become an operating theater under the control of a single supreme commander. That commander would be responsible for coordinating and directing all the fighting forces within it, regardless of nationality or service branch.[2]

Arcadia also created two new organizational bodies that set direction for U.S. and Allied strategy. The first was the Combined Chiefs of Staff (CCS). It brought together the senior U.S. and British service chiefs and provided "the constitutional framework for the combined direction of the war." King, Stark, Marshall, and Arnold were the initial American members. The second body was the Joint Chiefs of Staff (JCS); it allowed the U.S. members of the CCS to formulate and agree on U.S. strategy before meeting with their British counterparts. The JCS, in addition to representing the United States on the CCS, worked with the president to direct and coordinate U.S. national strategy.[3]

Initially, the decision to create the JCS did not align with the Navy's plans. King, Stark, and President Roosevelt were determined to avoid a repeat of the command challenges of World War I, when the Navy's civilian leadership had failed to effectively broker disagreements between high-ranking naval officers and introduce a coherent strategy. To prevent this problem, the three of them agreed to streamline and centralize American naval leadership.

On 12 March, the offices of COMINCH and CNO were combined and, two weeks later, King relieved Stark as CNO, becoming the only officer to serve as the Navy's commander in chief and CNO simultaneously.[4] Stark left for London to take command of U.S. naval forces in Europe, leaving King as the only naval officer on the JCS.

In the meantime, Marshall had recommended improving the JCS by turning it into a joint general staff with "a single head" who would be directly responsible to the president. King adamantly opposed this idea, and convinced Marshall to abandon it. However, the challenge Marshall hoped to address remained. The JCS needed a liaison officer who could "present the views of the JCS [to the president], expedite presidential decisions when necessary, and serve as the JCS spokesman."[5] By early summer, Marshall felt he had identified a solution that would also add another Navy voice to the JCS. He nominated retired admiral William D. Leahy, who was then ambassador to Vichy France, to be the liaison officer and de facto head of the JCS.

Roosevelt agreed. Leahy had been CNO before the war (1937–39) and was well known and trusted by the president and Admiral King. Leahy became Roosevelt's chief of staff and head of the JCS in July 1942. Leahy balanced the diverse opinions of his peers and offered sage advice to Roosevelt. Leahy's high regard for Nimitz—he considered the new CINCPAC one of "the best qualified [admirals] by experience, talent, and temperament"—helped Nimitz overcome doubts in Washington.[6]

## TENSION WITH WASHINGTON

But at the time of Arcadia, that was months in the future. In the meantime, President Roosevelt and Secretary Knox rashly expressed their impatience with the Navy's leadership in front of Churchill and his service chiefs. Roosevelt "rebuked the Navy for the succession of disasters in the Pacific, particularly the withdrawal of the Wake Island relief force." Knox expressed surprise and frustration that Pye had abandoned the island's defenders. Pye had earned a reputation for hesitancy and ineffectiveness. Roosevelt "wanted action" from PACFLT and its new commander.[7]

Halsey's raids were beneficial, but they were small comfort in the face of the inexorable Japanese advance. Rabaul fell on 23 January, Singapore surrendered on 15 February, and Japanese attacks isolated Java, preparing it for invasion. On 19 February, the *Kido Butai*—except for the Fifth Carrier Division, held back to guard against further American attacks—struck Darwin in northern Australia. The Malay barrier was broken, and Batavia, capital of the Dutch East Indies, was occupied on 5 March. Farther north, the Philippines were cut off. U.S. forces on Luzon retreated to the Bataan Peninsula. Important officials were evacuated, including Philippine president Manuel Quezon, Rear Adm. Francis W. Rockwell, commandant of the Sixteenth Naval District, and Gen. Douglas MacArthur, commanding general, U.S. Army Forces Far East. Bataan surrendered on 9 April. Gen. Jonathan Wainwright, who assumed command after MacArthur's departure, retreated to Corregidor, where he and his men held out for five more weeks.

In February, Roosevelt asked Secretary Knox to produce a list of the forty "most competent" senior naval officers. Knox convened a secret selection board composed of former fleet commanders—James O. Richardson, Edward C. Kalbfus, Harry E. Yarnell, Claude C. Bloch, and Joseph M. Reeves—as well as King, Stark, Rear Adm. Richard S. Edwards, King's deputy chief of staff for operations, and Rear Adm. Randall Jacobs, who had replaced Nimitz as chief of BuNav.[8]

Unsurprisingly, they all put King and Stark in the top forty. The remaining thirty-eight were selected by vote. A series of talented officers were identified; many would serve with distinction in the war. At the top of the list were Rear Adm. John H. Hoover, who would hold a variety of commands under Nimitz; Vice Admiral Halsey; and Capt. Charles M. "Savvy" Cooke, who would become King's chief planner. Others identified among the "most competent" were Vice Adm. Robert L. Ghormley; Rear Adm. Robert C. Giffen; Capt. Charles Pownall; Rear Admiral Fletcher; Rear Adm. Aubrey W. Fitch, who would later replace Brown as commander of TF 11; Capt. Marc A. Mitscher, who was working up the new carrier *Hornet*; Rear Admiral Turner, now King's assistant chief of staff; Vice Admiral Leary; and Rear Adm. Arthur S. Carpender.[9]

Although a number of Pacific Fleet officers—including Brown, Rear Adm. Leigh Noyes, Spruance, and Kinkaid—failed to make the list, the most significant exception was Nimitz. The board members felt he was "a paper-pushing personnel specialist who enjoyed the particular favor of President Roosevelt."[10] Nimitz's skill at managing personnel was not expected to translate to wartime command. The board's assessment explains why King felt he needed to work around and through Nimitz as he tried to protect lines of communication with Australia.

Those lines depended on a series of small and lightly defended islands stretching south from Hawaii: Palmyra, Christmas, Canton, Samoa, Bora Bora, Fiji, and New Caledonia. From Rabaul, the Japanese could strike southeast and attack these islands, cutting Australia off from the United States. The CCS reacted by establishing an independent naval command, the Anzac Area, directly under King. King informed Nimitz of the plan on 24 January and asked him to nominate a commander for the Anzac Area. King suggested Pye but failed to anticipate that Pye would be unacceptable to Roosevelt and Knox. Nimitz offered Admiral Leary, now available because *Saratoga* had been torpedoed. Leary became commander, Anzac Area (COMANZAC), in early February.[11]

In the meantime, Nimitz and his staff discussed their options. In late January, prompted by an alarming message from the ACNB indicating that "New Caledonia is practically undefended," they considered sending Brown's TF 11 to the southwestern Pacific. Pye recommended sending two carrier groups and operating them from Fiji and Samoa. McMorris and his War Plans Section disagreed for three reasons: two carrier groups would be insufficient to thwart a major Japanese offensive; the logistic situation in the South Pacific could not support them; and concentrating in the south would distract from the "primary task" of defending Hawaii. Instead, McMorris and his team proposed another strike in the Marshalls or a raid on Wake to divert enemy forces. Nimitz waited for the results of Halsey's strike before deciding.[12]

King used Nimitz's apparent indecision as an excuse to assert control of PACFLT striking forces. He directed Nimitz to cover two reinforcement convoys headed for the South Pacific with a carrier group. Nimitz sent Brown's TF 11 south on 2 February. Four days later, King went around Nimitz and ordered Brown to operate in the Anzac Area, justifying the decision by arguing that the "situation . . . requires prompt action to check [the] enemy advance." King also wanted Army B-17s sent south from Hawaii to give Leary a land-based striking force that could support Brown. On 8 February, Nimitz's command summary mentioned a dispatch from the War Department to Lieutenant General Emmons that made King's desire clear. Twelve of the bombers would go to Fiji. With the South Pacific reinforced, King urged Nimitz to take "vigorous offensive action" in the central Pacific. King felt he had the best perspective for how to use the fleet; the opinions of Nimitz and his staff were irrelevant.[13]

Nimitz recognized the challenge he faced. He knew King and Knox were losing confidence; they were all under enormous pressure. In a letter to his wife on 22 March, Nimitz said, "I'm afraid [Knox] is not so keen for me now as he was when I left—but that is only natural. . . . I will be lucky to last six months. The public may demand action and results faster than I can produce."[14]

## INTELLIGENCE REVEALS HALSEY'S IMPACT

Pressured by King to act, Nimitz and his staff examined a series of alternatives. McMorris and his War Plans Section produced a new estimate on 5 February. It highlighted the fact that the Japanese had been "successful in all their advances from Malaya to New Ireland." Halsey's and Fletcher's carrier raids had "apparently" diverted some Japanese planes, but they seemed to have no substantial impact on enemy plans. McMorris suggested two courses of action for slowing "and eventually stopping" the enemy advance. One was to reinforce the South Pacific; the other was "aggressive action in the [central] Pacific" to threaten the Japanese flank and protect the "vital territory" of Hawaii. McMorris and his section preferred the latter. They presented several options, including attacks on Truk, Saipan, the Bonins, the Marshalls, Eniwetok, and even Japan itself.[15]

Truk was a prime target. The base was "being used extensively" to support the Japanese advance south. A handwritten note on the estimate suggested the "very boldness of the operation would augur for its success." However, by sending Brown to the Anzac Area and ordering Nimitz to escort convoys to the South Pacific, King had made such a bold raid impossible. There were "not enough light forces [cruisers and destroyers] remaining to permit operational deployment of battleships" in the central Pacific. Instead, McMorris recommended attacking "the Bonin-Saipan Area with two carriers." Saipan was an "important administrative center" and striking targets so close to Japan was expected to have a powerful "psychological effect." Nimitz was not convinced; he did not believe an attack on Saipan would be worth the risk.[16]

On 7 February, Nimitz told King that there were "insufficient forces to conduct any offensive operations except hit and run raids" and that these "probably would not relieve the pressure" in the south. Instead of attacking in the central Pacific, Nimitz considered sending another carrier task force south to reinforce Brown. King disagreed. He urged Nimitz to act aggressively and relieve the pressure in the south. King believed Nimitz was a "fixer," a political officer who lacked the forcefulness to command in war. Accordingly, King was micromanaging Nimitz, undermining his authority, and issuing overly detailed instructions. Knox gave tacit approval to King's approach. If this behavior continued, Nimitz would lack the ability to flexibly respond to Japanese moves. He discussed the challenge with Pye, who had been serving as a senior adviser and attending Nimitz's morning conferences. Pye could explain to King how things appeared to Nimitz and his staff. Nimitz sent Pye to Washington on 9 February.[17]

That same day, Nimitz held a staff conference to examine alternatives, but "no satisfactory solution . . . could be reached." Discussions continued the following day, when Halsey, having returned from his raid in the Marshalls, joined them. They could not identify a suitable objective. On 11 February, their perspective changed dramatically. New intelligence from intercepted messages revealed that Halsey's strike had caused the IJN to withdraw their Fifth Carrier Division from offensive operations.[18]

When he realized his raids could have a major impact on Japanese plans and operations, Nimitz acted quickly and decisively. He planned an aggressive attack on Wake and Eniwetok with Halsey's and Fletcher's task forces, combined and redesignated as TF 16. If the raid into the Marshalls had diverted a Japanese carrier division, another bold strike might draw more forces north to protect their eastern flank. Halsey issued his operation order on 12 February, two days before his departure from Pearl Harbor. His Task Group (TG) 16.1, with carrier *Enterprise*, would strike Eniwetok on 25 February. Fletcher's TG 16.2, with *Yorktown*, would bomb and shell Wake at the same time. In his orders to Halsey, Nimitz preserved flexibility. Since little was known about Japanese installations, Halsey's orders allowed him to substitute other objectives—like Marcus Island—if attacking Eniwetok was "inadvisable." Submarine *Cachalot* scouted the targets and observed no activity on Eniwetok, which was surprising since it was believed to be a Japanese air base.[19]

In the meantime, Pye arrived in Washington and explained Nimitz's situation to King, his longtime friend and confidant. They discussed available intelligence, estimates of Japanese intentions, and if the results are any indication, command relationships in the Pacific.[20] Pye almost certainly pointed out how important it was to allow Nimitz to exercise his authority and initiative. Pye might even have reminded King of his own instructions regarding the "initiative of the subordinate" issued to the Atlantic Fleet a year before. Those instructions emphasized the importance of presuming subordinate commanders were competent, not "nursing" them, and being satisfied with their "acceptable solutions" even if they were not what higher echelon commanders would prefer.[21]

After talking with Pye and learning that Halsey's raid had caused the withdrawal of the IJN's Fifth Carrier Division, King developed a greater appreciation for Nimitz's perspective and agreed to give him some breathing room. On 15 February, King acceded that raids into the Mandates, like those currently under way, would be "considered sufficient" for the time being.[22] This was welcome news at Nimitz's headquarters. Based on *Cachalot's* reports, he changed his orders to Halsey and Fletcher. Halsey would attack Wake instead of Eniwetok. Fletcher would go south to rendezvous with Brown and seek opportunities in the Anzac Area.[23]

## RAIDING IN THE CENTRAL AND SOUTH PACIFIC

King had secured shipping for a substantial expedition to Noumea—a vital position along the route to Australia—by getting Marshall, Stark, and Arnold to agree to reduce the size of convoys destined for Iceland and Northern Ireland. It was essential that the Noumea convoy get through. To make sure it did, King expected Vice Admiral Leary to go to sea in his flagship, cruiser *Chicago*, and conduct a "strong and comprehensive" offensive to oppose any

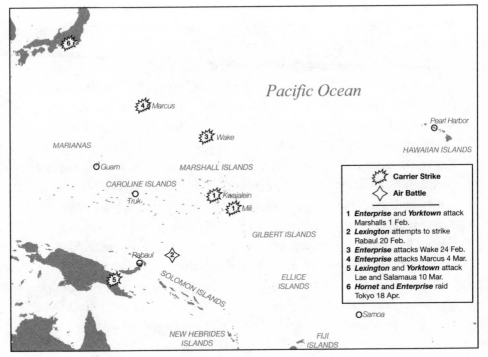

MAP 1. Pacific Fleet Carrier Raids, February–April 1942

Japanese moves south. Leary insisted on remaining at his headquarters in Melbourne where he could maintain "direct contact" with the Royal Australian Air Force, liaise with the Australian and New Zealand naval boards, and use "complete communications, intelligence, and operational facilities."[24]

Brown intercepted King's messages to Leary demanding offensive action and suggested raiding Rabaul, where Japanese shipping was concentrating. Events moved quickly after that. King ordered Brown to take charge of operations in the northern Anzac Area; Leary welcomed Brown's proposal and expanded on it, ordering him to make a coordinated strike with *Lexington* and land-based air. The dozen B-17s of Leary's command moved to Townsville in northern Australia; they would attack along with "all available" Australian planes. Brown would approach Rabaul from the northeast, through the gap between the Solomons and Carolines. The attack was planned for 21 February.[25] Nimitz, Leary, and King hoped that if Brown acted quickly, he might interrupt Japanese plans for attacking Timor.[26]

Japanese patrol planes sighted Brown's TF 11 the day before the scheduled attack. Capt. Frederick C. Sherman, Brown's flag captain, recommended that they proceed as planned, but Brown cancelled the raid, expecting enemy shipping at Rabaul to disperse. However, aware of the strategic importance of the effort and "in order to create as great an alarm and diversion as possible," Brown continued steaming toward Rabaul for several hours.[27] He did not expect to be attacked, but that afternoon, a flight of seventeen Mitsubishi G4M1 land attack planes approached. Coached onto the G4M1s by the carrier's fighter director, Grumman F4F fighters tore into the attackers. Lt. Edward H. "Butch" O'Hare was credited with five; his colleagues accounted for ten more. Only two G4M1s returned to Rabaul. Nimitz congratulated *Lexington*'s air group for their successful defense. However, even though his carrier was undamaged, Brown was shaken. He said that "due to the impossibility of effecting surprise," he would not attack Rabaul again until he had a second carrier group.[28]

Farther north, Halsey attacked Wake Island on 24 February. Damage was limited, but the raid kept the IJN's Fifth Carrier Division focused on defending the Japanese eastern flank; radio decrypts suggested they made a special effort to find Halsey. That was a strong signal that raids, no matter how little material destruction they caused, would divert the IJN's attention. Nimitz ordered Halsey to push ahead and "raid Marcus." A strike on Marcus, less than a thousand miles southeast of Tokyo, was sure to prompt a vigorous response. Halsey attacked before dawn on 4 March. After the island's defenders sent an "urgent message" requesting assistance, the Fifth Carrier Division, which had finally begun heading south, was rerouted to search for Halsey's force. Japanese offensive timetables were delayed by over a week.[29]

Brown's aborted attempt on Rabaul also delayed Japanese offensive operations. The air battle over TF 11 destroyed Rabaul's only striking force, rendering the base temporarily defenseless. While additional G4M1s rushed south, Japanese plans—including an assault on the north coast of New

Guinea—paused to await their arrival. In the meantime, Fletcher's TF 17 arrived in the Anzac Area. Brown, Leary, Nimitz, and King exchanged messages to determine how best to use the two carrier groups to strike the Japanese. Leary, assuming that Brown would be able to attack Rabaul with two carriers, advocated for another attempt; Nimitz "acceded to the idea," but pointed out that logistical constraints would force one task force to return to Pearl Harbor afterward. Brown was hesitant and clarified that he had "not intended" to recommend another strike on Rabaul.[30]

On 26 February, King tried to clarify command relationships in the Anzac Area. While Leary was ashore, the senior Pacific Fleet officer afloat would "exercise direct command" of the area's naval forces. King expected that officer to protect Allied territory through the "destruction of [Japanese] mobile forces, particularly carriers, cruisers, loaded transports, and long range bombers." Nimitz and his staff noticed that King left command relationships vague; that might have been deliberate. The lack of clarity gave King the ability to exercise direct control of Nimitz's striking forces.[31]

King ordered Brown to rendezvous with Fletcher and attack Japanese ships and bases in the Bismarcks-Solomons area "about" 9 March to cover the Noumea convoy. Brown planned to approach Rabaul from the south and attack from the Solomon Sea. As TF 11 and TF 17 moved north, Leary kept Brown apprised. Japanese forces were on the move again; an assault on the north coast of New Guinea was under way. Rabaul was largely empty of enemy ships, but an invasion force was at Salamaua. Brown immediately changed his plans and, reflecting King's emphasis on "mobile forces," made the invasion shipping his objective.[32]

On 10 March, Brown struck, capitalizing on the opportunity created by his aborted attack on Rabaul in February. Planes from *Lexington* and *Yorktown* flew over the mountains of New Guinea and attacked Japanese forces at Lae and Salamaua. They sank or damaged two-thirds of the invasion transports, crippling amphibious ships "needed for several pending invasions" and severely disrupting Japanese plans. It was "the first time the Allies had inflicted large-scale damage" on a Japanese operation. Rear Admiral Ugaki Matome, chief of staff of the Combined Fleet, expressed his frustrations in his diary: "It's annoying to be passive. Warfare is easier, with less trouble, indeed, when we hold the initiative."[33]

The raids initiated by Nimitz and King in February and March 1942 had an outsized impact. They resonated with the Navy's emphasis on aggressive action and continued to reinvigorate the Pacific Fleet's morale. At the same time, they focused Japanese attention on the Navy's mobile forces and exacerbated a growing schism in the Japanese command structure. In the coming weeks, the threat of Nimitz's striking forces would decisively change the IJN's strategic orientation.[34]

## FRACTURED JAPANESE STRATEGY

By the end of February 1942, the Japanese had begun to outrun their strategic plans. The IJN's operational policy called for occupying "key strategic locations in the southern region," establishing "a long-term and unassailable footing," and decisively attacking enemy naval forces to "crush their fighting spirit."[35] Initial Japanese offensives aligned with all three of these goals, but once key positions in the south were reached, divergent approaches began to emerge. The lack of a well-defined strategic vision—or an effective process for creating one—initially prevented any single one from becoming the dominant focus.[36]

Strategic decisions were ostensibly the responsibility of the Imperial General Headquarters (IGHQ), which was divided into IJN and Imperial Japanese Army (IJA) sections. The Naval General Staff was headed by Admiral Nagano Osami and strategic planning took place in Rear Admiral Fukudome Shigeru's First (Operations) Section. However, in practice, Fukudome's authority was "usurped" by Admiral Yamamoto and his Combined Fleet staff. They used Yamamoto's personal prestige and their string of early victories to argue that "the proper source of planning and execution" for IJN strategy should reside in the Combined Fleet. The "arrogance" of Yamamoto's staff led to a power struggle that fractured Japanese strategic decision-making.[37]

One alternative considered in the fleet was to halt offensive operations, establish an "unassailable footing," and prepare for the anticipated U.S. offensive. For decades, the IJN had been preparing to fight on the strategic defensive. They expected to defeat the U.S. Navy by combining attritional attacks with a decisive fleet engagement. Rear Admiral Kusaka Ryunosuke, chief of staff to Vice Admiral Nagumo Chuichi, commander of the *Kido Butai*, supported this idea, but IJN leadership was committed to maintaining an offensive posture, so it was never seriously entertained.[38]

Continuing to strike south would capture additional "strategic locations," such as northern Australia. However, the Imperial Japanese Army, which needed to approve IGHQ's strategic decisions and provide the troops, rejected the idea. Invading Australia would be a major logistical challenge, but it was even more problematic because the IJA's attention was focused on the Soviet Union. Although German forces had been stopped before Moscow in December, the Soviet Union was expected to fall in 1942. IJA officers "wanted to preserve the strength and freedom of action necessary" to quickly move against Russia if the Soviet Union collapsed. They would not provide invasion forces for Australia.[39]

The IJA was more receptive to an offensive in the Indian Ocean to occupy Ceylon, destroy the Royal Navy's Eastern Fleet, and force the collapse of British authority in India. The Combined Fleet already had plans to raid Ceylon, but the rapid fall of Malaya and neutralization of Singapore suggested a major offensive might destroy British political power in India. Rear Admiral Ugaki developed the concept, and it was explored in a series of war games in late February. However, Brown's abortive strike on Rabaul and Halsey's attack on Wake turned the Combined Fleet's attention to the east. The Ceylon raid would proceed, but there would be no assault on British India.[40]

Fukudome's Operations Section argued that additional "strategic locations" could also be seized to the southeast, neutralizing Australia not by invasion, but by cutting it off from reinforcement and resupply. On 29 January, IGHQ ordered Vice Admiral Inoue Shigeyoshi, commander of the Fourth Fleet, to seize Lae and Salamaua on the north coast of New Guinea; Tulagi, an anchorage in the Solomon Islands; and Port Moresby, on New Guinea's southern tip. This was the first step in an extended campaign. On 27 February, Inoue was ordered to prepare to occupy Ocean and Nauru Islands in the Gilberts. By 15 March, shortly after Brown's attack on Inoue's forces at Lae and Salamaua, Fukudome's Operations Section gained IJA and IGHQ approval to seize the "key localities" of New Caledonia, Fiji, and Samoa. If successful, this "FS Operation" would isolate Australia.[41]

However, aggressive Combined Fleet officers like Rear Admiral Ugaki wanted to focus on enemy naval forces and destroy them "before the cherry blossoms bloom."[42] They expected an offensive operation in the central Pacific to draw out the remnants of the Pacific Fleet. The basic concept had been developed before the war, but on 11 January, Ugaki began working on a more detailed plan. He hoped to capture Midway, Johnston, and Palmyra, establish air bases on those islands, and then "mobilize all available strength to invade Hawaii." The threat of invasion would force the Pacific Fleet to fight. Triumph in the ensuing "decisive battle" would allow Japan to force surrender terms on the United States and bring the war to a victorious conclusion.[43]

In early April, Yamamoto's staff officers argued for their plan at Naval General Headquarters in Tokyo. Critics pointed out that capturing Midway and other islands near Hawaii would be difficult because—unlike the objectives seized in the southern advance—they were beyond the range of land-based planes. It would be more effective, the critics argued, to draw out the U.S. carriers by threatening the lines of communication to Australia. Yamamoto and his staff were unmoved. They agreed the American carriers had to be destroyed, but felt the central Pacific was the best place to do it. In the face of Yamamoto's firm stance, the Naval General Staff acquiesced. They approved the operational plan on 5 April.[44]

Competing goals and failure to reach agreement led to a lack of strategic coherence. The IJN pursued three alternative strategies in parallel: Inoue's advance in the south, Yamamoto's offensive in the central Pacific, and a new concept, the capture of positions in the Aleutians to broaden the defensive perimeter. Yamamoto's striking forces were distributed among all three. Nimitz and King exacerbated the IJN's challenge. By raiding Japanese positions in the South Pacific, they demonstrated the importance of consolidating Japan's hold on the region and isolating Australia. At the same time, Halsey's raids in the central Pacific supported the Combined Fleet's argument that an offensive against the Pacific Fleet was essential to bring the war to a favorable conclusion. Nimitz's decision to use his limited forces in hit-and-run raids turned his aircraft carriers into a lodestone, an attractor that focused Yamamoto and his staff on the need to draw the Pacific Fleet into a decisive battle. This would give Nimitz an opportunity.[45]

## REORGANIZING PACFLT

After assuming command, Nimitz realized he needed to change how PACFLT gathered, assessed, and disseminated information. The prewar structure assumed that officers responsible for identifying and documenting effective practices—the foundations of tactical doctrine—would also be responsible for combat commands. The first weeks of the war had shown the inadequacy of this approach. Task force commanders who had administrative responsibilities could do their administrative work or command their forces; they could not do both. A new structure was needed to ensure PACFLT could effectively learn and rapidly improve.

On 1 January 1942, immediately after assuming command, Nimitz took his first step. He moved the Pacific Fleet's submarines out of the Scouting Force and made them an independent type command. Nimitz, an experienced submariner, knew that his boats could be an effective offensive weapon regardless of the overriding strategic situation, especially given the decision to execute unrestricted submarine warfare against Japanese commerce. By moving the submarine type command directly under CINCPAC, Nimitz was able to give the submarine force personal attention and maximize its potential.[46]

The other type commands were under the Pacific Fleet's main administrative and operational divisions, the Battle Force and the Scouting Force. Vice Admiral Halsey, for example, was commander, Aircraft, Battle Force, as well as commander of the *Enterprise* task force. Similarly, Rear Admiral Leary was commander, Cruisers, Battle Force, as well as a task force commander. When these officers were at sea, they took their staffs with them. In some cases, the administrative work of the type commands—ensuring the material upkeep of ships, assessing lessons, and revising tactical instructions—stopped. In others, it became the focus of the staff, distracting them from the task force's mission.[47] Nimitz took an initial step toward addressing this problem on 5 January, when he ordered Vice Admiral Brown to establish an administrative office ashore for cruisers of the Scouting Force.[48] On 17 January 1942, he ordered all the other type commands to do the same.[49]

However, after gaining experience with this approach, Nimitz realized additional changes were necessary. The Battle Force and Scouting Force created unnecessary overhead and restricted the flow of information, inhibiting the fleet's ability to rapidly make sense of emerging lessons. Nimitz eliminated them. He justified the decision in a detailed recommendation to King.[50] The CINCPAC staff took over the "administrative duties" of the Battle Force and Scouting Force. Their "operational functions" were divided among the fleet's task forces. The task force with the largest number of battleships—currently TF 1—became the operational equivalent of the Battle Force. Since Vice Admiral Pye had commanded the Battle Force before the war, Nimitz ordered Pye to take command of TF 1 in March.[51]

Nimitz also ordered Vice Admiral Brown—the commander of the Scouting Force—to take command of the Pacific Fleet's amphibious force when he returned from the South Pacific. Training for amphibious operations was one of the "operational functions" of the Scouting Force and, because Brown had extensive experience preparing for amphibious operations, Nimitz felt he was "the most suitable officer to command the amphibious force."[52]

These changes improved the ability of task force commanders to focus on operations. Their administrative work was delegated to type commands ashore dedicated to rapidly assessing lessons and promulgating new tactical doctrine. After King approved, Nimitz formally established the new Pacific Fleet structure on 10 April 1942:[53]

- Battleships, Rear Adm. Walter S. Anderson (soon to be Vice Admiral Pye)
- Carriers, Vice Admiral Halsey
- Cruisers, Rear Admiral Fletcher
- Destroyers, Rear Admiral Theobald
- Submarines, Rear Adm. Thomas Withers
- Patrol Wings, Rear Adm. John S. McCain
- Service Force, Vice Admiral Calhoun
- Amphibious Force, Vice Admiral Brown

The new structure increased the size of Nimitz's staff, but only slightly. When Nimitz assumed command on 31 December 1941, there were sixty-three officers on staff. By 30 July 1942, this number had increased to just seventy-nine, a growth of roughly 25 percent. Nimitz deliberately kept his staff small to accelerate information flows, quickly build shared understanding, and maintain a rapid feedback loop between his orders and their execution. Consistent delegation to subordinate commands—like the new shore-based type commands—was essential to this approach. They quickly began to absorb wartime lessons and modify tactical instructions accordingly.[54]

Nimitz's new organizational structure had significant benefits. During the rest of the war, operational commands "changed with bewildering frequency" depending on the needs of the moment. The administrative commands, in contrast, remained "relatively stable" ensuring a consistent approach to capturing lessons, identifying improvements, and disseminating new doctrines.[55] This enhanced the Pacific Fleet's combat power. As historian Ryan Grauer has argued, "[T]he way in which armed forces organize to manage information . . . conditions their combat strength."[56] Nimitz increased the combat strength of the Pacific Fleet by this important improvement in its organizational structure.[57]

## EMERGING INTELLIGENCE

Nimitz also enhanced the combat power of the Pacific Fleet by improving how intelligence information was used and disseminated. He focused on making the latest intelligence available to operational commanders. However, Nimitz's ability to do so was initially limited by the fractured nature of the Navy's intelligence organization. At the start of the war, there were three main stations responsible for gathering and assessing communications intelligence, Hypo, Cast, and Negat. Each of these names stood for a letter of the alphabet. Hypo ("H") was in Hawaii; Cast ("C") was in the Philippines, initially at Cavite and then Corregidor; Negat ("N") was at Main Navy, the Navy Department's headquarters in Washington. Negat housed the leadership of OP-20-G, the Navy's Code and Signal Section, part of the Office of the Chief of Naval Operations (OPNAV). Although all three stations intercepted and attempted to break the codes and ciphers of Japanese radio messages, OP-20-G segmented the work, giving each station slightly different responsibilities.[58]

In early 1941, Cast was ordered to focus on the IJN's operational code, JN-25(b). Since the Philippines were expected to face Japan's first offensive moves, the work of Cast emphasized real-time intelligence. They collaborated with the Far East Combined Bureau (FECB), a British joint intelligence operation whose "primary roles were to give early warning of Japanese attack, build an accurate Japanese order of battle . . . and provide operational intelligence once war had broken out." Cast's objectives were similar.[59]

Station Negat also worked on JN-25(b), but its approach was different. Negat tried to break the Japanese code by understanding its underlying structure and composition. The goal was a breakthrough like that achieved with the Japanese diplomatic code, called "Purple" by the Navy. Purple had been cracked through an intensive joint effort by OP-20-G and the Army's Signal Intelligence Service. Decrypts of Purple started to appear in September 1940 and were called "Magic." The intelligence they provided was extremely valuable and Purple became the focus of Negat's efforts. As war approached, the station "lacked the manpower necessary for a full-scale attack on JN-25(b)."[60]

OP-20-G had Hypo focus on IJN's administrative Flag Officers' Code. Because it was used infrequently, this code proved impossible to crack. Cdr. Joe Rochefort, who led Hypo's efforts, tried to provide useful intelligence by using traffic analysis to track the movement of IJN ships. Rochefort and his team analyzed who was sending messages and where they sent them from. Eventually, they discovered patterns in Japanese transmissions that allowed them to recognize specific ships—like carrier *Akagi*—from the unique styles of their radio operators. Rochefort used this information to predict Japanese moves and offered his assessments to Lieutenant Commander Layton and Admiral Kimmel. The value of Rochefort's analysis was questioned after the Pearl Harbor attack, but Hypo was given permission to work on JN-25(b) on 10 December. Rochefort immediately began to combine fragmented decryptions with traffic analysis to develop a broader picture of Japanese intentions.[61]

Nimitz was very supportive of these efforts. He had become familiar with the potential of signals intelligence in 1934 when he was captain of cruiser *Augusta*, flagship of the Asiatic Fleet. The IJN conducted operational maneuvers that year, and the Asiatic Fleet monitored radio traffic from the exercise, breaking IJN codes and using traffic analysis to create an accurate order of battle and track Japanese movements. That effort had been coordinated from

Nimitz's *Augusta* and he was fully aware of what the Navy's codebreakers could do.[62] Although IJN codes and communication methods had improved significantly in the intervening years, Nimitz quickly recognized the advantage Layton, Rochefort, and Hypo could give him. Nimitz reserved time in his schedule every morning for the latest intelligence briefing.

On 10 January, King tried to address the fragmented nature of intelligence work in the Pacific by making the Fourteenth Naval District, which contained Hypo, responsible for "coordination and dissemination of enemy activities at sea." However, he quickly changed his mind. On 20 January, King tried to assume more direct control of Pacific intelligence by transferring responsibility to the Southern Naval Coastal Frontier. Nimitz argued against it and succeeded in convincing King that Hypo, because of its "proximity to [the] theater of operations"—and his headquarters—should retain responsibility. King ordered Nimitz to issue a daily Pacific intelligence bulletin reflecting the best estimates of Station Hypo.[63]

Even though Rochefort's understanding of JN-25(b) was limited, his team quickly began to combine partial decryptions with their existing knowledge of context—the habits and procedures revealed through traffic analysis—to start to make sense of Japanese intentions. Hypo also used Rochefort's relationship with Layton to understand how the Pacific Fleet's operations fit into the emerging intelligence picture. With access to this "broad range of information sources," Hypo began to transform "information into intelligence."[64]

They had an initial success around 18 January when Rochefort identified a code group that translated to "invasion force." Messages indicated the invasion force had a specific designation represented by the letter "R." Rochefort concluded Rabaul was the Japanese objective and told Layton. Layton informed Nimitz a few days before the Japanese seized the base. Although Nimitz could do nothing to stop the Japanese assault, he acted on the new intelligence by ordering Halsey and Fletcher to strike more deeply into the Marshalls. Rochefort and his team proved that they could make sense of partially decrypted messages and provide real-time intelligence, giving Nimitz a distinct advantage.[65]

A new opportunity emerged in early March. Hypo discerned enough of Operation K, a raid on Pearl Harbor by two long-range Kawanishi H8K flying boats, to know that an attack was coming, but Rochefort and Layton remained uncertain "when and where" the Japanese would strike. Their planes took off from Wotje, refueled from submarines at French Frigate Shoals, and, struggling through clouds and rain, dropped their bombs harmlessly on Oahu in the early morning hours of 4 March. Nimitz was grateful for the early warning and recognized that the inability to discern the specifics of Japanese plans was an inherent part of the process. His confidence in Layton and Rochefort grew.[66]

Operation K provided Hypo additional details about Japanese code names. Afterward, the designator "AF" began to appear "more frequently in the Imperial Navy's radio traffic, clearly indicating a region the Japanese navy intended to visit." Inquiries about weather at AF on 9 March suggested another aerial attack. The next day, King suggested a renewed strike on Pearl Harbor might be planned. Rochefort thought the target was elsewhere. He informed Nimitz and King that "AF is probably Midway." The following morning, Midway's radar detected two incoming planes. One dropped away, but the other continued toward the island. Marine fighters intercepted it. Rochefort had been right, and now he and his team were confident they knew the JN-25(b) code groups for islands near Hawaii: "AF is Midway. AH is Hawaiian Islands. AI is Oahu (probable). AG is Johnston (question)."[67]

## RAIDS ON JAPAN AND CEYLON

In the meantime, a bold new plan had been devised to strike Japan. In January, King and his operations officer, Capt. Francis S. Low, discussed raiding Tokyo with Army medium bombers flown from Navy carriers. King thought it was possible and ordered Capt. Donald B. Duncan, his air operations officer, to study the problem. General Arnold "enthusiastically" supported the effort and provided the necessary planes—the North American B-25—and pilots. Flight training began in March at Eglin Field in Florida.[68]

On 19 March, Captain Duncan brought details of the plan to Pearl Harbor. Carrier *Hornet* would carry the B-25s and Lt. Col. James Doolittle would lead the raid. The bombers would strike Tokyo and other urban centers before landing in China. King expected carrier *Enterprise* to escort *Hornet* and Vice

Admiral Halsey to lead the strike force. Halsey was "enthusiastic" about the opportunity. Nimitz was more apprehensive; so was Draemel. Diverting two carriers to raid Japan increased the risk in the South Pacific. Only Fletcher's TF 17 would be available to oppose any Japanese advance in the south.[69]

Their concerns were overruled. The Doolittle Raid was a strategic necessity. By penetrating the Malay Barrier, the Japanese had exposed India to attack. The Royal Navy's First Sea Lord, Admiral of the Fleet Sir Dudley Pound, requested assistance from King, and King promised to do all that he could "to keep the enemy interested in the Pacific." He urged Nimitz to raid Japanese positions in the central Pacific with his battleships to draw out the Japanese, support the Doolittle Raid, and help relieve the pressure on the British in the Indian Ocean. Nimitz had no intention of doing so; the Pacific Fleet did not have enough destroyers to escort the battleships in a major operation. King acquiesced after reviewing Nimitz's sound written argument but insisted that Nimitz execute the Doolittle Raid.[70]

In the meantime, the Japanese initiated their Indian Ocean operation. The *Kido Butai*—less the carrier *Kaga*, refitting at Sasebo—reformed at Staring Bay off the southeast peninsula of Sulawesi. Vice Admiral Nagumo's departure was delayed slightly by the late arrival of the IJN's Fifth Carrier Division, held back because of Halsey's raids.[71] When Nagumo was ready, he took his ships into the Indian Ocean, planning to "conduct a surprise attack on the enemy fleet in the Ceylon area and destroy it." A second IJN force under Vice Admiral Ozawa Jisaburo would wreak havoc on Allied shipping in the Bay of Bengal.[72]

On 5 April, Easter Sunday, Nagumo's planes struck Colombo and triggered the "supreme crisis of the war for India."[73] The commander of the Royal Navy's Eastern Fleet, Admiral Sir James Somerville, knew the Japanese were coming and planned an ambush. However, because his intelligence anticipated the attack would come earlier, Somerville was out of position refueling when it came. Two British cruisers were sunk. Somerville tried to bring his carriers into range for a night attack, but lost track of Nagumo. The *Kido Butai* moved northeast. On 9 April, it struck Trincomalee, sinking the old carrier *Hermes*. In the meantime, Ozawa sank twenty-one merchant ships totaling nearly 100,000 tons. Allied shipping in the Bay of Bengal was "paralyzed." Somerville, unable to match the striking power of the Japanese carrier force and "shocked by the ferocity of the IJN strike," retreated to Kilindini Harbor in Kenya.[74]

While Nagumo struck Ceylon, Nimitz finalized plans for the Doolittle Raid. On 7 April, he issued his operation plan and ordered Halsey to strike Japan with TF 16. Nimitz gave Halsey estimates of current Japanese activity and the searches they might conduct. Planes from the Fifth Carrier Division were expected on Chichi Jima. *Kaga*'s air group was known to be in the Tokyo area. Heavy bombers were at Wake and Marcus. Bombers and long-range seaplanes were in the Marshalls. Nimitz drew Halsey's attention to a recent intelligence bulletin, which noted that enemy air searches extended seven hundred miles from Japan and a Japanese "auxiliary vessel" was approximately one thousand miles east-southeast of Tokyo transmitting weather reports.[75]

The auxiliary vessel was part of a Japanese picket line. On the morning of 18 April, TF 16 was pushing through heavy seas and steamed right into the pickets. Well-crafted plans to launch Doolittle's planes 450 miles away from Japan were rapidly altered. Radar allowed Halsey to avoid some of the pickets in the predawn darkness, but an aerial search made it obvious TF 16 would soon be sighted. Cruiser *Nashville* sank one enemy ship, but not before it sent a sighting report. Halsey, with Doolittle's agreement, decided to launch the B-25s once they were within 650 miles of Japan. Doolittle piloted the first plane off *Hornet*'s flight deck at 0725. Five hours later, bombs were falling on Tokyo, Kobe, Yokohama, and Nagoya.[76]

Although physical damage was slight, the raid delivered "shock and humiliation" that diminished the IJN's prestige and embarrassed its high command. Rear Admiral Ugaki recorded his embarrassment in his diary; the strike had "shattered" his "firm determination never to let the enemy attack Tokyo." Humiliation crystalized IJN strategic planning; before the Doolittle Raid there had been strenuous opposition to Yamamoto's plan to draw the Pacific Fleet into a decisive battle in the central Pacific; afterward, "no one [in the Japanese high command] could argue with effect" against Yamamoto's strategic concept. The Combined Fleet took the reins of Japanese war planning in the Pacific and made Midway its centerpiece.[77]

## CINCPOA AND COMSOPAC

After Vice Admiral Brown and TF 11 withdrew from the South Pacific, the difficulties King faced trying to coordinate operations from Washington became more apparent. In late March, Nimitz's intelligence and Leary's reconnaissance indicated the Japanese would begin "some kind of offensive" at the end of the month. Fletcher and TF 17 were at sea; he considered attacking a concentration of enemy ships known to be at Rabaul but assumed the Japanese would sight him on his approach, disperse their ships, and potentially damage *Yorktown* with their strike aircraft. Instead, he returned to Noumea to reprovision, anticipating he would strike the Japanese if they came south. Because he was observing radio silence, Fletcher did not communicate his intentions.[78]

While Fletcher was out of position, the Japanese advanced. They seized Bougainville and the anchorage at the Shortlands. When Japanese transports were sighted south of Bougainville, Leary, Nimitz, and King thought Fletcher was in an "excellent position to strike them." However, TF 17 was returning to Noumea. When Fletcher arrived there and explained that he was waiting for an opportunity to strike, King was furious. In a scathing message, he practically accused Fletcher of cowardice.[79]

Fletcher calmly explained that he had to reprovision because some of his ships had been at sea for two weeks. Also, it had not been a good opportunity to attack Japanese forces because they were advancing in short steps under the cover of land-based air from Rabaul. Even before Fletcher's explanation reached King, King had sent a more conciliatory note, acknowledging Fletcher's need to provision and stay ready for operations in the Coral Sea. "The situation in the area where you are now operating," King said, "requires constant activity of a task force like yours to keep the enemy occupied."[80]

It also required leadership and direction within the theater of operations. The friction between Fletcher and King illustrated the impossibility of coordinating the war in the South Pacific from Washington. Changes were already under way. King and his colleagues on the CCS and JCS agreed that the United States would assume overall responsibility for the Pacific and divide it into three theaters, Southwest (SWPAC), Southeast, and Pacific

Ocean Areas (POA). General MacArthur, who had arrived at Darwin on 17 March, was made commander of the Southwest Pacific (COMSWPAC), which included Australia, New Guinea, the Dutch East Indies, and the Philippines. Vice Admiral Leary became MacArthur's naval commander. The Southeast Pacific—the area south of the equator and east of Hawaii—was far from the combat zone; King initially oversaw its operations.

Nimitz was made commander, Pacific Ocean Areas (CINCPOA) on 3 April. He was instructed to divide his command into three areas: North (NORPAC), Central (CENTPAC), and South Pacific (SOPAC). Nimitz would personally oversee operations in CENTPAC and NORPAC, but because SOPAC was the site of so much activity, Nimitz was ordered to identify a subordinate officer to become "commander of the South Pacific Area [COM-SOPAC]," who would act under his "authority and general direction" to defend the lines of communication with Australia and eventually take the offensive against the Japanese. King expected it to be "a most difficult task." Nimitz initially nominated Pye to be COMSOPAC, but Knox and Roosevelt rejected him. Nimitz's second choice was Vice Admiral Ghormley; he became COMSOPAC on 10 April.[81]

The emergence of well-defined operating theaters was an important step that removed the uncertainty surrounding command relationships in the South Pacific. It kept King and his colleagues on the JCS and CCS focused on high-level strategy and delegated responsibility for operations to theater commanders. The decision to introduce two parallel theaters in the Pacific—POA under Nimitz and SWPAC under MacArthur—is generally interpreted as a departure from the sound military principle of unity of command. By establishing two theaters, the JCS created competition for scarce resources and failed to create a unified view of operations in the Pacific.[82] However, there is another way to view the decision. With two theaters, the Allied nations increased their options. Nimitz and MacArthur were urged to coordinate and cooperate, but they had the capability to operate independently. As supplies, troops, and equipment flowed into both theaters, the Japanese were ultimately faced with two independent opponents in the south—the coalition led by MacArthur and Nimitz's naval offensive. The benefits of this approach would begin to appear later in 1942.

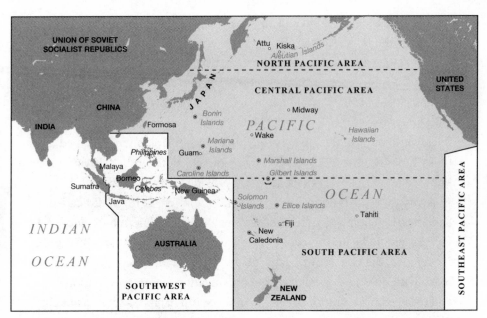

MAP 2. Pacific Theater Operating Areas

## CONFERRING WITH KING

In late April, Nimitz's intelligence organization gave him insight into an impending Japanese offensive. By the middle of the month, he knew that their incursion into the Bay of Bengal was over. By the 22nd, aided by the extensive radio traffic generated by the response to the Doolittle Raid, Station Hypo had discovered that the Japanese were going to attempt to capture Port Moresby by sea. It was a grave threat as well as an opportunity. With Port Moresby in their hands, the Japanese could threaten the lines of communication to Australia. However, Nimitz's staff recognized they had a chance to disrupt Japanese plans and destroy their striking forces.[83]

The enemy offensive was expected to commence "about May 3, 1942" and appeared to be aimed at the boundary between MacArthur's and Nimitz's commands. The Japanese were expected to support the operation with five carriers—*Zuikaku, Shokaku, Ryukaku* (an incorrect designation for the light carrier *Shoho*), *Kasuga Maru*, and *Kaga*—augmented by battleships, heavy cruisers, and other light forces. Land-based aircraft would cover from Rabaul. Although the Japanese had the initiative and were "flushed with victory," Nimitz resolved to exploit the opportunity by using all four of his carriers. Fletcher's TF 17 was already in the south. *Lexington* and TF 11, now commanded by Rear Admiral Fitch, would rendezvous with Fletcher soon. Halsey's TF 16, with *Enterprise* and *Hornet*, would head south as soon as possible. Together, they would oppose the Japanese advance. Nimitz's planners assumed that their "more resourceful and skillful personnel" along with "fairly accurate knowledge" of the enemy's plans would provide the margin of victory.[84]

Armed with this concept, Nimitz and members of his staff headed to San Francisco on 24 April to attend a previously scheduled conference with King; it would be an important milestone in the Pacific War. During the conference, the two admirals discussed the impending Japanese offensive along with questions of Pacific Fleet organization, command relationships, and the need to assume the offensive in the South Pacific as soon as possible. The most important decisions revolved around how to plan and coordinate the war in the Pacific. Nimitz and King entered the conference with differing views; they would leave with a shared understanding.[85]

King and Rear Admiral Turner, chief of OPNAV's War Plans Division, presented Turner's "Pacific War Campaign Plan." The plan outlined four operational phases. In the first, the United States and its Allies would hold their current positions and build up forces in the South and Southwest Pacific. During the second phase, dual offensives by Ghormley and MacArthur would capture Japanese positions in the Solomons, New Guinea, and the Bismarck Archipelago. Phase three involved an offensive in the Central Pacific Area, to capture the Marshall and Caroline Islands. Finally, in phase four, the Allies would advance through the Netherlands East Indies or the Philippines, cut Japan off from the resources of Southeast Asia, and impose a strangling blockade. Unlike prewar plans that had emphasized the primacy of the Central Pacific, Turner's plan focused on the south because Australia was an important ally. As CINCPOA, Nimitz was responsible for securing the lines of communication between Australia and the West Coast of the United States. That was one reason he was planning to concentrate all his carrier forces in the south to blunt the Japanese offensive. King reviewed the plan, withholding his approval while he considered the situation and assessed Nimitz's unanticipated aggressiveness.[86]

Nimitz and King also discussed the organization of carrier task forces, the use of battleships, and the limited pool of proven commanders. To maximize "flexibility," Nimitz and King expected to operate five carrier task forces in the Pacific, one for each large carrier. The task forces would normally operate in pairs for mutual support. Two new fast battleships, *Washington* and *North Carolina*, would arrive in the Pacific in August, about the time when offensive operations were anticipated. Before that, Nimitz would explore the possibility of sending a division of old battleships to SOPAC. The limited number of talented officers constrained Nimitz's options. He and King resolved to give promising younger officers opportunities to prove themselves. The best would advance; those who failed to measure up would be relieved.[87]

Fletcher received special attention. Both Nimitz and King "expressed uneasiness" about his handling of TF 17. They thought Fletcher might lack the necessary aggressiveness and discussed whether he ought to be relieved. However, they decided to wait until more information was available before making a decision. Nimitz almost certainly took the opportunity to let King know that his behavior, and his inflammatory message to Fletcher, could only have undermined the morale of the task force commander and his staff.[88]

Nimitz focused on "simplicity and directness" during this conference and showed he was "every bit as tough-fibered as Admiral King."[89] Although not documented in the record, Nimitz almost certainly confronted King about his tendency to micromanage operations and interfere with commanders at sea. King's behavior was inhibiting Nimitz's ability to act on emerging intelligence and thwart Japanese moves. Nimitz would have built on Pye's conversation with King in February and insisted—calmly, but compellingly—that he be able to position his forces as he saw fit. During their exchange, King realized that beneath Nimitz's calm outward demeanor was a determination to be relentlessly aggressive. The 22 April estimate was crucial in this regard; it demonstrated that Nimitz and his staff had identified the most likely target of the Japanese offensive and were actively preparing a counterstroke.

Nimitz left the conference uncertain if his plan to defend Port Moresby was approved. King was notoriously difficult to sway through oral argument; he needed time to digest alternative viewpoints and reach his own conclusions. It was not until Nimitz arrived back at Pearl Harbor on 28 April that he realized he had been successful and that King had approved his plan. The conference marked the beginning of a new relationship between the two admirals; three days of intense discussions had convinced King that he could trust Nimitz and his staff to fight the war with the necessary resolve. Nimitz quickly exploited the opportunity. Using the 22 April estimate as a guide, he issued his Operation Plan No. 23-42 on 29 April. It would trigger the Battle of the Coral Sea.[90]

## CONCLUSION

In the first four months of 1942, Nimitz faced three crucial challenges. First, he had to continue fighting the Japanese and seek opportunities to interfere with their plans. This was made easier after the strikes in February revealed that raids in the central Pacific influenced Japanese operations. Second, Nimitz had to win the confidence of his superiors. He had to convince American leaders, both military and civilian, that he was the right man to lead the Pacific Fleet and fight the war against Japan. This was not easy; Admiral King and Secretary Knox were especially difficult to satisfy and Nimitz found it challenging to overcome their doubts. Third, Nimitz had to reorganize the Pacific Fleet and improve its ability to process information and learn. Nimitz succeeded in all three areas by using his staff and supporting organization to rapidly identify opportunities and quickly act upon them.

Striking back at the Japanese would help Nimitz win the confidence of his superiors, so he prioritized it. When Nimitz learned that he could disrupt Japanese plans and force them to react, he planned more strikes to disrupt their decision cycle, delay their operations, and create new opportunities. Nimitz actively tried to transform the learning environment for the Japanese and make it more difficult for them to carry out the war based on their preconceptions. Journalist David Epstein has described this as a shift from a "kind" learning environment—where predictable patterns emerge in familiar contexts—to a "wicked" one, with unpredictable and unanticipated results. Nimitz and King, through their continuing pattern of carrier raids, tried to force the Japanese to react, think on their feet, and confront ever more complex challenges.[91]

Nimitz expected that would give him and his subordinates an advantage. Throughout the interwar period, the Navy had habituated officers to deal with "wicked" learning environments through the complex, open-ended Fleet Problems. Adm. David F. Sellers, when he was commander in chief in 1934, explained the approach well. He likened war to an unfolding story and believed "that training in making a continuous or running estimate of a situation that is changing from hour to hour" would be the best "preparation for war."[92] Nimitz and his staff, especially those who had studied their adversaries for some time, expected the Japanese to be less flexible and adaptive. Yamamoto, for example, was considered "relentless and impatient" and a "firebrand" who could be enticed to make poor decisions under stress.[93] Those poor decisions would create additional opportunities for Nimitz.

By April 1942, it was already happening. The IJN's failure to devise a coherent strategy for the next phase of the war, and the competition between the Combined Fleet Staff and Rear Admiral Fukudome's Operations Section, led to a dispersal of effort. The Combined Fleet sought a decisive battle in the central Pacific while the Operations Section focused on extending the offensive in the south. Although Yamamoto's Combined Fleet ultimately won the argument, by the time they had done so the IJN was already committed to the offensive against Port Moresby. This dispersed IJN forces at a critical time and would give Nimitz the opportunity to counter each move in turn.

By aggressively using his forces, Nimitz also convinced his superiors that he could successfully fight the war in the Pacific. The raids in the central Pacific, Brown's operations with Fletcher in the south, and the success of the Doolittle Raid all enhanced Nimitz's standing. King and Knox might not have initially evaluated Nimitz as one of the Navy's best admirals, but they acknowledged his accomplishments and made him CINCPOA in early April. They hedged their bets in the South Pacific, where the most intense fighting was expected, by creating a separate area command under Vice Admiral Ghormley.

Aggressive use of the Pacific Fleet's carrier task forces also revealed flaws in tactics, doctrine, and organizational structure. Nimitz improved information flows and deliberately increased the adaptive capacity of PACFLT by moving the administrative work of type commands ashore and flattening the fleet's organizational structure. These steps improved the fleet's ability to accumulate and share knowledge, enhancing its future combat potential.

# TAKING RISKS

*Enmesh the adversary in an amorphous,*
*menacing, and unpredictable world.*

—Col. John Boyd, USAF, Ret.[1]

B y the end of April 1942, Nimitz had achieved two crucial objectives. First, he had won the confidence of his superiors in Washington. Secretary Knox and President Roosevelt had chosen Nimitz to be CINCPAC as well as CINCPOA and given him responsibility for the Allied forces in the world's largest ocean. Admiral King had approved Nimitz's latest operation and was starting to grant him more leeway to exercise his initiative. Second, Nimitz had reinvigorated the Pacific Fleet through a series of aggressive operations and established a coherent vision for the future. He was focused on the IJN's *Kido Butai* and began to use the improving sensemaking capabilities of his staff to identify where and how he could win a victory against Japan's mobile striking force.

As he sought opportunities to defeat the *Kido Butai*, Nimitz emphasized the principle of "calculated risk." Because of how he used the term in his instructions before the Battle of Midway, it is generally assumed that Nimitz understood "calculated risk" to mean avoiding unnecessary losses: "[Y]ou shall interpret [calculated risk] to mean the avoidance of exposure of your force to attack by superior enemy forces."[2] However, his actions before and during that battle demonstrate that Nimitz's conceptualization of "calculated risk" relied upon an aggressive, offensive mindset intended to capitalize on the inherent uncertainty of war.[3] He focused his limited combat power at the decisive point and consciously accepted the risk of severe losses if his assumptions were incorrect. Nimitz's "calculated risk" was disciplined risk-taking in the extreme. He was willing to endanger future success to shape the current battlefield and maximize the potential for victory. Over the first few months of 1942, Nimitz had worked to impress this orientation on the Pacific Fleet, leveraging the established heuristic emphasizing aggressive offensive action. In May and June, he and his subordinates would use that mindset to win a pair of victories that transformed the war in the Pacific.

## RECONFIGURING THE STAFF

Nimitz allowed his inherited staff members to redeem themselves by keeping them on for a time, but as the year progressed, he gradually took steps to ensure that the Pacific Fleet staff more closely reflected his aggressive mindset. A staff organization must become a sensemaking structure. Staff members bring newly emerging information into their deliberations and help the head of the organization determine how to act upon it. Members of a staff also mediate their commander's will; they help to create a "bond of kinship" between the commander and the rest of the organization by fostering shared understanding and mutual respect. Once Nimitz felt that he had established sufficient "bonds" with his inherited staff members, he began to bring in new personnel that could maximize his staff's potential. As he told his wife, the "staff will gradually change from those I found to those I choose."[4]

The aggressive Captain McMorris was detached and sent to sea, a necessary step for future promotion. McMorris' able assistant, Lynde McCormick, became head of War Plans. Vice Admiral Pye, former commander of the Battle Force, was detached in late March; Nimitz made him commander of TF 1, containing the Pacific Fleet's remaining battleships. On 14 May, Nimitz replaced Rear Admiral Withers, his submarine force commander, with Rear Adm. Robert H. English. Withers had blamed his captains for the limited success of the submarines; Nimitz wanted better results and expected English to deliver them. Nimitz also wanted a commander of the Fourteenth Naval District who could collaborate more effectively. He asked King to replace Bloch, and on 2 April, Rear Adm. David W. Bagley became the new district commandant.[5]

Although Nimitz used both his Plans and Operations Sections to assess options and craft orders for his task force commanders, he began to use them differently. The conservative and methodical Draemel, head of Operations, became responsible for routine and predictable—but no less essential—orders, such as assigning convoy escorts, scheduling training sorties, and detailing ships for supply runs. Nimitz relied on War Plans—initially led by McMorris and later McCormick—to direct major task force operations. This division made sense. Although Nimitz worked well with all of his staff, McMorris and McCormick had the temperament Nimitz desired. They were aggressive, they wanted to get at the Japanese, and they embraced Nimitz's conception of risk. It was through their War Plans Section that Nimitz crafted and executed the decisive operations of May and June 1942.

Nimitz could take this approach—which directly reflected the personalities of his staff members—because there was no established precedent, no standard, for Navy staff organizations. As a Naval War College lecture in 1944 noted, "The Navy has no definitely prescribed staff organization or staff procedure." The lack of a "plan or organization for staff functions in war" meant that Nimitz could delegate authority and responsibility based on the dispositions of his staff members, giving specific tasks to those who were best suited to carry them out. The emerging organizational structure reflected these decisions, codifying relationships and patterns of interaction that had already been established. Form followed function at this early stage of the war. Nimitz's decision to organize this way made sense; there was little time to do otherwise.[6]

Nimitz brought in one of "his men" in March 1942. Capt. Lloyd J. Wiltse had been gunnery officer of cruiser *Augusta* under Nimitz in the early 1930s and served in BuNav before the war. Nimitz made him assistant chief of staff. Wiltse became responsible for all staff administration, relieving Draemel of that burden and allowing him to focus his attention on operations. This arrangement allowed Nimitz to comfortably delegate and focus on the most pressing issue: how to use emerging intelligence to create an opportunity to defeat the *Kido Butai*. While Draemel and Wiltse managed "regular" operations, Nimitz, McCormick, and the War Plans Section explored how to counter IJN moves.

As he made these adjustments, Nimitz began to introduce and reinforce a particular culture and mindset. He built on his reputation as an honest broker, using it as a foundation to establish extremely high expectations and implicit standards for learning and failure. Lloyd Mustin, who had served with Nimitz in the early 1930s, emphasized Nimitz's approach as never being content with "anything short" of "as close to perfection as human limitations permit." Officers within Nimitz's previous commands who failed to embrace this perspective were quietly removed. "Nimitz was very direct and completely ruthless," Mustin recalled. Once he was confident that he had restored the morale of his staff, Nimitz worked to bring these expectations to the Pacific Fleet.[7]

Nimitz's approach explicitly encouraged risk-taking and more rapid learning, effectively creating an environment that recognized the two categories of "failure" Harvard professor Amy Edmondson has identified as essential for organizational learning. Failures that revealed new lessons were expected and the learning from them was valued. Failures that were attributable to inadequate skill or inappropriate orientation were sanctioned, and the officers responsible for them were quietly removed or given positions of lesser responsibility. Nimitz took this step with Bloch, and he made sure that Pye and Draemel were in roles that fit their abilities. Halsey's aggressiveness, even as it revealed flaws in his tactics and doctrine, was rewarded. As Edmondson has explained, this dual approach to failure—celebrating unexpected learning while sanctioning attributable mistakes—helps an organization learn more rapidly and creates an environment more receptive to risk-taking. Nimitz incorporated this dualistic conception of failure, and he used it to enhance the performance of his staff and his subordinates.[8]

## CARRIER DUEL IN THE CORAL SEA

Even before he formally assumed command as CINCPOA, Nimitz began to assert greater authority over operations in the South Pacific. Vice Admiral

Ghormley was still on his way south and King could not exercise effective control from Washington; he delegated to Nimitz. Nimitz issued Operation Plan No. 23–42 on 29 April, designed to oppose the enemy offensive against Port Moresby. He hoped to combine Halsey's TF 16—carriers *Enterprise* and *Hornet*—and Fletcher's TF 17—carriers *Lexington* and *Yorktown*—together into a powerful striking force and "check [the] further advance of the enemy in the New Guinea-Solomon area." However, as Nimitz and his staff feared, they were "unable to send enough forces to be *sure* of stopping the expected Japanese offensive." Halsey had to return from the Doolittle Raid before he could head south. He would not arrive in time; Fletcher fought alone.[9]

Nimitz gave Fletcher an outline of anticipated Japanese operations on 21 April that identified their "probable primary objective" as Port Moresby. The Japanese had been considering an operation against Port Moresby for some time; Vice Admiral Inoue had been ordered to seize it "if at all possible" in late January. By late April, he was ready. The Fourth Fleet's lone carrier, *Shoho*, would screen the invasion fleet, but was inadequate to secure aerial superiority. In early April, Yamamoto's staff had planned to augment the invasion forces with *Kaga*, but on 10 April, he and his staff decided to use Rear Admiral Hara Chuichi's Fifth Carrier Division—*Shokaku* and *Zuikaku*—instead. If the Americans appeared in force, Hara's two carriers would overwhelm them. The Combined Fleet staff also augmented Inoue with the land-based planes of the 25th Air Flotilla.[10]

Inoue devised a phased operation and issued his "Operational Order No. 13" on 23 April. He would send a force under Rear Admiral Shima Kiyohide east to occupy Tulagi in the Solomons on 3 May and then Ocean and Nauru in the Gilberts by mid-month. In the meantime, the Moresby Invasion Force under Rear Admiral Goto Aritomo would seize and occupy the main objective on 10 May. Rear Admiral Takagi Takeo would command the striking force with Hara's Fifth Carrier Division. They would support the Tulagi invasion and then sweep into the Coral Sea from the east, destroy any enemy forces encountered, and ensure the capture of Port Moresby by neutralizing Allied air bases in northern Australia. Hara felt striking the Australian bases would risk his carriers unnecessarily; Yamamoto agreed, and the attacks were called off. Inoue tasked his land-based planes with suppressing the Australian bases. To augment their numbers, Takagi was ordered to ferry additional fighters to Rabaul.[11]

Fletcher expected to face up to four IJN carriers: *Shokaku*, *Zuikaku*, *Ryukaku*, and *Kasuga Maru*. Nimitz thought there might be as many as six. Because aerial reconnaissance from MacArthur's SWPAC had been unreliable, Fletcher assumed control of twelve PBYs at Noumea. They would patrol the Coral Sea. Fletcher planned to keep both of his carriers together inside a single screen, an early departure from prewar doctrine that emphasized dispersal in the face of enemy attack. Fletcher also created two surface action groups, an Attack Group under Rear Admiral Kinkaid and a Support Group under Rear Admiral John G. Crace, Royal Navy (RN). Either could be detached if circumstances warranted; the Attack Group paired heavy cruisers and destroyers in a "Night Search and Attack" organization.[12]

Fletcher and Rear Admiral Fitch rendezvoused three hundred miles northwest of New Caledonia on 1 May. In rough seas, they fueled from the oilers *Neosho* and *Tippecanoe* the next day. *Yorktown* and her escorts finished and were ready for action that evening. When Shima's assault on Tulagi took place as planned on 3 May, Fletcher estimated he could move north with *Yorktown*, strike, and regroup before the main Japanese effort began. Nimitz, aided by Station Hypo's recovery of the Japanese operation order, correctly assessed that it was already under way. Fletcher opened the Battle of the Coral Sea by attacking Shima's invasion force on 4 May. The strike brought elation to Yamamoto's headquarters; the Fifth Carrier Division was in position "to catch and destroy the enemy aircraft carriers that have eluded us since the beginning of the war."[13]

To try to prevent the Japanese from using overwhelming force against Fletcher and keep Yamamoto guessing as to the location of Pacific Fleet striking forces, Nimitz planned to raid Japanese fishing vessels—believed "to be armed, . . . officered by Japanese naval reservists, and escorted by naval vessels"—in the North Pacific. Nimitz ordered light cruiser *Nashville* to carry out the operation on 2 May. On her way north, *Nashville* stopped at Midway to refuel and grounded. She was unable to carry out the plan, but Nimitz and his staff continued to try to distract the Combined Fleet and disperse Japanese efforts.[14]

In the meantime, MacArthur's planes had sighted *Shoho* off the west coast of Bougainville; the sighting report was passed to Fletcher and Fitch along with indications that it was a much larger carrier, possibly *Kaga*. Aware that a carrier battle was looming, Fletcher put his operation order into effect, merged his two carrier task forces into TF 17, made Fitch responsible for air operations, and readied his surface action groups for independent action. Hypo misread Hara's instructions and believed his carriers would attack Allied air bases. That pulled Fletcher toward the Louisiades as he sought to flank approaching Japanese forces. Early on 7 May, he ordered Crace to take his Support Group and "destroy enemy ships reported passing through Jomard Passage." Crace would, hopefully, prevent a successful invasion even if *Enterprise* and *Lexington* were disabled or distracted by a carrier duel. Later that day, TF 17 planes sank carrier *Shoho* while Hara's aircraft crippled oiler *Neosho* and sank destroyer *Sims*. Inoue postponed the Moresby landings for two days to allow his forces to regroup and give Takagi time to deal with the American carriers. Goto withdrew to the northwest.[15]

On 8 May, the carrier forces exchanged simultaneous blows. When Fitch's strike arrived, *Zuikaku* moved under a rain squall and escaped. *Shokaku* was hit by three bombs and set ablaze. Takagi concluded he lacked the planes for a second strike and, deeply worried about fuel, retired to the north. He believed he had damaged the two U.S. carriers sufficiently to sink them. He was wrong. Two torpedo hits on *Lexington* flooded compartments, reduced her speed, and opened leaks in aviation gas tanks, but she was still able to make way. The more maneuverable *Yorktown* had nimbly avoided torpedoes, but a bomb hit and several near misses had reduced her speed to twenty-five knots. Fletcher cleared the area and prepared to strike the Moresby invasion convoy if it came south again.

It did not. Inoue, lacking air cover for his invasion forces, wary of Allied land-based air, and apprehensive of the threat presented by Crace's Support Group, decided to formally postpone the Moresby operation. Fletcher and his team had won the Battle of the Coral Sea. However, Inoue still intended to occupy Ocean and Nauru. He scheduled that operation for 15 May.

At Pearl Harbor, Nimitz initially felt that the "situation was generally favorable." The Japanese were withdrawing and both U.S. carriers appeared to have survived. However, the situation shifted dramatically after a series of gasoline explosions and fires consumed *Lexington*. Nimitz explained to King that *Lexington* was "one fifth our carrier strength in Pacific" and, assuming *Shoho* was a large carrier, the Japanese had also lost approximately one-fifth of their carrier force. It was an unacceptable exchange. "We can not," Nimitz concluded, "afford to swap losses with this ratio." He asked for more planes to offset Japanese superiority in land-based aircraft and augment the operations of his remaining carriers. Nimitz also looked for opportunities to secure a more favorable exchange the next time PACFLT fought Japanese carriers.[16]

## EMPLOYING UNITY OF COMMAND

As a theater commander, Nimitz emphasized decentralized and unified command throughout his area of operations. To Nimitz, "unity of command" meant that each of his subordinate commands would have a single officer in charge who would command all forces allocated to him, regardless of their nationality or service branch. This held true for large commands, like the South Pacific Area, as well as smaller ones, like the islands of the South Pacific. This approach was a deliberate decision, one intended to foster the initiative of subordinates, modularize the theater's command structure, and make it easier to plan and conduct operations.

King understood its importance. He worked with Marshall to ensure coordinated joint action would be taken if areas like Hawaii or the West Coast were threatened. On 1 May, King informed Nimitz that "all Army air units" that would operate "against enemy seaborne activities" would fall under sea frontier commands. Naval officers in the Pacific would assume control of Army planes and pilots. This was an important step that gave Nimitz the ability to begin to maximize the potential of land-based planes in the Pacific. He and his staff hoped that a more unified approach, with more Navy influence on exercises and training, would increase the effectiveness of the Army's aerial attacks against enemy ships.[17]

In the South Pacific, the geographic distribution of Allied bases made unified command essential. Nimitz established a joint command at each island. Maj. Gen. Alexander Patch took command of Noumea; Brig. Gen. Henry Larsen, USMC, assumed command of Samoa; and Brig. Gen. Benjamin C. Lockwood Jr. took command of Tonga. Nimitz consistently delegated authority to subordinates and trusted them to carry out their missions. In the South

Pacific, they focused on organizing their defenses, establishing base facilities, and building airfields. In Hawaii, the immediate need was for more effective search and attack. Nimitz consolidated his long-range air forces by placing the heavy bombers of the VII Bomber Command under Rear Admiral Bellinger, who was now commanding all the Pacific Fleet's patrol wings. This integrated Army and Navy planes into a comprehensive search and striking force.

Nimitz's approach contrasts markedly with that taken by General MacArthur in the Southwest Pacific. While Nimitz stressed unification at all levels of his command hierarchy, MacArthur unified command only at his personal level. The result was an overly centralized command structure that made planning and conducting operations more difficult; in MacArthur's area, success relied on coordination generated from personal relationships, not organizational structure.[18] Nimitz recognized the importance of relationships, but deliberately used organizational structure to enhance effectiveness by creating subordinate "modules" throughout his command hierarchy. This increased the flexibility, responsiveness, and adaptive capacity of his theater. He encouraged his subordinates to leverage their creativity and make the most of their newly joint commands. The importance of this distinction cannot be overemphasized. The complexity of the challenge faced in the larger and more distributed Pacific theater made it essential to effectively leverage decentralized command; Nimitz could not have addressed his needs with MacArthur's more centralized approach.

On 2 May, Nimitz made a personal inspection of one of the many islands with a unified command structure, Midway. Positioned at the extreme northwestern end of the Hawaiian chain, Midway is thirteen hundred miles from Oahu. Nimitz and his staff considered it a "possible objective" for a surprise Japanese carrier raid. After his visit, Nimitz was confident it could resist a "moderate attack," but he took immediate steps to augment its defenses. Nimitz requested more troops and equipment from Admiral King. King was doing what he could; he ordered the small carrier *Wasp* sent to the Pacific, but there were too few escorts and skilled sailors to meet PACFLT's needs.[19]

## AN IMPENDING JAPANESE OFFENSIVE

After Coral Sea, Nimitz ordered Fletcher to withdraw. Although King and Nimitz expressed concerns about Fletcher's aggressiveness, it was clear he had won a strategic victory. Nimitz's approach of setting clear expectations, empowering his subordinates, and seizing emerging opportunities was starting to bear fruit. Although he desperately wanted a better exchange ratio, at Coral Sea the Japanese had been turned back for the first time. Nimitz's next challenge was deciding where to position his talented subordinates to win another victory.

The Japanese appeared to be planning a set of integrated offensives across the Pacific. The "#2 KING [for the letter K] Campaign" first appeared in CINCPAC intelligence briefings on 6 May. The campaign's objective was uncertain, but a supporting operation—the seizure of Ocean and Nauru—was much better understood. Inoue was expected to attack on 17 May. The Japanese "striking force," the *Kido Butai*, appeared to be preparing to commence offensive operations a few days later, on 21 May. Nimitz had to quickly discern where they would strike and how he would counter. In the meantime, Halsey's TF 16 arrived in the South Pacific. He was well positioned to thwart Inoue's plans. Nimitz gave Halsey the necessary details and he moved into position to ambush Inoue's forces on 13 May.[20]

That day turned out to be momentously important. The Japanese supply ship *Goshu Maru*, anchored at Wotje, received an important message about bringing supplies to "AF" for the "K campaign." Commander Rochefort quickly tied the two together. The "#2 KING Campaign" was associated with "AF," the Japanese designator for Midway. Layton quickly brought the new information to Nimitz's attention. Nimitz wanted validation that he could use it as a basis for planning. He sent McCormick to meet with Rochefort and talk through the details. McCormick was convinced. The CINCPAC intelligence briefing the next day documented the new intelligence. The Japanese were planning "a campaign designed to take Midway and Dutch Harbor, followed by an assault on Oahu."[21]

Nimitz acted quickly. He correctly assessed that if the Japanese sighted Halsey's carriers, Inoue might not move against Ocean and Nauru. That evening, Nimitz sent an "eyes only" message to Halsey asking him "to ensure that the enemy located TF 16 the next day."[22] In parallel, Nimitz worked to convince King of the emerging opportunity. Although King had recognized the threat to Hawaii, he had a standing requirement that a carrier force remain in the South Pacific.

In a detailed message the evening of 13 May, Nimitz presented his assessment and urged King to be more open to flexible employment of the carrier groups. Nimitz wanted his "striking forces in a state of maximum mobility" so that they could seize emerging opportunities and—as his 1923 thesis said—"surprise and deceive the enemy as to the plan of battle, and method and point of attack."[23] That meant moving Halsey and his carriers to the Central Pacific Area to oppose the impending attack on Midway. Nimitz told King that "in view of carrier situation which will exist until *Saratoga* and *Wasp* are available . . . believe [your] instructions . . . to maintain a [carrier task] force . . . in [the] South Pacific Area should be reviewed." Nimitz stressed that there was not much time to get Halsey in position before the Japanese struck.[24]

Nimitz was being disingenuous. Although he appeared to be collaboratively working the problem, Nimitz had already decided what to do. His message to King established the foundation for plans that were already in motion. Before King could respond, Halsey was sighted "500 miles Southeast of Tulagi" by Japanese patrol planes, exactly as Nimitz intended. As expected, Inoue "immediately cancelled the invasion" of Ocean and Nauru and prepared for battle. This gave Nimitz the opening he needed; on the afternoon of 15 May, he instructed Halsey to "proceed to Hawaiian Area."[25] Nimitz explained these orders to King directly:

Present indications [are] that there may well be three separate and possibly simultaneous enemy offensives. One involving cruisers and carriers against the Aleutians, probably Dutch Harbor. Second against Port Moresby involving present forces [in] that area, probably reinforced. Third against Midway–Oahu line, probably involving initially a major landing attack against Midway for which it is believed the enemy's main striking force will be employed. The time these offensives will be delivered is not clear but believe sighting Halsey in South yesterday caused postponement Ocean and Nauru Operations and will expedite Northern and Central Operations. My orders to Halsey . . . based on fact third offensive is against the most vital area and the mobile forces available to use are insufficient to effectively oppose all three offensives.[26]

This message best expresses Nimitz's view of calculated risk. Unable to defend everywhere, he had to decide where to position the Pacific Fleet for a counterblow. Since the Japanese assault against Midway was the greatest threat—and greatest opportunity—he would concentrate against it.

King was not convinced. In his response to Nimitz's message of 13 May, King felt the greatest threat was in the south. He assumed that in addition to Port Moresby, the Japanese might strike "either Northeast Australia or New Caledonia and Fiji." Midway would be a diversion. However, King respected Nimitz's assessment and gave him permission to "temporarily" remove carriers from the South Pacific, retroactively authorizing actions Nimitz had already taken.[27]

The specific sequence of these messages is crucial. When read in the order of their timestamps, they give the impression that Nimitz explained the situation, King approved Halsey's move north, and then Nimitz ordered it. This is how they are typically interpreted.[28] However, a close reading reveals that Nimitz sent his messages of 15 May before reading King's response. Nimitz acted on his own initiative to order Halsey back from the South Pacific and retroactively justified it to King. Nimitz's message to King the evening of 13 May was not a request for permission; it was a statement of intent. As soon as Nimitz confirmed that Halsey's sighting had delayed Inoue, he ordered Halsey north. A correct understanding of this sequence reveals Nimitz's aggressive determination and the assertive stance he was taking with King.[29]

When Nimitz next responded to King, he made three points. First, Nimitz emphasized his assessment that the Japanese would "try to capture [the] vital Hawaiian Area . . . before reinforcements afforded by our war production can be received." Second, he explained that he would "return Halsey to [the] Southwest" and act in concert with MacArthur if the Japanese did move south. Finally, Nimitz noted that *Yorktown* could probably be repaired at Pearl Harbor in a "reasonably short time." If the carrier was ready in time, she would increase Halsey's striking power by 50 percent.[30]

King once more demonstrated that he could revise his assessments when given sufficient time and evidence. By 17 May, he agreed with Nimitz's interpretation of Japanese plans and threw his support behind Nimitz's preparations. King instructed the commanders of the Western Sea Frontier and Northwestern Sea Frontier to support Nimitz and placed all forces in those areas at Nimitz's disposal. He also ordered "full coordination" with the Army, especially in Alaska. King warned Nimitz that the enemy appeared intent on trapping and destroying "a substantial portion of the Pacific Fleet" and ordered him to create a North Pacific Force to help defend Alaska.[31]

To eliminate any lingering doubts as to the intended target, Lt. Cdr. Jasper Holmes, one of Rochefort's team at Station Hypo, devised a clever scheme. Holmes knew that Midway used an evaporator plant to provide its freshwater supply. He proposed telling Midway to report in plain language that the plant had broken down; this could be done without risk of interception by using the submarine cable connecting Midway with Hawaii. Rochefort brought the idea to Layton, who proposed it to Nimitz. Nimitz authorized the plan, and the message was sent on 19 May. Midway sent the report; the Japanese intercepted it, and dutifully arranged to provide a water ship for "AF." Allied codebreakers at Belconnen and Hypo intercepted these transmissions the next day, confirming Midway as the objective of the Japanese operation.[32]

## THE COMBINED FLEET PLAN

In the aftermath of the Doolittle Raid, the center of gravity for IJN strategic planning shifted to Yamamoto and his Combined Fleet staff. For the war's "second phase" they focused on "luring the main strength of the US fleet into . . . a short-term decisive battle through attacks against places like Midway and Hawaii."[33] To prepare for these operations, Yamamoto brought together his fleet and force commanders on 18 April. He shared his personal assessment that "Second Phase Operations" required the Combined Fleet to "take the offensive" before the United States could bring the full extent of its industrial power—"from five to ten times ours"—to bear. "It is absolutely necessary," Yamamoto concluded, "that our naval air power overpower the enemy." He would seize Midway and, as King correctly deduced, use it to draw out the remnants of the Pacific Fleet and destroy them. The *Kido Butai* and the Main Body of the Combined Fleet would "overpower the enemy," demonstrate Japanese martial and moral superiority, and bring the war to a conclusion by crushing the "morale of the United States."[34]

However, to gain approval for his plans, Yamamoto had to make concessions. The most significant was acceding to the desire of Naval General Headquarters to seize positions in the Aleutian Islands. Conceived as a "means of forestalling U.S. offensives . . . toward northern Japan," the Aleutian offensive was timed to occur simultaneously with Yamamoto's Midway operation. Nothing more clearly illustrates the fractured nature of Japanese strategy. While the Aleutian operation was defensive and designed to expand the Empire's protective perimeter, Yamamoto's Midway plan was purely offensive. If successful, it would obviate the need for additional defensive positions by knocking the United States out of the war. Unsurprisingly, Yamamoto made Midway his main effort and assigned limited forces to the Aleutians.[35]

The combined effort became the "MI–AL Operation." As originally conceived, offensive operations in the Aleutians and against Midway would occur simultaneously, on 3 June. Vice Admiral Hosogaya Boshiro, commander in chief of the IJN's Fifth Fleet, would execute operations in the north. He planned three different phases of operations. In the first, he would seize Kiska, occupy Attu if possible, destroy installations on Adak, and raid the American base at Dutch Harbor. During the second, Hosogaya expected to consolidate his newly occupied positions and defeat any counterattacks. The third phase was a revision to a more static defensive strategy, intended to occur by 20 June.

Farther to the south, a series of coordinated operations would occupy Midway and seek battle with the Americans. Nagumo's *Kido Butai* would approach the atoll from the northwest. Yamamoto had intended to use all six of his large carriers, but damage to the Fifth Carrier Division at Coral Sea limited him to just four. Confident that Hara had destroyed two U.S. carriers, Yamamoto expected four carriers to be sufficient for Nagumo's task. His planes would knock out Midway's defenses on 3 June. Additional attacks would follow until the invasion, scheduled for 6 June. Rear Admiral Tanaka Raizo's transports would bring the assault troops; they and Vice Admiral Kurita Takeo's Close Support Group would approach the island from the west-southwest. Combat engineers were expected to quickly turn Midway into a "major outpost," ready to participate in the battle to destroy the Pacific

Fleet. Vice Admiral Kondo Nobutake's Invasion Force Main Body would act as bait and lure Nimitz's forces north. Once the Americans were within range, Kondo and Yamamoto would combine into a powerful battle line. Under the cover of Nagumo's carriers, the Combined Fleet's battleships would shatter the American forces. Yamamoto brought his staff and subordinates together in early May to rehearse the operations and develop detailed plans.[36]

The Combined Fleet's Midway exercises have been criticized as "fanciful" and unrealistic. The lack of realism was a result of the prevailing strategic situation. Yamamoto had assumed control of IJN planning through his personal prestige. Having staked his reputation on the offensive in the central Pacific, Yamamoto could not now fail to deliver. Accordingly, the exercises focused on how best to execute his plans and failed to assess their viability. There was no time for major revisions or reassessments. Ugaki's diary reflected this emphasis. He recorded that "delay would only benefit the enemy," and that "every effort" had to be made in preparation, training, and crafting detailed plans. If the American carriers appeared in an unanticipated position or were able to attack by surprise, Yamamoto's subordinates expected to find a way to triumph with their superior forces.[37]

However, Yamamoto and his staff did make some adjustments. While they went through their chart maneuvers, the Battle of the Coral Sea began. News of Fletcher's planes striking Tulagi came as a surprise; to help mitigate a similar surprise off Midway, the staff decided to carry out an aerial reconnaissance of Pearl Harbor prior to the first attacks "to confirm the presence of American aircraft carriers." If they were not there, then additional precautions would need to be taken. This reconnaissance effort was planned as a repeat of March's Operation K, with long-range H8K flying boats refueling from submarines at French Frigate Shoals before continuing on to Oahu. The Combined Fleet issued their preliminary orders for the "MI–AL Operation" on 5 May; the modifications devised during the wargames, including the "Second K Operation" followed three days later.[38]

Submarines were an important part of the plan. Yamamoto ordered the Sixth Fleet, his submarine force, to refuel the H8Ks at French Frigate Shoals and to form two scouting lines, designed to cover the most likely approach routes from Pearl Harbor. One was north of Oahu; the other was to the west. Additional submarines would scout Midway and the Aleutians. These submarines would act as a reconnaissance and attack force, locating Nimitz's ships and reducing their number before the final showdown with the Combined Fleet.

## THE CINCPAC ESTIMATE

Nimitz and his staff examined the latest intelligence and debated how to deal with the impending Japanese offensive. As usual, this involved a detailed estimate from Captain McCormick's War Plans Section. Their "Attack on Hawaiian and Alaskan Bases" was ready on 26 May. McCormick and his team were remarkably perceptive regarding the logic behind the timing of the Japanese offensive. "The enemy," they wrote, "knows our building program." The construction under way in American shipyards would make the Pacific Fleet the largest in the world within two years. Therefore, Japanese offensive operations "should be conducted at the earliest possible time" while U.S. defenses were "inadequate" and the IJN held the initiative. McCormick's estimate concluded that the Japanese would "attempt to capture Midway" and use it as a base for "subsequent operations against Oahu." Simultaneously, the Japanese would attempt to "capture an advanced position" in the Aleutians.[39] McCormick's reasoning mirrored Yamamoto's presentation to the Combined Fleet the month before. Both knew the Japanese could not triumph in a war of attrition against the United States.

However, McCormick acknowledged the significant risk that PACFLT was basing its plans on a "sole source of information," the intelligence provided by Station Hypo and other nodes of the Allied signals intelligence network. If they were incorrect—if the Japanese were mounting a massive deception campaign—Nimitz's carriers might be drawn into a trap. However, Nimitz and most of his staff believed the intelligence was correct and that they had a great opportunity.[40]

King declared a state of "fleet opposed invasion" on 14 May, giving Nimitz full authority over all air and naval forces in the Hawaiian Islands and allowing him to avoid one of the problems encountered in the Coral Sea, divided command of sea and air forces. Prewar tactics had emphasized the use of multiple "factors of strength" in combination; Nimitz exploited this concept to the fullest and packed the area around Midway with forces that could seek out and attack the Japanese. Rear Admiral Bellinger sent a substantial contingent of bombers and seaplanes to Midway. He held other aircraft in reserve around Oahu, ready to support Midway and guard Pearl Harbor. Once at Midway, Bellinger's planes joined many other fighters, torpedo planes, and dive-bombers. Capt. Cyril T. Simard commanded the island's defense; when the battle began, he had 127 combat aircraft.[41]

Rear Admiral English deployed twenty-five submarines to support Midway and the Aleutians. At the time of McCormick's estimate, five boats were already patrolling the approaches to Midway. Eight more were at Pearl Harbor ready to join them. When the Japanese arrived, English had twelve submarines stationed off Midway, four north of Oahu, and three in the areas in between. English arranged the submarines at Midway in a series of arcs to the north and west of the island. Nimitz expected them to close and attack using "division tactics" once they contacted the enemy. *Cuttlefish* was positioned much farther west, at an expected enemy rendezvous point.[42]

The most powerful blows were expected to be delivered by Halsey's TF 16. Nimitz planned to position Halsey northeast of Midway as soon as possible. If *Yorktown* was able to join the fight—still uncertain when the estimate was drafted—Fletcher and TF 17 would accompany him. Nimitz's other carrier, *Saratoga*, was still being repaired on the West Coast; she was expected to be ready on 5 June. Nimitz anticipated rushing *Saratoga* to the combat zone but did not expect her to arrive in time. With the extent of *Yorktown*'s damage still uncertain, Nimitz prepared to ambush the four most experienced carriers of the *Kido Butai* with just two of his own. He was ready to take this risk because he had faith in the total collection of forces at Midway and the acumen of his subordinates. It was an extremely bold decision. It also reflected the limitations of Nimitz's intelligence; he was unaware that Yamamoto was bringing the Combined Fleet's main body to the battle and had no plans to fight it.

Nimitz attempted to mitigate risk by preparing for a variety of contingencies. He put the Pacific Fleet's amphibious force, currently training in San Diego, on forty-eight hours' notice. Should the Japanese successfully land on Midway, the amphibious force would "retake any positions captured by the enemy." In the meantime, the island's nearly three thousand defenders, under the leadership of Col. Harold Shannon, USMC, worked diligently to make that unnecessary.[43]

To guard against the threat to the Aleutians, Nimitz created TF 8, the North Pacific Force, under Rear Admiral Theobald and gave him authority to coordinate all air and naval forces in the area. Nimitz expected Theobald to use his land-based air to locate and strike the Japanese as they approached. The poor weather in the north would hopefully mitigate the offensive capabilities of the IJN's carriers. If they closed the Alaskan mainland, Theobald was expected to mount coordinated strikes with his planes and surface ships. Nimitz anticipated Theobald's forces would turn back any attempted invasion, but Nimitz kept TF 8 small to strengthen his hand at Midway.

McCormick's estimate accurately reflected Nimitz's basic concept for the coming battle, attrition guided by calculated risk: "We cannot now afford to slug it out with the probably superior approaching Japanese forces. We must endeavor to reduce his forces by attrition—submarine attacks, air bombing, attack on isolated units. The principle of calculated chance is indicated. . . . If attrition is successful, the enemy must accept the failure of his venture or risk battle on disadvantageous terms." Nimitz would use his carriers, submarines, and land-based planes to ambush the *Kido Butai*. He would refuse any surface action. In later discussions with his staff and subordinates, Nimitz reframed the concept of "calculated chance" as "calculated risk."[44]

The "principle of calculated risk" has been extensively discussed, but never placed in appropriate context.[45] Nimitz's perspective was well summarized in his 15 May message to King, when Nimitz said that his forces were "insufficient to effectively oppose all three [Japanese] offensives." Unable to defend everywhere, Nimitz used available intelligence and the diverse perspectives of his staff to identify the most fruitful opportunity—an ambush off Midway—and positioned his forces for maximum effect. As valid as this decision appears in hindsight, it was a significant gamble and not an obvious choice at the time. Nimitz's "calculated risk" was disciplined, deliberate, and extremely bold.[46]

### FINAL APPROACH

When Halsey returned to Pearl Harbor on 26 May, he was sick and suffering from severe dermatitis. "Gaunt, exhausted, and irritable," Halsey was in no

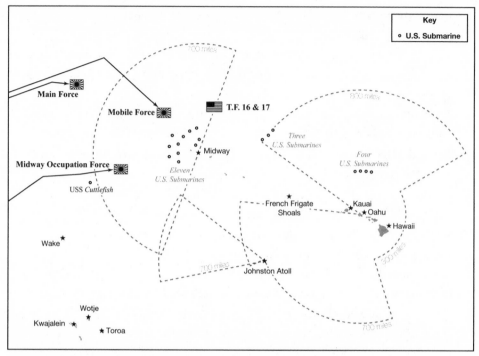

MAP 3. Nimitz's Dispositions for the Battle of Midway, June 1942

shape to command. Nimitz could have replaced him with Rear Admiral Noyes, Halsey's shore-based administrator, or Rear Admiral Bellinger, but Halsey recommended Spruance, his cruiser commander. Halsey provided an official letter, praising Spruance's "outstanding ability . . . , excellent judgement, and quiet courage." Nimitz was surprised, but he had confidence in Spruance—Nimitz was already planning to make him CINCPAC chief of staff—and went along with Halsey's recommendation. By taking command of TF 16, Spruance provided an excellent example of the resilience and adaptive capacity created by Nimitz's decision to have each carrier task force led by a pair of admirals, one commanding the task force and another commanding the screening vessels. Spruance was thoroughly familiar with TF 16 and its operations; he seamlessly stepped into Halsey's place, integrated with TF 16's staff, and demonstrated the wisdom of Nimitz's approach during the battle.[47]

On 27 May, Nimitz issued his Operation Plan 29-42 and held a conference to discuss it with his principal subordinates, including Lieutenant General Emmons, Spruance, and Fletcher. Nimitz framed the opportunity and made space for everyone to share their thoughts: "All hands expressed their views and were given a very clear explanation of the problem." Nimitz's operation plan succinctly described the mission, provided necessary details, and granted his subordinates great flexibility. The Japanese were expected to suppress Midway through shore bombardment and carrier strikes "so incessant as to prevent refueling and rearming" of defending planes. Japanese focus on Midway would create the opportunity for an ambush, but once PACFLT carriers were sighted, they were certain to "become the primary" target. Still, the risk was great, and accepting it had taken a toll on Nimitz. Fletcher observed that he was not his usual, calm self; Nimitz appeared agitated and "exceptionally disturbed."[48]

But there was cause for optimism. *Yorktown* had arrived at Pearl Harbor that morning, a day earlier than anticipated. Fourteen hundred workers immediately boarded the damaged carrier and set to work. The next day, *Yorktown* entered drydock for repairs to her hull. In little more than forty-eight hours, by 0900 on 30 May, *Yorktown* was ready to sail. Her air group was augmented with planes from *Saratoga*, giving *Yorktown* a full complement. Nimitz praised the men of TF 17 as they departed: "Your work in the Coral Sea against heavy odds was magnificent. . . . You outfought an able enemy and inflicted severe losses. . . . As you go out to meet him again, I have great confidence in your courage, skill, and ability to strike even harder blows. Good hunting and good luck." Fletcher headed north to join Spruance, who had sailed the day before. They would rendezvous northeast of Midway at "Point Luck," where Fletcher would assume command of the combined striking force.[49]

Nimitz ordered Fletcher and Spruance to "inflict maximum damage on the enemy" through "strong attrition tactics" and avoid "decisive action." At Point Luck they could sit out of range, on the flank of the Japanese striking force, and move to strike if favorable circumstances developed. While Fletcher and Spruance waited, Midway's planes searched for the enemy. Long-range patrols, out to seven hundred miles, were expected to find the enemy carriers early in the morning, potentially before they launched their strikes. English told his submarines to pursue the enemy aggressively and "press home all attacks." Nimitz expected to be kept "fully informed of air searches and other air operations." He would assess incoming information and coordinate operations from the submarine base at Pearl Harbor. Others would fly the planes and conn the ships, but Nimitz—as the officer best positioned to keep abreast of the entirety of the developing situation—would lead his fleet in battle.[50]

Farther west, a series of unanticipated delays and difficulties interfered with Yamamoto's plans. Nagumo needed more time than expected to provision and prepare; he asked to delay the *Kido Butai*'s sortie by a day. Yamamoto acquiesced, but kept the existing timetable for the operation; the amphibious assault could not be moved because it relied on favorable tides. Nagumo would have less time to suppress Midway's defenses. The Sixth Fleet's submarines also left late and missed the opportunity to sight TF 16 and 17 as Fletcher and Spruance left Pearl Harbor. The error was compounded by failure to report the delay, leaving Yamamoto ignorant of the fact that his submarine scouting lines were out of position. Another scouting effort was thwarted when Nimitz stationed seaplane tenders at French Frigate Shoals. When Japanese submarines arrived, they realized they could not surface and refuel the seaplanes as intended. The Second K Operation was cancelled on 31 May, preventing the Japanese from reconnoitering Pearl Harbor.[51]

Despite these reconnaissance failures, the Combined Fleet moved ahead. Intercepted radio traffic led Ugaki to suspect that the Americans were "preparing to meet us." However, this was exactly what he and Yamamoto had anticipated. They wanted to draw out the Americans, and if the enemy came to Midway's defense earlier than anticipated, so much the better. The result would be the same. All IJN forces continued to close, anticipating that searches from Midway would only reach five hundred miles. They failed to entertain alternative possibilities.[52]

Over the next several days, as circumstances unfolded as his intelligence predicted, Nimitz's confidence increased. On the afternoon of 30 May, he told his subordinates that he anticipated a Japanese landing attempt on 5 June and the first "preliminary attacks" on 2 or 3 June. The enemy invasion forces were expected to refuel in a position to the west on 31 May or 1 June; Nimitz thought it might be a good opportunity for an attack by B-17s. On 2 June,

Nimitz suggested Fletcher take his task forces west "to insure" they would be "within early striking distance" of the enemy carriers; as he had in January, before Halsey's strike into the Marshalls, Nimitz used his best intelligence to urge his subordinates to take more aggressive action. Instead of waiting on developments, Fletcher would be ready to strike almost immediately. Nimitz also sent more details of Japanese plans; "they are even bringing guns captured on Wake to defend our islands," he said. He closed with encouragement: "Confident you have the stuff to smear their plays. Watch for razzle dazzle."[53]

Following Nimitz's suggestion, Fletcher moved west. He kept the two carrier task forces separate, positioned TF 17 ten miles north of Spruance's TF 16, and introduced a straightforward division of labor. Fletcher would use *Yorktown's* planes to search for the enemy while Spruance kept *Enterprise* and *Hornet* ready to strike as soon as the Japanese carrier force was sighted. Everything now depended on locating their carriers. Nimitz, Fletcher, and Spruance suspected the Japanese might operate their carriers in two groups, one close to Midway and the other in distant support. On 2 June, Nimitz reminded Simard that the "successful and timely employment of striking forces" depended on "reliable combat intelligence" from his scouting operations. Fletcher and Spruance would have one good chance to catch the *Kido Butai* unaware. "Reports," Nimitz stressed, "must get through promptly."[54]

## DANGER IN THE ALEUTIANS

In the Aleutians, the declaration of a state of "fleet opposed invasion" put Rear Admiral Theobald in command of all naval and air forces. Nimitz instructed Theobald to establish a joint defense with Brig. Gen. William C. Butler, commander of the Eleventh Air Force, Capt. Leslie E. Gehres, commander of Patrol Wing Four, and Capt. Ralph Parker, commander of the Alaskan Sector. Nimitz wanted Theobald to create a joint task group with all his planes under Butler. Instead, Theobald decided to "assert his prerogative discreetly . . . by persuasion rather than command." He failed to establish unified command.[55]

When he reached Kodiak on 27 May, Theobald conferred with Butler, Parker, and Gehres and devised a plan to repulse the Japanese offensive. Theobald divided his forces into six main groups. The Main Body contained

Theobald's five cruisers and their escorting destroyers; Theobald would command them personally, patrol south of Kodiak, and look to "exploit opportunities." Parker's patrol craft would form a Surface Search Group and act as pickets. Gehres would operate Theobald's Air Search Group, composed of Navy PBYs and a few B-17s, many equipped with radar. They would scout for the enemy. Butler's Air Striking Group, with the Army bombers and fighters, would attack the Japanese once they were found. Theobald also created a Destroyer Striking Group based at Makushin Bay on the island of Unalaska, ready to attack enemy forces approaching Dutch Harbor. His last group was his submarines, "disposed in the hope of intercepting the enemy." Nimitz "generally" concurred with Theobald's concept and, in his typical way, expressed confidence in him.[56]

Unfortunately, Theobald's dispositions were ill suited to meet the Japanese attack. In mid-May, Nimitz and his staff began to recognize that the islands of Attu and Kiska were likely Japanese objectives. They alerted Theobald of their suspicions on 28 May, but he ignored them. Instead, Theobald assumed the Japanese would strike the objectives King had identified—Dutch Harbor, Kodiak, and the approaches to the continent—and positioned his forces accordingly. On 1 June, confident in his arrangements, Theobald boarded his flagship *Nashville* and headed to sea. When the Japanese attack came on 3 June, Theobald was too far to the east and out of position; forced to maintain radio silence while at sea, he was also unable to coordinate his forces.

Vice Admiral Hosogaya struck Dutch Harbor on schedule with his Mobile Force, light carriers *Ryujo* and *Junyo*, commanded by Rear Admiral Kakuta Kakuji. The weather in the Aleutians was consistently difficult; *Junyo*'s strike group turned back. *Ryujo*'s planes found clear skies over the target and "inflicted considerable damage," but the limited strength of the attack—just four bombers and twelve fighters were reported—suggested that it was a "preliminary feeler" and that the "main carrier attack" would come the next day. Unlike Nimitz, Theobald did not maintain a plot with a comprehensive view of enemy dispositions; this limited his situational awareness and led to confusion and wasted effort. Gehres, for example, incorrectly assumed the Japanese were operating two carrier groups, one to the north in the Bering Sea and another to the south.[57]

Kakuta planned another strike, this time against Theobald's Destroyer Striking Group, but bad weather prevented it. In the meantime, an Eleventh Air Force plane apparently found Kakuta, but it could not maintain contact. PBYs found his carriers the next day southwest of Dutch Harbor. Bombers took off to attack, but poor weather hampered their efforts and contact was lost before they could arrive; most returned to base without sighting anything. After contact was regained later in the day, another strike went out. A few planes managed to attack, but none scored any hits.

Kakuta spent the morning of 4 June preparing to strike Adak. Terrible weather was forecast over that island, so he attacked Dutch Harbor again that afternoon. While his ships dodged the sparse American attacks, Kakuta's planes set fire to the harbor's fuel stowage, destroying 22,000 barrels. Vice Admiral Pye, who had been informed by Theobald's subordinates of the Japanese attack, incorrectly assumed the Japanese would raid the West Coast. Pye took TF 1 and its old battleships out of San Francisco and assumed a "support position" one thousand miles west of the California coast.[58] Theobald, frustrated at his forces' inability to fight off the Japanese, took *Nashville* to Kodiak, arriving there the next morning.

On 5 June, after "forty-eight hours [of] continuous flying and fighting," Gehres and his men were reaching the limits of their endurance. Only fourteen of his twenty aircraft were still operational; losses were mounting, and they had "not yet struck [an] effective blow." Gehres requested replacements before the Japanese could get away, but they seemed to have already disappeared. Theobald felt his dispositions were still adequate to keep the Japanese from achieving their objectives and told Nimitz that he had "no reason to alter" them. Theobald also suggested that because the attacks had been relatively minor, the Japanese effort in the Aleutians might be a "diversion" and that their carriers might be heading for Midway.[59]

## VICTORY UNFOLDS

With all the pieces set, the Battle of Midway developed quickly, and much as Nimitz's plan envisioned. He and his staff maintained a clear sense of the unfolding engagement at Pearl Harbor, using a large plot "laid over plywood across a pair of sawhorses."[60] They monitored sighting reports, refined them, and rebroadcast essential details to Simard, Fletcher, and Spruance. Although not always necessary because several of the carriers monitored the search plane frequency, Nimitz's messages enhanced his subordinates' situational awareness and allowed a more concerted approach to battle, especially in its early hours.

The first sighting report came on the morning of 3 June. At about 0930, one of Simard's PBYs found Tanaka's invasion convoy seven hundred miles from Midway on bearing 261 degrees. Nimitz correctly ascertained that this was the enemy "occupation force" and broadcast that information to his task force commanders. The "striking force," Nimitz reminded them, was "expected to be separated." Nimitz summarized the situation for King and sought to prevent him from interfering by explaining that events were developing as anticipated. The enemy had been sighted in the Aleutians, but their "attack force" in those waters had not been located. The Midway "occupation force" had been identified and B-17s were on their way to attack it; however, the "striking force" had not yet been found. Nevertheless, Nimitz was so confident he was "beaming." The events of the day had confirmed his staff's assessment and validated their preparations.[61]

While Simard and English worked to attack the enemy occupation force, Nimitz informed his subordinates that the "carriers, our most important objective, should soon be located. Tomorrow may be the day you can give them the works." Nimitz and his staff expected the Japanese carrier attack on Midway at dawn the next day, but they still faced a great deal of risk and uncertainty. It was essential that the next morning's searches locate the enemy carriers. Anticipating they would, Nimitz slept on a cot in his office.[62]

At 0534, a PBY found the Japanese carriers; a second amplified the sighting less than thirty minutes later: "two carriers and battleships bearing 320 degrees, distance 180 [miles], course 135, speed 25." The location was almost exactly where Nimitz and his staff expected the IJN carriers to be found. Simard reported he was "shooting the works." Nimitz rebroadcast the sighting report to his task force commanders, trusting they would know what to do. English acted quickly; he ordered nine submarines of his Midway Patrol group to "go after them."[63]

Fletcher reacted even faster. At 0607, he ordered Spruance to "proceed southwesterly and attack enemy carriers when definitively located."

*Enterprise*'s radio operators had intercepted the sighting reports, so Spruance was ready. He pulled out a blank maneuvering chart and "calmly" plotted the relative positions of TF 16, Midway, and the enemy carrier groups. "Using his thumb and index finger as dividers, he estimated the distance was about 175 miles," the maximum range of his fighters and torpedo bombers. Spruance needed to close. He took TF 16 toward the enemy at twenty-five knots; an hour later, at 0706, the strike started taking off.[64]

In the meantime, Nagumo tried to make up for lost time by aggressively suppressing Midway's defenses and destroying its airplanes. His initial strike on the island did "considerable damage," but Midway struck back. From about 0700 to 0830, a motley collection of Simard's planes attacked the *Kido Butai* from various angles and altitudes. The steady stream of uncoordinated attacks convinced Nagumo of the need for a second attack, kept his carriers off balance, and forced him to operate "reactively."[65]

Nagumo had cruiser floatplanes searching to the east, but a combination of late starts, bad weather, and the inherent challenges of overwater searches kept them from sighting TF 16 or 17 before Nagumo's attention became firmly focused on Midway. He ordered the planes he was holding ready to attack enemy ships rearmed for another strike on the island. When one of the scouts finally located TF 16 and reported it as "ten enemy surface units," Nagumo stopped the rearmament of his planes, asked for amplification, and ordered more extensive reconnaissance of the area. When the scout reported "what appears to be a carrier," Nagumo resolved to attack as soon as possible, but with B-17s overhead and his planes from the Midway strike waiting to land, he had to wait.[66]

The *Kido Butai*'s fate was already sealed. Nagumo started recovering his planes at 0837. Once landing operations completed, he altered course to close the range before launching his attack, but at 0918, before his strike aircraft were spotted, Lt. Cdr. John C. Waldron's Torpedo Squadron Eight appeared. They were the first of Spruance's planes to attack. Rear Adm. Marc Mitscher, *Hornet*'s commanding officer, had sent her planes to the expected position of the second IJN carrier group; most missed Nagumo to the north. Waldron, a "highly aggressive officer," followed his instincts, broke formation, and led his "well trained squadron" right to the Japanese. Attacking "without hesitation,"

Waldron's squadron was annihilated by the *Kido Butai*'s defending fighters. Although they scored no hits, Waldron and his men filled the lull between Midway's attacks and those from *Yorktown* and *Enterprise*.[67]

As *Enterprise*'s Torpedo Squadron Six attacked and was similarly destroyed, Nimitz was "frantic." The Japanese carriers had appeared as expected, but the initial attacks had failed to deliver any telling blows. That changed rapidly shortly after 1000. *Enterprise*'s dive-bombers, Bombing Six and Scouting Six, under the command of Lt. Cdr. Clarence Wade McClusky Jr., approached the *Kido Butai* from the south-southwest. Nearly simultaneously, *Yorktown*'s strike group, launched by Fletcher at 0838, closed from the southeast. *Yorktown*'s group was a cohesive formation with a dive-bomber squadron, a torpedo squadron, and a fighter squadron.[68]

For the first time, the *Kido Butai* faced a coordinated attack from multiple squadrons, and its defenses were overwhelmed. *Yorktown*'s Torpedo Squadron Three drew Japanese attention to the wavetops while *Enterprise*'s dive-bombers used scattered clouds to avoid detection. They crippled *Kaga* with bombs that destroyed her bridge, wrecked her flight deck, and started terrible fires. A few minutes later, *Yorktown*'s dive-bombers hit *Soryu* with three bombs and turned her flight deck into a "sea of fire." Above *Kaga*, Lt. Richard H. Best, commander of *Enterprise*'s Bombing Six, noticed that Nagumo's flagship *Akagi* was not being attacked. He and two of his squadron switched targets. One of their bombs exploded in *Akagi*'s upper hangar and started a fire that quickly raged out of control. By 1030, all three carriers were crippled.[69]

While Nagumo transferred his flag to cruiser *Nagara*, his subordinates struck back. *Hiryu* began launching a partial strike of Aichi D3A dive-bombers and escorting fighters at 1054. Nakajima B5N torpedo bombers would follow in a second wave. Station Hypo intercepted a plain language Japanese transmission requesting the "position [of] enemy carriers," so Nimitz broadcast a warning that the strike was coming. Nagumo intended to follow these strikes with an attack by his surface ships. In the meantime, Lt. Cdr. William Brockman compounded Nagumo's difficulties by bringing submarine *Nautilus* into attack position. Brockman fired three torpedoes at the doomed *Kaga*. One hit but failed to detonate. Brockman incorrectly reported he had mortally wounded the carrier.[70]

Fletcher still assumed that the Japanese were operating in two carrier groups. He knew the two carriers reported by Midway were damaged but had "no indication of [the] location" of the others. Anticipating the need for additional searches, he had held half of *Yorktown*'s dive-bombers in reserve. Confident that a Japanese strike was inbound, at 1133 he sent them searching to the northwest. Soon thereafter, *Hiryu*'s strike appeared on *Yorktown*'s radar. Nimitz's headquarters received a hastily coded message from an unknown originator: "Am being attacked by a large number of enemy bombers." It was *Yorktown*.[71]

Defending fighters broke up the attacking formation, but *Hiryu*'s dive-bomber pilots demonstrated why they were considered the best in the fleet. Three hits and two near misses started fires and brought *Yorktown* to a halt. Fletcher transferred his flag to cruiser *Astoria* and transferred tactical command to Spruance. Damage control parties extinguished *Yorktown*'s flames, repaired the flight deck, and got the carrier under way just in time to meet *Hiryu*'s next wave. To the Japanese pilots, *Yorktown* appeared undamaged, so they thought they were attacking a "second" American carrier. The antiaircraft fire "was so heavy that observers thought it incredible that any [attackers] got through." Two torpedoes hit *Yorktown*'s port side at 1445, knocking out power and starting a list to port that quickly reached 23 degrees. Capt. Elliott Buckmaster, fearful she would capsize, ordered the ship abandoned at 1500.[72]

With successful attacks against "two enemy carriers," Yamamoto remained optimistic. At 1655, chief of staff Ugaki asked his counterpart on Nagumo's staff if it would be possible to use the base at Midway tomorrow. Ugaki and Yamamoto, although aware of the damage to the *Kido Butai*, still believed that the operation could be brought to a successful conclusion. If there were only three American carriers—which appeared most likely—then the odds were now roughly even. Success would go to the side that was first to strike. *Hiryu* prepared for a dusk attack against the remaining U.S. carrier.[73]

Fletcher's decision to preserve adaptive capacity by holding back half of *Yorktown*'s dive-bombers proved crucial. Prior to the second attack on TF 17, Spruance assumed that "all four enemy carriers" were "badly damaged." He and his staff paused, doubting the need for further attacks. The second strike on *Yorktown* validated Fletcher's suspicion that at least one Japanese carrier was "still on [the] loose." His scouts found *Hiryu* at 1430. Spruance immediately launched a strike. When it arrived, *Hiryu* was preparing her attack. Four bombs crashed into *Hiryu* and started a crippling conflagration. The *Kido Butai* had been destroyed.[74]

As the day ended, Nimitz sent a message of encouragement to his task force commanders and prepared them for another day of combat: "You who participated in the Battle of Midway today have written a glorious page in our history. I am proud to be associated with you. I estimate that another day of all-out effort on your part will complete the defeat of the enemy." He also broadcast his current assessment to his subordinates and Admiral King. The concentrated attacks on the Japanese striking force had apparently left three carriers burning. However, Nimitz correctly assessed that Yamamoto would persist despite his losses. "Believe enemy will," Nimitz concluded, "continue duel with our two remaining carriers" and "proceed with landing attack on Midway." Nimitz was "certain" the Japanese still had "at least one carrier able to operate aircraft." To balance the loss of *Yorktown*, Nimitz planned to bring *Saratoga* and TF 11 into the battle as soon as possible.[75]

Spruance broadcast details of his final strike, which left another enemy carrier burning, and requested Midway's morning searches provide details on "enemy units still available for attack." Then he moved east to keep his distance from IJN surface forces. Nagumo initially tried to retrieve some semblance of a victory by gathering his forces and seeking a night surface battle. Yamamoto supported this course of action, ordering his task forces to "immediately contact and attack the enemy" at 1915. These exhortations were unrealistic; the IJN had no hope of catching Spruance that night. After *Hiryu* was mortally wounded, Nagumo realized this fact; he ignored the order to attack and withdrew.[76]

Once Nimitz received news of Spruance's final attack of the day, he reassessed and shared the good news that "four enemy carriers [were] probably accounted for." But his assumption that the Japanese would press ahead was correct. Kurita's bombardment force closed Midway, other ships searched for Fletcher and Spruance, and submarine *I-168* briefly shelled the atoll. However, by 0015 on the morning of 5 June, it was clear to Yamamoto and his staff that their forces would be dangerously exposed when daylight came.

They ordered them to fall back on the main body. Kurita reversed course, inadvertently heading directly toward the surfaced submarine *Tambor*, which had been shadowing his cruisers. As they maneuvered to avoid *Tambor*, *Mikuma* and *Mogami* collided. Kurita ordered two destroyers to escort the damaged cruisers to safety.[77]

*Tambor* failed to attack but reported "many unidentified surface ships" just ninety miles west of Midway; their proximity, and the lack of specific details as to their course, convinced Nimitz and Simard that the Japanese were intent on assaulting the atoll. They contracted their defense and prepared to repulse the invasion. When Nimitz later discovered the flaws in *Tambor's* sighting report, he was "irate" because it led English to move his submarines just twelve miles from Midway and Simard to send his morning searches out to only 250 miles. These arrangements prevented Nimitz from fully capitalizing on the success of 4 June. As he later told King, "[O]ur forces should have destroyed many enemy ships on 5 June."[78]

Simard's morning searches "made it clear that the Japanese had reversed course." They only found Kurita's cripples; Midway planes attacked *Mikuma* and *Mogami* but scored no hits. Spruance pursued the retreating Japanese and launched an attack that afternoon, apparently against the damaged *Hiryu*, but by the time the planes arrived at 1715, the carrier had sunk. The next morning, Spruance launched a search that discovered *Mikuma* and *Mogami*, still slowly attempting to escape. Strikes hit both cruisers; *Mogami* was able to withdraw, but *Mikuma* was sunk.[79]

Nimitz realized the extent of the victory by the evening of 5 June. There had been no air attack on Midway since the previous morning and "no enemy aircraft were evident," indicating that all four Japanese carriers were disabled or sunk. The enemy was "heading westward." In a message to King on 6 June, Nimitz indicated that he intended to pursue the Japanese in the Aleutians "if situation continues favorable in Midway area." As the full picture of the victory emerged, 4 June was recognized as a "great day for the American Navy."[80] This was despite the loss of the damaged *Yorktown*, which had been torpedoed and sunk by submarine *I-168*.

*Saratoga* arrived at Pearl Harbor on 6 June, and Nimitz sent her north. He would use her planes to bring *Hornet* and *Enterprise* up "to best practicable air strength" and then integrate *Saratoga* into TF 17. While Fletcher headed back to Pearl Harbor for replenishment, Spruance and TF 16 would operate under the command of Rear Admiral Theobald to "seek out and destroy enemy forces in the Aleutian area." King agreed with Nimitz's decision to send a "strong task force north." However, by 10 June, it was apparent that the threat in the Aleutians was insignificant compared to that in the South Pacific. Nimitz ordered Spruance to return to Pearl Harbor.[81]

Nimitz summarized his reasoning in a message to Admiral King: "I consider that his [the enemy's] drive for Moresby and/or other Southern bases . . . is a greater threat to our interests. I therefore propose to return Task Force 16 and the Fleet units of Task Force 8 to Pearl in preparation for future operations and will employ only submarines and shore based air against the enemy" in the Aleutians. Nimitz once more focused on "calculated risk." He would place his limited forces where they could have the greatest impact and maximize his potential opportunities. King approved; with the decisive success of Midway, he could hardly do otherwise.[82]

## CONCLUSION

Victories in the battles of May and June transformed the war in the Pacific. Before Midway, the unprecedented striking power of the *Kido Butai* gave the IJN the initiative and allowed Yamamoto to control the fighting. To have a hope of winning, Nimitz had to blunt that power. He understood this immediately; in early January, he told Lieutenant Commander Layton to "be the Admiral Nagumo of my staff" and "see the war . . . from the Japanese viewpoint."[83] The focus on Nagumo was deliberate and calculated. Nimitz wanted to destroy the *Kido Butai*. When intelligence provided the opportunity for an ambush, he seized it. The victory at Midway "shattered" the IJN's striking force and gave Nimitz the opportunity to initiate offensive operations.

Through the lens of victory, it is difficult to appropriately frame the magnitude of Nimitz's gamble at Midway. He stripped defenses from other sectors, deployed a minor force in the Aleutians, and concentrated virtually everything around the small atoll. Even if *Yorktown* had not been repaired in time, Nimitz was willing to fight with just two carriers against the IJN's best four. Edmondson's research into organizational learning and innovation has stressed the importance of risk-taking; although her comments are intended for modern businesses, they reflect Nimitz's approach to battle: "Playing not to lose is a mindset that focuses, consciously or not, on protecting against the downside; playing to win, in contrast, is focused on the upside, seeks opportunity, and necessarily takes risks."[84] At Midway, Nimitz played to win.

Nimitz could confidently take such risks because he had brought a coherent approach to the Pacific Fleet that resonated with his aggressive disposition. He had reconfigured his staff, identified effective subordinates, and achieved a shared understanding with Admiral King. This created space for "calculated risk" at Midway. "Orientation," John Boyd argued, "is the center of gravity for command and control, the key factor" that determines whether one can "exploit" the variety inherent in rapidly changing circumstances.[85] Nimitz knew this. He deliberately fostered his command's ability to reorient and increased his subordinates' ability to act in concert toward mutual goals. Nimitz did this through increased trust, prompted through collaboratively developed shared understanding. He valued diverse perspectives and opinions, welcoming them in his regular morning conferences, and it was in those sessions where he set clear expectations. This allowed Nimitz, the members of his staff, and his chief subordinates to collectively make sense of the unfolding war and act coherently.

Their success at Midway was the culmination of efforts that began much earlier. Foremost among them was the Navy's emphasis on aggressive action to seize and hold the initiative in battle. The series of uncoordinated strikes the morning of 4 June failed to hit Nagumo's carriers, but they kept him occupied, forced him to react, and prevented him from launching a strike against Fletcher and Spruance until dive-bombers from *Yorktown* and *Enterprise* crippled three of his carriers. By employing "calculated risk" and bringing virtually all his mobile forces to Midway, Nimitz increased the likelihood of this outcome, but the victory was a narrow one. English's submarines accomplished very little, the slow torpedo bombers were overwhelmed, and the strikes from Midway, as important as they were, were largely ineffective. Nimitz needed everything he had to win.

That victory was possible because in the months prior, Nimitz had endeavored to, in the words of Boyd, "enmesh the adversary in an amorphous, menacing, and unpredictable world."[86] Nimitz and King had used their mobile forces to initiate a series of attacks on Japanese forces and positions, creating uncertainty about where they might be and when they would strike next. Unwilling to tolerate this threat, and unable to reconfigure his basic plan for winning the war, Yamamoto resolved to destroy the Pacific Fleet's mobile task forces. He used his prestige and strong personality to take advantage of the fractured nature of Japanese strategy to seek a battle in the central Pacific. This gave Nimitz the opportunity he needed.

War is a complex and uncertain endeavor. It would be inappropriate to suggest that Nimitz relied on chance at Midway, but he recognized its importance. He worked diligently to maximize the odds of success by drafting a straightforward plan, ensuring his subordinates understood his intent, positioning them appropriately, and doing his best to maintain situational awareness as the battle developed. Much as he had after Halsey's raid into the Marshalls, Nimitz allowed others to receive accolades for the victory, but it was he and his staff that won Midway by identifying the opportunity and orchestrating the battle. Fletcher, Spruance, Simard, and many others made vital decisions, but Nimitz led them. Soon after the battle, Cdr. Vincent Murphy, a member of McCormick's War Plans Section, wrote, "Nimitz gets better and better as he goes along, and I believe is going to make a really great Commander in Chief. He was a Rock of Gibraltar during the Midway show, did not hesitate to take legitimate chances, and was relentless in pursuit."[87] Nimitz had won his victory; now, he had to capitalize on it to seize the initiative in the Pacific.

# SEIZING THE INITIATIVE

*We have made a start and have gotten a toe hold . . .*
*from now on [we] will be in constant battle.*

—Adm. Chester W. Nimitz[1]

The defeat of the *Kido Butai* at Midway created an opportunity. Nimitz and his subordinates now had the space to do two things. First, they could take the offensive and seize the strategic initiative. Second, they could absorb lessons from the initial battles and reconfigure the Pacific Fleet. Although prewar plans assumed the Navy would advance through the Japanese-held islands of the Central Pacific, the first offensives would take place in more distant areas. In the north, Rear Admiral Theobald struggled to work with the Army and extract the Japanese from the Aleutians. In the south, Vice Admiral Ghormley led "Task One," which became Operation Watchtower, the recapture of the anchorage at Tulagi and the occupation of Guadalcanal in the Solomon Islands.

Operation Watchtower was prompted by Admiral King, who was worried about a Japanese push toward Fiji and New Caledonia and keenly aware of the need to protect the lines of communication between Australia and the West Coast of the United States. King ordered Nimitz to prepare for the offensive in late June 1942, before gaining approval from his peers on the JCS.

After a joint directive was issued in early July, signals intelligence alerted King and Nimitz to the fact that the Japanese had begun building an airfield on Guadalcanal. Capturing it became a principal objective of Watchtower. Nimitz, Ghormley, and their subordinates knew they were in a race against the Japanese; they acted accordingly.

During the initial phase of the offensives in the North and South Pacific, Nimitz adhered to two of his key principles. He delegated authority to his subordinates and continued to employ "calculated risk." Once Nimitz had determined how the Pacific Fleet's limited forces would be allocated, Theobald and Ghormley assumed responsibility for planning their operations, configuring their task forces, and orchestrating their assaults. Nimitz used "calculated risk" by deliberately concentrating his forces for maximum advantage; as the operations in the south drew the attention of the Japanese, Nimitz recognized that if he could win a campaign of attrition there, he could take control of the war in the Pacific. Just as he had at Midway, Nimitz subordinated everything to the key campaign—the fight in the Solomons.

Nimitz recognized the emerging opportunity in the south because even in this most challenging and dynamic phase of the war, Nimitz remained focused on ensuring that he and his organization would be able to quickly make sense of rapidly changing circumstances and take advantage of them. Nimitz actively sought the capability that David Woods, an expert in sociotechnical systems, has termed "graceful extensibility." Woods defines it as "the ability of a system to extend its capacity to adapt when surprise events" occur and relates it to "adaptive capacity." A system with graceful extensibility can "extend the range of its adaptive behavior" and overcome unanticipated circumstances.[2] By deliberately creating such adaptive capacity within his organization, Nimitz increased his command's ability to learn, improve, and reconfigure itself based on new information. The active search for graceful extensibility was crucial. The Japanese were also adapting their techniques and incorporating lessons; Nimitz needed to be able to learn faster.

## GATHERING LESSONS AND REORGANIZING

After Midway, Nimitz and his staff built on a learning system developed in the interwar period. In peacetime, the learning system had used exercises to regularly refine practices, procedures, and doctrines. Nimitz and his staff took a similar approach but used wartime experience instead of exercises; to aid the process, they introduced an improved format for capturing lessons in action reports. By mid-1942, they were ready to introduce several valuable changes.[3]

One of the most important involved the coordinated use of airpower. At the Battle of Coral Sea, Fletcher had used scouting reports from land-based planes to "deliver his highly successful attack against . . . Tulagi and to . . . time the battle with [the] enemy carriers." However, better coordination was needed and unified command of land-based planes, as Nimitz employed at Midway, was essential. Rear Admiral McCain was appointed commander, Aircraft, South Pacific (COMAIRSOPAC) in late May and given control of all land planes and seaplanes in the South Pacific. Coordination between carriers was also important; at Midway, TF 16 and 17 had operated under their own task force instructions. On 2 July, Nimitz issued standard cruising instructions for all his carrier task forces, to make it easier for them to operate together.[4]

Coral Sea had also shown the potential of fighter planes to protect their carriers. Fighter directors on board ship could use radar plots to vector the planes and intercept incoming enemy strikes. Although there were flaws in the process and no standardized procedures yet, effective fighter direction techniques were emerging. Nimitz recommended doubling the number of fighter aircraft on board the carriers, from eighteen to thirty-six, to allow larger and more widely dispersed combat air patrols, increasing the chances of an effective interception. Other types of planes were showing their strengths and limitations. The Douglas TBD torpedo bombers used at Midway were "fatally inadequate." They would be replaced by the Grumman TBF. PBYs were "excellent for long range search" but could not maintain contact in the face of enemy fighters. Nimitz requested Army B-24s, which had long range, more defensive armament, and higher speed, making them "well adapted to this service."[5]

The hasty preparation for Midway had demonstrated the importance of keeping carriers and their air wings separate and modular. Nimitz had been able to fill out *Yorktown*'s air group with *Saratoga*'s planes because of this modular approach. However, more disciplined and consistent procedures were needed to ensure carriers could be kept fighting if their aircraft were lost in combat. In a mid-June message to King, Nimitz explained that "war experience" had "demonstrated the necessity for trained carrier replacement groups." He planned to keep whole air groups ready to rotate in and out of carriers, a form of adaptive capacity that would allow him to overcome the challenges that lay ahead.[6]

The victories at Coral Sea and Midway would have been impossible without timely intelligence, especially from Station Hypo. Nimitz wanted to build on their work by creating an "Intelligence Center" that would provide a true joint assessment based on all available intelligence sources. The new Intelligence Center, Pacific Ocean Areas (ICPOA) was officially established on 25 June 1942 and, although it was under administrative control of the Fourteenth Naval District, Nimitz directed its operations. He and his staff identified the center's targets and were its primary customers. From its beginning, ICPOA emphasized drawing from a diverse set of sources to create a comprehensive intelligence picture that could augment planning throughout the theater.[7]

Nimitz also sought to augment planning by appointing Rear Admiral Spruance CINCPAC chief of staff. Spruance brought a methodical perspective that increased the sophistication and diligence of Nimitz's planning. Although Spruance was largely unfamiliar with Nimitz, he quickly became impressed with Nimitz's "keen, well-stocked, and determined intellect." Nimitz's aggressiveness also left a profound impression; Spruance later recalled that Nimitz's "first reaction each time we thought of a way to hit the Japanese" was "Let's go and do it!" To give Spruance and the rest of his staff more space to collaborate, in late August, Nimitz moved his headquarters to a new building on the side of Makalapa Crater. Spruance's dark, strong coffee—brewed with beans from the South Pacific—proved too potent for most but served as a memorable initiation ritual for staff members and visitors.[8]

Nimitz gave himself the time and space for creative problem solving by adopting a well-structured daily routine with time dedicated to recreation and social activities. At 1000, after his morning conference, he took a break for about an hour. In stressful times, he spent it on the pistol range. When he was more relaxed, Nimitz played horseshoes. At 1100, Nimitz met with newly arrived commanding officers; he wanted to "size them up," hear their ideas—Nimitz claimed that "some of the best help and advice" he received came from junior officers—and establish a personal relationship. Nimitz kept his afternoons unstructured. Some were spent in planning conferences; others were dedicated to reviewing plans in private. On quiet days, Nimitz's day typically ended by 1630, which gave him time for exercise before a cocktail hour and dinner. Nimitz enjoyed playing tennis, swimming, and going for long walks; Spruance became a favorite walking partner. On the weekends, Nimitz often visited the home of Sandy and Una Walker at Muliwai to gain some distance from his daily routine. Although Nimitz and his staff worked seven days a week, and often well into the evenings, the focus on keeping "body and nerves in shape by taking exercise and relaxing" made the effort sustainable and allowed Nimitz to identify how best to—as a sign outside his office read—"grasp time by the forelock."[9]

Back in Washington, King felt more could have been done to employ destroyers in night search and attack missions, both at Coral Sea and Midway. Nimitz reserved judgment until he could learn more from his carrier task force commanders. On 17 June, he shared his assessment with King. Nimitz pointed out that the range and speed of modern planes "greatly curtailed such attack opportunities" making them "prohibitive unless destroyers are present in numbers considerably in excess of defensive screen requirements." That had not been the case. However, Nimitz acknowledged that "modern naval warfare will continue to present tactical situations favorable to night destroyer attacks" and that his task force commanders could be "counted on to exploit favorable opportunities." Presciently, he expected more to arise during "our aggressive operations of the future."[10]

## WAR IN THE NORTH

Despite access to intelligence that accurately predicted Japanese intentions, Theobald's dispositions failed to prevent Vice Admiral Hosogaya from seizing Attu and Kiska on 7 June. For the next several months, the Japanese positions on these islands were the focal point of the war in the north.[11] Captain Gehres of Patrol Wing Four was the first senior officer to recognize what the Japanese had done. When weather reports stopped arriving from Attu and Kiska, Gehres moved tender *Gillis* to Atka Island and had his PBYs scout to the west. On 10 June, they sighted Hosogaya's invasion forces in Kiska harbor. With Theobald still at sea, Nimitz ordered Theobald's planes and submarines to "bomb the Japanese out of Kiska" and cut off their supplies and reinforcements. Unfortunately, the "Kiska Blitz" did not stop the Japanese from securing the island. They used their own seaplanes to force Gehres to withdraw *Gillis*.[12]

Theobald moved ashore, put Rear Adm. Poco Smith in command of his surface striking group, and finally unified command of his air forces under General Butler, as Nimitz had originally directed. However, Theobald failed to establish an effective working relationship with the Army's ground force commander, Maj. Gen. Simon B. Buckner. Buckner, responsible for the Alaskan Defense Command, reported to Lt. Gen. John L. DeWitt, head of the Western Defense Command based in San Francisco. Although Theobald and Buckner operated in the same theater in pursuit of a single goal, their respective chains of command met only at the JCS, where DeWitt's and Nimitz's superiors, Marshall and King, set the nation's strategic direction. Growing animosity between Theobald and Buckner seriously complicated efforts to extract the Japanese from the Aleutians.[13]

Nimitz, King, and Theobald explored their options. Nimitz wanted to use a Marine Raider battalion and recapture Kiska before the Japanese consolidated their position. King felt the Raiders would be more useful in the south. Instead, he suggested a preliminary operation to establish an airfield closer to Kiska so that Theobald could impose a strangling blockade. Although DeWitt and Buckner agreed, they were not ready for such a move, so King recommended an interim strategy of attrition. Theobald, however, wanted to act quickly. He requested major reinforcements—including the Pacific Fleet's carriers—to retake both islands immediately, without the Army's help. Theobald's concept would have meant a major reconfiguration of Pacific strategy; Nimitz rejected it. He was growing impatient with Theobald's unwillingness to craft joint solutions with the Army, but because Theobald and King were old friends, Nimitz had to approach the situation cautiously.[14]

On 27 July, Theobald attempted a naval bombardment of Kiska. It ended in disaster. Thick fog forced the ships to turn back; destroyer minesweeper "*Lamberton* . . . turned prematurely [and] rammed [destroyer minesweeper]

*Chandler*." Two other ships also collided. Nimitz sent Theobald encouragement, but also began to make uncharacteristically detailed suggestions. Nimitz no longer expected Theobald to take the initiative. The CINCPAC staff agreed; they noted that Theobald had a habit of "marking time." Nimitz regularly pressured Theobald to act, and eventually, his ships successfully bombarded Kiska on 7 August, an attack timed to coincide with the offensive in the Solomons.[15]

In the meantime, the JCS began to pursue King's strategy. On 25 July, they ordered a "joint investigation . . . of Tanaga and Adak Islands" to determine which would be most suitable for an airfield. Rear Adm. John W. Reeves, who had commanded the Alaskan Sector since late June, was ordered to collaborate with Buckner and identify the best location. After Reeves completed the survey, DeWitt recommended occupying Tanaga, and the JCS, assuming this reflected a consensus opinion, ordered Theobald to undertake the operation. Theobald sent a flurry of messages opposing the move and claiming that DeWitt's suggestion was "entirely unilateral" and "disregarded" Reeves' survey. Although Reeves did not agree with all Theobald's points, he did recommend Adak instead of Tanaga because of its superior harbor.[16]

Theobald went further. He resurrected his request for carrier support and used it to question Nimitz's leadership. "Large scale naval commitments in two widely separated areas," Theobald argued, "violates fundamental principles [of] naval strategy." Because the Pacific Fleet lacked the "preponderance" of naval strength necessary to support his preferred course of action, Theobald preferred not to advance at all. In his response, Nimitz gave Theobald a chance to reconsider his perspective by graciously assuming that Theobald's messages had been written before he had seen the JCS directive to seize Tanaga. Theobald ignored the opening and remained intransigent. He was determined to escalate the issue of interservice collaboration to Nimitz and King, forcing them to make decisions that were his own responsibility. Nimitz demanded progress. He ordered Theobald to make a detailed inspection of Tanaga. It supported Reeves' original recommendation. Tanaga's harbor was unsuitable; Adak was the better location.[17]

DeWitt objected and pulled Nimitz into the debate. DeWitt preferred Tanaga because it was closer to Kiska, an air base could be built there faster, preparations for its occupation were already "far advanced," and if they did not occupy it, the Japanese might get there first. However, DeWitt was willing to be flexible; he told the JCS that he would "support [the] Adak operation" if the Navy assumed the risk and provided "constant protection" until the airfield was operational. Nimitz agreed. The JCS officially substituted Adak for Tanaga on 18 August. Theobald planned the operation for 30 August and pessimistically assumed he would have to cover the island until the end of October. Army engineers worked faster than anticipated; they drained a lagoon and had the airfield operational by 10 September. On 14 September, newly arrived planes made a "maximum effort" raid against Kiska, sinking two ships, setting three others afire, and wreaking havoc with Japanese installations. It was the most effective strike on Kiska to date. Progress was being made, but Nimitz recognized that he needed a more effective leader to execute his vision in the North Pacific.[18]

## LOGISTICS AND OFFENSIVE PREPARATIONS

After Midway, Allied commanders moved quickly to take the offensive. MacArthur asked the JCS for reinforcement so that he could "immediately" attack "the New Britain-New Ireland area." On 8 June, Ghormley forwarded MacArthur's message to Nimitz. In it, MacArthur claimed he lacked the means to take offensive action; he wanted Nimitz's striking forces, including two carriers and a division trained in amphibious operations. MacArthur promised to use them to "force the enemy back 700 miles to his base at Truk." He did not wait for a response before sharing his plan with the press. By 20 June, Nimitz was hearing about MacArthur's impending offensive on the radio.[19]

Nimitz and his staff also recognized the opportunity, but they felt the best course of action was an offensive in the South Pacific under Nimitz's operational control. In late June, McCormick's War Plans Section investigated the possibilities. Now that four carrier task forces were available, they recommended sending two to the Coral Sea in early July to contest "further Japanese advances" in that area. Sometime in August, those task forces would be relieved by the other two; when that happened, there would be an overlap of "about four days" when all four carrier task forces would be in the south.

McCormick and his team suggested "a major offensive" during this window. The concept resonated with Nimitz's aggressive disposition and aligned with plans Admiral King already had in motion.[20]

On 24 June, just two days after McCormick and his team delivered their recommendations, King ordered Nimitz to prepare for the "seizure and initial occupation of Tulagi and adjacent islands" in the Solomons. Ghormley's South Pacific Amphibious Force would deliver the 1st Marine Division to the objective area while "at least two carriers" covered the move. King expected MacArthur to play a supporting role; Army troops from the Southwest Pacific would consolidate the newly occupied positions, freeing the Marines for the next major advance. Time was of the essence; King wanted Nimitz to aim for a target date of "about August 1st." Nimitz was happy to oblige.[21]

On 10 June, King sent a message to Stark in London, hoping that the Royal Navy's Eastern Fleet would attack Japanese positions, perhaps Timor or the Andaman and Nicobar Islands, at about the same time. The Royal Navy was focused elsewhere. June and July 1942 marked the "absolute nadir" of "Britain's fortunes on land and sea." Malta, the key to the Mediterranean, had to be resupplied. Attempts were made in June, but they had been "disastrous failures." Another major effort—Operation Pedestal—was planned for August. Despite their limited capabilities, the British did agree to mount a diversion to support Ghormley. Three decoy convoys would depart Madras, Trincomalee, and Vizagapatam on 1 August and head toward the Andaman Islands before reversing course about twelve hours later. Although the British considered the operation successful, there is little evidence that the convoys—or the radio deception campaign that followed—had any significant impact on Japanese operations.[22]

King's determination to take the offensive outpaced the JCS' ability to plan. After sending his orders to Nimitz, King retroactively sought approval from his peers. The ensuing negotiations were intense, but necessary to meld the "Germany First" strategy with coherent action in the Pacific. General Marshall had asserted his service's dominance in the European theater; King wanted similar recognition for his in the Pacific. However, MacArthur believed it was his prerogative to lead the offensive, and because New Guinea and most of the Solomon Islands were in the Southwest Pacific, Marshall initially agreed. King insisted that it be a Navy operation and resolved to proceed against Tulagi without MacArthur's support. When MacArthur heard this, he refused to have anything to do with the operation "except under direct orders from Marshall."[23]

Marshall adopted a conciliatory stance; he smoothed things over with MacArthur and created space for King to compromise. The operation was ultimately divided into three "tasks." Ghormley, under Nimitz, would lead Task One and seize "the Santa Cruz Islands, Tulagi, and adjacent positions." MacArthur would lead Tasks Two and Three. First, he would advance along the northeast coast of New Guinea and capture the rest of the Solomon Islands; then, he would retake Rabaul. King transmitted the JCS "joint directive" outlining these tasks on 2 July. In effect, the JCS had created specific guidance for the second phase of Rear Admiral Turner's "Pacific War Campaign Plan."[24]

Operation Watchtower, the code name for Task One, was tentatively set for 1 August. The boundary between Nimitz's theater and MacArthur's was shifted west to longitude 159° E to ensure the entirety of Guadalcanal and Tulagi were within Nimitz's theater. Nimitz was instructed to choose a commander to lead Task One, but it was obvious it would be Ghormley; no other officer was as well prepared or positioned. The JCS ordered MacArthur to support the effort with the naval and air forces of the Southwest Pacific. They also ordered the designation of "a Commanding General Army Forces" in the South Pacific who would assist Ghormley with "the preparation and execution of plans" and "coordinate and supervise the administration, logistics, and training of all Army ground and air troops within the area." Marshall chose Major Gen. Millard F. Harmon; he became commander, Army Forces South Pacific, on 4 July.[25]

Unlike their foes, the Japanese high command failed to recognize the full significance of the defeat at Midway. There were several reasons. One was secrecy; while U.S. officers allowed their success to spread through Allied commands and newspapers, the Japanese kept their losses hidden. During a joint command liaison meeting that discussed the battle on 10 June, IJN officers concealed specifics from their colleagues in the IJA. Even Emperor Hirohito helped ensure that "news of the disaster was tightly controlled."

Official records were manipulated to mask the defeat. Carriers *Akagi* and *Hiryu* were initially kept on the IJN's registry and listed as "heavily damaged" until they were quietly removed long after the battle. A determination to remain on the offensive prevented serious retrospection; Yamamoto, having wrested control of the IJN's strategic planning through personal prestige, could not admit defeat without jeopardizing that privileged position. Accordingly, the IJN continued to maintain an aggressive stance toward future operations. Plans assumed just a two-month delay—from July to September—would be enough time to build up sufficient air strength to mount the operation to seize Fiji and Samoa. This concept was only abandoned in early July when it became clear that it was impossible. The attempt to seize Port Moresby, however, would continue, this time by an overland route.[26]

While preparing for his offensive, Ghormley had to rely on a series of widely distributed anchorages and newly emerging bases that secured the lines of communication to Australia. Distances were enormous. From the Pacific Fleet's base at Pearl Harbor, it was 2,276 miles to Samoa, 3,400 miles to Noumea, and 4,410 miles to Port Moresby. Sailing these distances took immense quantities of fuel. The Japanese faced similar challenges, but their bases were closer. Rabaul to Port Moresby was 950 miles by water, and Rabaul to Truk, the major Japanese fleet base, was just 795 miles. Compounding their advantage, the IJN had built a fleet of high-speed oilers that could refuel their mobile forces at sea. Nimitz's Pacific Fleet, although practiced at underway refueling, lacked a comparable capability. His oilers could support raids and defensive battles, but not sustain operations comparable to the *Kido Butai*'s wide-ranging thrusts. In the South Pacific, Nimitz and his team would rely heavily on bases and a rapid logistical buildup.[27]

When he assumed command in the South Pacific, Ghormley created a South Pacific Service Squadron modeled on PACFLT's Service Force. Commanded by Vice Adm. William Calhoun, PACFLT's Service Force was divided into four Service Squadrons (SevRons). SevRon 2 contained repair, salvage, and hospital ships; SevRon 4 provided drydocks and storage facilities for mobile advanced bases; SevRon 6 performed offensive and defensive mining; and SevRon 8 transported bulk fuel and refueled task forces at sea. To share the latest lessons, Nimitz had Calhoun write up the details of his approach, particularly the operations of SevRon 8, and share them with Ghormley. The lack of oilers would be addressed by establishing an advanced fueling base at Bora Bora with capacity for 120,000 barrels, about the capacity of a fast fleet oiler.[28]

King helped ensure coherent effort by issuing a "Joint Logistic Plan" for the South Pacific on 15 July. It addressed the redundant and duplicative processes used by the Army and Navy and introduced an integrated approach to logistics for the entire area. A Joint Purchasing Board was established in Wellington; it would be the initial source of supply and anything it could not provide would be sourced from the United States. Ghormley's Service Force distributed materials and managed the process; they tried to maximize shipping efficiency by minimizing turnaround times, dispatching full ships whenever possible, and closely collaborating with existing Allied "shipping agencies."[29]

The Joint Logistic Plan was an example of King's proactive approach to logistical planning and administration. The executive order that merged the offices of COMINCH and CNO also created a new position, the Vice Chief of Naval Operations (VCNO). The VCNO headed the CNO staff and focused on the daily direction of OPNAV, allowing King to "concentrate upon the strategic direction of the war." He was fortunate to have a very capable VCNO, Vice Adm. Frederick J. Horne, who brought a methodical and well-organized approach to the Navy's logistical planning and administration.[30]

A tentative network of bases sprang up across the South Pacific. Where the Army already had airfields for their air ferry route to Australia—Christmas Island, Canton, Fiji, and New Caledonia—they led development. The Navy established flanking positions at Samoa, Palmyra, and Johnston. Joint bases were established at Bora Bora, Tongatabu, Efate, and Espiritu Santo. Ghormley called for "a large scale" construction program, but progress was slow. The bases initially suffered from limited facilities, poor infrastructure, and unanticipated construction delays. Although Nimitz had authorized Naval Construction Battalions—"CBs" or Seabees—as chief of BuNav in October 1941, there were few available, so combat troops had to be diverted to "labor alongside the service personnel." A new infantry division—the Americal—was formed at New Caledonia to guard the vital harbor at Noumea. Facilities there were "very unsatisfactory," and unloading was unable to keep pace with arriving material. Supplies for Ghormley and MacArthur stacked up while service troops and their officers struggled to overcome "the multitudinous and complex problem" of creating bases out of nothing.[31]

## SECOND CONFERENCE WITH KING

In early July, Nimitz and King met again in San Francisco. They discussed a variety of topics but focused on two main themes. The first was officers, their ranks, and the relationship between ranks. The second was the impending offensive in the South Pacific. For certain parts of the conference, other officers attended, including Captain McCormick, Rear Admiral Turner, who would assume command of Ghormley's amphibious forces, and Vice Admiral Pye, who was already in San Francisco with TF 1.

The seaplane carrying Nimitz and McCormick to the conference struck debris while landing in San Francisco Bay and crashed. Nimitz's behavior during the incident reveals much about his leadership. McCormick suffered two cracked vertebrae. One of the pilots was killed. Nimitz was bruised but escaped serious injury. As the inverted plane started to fill with water and sink, the passengers and crew made their way onto the wing. Nimitz refused to get into a rescue boat while men were still inside the plane. "Each time a corpsman with an armful of blankets draped one around Nimitz's shoulders, the admiral took it off and wrapped it around an injured man." After a young seaman told Nimitz to "get the hell out of the way," he finally donned a blanket and stepped into a boat. As it pulled away, Nimitz remained standing so that he could watch the rescue efforts. The coxswain yelled at him to sit down for his own safety. After Nimitz sat down, his uniform sleeve insignia peeked out from under the blanket. The coxswain saw it and tried to apologize. With humility and respect, Nimitz said, "Stick to your guns. You were quite right." Once at the dispensary, he refused to change out of his wet clothes or leave until he had checked on all the injured men from the plane.[32]

During the conference, Nimitz and King discussed their talent pool and how to reconfigure it to encourage more desirable outcomes. Nimitz needed more task force commanders; King suggested using sea frontier commanders to increase the number of officers Nimitz could choose from. Nimitz also wanted more aggressive submarine commanders to accelerate the war against Japanese commerce. King was willing to transfer some from the Atlantic Fleet if necessary. Some officers received special scrutiny. Nimitz and King were dissatisfied with Theobald, but "agreed to reserve judgment . . . pending further developments." Halsey was still ill; Fitch would become Nimitz's senior air officer if Halsey did not return. Marc Mitscher had been assigned a carrier task force but was now commanding Patrol Wing 2. Newly promoted Rear Adm. George D. Murray, the former captain of carrier *Enterprise*, was available for task force command. Throughout these discussions, Nimitz and King balanced structure—and the creation of the right roles—with personalities as they endeavored to place officers in the positions that best fit their talents.[33]

When they turned to the impending offensive in the south, Nimitz and King reviewed the current state of their plans. Turner acknowledged that the available troops, ships, and aircraft lacked adequate training, but believed there was "sufficient time, before August 1st, to remedy training deficiencies." He would have the opportunity to prove it by commanding Ghormley's amphibious forces and executing the assault.[34] After the successful completion of Task One, "strategic direction" would shift to MacArthur. Ghormley would still be under Nimitz's command, but they would have to coordinate with MacArthur and advance toward Rabaul through the Solomons. King explained to Nimitz that the JCS' instructions would prevent MacArthur from "making unreasonable demands" of PACFLT naval forces.[35]

King was apparently envisioning a large flanking maneuver—one that would advance north after capturing Rabaul to strike Truk, Guam, and Saipan, avoiding the defensive network the Japanese had created in the Marshall and Gilbert Islands. The many anchorages and airfields of that network allowed the Japanese to quickly concentrate their forces and strike back against any offensive operation. In a paper prepared for the conference, Pye noted that any "attempt to seize any of the Marshall or Caroline groups without long extended operations to neutralize the enemy's well-established air bases, might result in defeat." It would be like Midway in reverse. Nimitz and King agreed. Instead of attacking the network of bases directly, King wanted to outflank it by advancing on Truk from the south and cutting off the network's source of supply. Japanese positions in the Marshalls could then be left to "wither on the vine" or could be occupied once they had been weakened. King's concept was an early expression of the "island hopping" strategy employed later in the war.[36]

To support Ghormley's offensive, Nimitz planned three diversionary operations. The first was an attempted repeat of *Nashville*'s raid on Japanese fishing vessels. Cruiser *Boise* was instructed to leave Pearl Harbor 27 July, attack the "line of sampans and small cargo ships . . . eight hundred miles east of Honshu," and "create the impression that a striking force" was approaching Japan. To draw more attention to *Boise*'s operation, Nimitz planned to bomb Wake with B-24s shuttling through Midway. The second diversion was a raid on the Gilberts. Before Midway, Nimitz had considered using the 1st Marine Raider Battalion "against advanced and semi-isolated enemy bases." At the conference, he told King that the Japanese seaplane base at Makin would be a good target. The 1st Marine Raider Battalion was headed to Tulagi with Turner, so Col. Evans F. Carlson's 2nd Marine Raider Battalion attacked Makin the night of 16 August from the large submarines *Nautilus* and *Argonaut*. They seized control of the island and then withdrew. Nimitz expected Theobald to mount the third diversion, ordering him to apply "continuous pressure" on the Japanese through "strong diversional attacks on Kiska and/or Attu" and timing one to coincide with Ghormley's offensive. The bombardment of 7 August described above was the result.[37]

Rapid success was considered essential for Ghormley's offensive. If all went well, the three diversionary operations would keep the Japanese blind to the true threat until the Marines had consolidated their positions. Then attention could turn to Task Two. All conference attendees expected to move with unrealistic speed. Turner hoped to get airfields operating at each new location within a week after its capture, a completely unworkable expectation that reflected his ignorance of the challenges in the South Pacific. Before leaving for Pearl Harbor after the conference's first day, Turner suggested building an airfield on Guadalcanal, across the sound from Tulagi. It was an excellent idea and the Japanese knew it. The next day, on 5 July, Station Hypo alerted Nimitz and King that the Japanese were building an airfield on Guadalcanal. Before the conference adjourned, King and Nimitz deleted the Santa Cruz Islands from Task One and substituted Guadalcanal so they could seize it.[38]

The emphasis on speed remained as planning became more detailed. When Turner arrived at Pearl Harbor, he "immediately" drafted an estimate with Nimitz's staff. It noted that military operations had a tendency "to wait until everything is absolutely perfect," but "conditions will never be perfect, and we cannot afford to miss any chance while waiting for perfection." Turner, Nimitz, and his staff consciously traded thorough preparation for time. They recognized the importance of making progress to end the war and "its terrific drain on our national resources." By moving quickly, they could seize the moment and strike while the Japanese were "extended and disorganized." On 6 July, to ensure rapid success, Nimitz departed from McCormick's latest concept, which had called for two carrier task forces to support the operation, and committed three—Fletcher's TF 11, with *Saratoga*, Noyes' TF 18, with *Wasp*, and Kinkaid's TF 16, with *Enterprise*. Optimistically, Nimitz, Turner, and his staff assumed that the 1st Marine Division and its supporting echelons would be relieved by a defense battalion five days after landing.[39]

Intelligence supported their desire to move quickly. The Japanese appeared to be preparing to "eliminate [Port] Moresby and get near enough to strike at . . . our Australian communications." This assessment was correct. The Japanese Seventeenth Army, which had been formed to occupy positions in the South Pacific, was ordered to attack Port Moresby "with all haste and . . . firm resolve." It would move to advanced positions at Buna and Milne Bay and then trek across the Owen Stanley Mountains to come at Moresby from the northeast. The opposing sides were in a race to seize the initiative.[40]

## DETAILED PREPARATIONS

As Ghormley prepared for the offensive, he became pessimistic about Watchtower's prospects. On 8 July, he traveled to Melbourne to confer with MacArthur. They concluded "the depth of . . . existing hostile reconnaissance" made surprise "improbable." The Japanese would detect Turner's approach and quickly counterattack. MacArthur did not think his planes could "interdict hostile air or naval operations" and Ghormley expected the carrier task forces to be drawn off to fight their opposite numbers, leaving the assault forces dangerously exposed. Ghormley and MacArthur told Nimitz and King that "without a reasonable assurance of adequate air coverage" the operation posed grave risks. They wanted to delay the operation to allow them to build up greater strength. In the interim, they proposed minor operations employing infiltration tactics.[41]

Nimitz and King overruled these concerns. "It is necessary," King argued on 10 July, "to stop without delay the enemy's southward advance." Nimitz continued his preparations and officially designated Ghormley the commander of Task One. Nimitz ordered Ghormley to use the three carrier groups—operating under Fletcher's tactical command—and Turner's amphibious force to "seize and occupy . . . Tulagi and adjacent positions in order to deny that area to Japan." Nimitz closed with a motivational statement typical of his style: "I have full confidence in your ability to carry this operation to successful conclusion." Ghormley continued to harbor doubts and expressed concern about Japanese land-based strike aircraft. In response, Nimitz arranged to send thirty-five additional B-17s to the South Pacific. With the bulk of his striking forces concentrated there, the Hawaiian area was "most vulnerable." Nimitz accepted the risk.[42]

However, in an official letter to King, Nimitz expressed his own doubts. Ghormley had what he needed to initiate Task One, but it was "unsafe to assume," Nimitz argued, "that the enemy will not exert every effort to recover the [occupied] positions." Losses were certain; they might be heavy. "Unless these losses," Nimitz continued, "are made good by a *steady flow* of replacements . . . not only will we be unable to proceed with Tasks Two and Three of this campaign, but we may be unable even to hold what we have taken." Nimitz recommended "immediate steps" to ensure that steady flow was established. He had already ascertained that victory in the South Pacific would go to the side that could keep men and material fighting in the theater.[43]

Ghormley developed a plan for an offensive through the Solomons and shared it on 29 July. After seizing Tulagi, he expected to advance using land-based air and infiltration tactics to avoid tying down Nimitz's "large ships" and "carrier support." However, Ghormley remained focused on the primary mission specified in his original orders: "the defense of the sea lanes to Australia and New Zealand." He retained a defensive orientation and felt the advance in the Solomons was secondary. On this point, Ghormley and Nimitz were fundamentally misaligned.[44]

As Ghormley advanced his headquarters from Auckland to Noumea, his defensive posture filtered his view of information. At Noumea, it was easier to confer with his subordinate commanders, like Rear Admiral McCain, Major General Harmon, and Maj. Gen. Alexander M. Patch, commander of the American Division, but Ghormley became increasingly focused on the limitations of his command. He was convinced that he had too few men and too little material, that his port organization was deficient, and that he lacked the necessary fuel to meet his commitments. The scene at Noumea—rapidly becoming the most important port in the South Pacific, both for Ghormley's command and MacArthur's—did not help. Supplies were stacking up ashore, unable to move forward rapidly enough.[45]

Ghormley's decision to command from his flagship *Argonne*, an old submarine tender commissioned in 1921, made the situation worse. Although *Argonne* had a variety of command facilities, she could not house the entire COMSOPAC staff or support all its radio traffic. Communications slowed, and command, control, and coordination became difficult. Ghormley did not seem to realize that failure to establish headquarters ashore unnecessarily constrained his ability to command, kept him and his staff from getting regular exercise, and reinforced his defensive orientation. It also limited the effectiveness of his chief of staff, Rear Adm. Daniel J. Callaghan. Callaghan had been hand-picked because he was an empathetic team builder with "driving energy" and "offensive spirit." Callaghan was expected to balance out Ghormley's "remote" and studious style. Had Ghormley moved ashore, Callaghan's positive influence might have infected the whole staff and led to the development of the adaptive capacity necessary to keep pace with the changing nature of the conflict in the South Pacific.[46]

Ghormley delayed Watchtower's target date until 7 August to give his forces more time to prepare. On 17 July, he issued his operation plan. It was brief and divided tasks between his two main forces, Fletcher's TF 61 and McCain's TF 63. McCain would use his planes to scout, attack approaching enemy forces, and provide on-call support. Fletcher's expeditionary force was divided into the three carrier groups and Turner's assault forces. Together, they would "capture [and] occupy [the] Tulagi area and [the] adjoining portion [of] Guadalcanal." Ghormley ordered the Marines to "defend until relieved."[47]

Ghormley's subordinate commanders gathered on 26 July in the Fijis to work through the details. Fletcher, the senior officer present, presided. He was joined by Callaghan—representing Ghormley, who felt too pressed for time to attend—McCain, Turner, Kinkaid, Rear Admiral Victor A. Crutchley of the Royal Navy, commanding MacArthur's TF 44, and Maj. Gen. Alexander A. Vandegrift, commander of the 1st Marine Division. Their discussion became "animated" when Turner said unloading operations would take five days. Fletcher planned to withdraw the carriers after two. Vandegrift emphasized it was a substantial occupation, not a small raid. Fletcher agreed to keep the carriers on station for a third day. The emphasis on moving quickly, pushed by Nimitz and his staff, left many details undone and important questions unanswered. The failure of Fletcher and Turner to agree on how long to cover the landing forces would threaten the viability of Vandegrift's position.[48]

However, timing was crucial. The day after the conference, Ghormley's intelligence suggested the Japanese were about to begin a major operation. He urged Fletcher to expedite his plans. In mid-July, the IJN had created an "Eighth Fleet" at Rabaul and Nimitz's intelligence organization had observed its steady reinforcement. In an estimate issued 1 August, Captain McCormick anticipated the Eighth Fleet would support an advance toward "the New Hebrides and to New Caledonia." The new airfield under construction at Guadalcanal was expected to cover the movement. From Washington, King reiterated the importance of not delaying the offensive "beyond August 7th." Operation Watchtower would collide directly with these Japanese plans.[49]

## THE TOE HOLD

On 7 August, Rear Admiral Turner's amphibious forces steamed into Savo Sound and assaulted Japanese positions at Guadalcanal and Tulagi. Resistance on Guadalcanal was slight. At Tulagi and nearby islands, the Japanese fought fiercely from prepared positions, forcing the Marines to extract them at close quarters. King's sense of timing was perfect. "The high command in Tokyo was stunned." They "were utterly unable to conceive" that Nimitz and his forces could mount an offensive in such strength. An initial counterattack was made by land-based planes from Rabaul later that day. They hit destroyer *Mugford*, but Fletcher's fighter umbrella prevented further damage. Turner requested "scouting against [the] approach [of] enemy surface forces from westward." He was right to be concerned. Vice Admiral Mikawa Gunichi, commander of the Eighth Fleet and Outer South Seas Force, had gathered a mixed group of seven cruisers and one destroyer and headed for Savo Sound. While Mikawa approached, Japanese air strikes on 8 August disabled a destroyer and set a transport ablaze. Most of the attacking planes were destroyed. Initial reports of success buoyed Nimitz's outlook; he asked King to allow Ghormley to "extend control . . . northwest along the Solomons" and consolidate his position.[50]

It was too early for such optimism. That night, during the Battle of Savo Island, Mikawa's force attacked Turner's screen. Radar pickets failed to give warning and tired officers, strained from continual watches over the past several days, did not react effectively until it was too late. The scope of the defeat first appeared at CINCPAC headquarters in a report from Fletcher: "*Chicago* hit torpedo, *Canberra* on fire. . . . More of our ships in trouble. . . . *Quincy* sunk. . . . *Vincennes* sunk by gunfire and torpedoes. Casualties heavy. . . . *Astoria* has fire in wardroom." *Astoria* would not survive. Of the five cruisers in Fletcher's message, four were lost. Only *Chicago* survived. The shocking and humbling defeat broke Ghormley's confidence. He was convinced that the Solomons were too dangerous for his ships and told Nimitz that he would hold his naval forces back until he had enough planes to secure communications with Guadalcanal. Nimitz had no more planes to send—he had stripped Hawaii of aircraft and was operating with "no reserve for losses"—but he sent the modern battleships *South Dakota* and *Washington* as soon as they arrived in the Pacific.[51]

On Guadalcanal, Vandegrift had secured Guadalcanal's airfield, but the Japanese faded into the jungle and disappeared before his patrols. Vandegrift lacked the strength to secure the whole island. Instead, he established a perimeter at Lunga Point and patrolled the surrounding area aggressively. Ghormley ordered Vandegrift to prepare for a Japanese counter-landing. Nimitz felt it was essential to prevent one; he told Ghormley to use his carriers to keep Japanese assault forces away. Ghormley passed these instructions to Fletcher, who was to balance fighting enemy carriers with destroying any "hostile attack force." Vandegrift realized the Japanese had planned to turn Guadalcanal into a "major base" and was convinced they would try to recapture it. He asked Turner to bring up an additional regiment to help defend the perimeter.[52]

The Japanese quickly prepared a counteroffensive. By 11 August, Nimitz's intelligence organization had detected the formation of a "strong striking force." According to Nimitz's best estimates, the attack would come within seven to ten days; he ordered Ghormley to resist with "every means available." Nimitz hoped Boise's diversion would help. Although the cruiser had not sunk any picket vessels, her messages had given the Japanese the impression that another carrier raid was about to strike Japan. It looked as if the Japanese had "hurriedly loaded three carriers" to fend off the attack. Nimitz's intelligence organization exploited the resulting messages to learn more about IJN communications and force structure.[53]

With the pressure mounting, King began to question Nimitz's decisions. King thought concentrating carriers in the south would "unduly expose [the] Hawaiian area." Instead of carriers, he wanted Nimitz to send "three to five" of the old battleships to the South Pacific. In his response, Nimitz once more demonstrated his disciplined approach to risk. He was determined to concentrate his forces where they would be most effective. The Japanese could raid Hawaii or Midway, but that would not alter the strategic balance. "Maximum carrier strength" was needed in the South Pacific, along with "shore-based air, . . . fast forces, . . . [and] new battleships." The old battleships consumed too much fuel and water for the limited logistical infrastructure of the South Pacific to keep them operating off Guadalcanal. However, to mollify King, Nimitz agreed to move them from the West Coast to Pearl Harbor as a potential check against a Japanese raid.[54]

Although Nimitz remained familiar with the details of the emerging struggle in the south, he refused to be consumed by it. On 13 August, Nimitz drew King's attention to the fact that the Japanese focus on Guadalcanal ought to make it easier for MacArthur's forces to advance against the Japanese in New Guinea. King brought the concept to the JCS and two days later they directed MacArthur to push ahead with the "seizure and occupation of

Lae, Salamaua, and the northeast coast of New Guinea." When MacArthur hesitated because his naval forces were supporting Ghormley, Nimitz ordered Ghormley to return them. MacArthur used them to support his operations in Milne Bay, where the Japanese had landed on 26 August.[55]

McCain had just enough time to get Guadalcanal's airfield operational before the Japanese attack. He sent four destroyer transports to the island on 15 August. They brought aviation gasoline, bombs, and construction specialists. Nimitz warned Ghormley the attack could come as early as 20 August. That very day, escort carrier *Long Island* ferried a group of Marine aircraft to the island. Henderson Field, named for Maj. Lofton Henderson, USMC, who died leading scout bombers against the *Kido Butai* at Midway, was operational.[56]

On 18 August, Ghormley issued a brief operation order with his plan to repulse the Japanese attack. Fletcher's three carrier task forces—with *Saratoga*, *Enterprise*, and *Wasp*—would "destroy hostile forces prior to their arrival" off Guadalcanal; Vandegrift would defend his occupied areas; and Turner would "expedite [the] movement [of] food and ammunition" to the Marine defenders. MacArthur was expected to assist by interdicting Japanese movements with his submarines and aircraft. Four days later, Ghormley amplified his instructions and informed Fletcher that "indications point strongly to enemy attack in force . . . 23–26 August."[57]

Unknown to Ghormley and Vandegrift, the Japanese had already made their initial counter-landings. On the night of 18 August, Rear Admiral Tanaka Raizo's Destroyer Squadron Two had ferried a contingent of the 5th Special Naval Landing Force to Guadalcanal and put them ashore west of the Marine perimeter. The following night, a substantial portion of Colonel Ichiki Kiyono's 28th Infantry Regiment, originally scheduled to assault Midway, landed at Taivu Point, east of Vandegrift's position. With his patrols suggesting a growing Japanese presence in the area, Vandegrift responded aggressively. A reconnaissance in force dispersed the naval infantry in the west. A patrol to the east ambushed a group of Ichiki's men and captured his plans. When Ichiki attacked the night of 20 August, the Marines threw back the assault and annihilated his force.

Ichiki was the advance guard of a major operation. The rest of his regiment and the remainder of the 5th Special Naval Landing Force would be brought to Guadalcanal on board transports commanded by Rear Admiral Tanaka, part of Mikawa's Eighth Fleet. Tanaka's movement was covered by three separate forces. Vice Admiral Kondo Nobutake commanded the Advanced Force, a powerful surface strike group positioned 110 to 150 miles ahead of Vice Admiral Nagumo's Main Body. Nagumo would use carriers *Shokaku* and *Zuikaku* to smash the American carriers. Nagumo had a second carrier group, with light carrier *Ryujo*, commanded by Rear Admiral Hara Tadaichi; he would suppress Henderson Field and make sure the transports got through.[58]

Allied scout planes found Tanaka's transports on 23 August, opening the Battle of the Eastern Solomons; Fletcher and Vandegrift launched strikes, but Tanaka reversed course before the attack could arrive. Since no searches had located the enemy carriers, Fletcher decided to send Rear Adm. Leigh Noyes' TF 18 with *Wasp* south to refuel. The next day, McCain's search planes found Hara, Kondo, and Nagumo's battleships, but the big Japanese carriers remained beyond their range. Fletcher launched searches and strikes, crippling *Ryujo* and locating *Shokaku* and *Zuikaku*. Scout bombers attacked *Shokaku* after sighting her, but did little damage; radio interference prevented their reports from reaching Fletcher in time for a follow-up strike. In the meantime, Nagumo's planes attacked Kinkaid's TF 16. Carrier *Enterprise* was hit by three bombs in close succession; with her flight deck temporarily disabled, some of her planes went to Henderson Field. That evening, Fletcher withdrew to fuel while TF 18 moved up to support Guadalcanal.

The Japanese erroneously believed they had set two carriers afire and won a significant victory. Kondo advanced, seeking a night action. A line of Japanese submarines patrolled south of Guadalcanal to cut off Fletcher's escape. Convinced that the IJN had achieved aerial superiority over Guadalcanal, Mikawa ordered Tanaka to proceed. Mikawa was wrong; on the morning of 25 August, planes from Henderson Field, including those from *Enterprise*, attacked. They crippled one large transport, hit a second, and damaged Tanaka's flagship, cruiser *Jintsu*. B-17s from Espiritu Santo attacked while destroyer *Mutsuki* was stopped to rescue survivors and sank her. Tanaka and his surviving ships withdrew. The first Japanese effort to recapture Guadalcanal had been defeated.[59]

## DESPERATE DEFENSE

Officers reacted to the victory at the Eastern Solomons differently depending on their position and orientation. Nimitz was characteristically aggressive. On the evening of 25 August, he told King that it was essential to "not let this offensive die on the vine." Nimitz felt the "moderate losses" sustained so far were acceptable, but immediate reinforcement was necessary. If King could provide replacement aircraft, Nimitz was ready to send B-17s, PBYs, and fifty more fighter planes to Ghormley. Under Secretary of the Navy James Forrestal was visiting the South Pacific at this time, and he threw his weight behind Nimitz's request. Speaking for the Army, Marshall agreed to allow Nimitz to move "any aircraft . . . necessary" and authorized the transfer of thirty-five B-24s to Hawaii.[60]

King was more apprehensive. Like Ghormley, he felt the long lines of communication in the South Pacific were vulnerable. King's "growing conviction" was that the Japanese would push past Guadalcanal and attack Samoa or Fiji, severing Ghormley and MacArthur's communications with the West Coast. Nimitz disagreed. He acknowledged that the Japanese could attack South Pacific bases, but they were unlikely to do so because it would place "strong forces" on their flank, tax them logistically, and leave a "more important" objective—the Pacific Fleet's carriers—untouched. Cognizant of the difficulties Ghormley was having with logistics, Nimitz was convinced that even if the Japanese raided Samoa or Fiji, they would be unable to occupy them.[61]

Turner's confidence was tempered by the first weeks of the campaign. He selectively recalled his earlier arguments, contending that he had warned that the offensive would require "continuous support by strong naval and air forces" to succeed. However, Turner remained characteristically aggressive. He felt Guadalcanal was "a golden military opportunity." The island was "an unsinkable aircraft carrier" that could be "multiplied into an invincible fleet" with "determined support." Turner pressured Ghormley to provide it.[62]

Nimitz recognized the challenge and the opportunity. The Japanese were focused on the fight for Guadalcanal. What he and other senior officers had expected to be a quick offensive movement was turning into an attritional campaign "more vital to the prosecution of the war in the Pacific than any other commitment." Success would give the victor the initiative in the Pacific, and success would be determined by which side could maintain fighting strength in those distant waters. Nimitz was determined that it would be his Pacific Fleet. In anticipation of the need, he had already recommended sending additional advanced base materials and construction battalions south.[63]

Keeping Vandegrift supplied was a tremendous challenge. As Ghormley explained in mid-August, there was "nothing [in the way of] . . . unloading equipment" at Guadalcanal. He asked Vice Admiral Horne for "pontoon wharves and barges" to allow more rapid unloading there and at other South Pacific bases. Japanese interdiction efforts compounded the difficulties. Their strike aircraft and submarines regularly attacked ships in the waters off Guadalcanal. In mid-August, a torpedo "barely missed" supply ship *Fomalhaut*. Destroyer *Blue* was hit the night of 21 August and had to be scuttled. On 30 August, destroyer transport *Colhoun* was bombed and sunk. The Japanese established a seaplane base at Rekata Bay on Santa Isabel Island and used it to mount additional attacks. While their planes dueled with those on Guadalcanal, Ghormley urgently requested patrol vessels to help keep the Japanese submarines at bay. Nimitz sent all he could spare.[64]

Japanese submarines scored a major success on 31 August, when *I-26* torpedoed carrier *Saratoga*. Although structural damage was limited, the explosion's concussive force damaged *Saratoga*'s electric propulsion system. She withdrew to the West Coast for repairs. What had been a four-carrier Pacific Fleet was now, with the temporary loss of *Enterprise* and *Saratoga*, down to just two.[65]

At the end of August, Nimitz asked McCormick to produce another estimate. McCormick was confident the Japanese would mount "an all-out offensive to recapture [their] lost positions in the Solomons." They were concentrating "a large portion" of their "air and surface units" in the South Pacific, including "at least three" carriers. Troops were coming to Rabaul from "as far west as the N.E.I. [Netherlands East Indies] and Philippines." However, the Japanese might strike alternative targets. They could raid Espiritu Santo, perhaps in concert with "a major attack" on Guadalcanal. The Japanese might also occupy Ndeni, the largest of the Santa Cruz Islands. In addition to these dangers in the south, McCormick's estimate also highlighted the "extreme vulnerability" of Hawaii. To mitigate that risk, Nimitz prepared the old battleships of TF 1 to act in concert with land-based air and repel any raid against the Hawaiian Islands.[66]

McCormick's estimate justified Nimitz's decision to focus his striking forces in the south. *Hornet* left to join *Wasp*, leaving no carriers in the Central Pacific Area. When *Enterprise* and *Saratoga* came north for repairs, their air groups stayed in the south. Nimitz asked King for more Army aircraft to reinforce them, arguing that "success [in the] present campaign" would depend on a "steady flow" of "suitable Army aircraft with trained pilots." His request ended on a typically positive note. Since Cactus was the code name for Guadalcanal, Nimitz told King, "Let's give Cactus the wherewithal to live up to its name." Ghormley made similar requests of MacArthur, asking him to spare high-performance fighters; all the Army fighters McCain had sent to Guadalcanal were already out of commission.[67]

Nocturnal dominance of the waters around Guadalcanal allowed the Japanese to reinforce and resupply their troops. Large transports were too slow to avoid daylight attacks from Henderson Field, so the Japanese made "continuous small landings during darkness" with destroyers. The defenders of Guadalcanal called this the "Tokyo Express." Vandegrift knew the Japanese were building up strength and preparing to attack. He asked Turner to bring an additional regiment, the 7th Marines, to allow for a more "active defense." Turner was hesitant; on the night of 4 September, he lost two more destroyer transports, *Little* and *Gregory*, to Japanese ships off Guadalcanal.[68]

King and Nimitz were frustrated. They could not understand why Ghormley was allowing Japanese ships to operate at night with impunity. On 7 September, Ghormley finally created a surface action group, TF 64, under Rear Adm. Carleton H. Wright. Ghormley ordered Turner to use TF 64 to escort resupply operations, intercept Japanese reinforcement convoys, and "destroy promising enemy targets." However, Ghormley's orientation remained defensive. Fearing the Japanese would seize Ndeni, he ordered Turner to prepare to occupy it with the 7th Marines. Ghormley and his staff were reacting to events and failing to see the bigger picture. They had not yet discerned that the key to success was, first and foremost, the airfield on Guadalcanal.[69]

McCain had. He visited Guadalcanal at the end of August and recognized that Henderson Field could become "a sinkhole for enemy air power." He pushed for reinforcements. The Seabees of the 6th Naval Construction Battalion arrived soon thereafter; they built an auxiliary airstrip in a week, providing redundancy in case of bombardment and allowing more planes to take to the air simultaneously. On 3 September, Brig. Gen. Roy Geiger, commander of the 1st Marine Air Wing, took control of Guadalcanal's air operations. Eight days later, planes from *Saratoga*'s air wing arrived. Both Turner and McCain came with them to get a firsthand sense of the situation on the island.[70]

On the night of 12 September, Turner and McCain were in the Marine perimeter when the Japanese ground offensive struck. Major General Kawaguchi Kiyotake had gathered a sizable force west of Vandegrift's position and marched inland, circling around to attack from the south. Kawaguchi planned to break through the Marine defenses, seize a ridgeline that dominated the airfield, and sweep Vandegrift into the sea. Supported by a naval bombardment, Kawaguchi's preliminary blow fell on Col. Merritt A. Edson's Raiders and Parachutists, who staunchly defended the ridge. Impressed by the ferocity of the Japanese attack, Turner conferred with Vandegrift the next morning. The two agreed "that at least one more regiment" was "essential" to defend Guadalcanal; Turner and McCain left that day, determined to bring the 7th Marines to Guadalcanal as soon as possible.[71]

Soon after sundown, another more determined attack on the ridge began. Waves of Japanese came at the Marines, who used rifles, grenades, and ultimately bayonets to fend them off. Edson's grip on the ridge became precarious. At the climax of the battle, he and Maj. Kenneth D. Bailey stood atop the ridge, organizing counterattacks and encouraging the Marines to resist all that Kawaguchi and his veteran troops could muster. Victory at "Edson's Ridge" saved Henderson Field, but barely; the situation on Guadalcanal was desperate and the initiative in the Pacific hung in the balance.

## CONCLUSION

By mid-September, the situation in the Pacific was precarious. Nimitz and his subordinates had seized the opportunity won at Midway and initiated a major offensive, focusing Japanese attention on the South Pacific. However,

Vandegrift's tenuous hold on Guadalcanal and its vital airfield was at risk. If Ghormley and his forces could not overcome Japanese dominance of the waters surrounding the island and keep supplies flowing to the Marines, the Japanese would retake Guadalcanal, defeat the offensive, and turn their attention to New Guinea and the vital lines of communication between the West Coast and Australia.

Nimitz and his staff used their adaptive capacity to quickly recognize that Turner's plan for a series of quick offensive movements had degenerated into an attritional struggle. Victory would depend on which side maintained a "steady flow" of ships, planes, men, and other vital supplies to Guadalcanal. That would require two things. First, the effort in the South Pacific had to be given priority, so that the necessary materials could be routed to the theater in sufficient quantities. Second, once they arrived, Ghormley's logistical infrastructure had to get those materials where they were needed in time to make a difference. Logistics in the South Pacific remained extremely challenging; much more work was necessary to ensure that Ghormley and his forces could keep fighting.

This development played to the Navy's strengths. Although the IJN was superior in many important respects, including the striking power of its carrier aviation and its capability to refuel while under way, it lacked the infrastructure to sustain a major counteroffensive at Guadalcanal. By initiating a campaign of attrition in the South Pacific, far away from sources of supply and material, the Pacific Fleet had reconfigured the war and brought it into line with its established plans. The Navy had conceived of the Pacific War as a "campaign" for decades and used that paradigm during its interwar planning.[72] As a result, it was better prepared for the kind of fighting that emerged in the South Pacific and quicker to adapt to its needs. The sophisticated capabilities of the IJN, in contrast, would begin to falter under conditions of sustained stress.

Nimitz recognized this emerging dynamic because, although he was mindful of day-to-day operations in the North and South Pacific, he kept his distance from them. He and his staff preserved their ability to accurately assess the evolving situation. That helped Nimitz recognize that victory in both areas would require leadership more closely aligned to his own disposition. In the north, Theobald was too inflexible. He had failed to cooperate with Buckner to develop a joint approach for fighting the Japanese. Although the occupation of Adak had dramatically improved the situation, Theobald's unilateral approach continued to undermine prospects for success.

In the South Pacific, the situation was dire. Ghormley's defensive disposition, methodical approach, and unwillingness to move his headquarters ashore had fostered an unacceptable level of passivity. Unlike his subordinates McCain and Turner, Ghormley had not visited Guadalcanal. He had too little appreciation for the strength of Vandegrift's position and the increasingly desperate situation on the island. Rather than approaching the situation at Guadalcanal with "calculated risk," Ghormley did the opposite. He hedged his bets and held forces back to respond to the inevitable onslaught if the Japanese recaptured the island. Unlike Nimitz, Ghormley had failed to develop graceful extensibility within his command. He was too enmeshed in details and was unable to quickly identify opportunities or adapt to changing circumstances. Ghormley could not see that Henderson Field was the key to the struggle and that it hung in the balance.

Nimitz could. By consciously growing the adaptive capacity of his staff, Nimitz could observe developments, rapidly make sense of them, and take coherent action in pursuit of his goals. He recognized that Guadalcanal had become the key to the Pacific, and although Nimitz remained predisposed to allow his subordinates to exercise their initiative and operate with broad, general direction, he had started to realize he would need to inject himself into the struggle for the South Pacific. How he chose to do that would have decisive implications for the future of the campaign.

# ADJUSTING THE SYSTEM

*Success is won, not by personnel and materiel in prime condition,*
*but by the debris of an organization worn by the strain*
*of campaign and shaken by the shock of battle.*

—Sound Military Decision[1]

N imitz had marshaled his forces and aggressively taken the offensive.
Operation Watchtower began just eight months after Pearl Harbor
and caught the Japanese off guard. A much smaller but similarly
determined effort was under way in the Aleutians, where the occupation of
Adak had provided a base for attacking and blockading Japanese positions.
However, the initiative in the Pacific still hung in the balance. The IJN's
Combined Fleet was determined to recapture Guadalcanal and cut the link
between Hawaii and Australia.

Nimitz recognized the opportunity. The struggle in the South Pacific had
drawn the Japanese into an attritional struggle in a remote part of the world
far from established bases and at the end of lengthy supply lines. This played
to the Navy's strengths and capitalized on decades of campaign planning.
Nimitz knew that if he could concentrate overwhelming force at Guadalcanal,
his forces would triumph. However, he could not give Vice Admiral Ghormley
everything he wanted. King and his colleagues on the JCS had to balance the
needs of the Pacific against the commitment to establish a second front in

North Africa in 1942. Still, Nimitz gave Ghormley virtually all that he had, denuding the defenses of Hawaii and other vital areas.

To triumph at Guadalcanal and to accelerate operations in the North Pacific, Nimitz had to find inspiring and determined subordinates who could act on his vision. In the South Pacific, that required an aggressive mindset. In the Aleutians, it meant developing a collaborative partnership with the Army and adopting a holistic view of joint operations. In the coming months, after much "anguished consideration," Nimitz selected and appointed commanders who could meet these needs. He would work with and through them to drain Japanese strength, seize the initiative in the Pacific, and set the stage for much more powerful offensives in 1943.[2]

## SEPTEMBER CONFERENCE WITH KING

On the evening of 6 September, Nimitz and McCormick flew to San Francisco for another conference with King. Halsey had recovered from his dermatitis and joined them. They focused on the situation in the South Pacific. The original concept of three tasks that would be executed in quick succession had been disrupted by the intensity of Japanese counterattacks. King bluntly declared that Tasks Two and Three were "out the window." He and Nimitz criticized Ghormley for holding back his surface forces, refueling his ships "at inopportune times," and failing to coordinate his operations. TF 64, Ghormley's surface striking force, was formed "one month late." He needed to take more "calculated risks."[3]

MacArthur was not helping. His domineering style made him difficult to deal with and he appeared more focused on self-aggrandizement than victory. King had decided to replace Vice Admiral Leary, MacArthur's naval commander, with Vice Adm. Arthur S. Carpender in the hope of improving working relationships in the Southwest Pacific. To counterbalance MacArthur's manipulative press releases, Nimitz and King agreed to issue their own, highlighting Vice Admiral Brown's sixty-day cruise in the South Pacific and Rear Admiral Fletcher's 101 days at sea earlier in the year. King and Nimitz considered shifting the boundary between Ghormley's and MacArthur's commands westward to give Ghormley more "freedom," but decided against it because of the "protests" MacArthur was sure to make.[4]

Personnel assignments were another major item on the agenda. The most significant shift was Rear Adm. John H. Towers' upcoming transfer to the Pacific. Currently head of the Bureau of Aeronautics (BuAer), Towers was a talented administrator and a strong proponent of military aviation. King found him abrasive and wanted him out of Washington. Towers became commander, Aircraft, Pacific Fleet (COMAIRPAC) and regularly attended Nimitz's morning conferences. Rear Admiral Fitch, who had been commanding the Pacific Fleet's aircraft, went to the South Pacific and relieved Rear Admiral McCain as COMAIRSOPAC. McCain came to Washington and occupied Towers' former billet. With Leary once again available for task force command, Nimitz assigned him to TF 1 and made him head of PACFLT's Battleship Type command. Leary relieved Pye, whose performance during Midway had disappointed Nimitz. Pye became president of the Naval War College.[5]

When they discussed the Aleutians, Nimitz and King focused on command relationships. Theobald was creating unnecessary tension with the Army and failing to collaborate with generals Buckner, Butler, and DeWitt. DeWitt planned to occupy the Pribilof Islands in the Bering Sea to provide an air base west of Alaska, but Theobald felt he lacked the ships to support the operation. Instead of working with DeWitt, Theobald complained to Nimitz and promised to "take no action" until Nimitz responded. After reviewing the JCS directive for the Aleutians, Nimitz and King agreed that Theobald had authority over the Pribilof move, not DeWitt. Nimitz sent a dispatch to that effect. However, both Nimitz and King acknowledged that unless relations improved, they would have to make a change.[6]

Nimitz told King that he needed more forces, especially land-based planes and high-speed tankers. King assured him that reinforcements were coming. During his tour of the Pacific, Under Secretary Forrestal came to appreciate Nimitz's difficulties. Nimitz had explained to Forrestal that the new fast battleships—*Washington*, *South Dakota*, and *North Carolina*—were extremely useful, but they taxed his logistical capabilities because of their appetite for fuel. He needed more tankers to keep them operating in the South Pacific. Forrestal made the necessary tankers available before returning to Washington. More fast battleships were coming; King agreed to send another to PACFLT during the conference. Numbers would help Nimitz make up for combat damage and accidents; while leaving Tongatabu on 6 September, *South Dakota* grounded and had to return to Pearl Harbor for repairs.[7]

## SAGGING MORALE IN THE SOLOMONS

By mid-September, Ghormley was showing signs of strain. In a message to Nimitz and King on the 11th, he described his difficulties. The "food situation" on Guadalcanal was "not good." His transports could only visit the island "during daylight" because of the Japanese blockade, and air raids frequently interrupted their unloading. At Turner's urging, Ghormley had agreed to send the 7th Marine Regiment to Guadalcanal to shore up Vandegrift's position, but they might not arrive before the next Japanese offensive. Ghormley was passive and reacting to Japanese moves.[8]

In his letters, Ghormley's tone was defeatist. In one to Nimitz dated 7 September, Ghormley complained that King did not appreciate his challenges. The Japanese had "many more carriers"; if they used them "properly they could raise havoc." It was "too dangerous" to send surface forces to Guadalcanal at night, patrol planes and pilots were getting "worn down," and resupplying Vandegrift was a "big risk." The Army was holding back high-performance fighters and leaving him to hang on "by a shoestring." Although Ghormley's intent was to provide an honest view of the situation, his tone and substance created a profoundly negative impression.[9]

Fortunately, Ghormley's subordinates had a very different attitude. Vandegrift, McCain, and Turner were determined to hold Guadalcanal. While Colonel Edson and his men repulsed Kawaguchi's efforts to storm "bloody ridge," Turner brought up the 7th Marines, escorted by TF 64. Rear Admiral Noyes, commanding TF 61 with the carriers *Wasp* and *Hornet*, covered the move and prepared to attack any Japanese task force that came within range. Although he expected to be outnumbered, Noyes knew he could augment his striking power by using Henderson Field. He delivered Marine F4Fs to Guadalcanal on 12 September and launched a strike against approaching Japanese task forces the next day, but when word of Kawaguchi's defeat reached them, the enemy ships withdrew.[10]

On 15 September, Noyes was still in position to cover Turner's reinforcement effort. *Wasp* was sighted and attacked by submarine *I-19*. At least two torpedoes hit *Wasp*, triggering explosions and fires that doomed the ship. Torpedoes also struck battleship *North Carolina* and destroyer *O'Brien*. With *Enterprise* and *Saratoga* undergoing repairs, *Hornet* was the only operational carrier remaining in the Pacific. King strongly suggested that Ghormley keep his carriers in protected anchorages "except when employed for specific tasks." This was a disingenuous and reactionary chiding; Ghormley had been responding to aggressive Japanese moves, but he ordered Rear Admiral Murray, commander of the *Hornet* task force, to remain close to Espiritu Santo.[11]

MacArthur also felt the situation was bleak. In a message to Marshall, he emphasized the vulnerability of his command and asked for assurances that the Pacific Fleet would come to his aid if the Japanese made a "seaborne attack on New Guinea." King delegated the response to Nimitz. In his reply, Nimitz addressed MacArthur's concerns. If the Japanese attacked, MacArthur's search planes would find them and Ghormley would attack their flank. In the meantime, the "first duty of SOPAC naval forces [was the] protection of Guadalcanal." Nimitz believed that "sufficient pressure in [the] Solomons" would "prevent [a] landing attack in force against [Port] Moresby." MacArthur was not satisfied; he continued to agitate for more naval and amphibious forces—but Nimitz's perspective was an astute framing of the strategic situation.[12]

## NIMITZ VISITS SOPAC

After his conference with King, Nimitz met with Major General Emmons, commander of the Army's Hawaiian Department. While Nimitz had been in San Francisco, Emmons had toured the South and Southwest Pacific. He returned "infected with the wave of pessimism that permeated" those commands. MacArthur told Emmons that the Japanese could take New Guinea at "any time," that Ghormley's "positions in the Solomons are very precarious," and that "as soon as the Japanese clear us out of the Solomons they will attack Hawaii."[13]

On 20 September, Gen. Henry "Hap" Arnold, commander of U.S. Army Air Forces and member of the JCS, arrived in Hawaii. He was headed to the South and Southwest Pacific to assess aircraft needs. Arnold was concerned when he heard Emmons' negative assessment and asked Nimitz for his views. Could Vandegrift hold Guadalcanal? Nimitz thought so. If Turner could keep the Marines resupplied, and if Geiger and Fitch could control the skies above Guadalcanal, the Japanese would expend their forces in futile attempts to retake the island.[14]

However, Nimitz resolved to visit the South Pacific to get a firsthand look at the situation and to inspire Ghormley and his subordinates. On 24 September, Nimitz and select members of his staff—Col. Omar T. Pfeiffer, USMC, his senior Marine officer; Capt. Ralph A. Ofstie, USN, his air officer; Capt. William M. Callaghan, USN, an expert on refueling and logistics; Capt. John R. Redman, USN, his communications officer; and Lieutenant Lamar, his aide—left for the South Pacific. Nimitz chose this team specifically because Ghormley was facing challenges in each of these areas; he wanted their expertise to help evaluate the situation, make solid recommendations, and create a comprehensive estimate.[15]

The next day, during a layover on Palmyra, Nimitz met with McCain and Noyes, who had stopped over on their way back to Hawaii. McCain told Nimitz and his staff that planes had to be kept flowing into Guadalcanal. Henderson Field couldn't handle many at once, "but you have to be ready to feed them in all the time." Pilots also needed to be regularly replaced; they were under severe strain from Japanese attacks day and night. McCain confirmed that there was a sense of pessimism in SOPAC, but he was not afflicted by it. Neither was Vandegrift; he was "not worried about holding" Guadalcanal, but Japanese reinforcements had to be stopped. If Geiger and his pilots could achieve aerial superiority, McCain believed victory would follow.[16]

Nimitz and his party arrived at Noumea on 28 September and the "principal conference of [the] tour" soon began on board *Argonne*. The main attendees were Nimitz, Ghormley, Turner, Harmon, Arnold, and two members of MacArthur's staff: Maj. Gen. Richard K. Sutherland, USA, the SWPAC chief of staff, and Maj. Gen. George C. Kenney, USA, the SWPAC air commander. Other attendees included members of the respective staffs. MacArthur and Nimitz demonstrated their different styles by how they approached the conference. Although MacArthur had been invited, he felt SWPAC required his attention and sent staff members. Nimitz was intent on showing leadership, inspiring his subordinates, and building consensus; he attended in person.[17]

Nimitz opened the conference by explaining that "the purpose" was to gain a better understanding of "conditions in the SOPAC area" and "the problems of Admiral Ghormley and General MacArthur." Ghormley described how the Marines at Guadalcanal were "under constant pressure" and resupply was "most difficult." Sutherland felt the major challenge in SWPAC was the movement of supplies and reinforcements. There were 55,000 men at Port Moresby. They required one thousand tons of shipping each day. However, SWPAC naval forces were limited. If the Japanese mounted a major operation, Sutherland believed they could seize Port Moresby from the sea.[18]

Nimitz used this opportunity to share his assessment that Guadalcanal was the key to both theaters. The Japanese lacked the air strength for a naval operation against Port Moresby. An assault overland from the north, along the Kokoda Track, was more likely. After Sutherland confirmed SWPAC was prepared for this contingency, Nimitz continued. The Japanese were far more likely to use their naval forces in the Solomons, where they had greater freedom of movement and less risk from Allied airpower. That was why Nimitz was employing "calculated risk" and sending nearly all his fighting strength to the South Pacific. Sutherland's attempt to argue for increased naval forces in SWPAC reinforced Nimitz's point. Guadalcanal, Sutherland said, "is covered by the whole navy except TF 1." Exactly; that was where the IJN was most likely to strike.[19]

As the discussions turned to details, Nimitz asked pointed questions. If the hold on Guadalcanal was tenuous, why was so much being held in reserve? What kept the Army division on New Caledonia from reinforcing Vandegrift? What about planes? Arnold noticed that a large number were being held back; he was hesitant to authorize more until Ghormley used what he had. Nimitz wanted to know why Ghormley wasn't using his surface forces to prevent Japanese night landings and naval bombardments. Battleship *Washington* was a perfect example; Nimitz was surprised the ship was being held at Tongatabu, too far away to do much good. Ghormley pled fuel difficulties, but Nimitz pressed. Why did the Japanese own the waters off Guadalcanal?[20]

Ghormley's answers showed his fatigue and strain. He had built no time into his schedule for relaxation or reflection, the downtime so essential for processing complex challenges and identifying creative solutions. Instead, he obsessed over details and worked himself into ineffectiveness, constantly worried that the Japanese would break through his defenses. The aggressive, creative approach Ghormley had envisioned before the offensive began was absent. His low morale was palpable to the other attendees. Twice during the conference, Ghormley reacted negatively to incoming messages; "My God," he asked at one point, "what are we going to do about this?"[21]

Nimitz's attitude was fundamentally different; he repeatedly emphasized the importance of coming to grips with the Japanese and defeating them. During a discussion of the attritional air war raging in both theaters, Nimitz emphasized that the enemy "won't be left alone" and that "we must go on with offensive action and hit him wherever we find him." Accordingly, the discussion turned to Rabaul, the ultimate objective of the offensive. Turner described his strategy for an advance in the Solomons, suggesting that the natural harbor at the Shortlands was the key to the island group. Kenney argued that seizing Buna and occupying the north coast of New Guinea would be sufficient. Turner bristled. "Well," he asked, "why don't you take such a position on the north coast of New Guinea?" That gave Kenney the opportunity to revisit Sutherland's point that MacArthur needed more naval forces. A rapid advance to the north coast would require a major amphibious operation.[22]

Nimitz deftly moved past these disagreements and reframed the discussion. The Japanese could not afford to allow Ghormley to consolidate his position at Guadalcanal; they had to strike "while time is in their favor." Nimitz once more stressed that Guadalcanal was the key to both theaters; if they could stop the Japanese "at the corner," it would prevent them from moving against Port Moresby, Noumea, or other positions farther south. The attritional struggle currently under way favored U.S. forces because of the reinforcements that were coming from American shipyards and factories; the Japanese were not expected to keep pace. Guadalcanal was an opportunity to bleed them white.[23]

## ON TO GUADALCANAL

After the conference, Nimitz flew on to Espiritu Santo and met with Fitch, newly installed as COMAIRSOPAC. The next morning, Nimitz and his party flew to Guadalcanal in a B-17. Vandegrift welcomed the newcomers. Despite heavy rain, Nimitz insisted on touring the perimeter, flight operations, and Edson's Ridge. Nimitz was pleased with the confidence expressed by Vandegrift and his chief subordinates. In the evening, the two spoke alone. Vandegrift needed more support. He needed more men to strengthen his defenses, more planes to beat off the regular Japanese raids, and more aggressive action from the Navy. Vandegrift felt the most important lesson of the campaign thus far was the failure of senior naval officers to support his position on Guadalcanal. Japanese ships regularly arrived off Guadalcanal, offloading supplies and shelling Marine positions under cover of darkness. A more aggressive response could prevent that or make the Japanese incursions more costly. Nimitz was noncommittal, but Vandegrift felt he had gained an important ally.[24]

Nimitz was back at Noumea on 2 October. While there, he held another conference with Ghormley, Callaghan, Turner, and various staff members. Nimitz was convinced Guadalcanal could be held. He expected Ghormley to exercise more leadership and become better informed. "I want you to go up and see conditions [on Guadalcanal] for yourself," Nimitz told him, "Callaghan can take care of things here while you are away." Nimitz presented a series of recommendations from his staff for strengthening Guadalcanal, including all-weather runways, bulk storage for aviation gasoline, Quonset huts for dry housing, improved cargo handling facilities, and a salvage tug for Tulagi. Nimitz wanted Ghormley to shift the main SOPAC supply base from Auckland, which was "too far back," to Espiritu Santo. It had good roads and space for development.[25]

When the discussion shifted to future operations, Nimitz allowed Ghormley to lead. His outlook remained pessimistic. Ghormley complained, for example, that MacArthur had not provided "his plan for getting . . . to Rabaul." Ghormley was only able to focus on the strategic picture briefly before descending into detail. Stabilizing the situation at Guadalcanal was "a big job" that would "take time." Rabaul was less an objective than a threat; Ghormley emphasized the size of the Japanese garrison and how easily they could move troops to Guadalcanal. King had asked Ghormley for a plan and schedule of future operations on 15 August; he had not provided it, arguing that "our present operations have not yet reached the point where such plan and schedule would be worthwhile."[26]

When Nimitz tried to prompt discussion of such plans, Turner first blamed the Marines for not consolidating their position more quickly. "We have not made further progress in Cactus," he contended, "due to our ignorance and lack of skill." Then Turner proposed using Guadalcanal as a "spring board" to seize a series of mutually reinforcing positions in the Solomons. Nimitz valued Turner's aggressiveness but expressed his "high regard" for the Marines, emphasized Vandegrift was "offensive minded," and implied Turner's criticisms were disingenuous. Nimitz asked about reinforcing the Marines with the Army, the 2nd Raider Battalion, and New Zealand troops. Beyond being hesitant to use New Zealanders, Ghormley had no clear plans. Turner was against employing the 2nd Raiders on Guadalcanal and apparently had not considered using the Army. Nimitz closed the conference by urging Ghormley to "use all the resources . . . available" to secure Guadalcanal. Several days later, driven by this prompting, Ghormley decided to send the 164th Infantry Regiment of Patch's Americal Division to Guadalcanal. Turner would lead the convoy and Ghormley's TF 64, now commanded by Rear Adm. Norman Scott, would cover the move.[27]

Nimitz returned to Pearl Harbor on 5 October. He summarized his impressions in an official letter to Ghormley on 8 October. Nimitz reiterated his priorities for Guadalcanal and stressed the importance of visiting the island, "which I hope you will not delay too long in doing." Nimitz urged Ghormley to take "calculated risks" and use his task forces to damage enemy ships and disrupt the Tokyo Express. To help with logistic matters, Nimitz was sending Capt. Worrall R. Carter to SOPAC. Carter would assume command of the area's naval bases and improve the theater's logistics. Nimitz also told Ghormley that he was sending a copy of the letter to King, so that "if he does not agree or thinks that I am too reckless, there will be opportunity to take corrective measures." That was disingenuous; King would never accuse Nimitz of being too reckless. Instead, Nimitz shared the letter with King to make his increasing frustration with Ghormley known.[28]

## BLEAK OCTOBER

The first conference with Nimitz had prompted Ghormley to action. On 1 October, he ordered Murray to take TF 17 and raid the Japanese base at Buin-Faisi on the southern tip of Bougainville. The anchorage was "the main staging area for the fast warships of the Tokyo Express" and Murray was instructed to target enemy shipping. Ghormley asked Fitch and MacArthur to aid Murray by suppressing nearby Japanese air bases. Murray approached the target at high speed the night of 4 October. Weather conditions were "unsettled" when *Hornet's* planes took off but were expected to be better over the target. Instead, the weather worsened. Pilots became separated and had difficulty identifying targets. Hits were claimed on a "heavy cruiser" and four transports, but the Japanese recorded damage to just two destroyers.[29]

Nimitz praised the aggressive operation. Even though the weather had kept Murray's pilots from inflicting serious damage, they had suffered no losses. Nimitz agreed with Murray's conclusion that "every opportunity should be seized to assign offensive missions to carrier task forces" and make surprise attacks. Ghormley, however, remained focused on the defensive. Desperate to preserve *Hornet*, he ordered Murray to operate far south, between New Zealand and Australia. Nimitz and his staff felt TF 17 ought to be at Espiritu Santo, ready for offensive operations.[30]

While Nimitz was in SOPAC, his intelligence organization compiled a list of Japanese units and drafted an "Estimate of Enemy Capabilities." Both documents supported Nimitz's decision to focus on Guadalcanal to exert "continual pressure" on the Japanese. They were concentrating major naval forces at Truk, apparently for an "all-out effort" against Guadalcanal, New Guinea, or both. That meant there would be no enemy attack on Hawaii or "toward India." However, the Japanese had recently changed their codes and call signs, making it impossible for the CINCPAC intelligence organization to "analyze current Japanese moves" with certainty. Nimitz agreed with the estimate and accepted the risk. He sent the *Enterprise* task force, commanded by Rear Admiral Kinkaid, to the South Pacific. Vice Admiral Halsey, now fully recovered, would follow and take command of the combined carrier striking force with *Enterprise* and *Hornet*.[31]

In the meantime, Scott's TF 64 demonstrated that a well-drilled force could defeat the Japanese at night. At the Battle of Cape Esperance, fought during the night of 11–12 October, Scott's column surprised a bombardment force led by Rear Admiral Goto Aritomo. Scott sank cruiser *Furutaka* and destroyer *Fubuki*, and heavily damaged Goto's flagship *Aoba*. The Japanese admiral died on the bridge of his ship, convinced that the melee was the result of friendly fire. In return, destroyer *Duncan* was sunk and light cruiser *Boise* seriously damaged. Cape Esperance was a much-needed victory that helped ensure the safe arrival of the 164th Infantry Regiment at Guadalcanal.[32]

However, two nights later the Japanese proved they still dominated the waters off the island. Rear Admiral Kurita Takeo took two battleships, *Kongo* and *Haruna*, into Savo Sound and bombarded Vandegrift's positions for ninety minutes, wrecking planes, killing men, and incinerating vital aviation gasoline. According to Rear Admiral Ugaki, Yamamoto's chief of staff, the bombardment was "splendid" and turned "the whole area of the airfield . . . into a mass conflagration." The Japanese coordinated the bombardment with air raids that tore gashes in the runway.[33]

To Nimitz and his staff, these attacks signaled the start of another enemy offensive. The sighting of a Japanese convoy confirmed it. The situation was urgent; Geiger was down to just thirty-seven planes and only seven strike aircraft. His men siphoned gasoline from damaged planes and attacked the approaching transports. Their desperate effort had little effect. Fitch flew more bombers and gasoline to Henderson, but the Japanese returned for another bombardment that night and wrecked more planes and vital equipment. The next day, six Japanese transports unloaded at Tassafaronga Point.[34]

At Pearl Harbor, the situation looked bleak. The Japanese were operating two "major forces" in the South Pacific with an estimated six battleships, one carrier, and supporting light forces. Ghormley believed an "all out enemy effort" was under way to seize Guadalcanal and "possibly other positions." He requested immediate reinforcement. When Fitch's scouts located the enemy carrier force, Ghormley assumed the Japanese were about to raid Espiritu Santo and evacuated the harbor. Nimitz's assessment was grave; the optimism he had recently displayed was gone: "It now appears that we are unable to control the sea in the Guadalcanal area. . . . The situation is not hopeless, but it is certainly critical."[35] Something had to be done.

## NIMITZ'S DECISION

During his visit to the South Pacific, Nimitz had developed a much better understanding of the situation. However, he had failed to inspire Ghormley. Nimitz had repeatedly used his leadership skills to get the best from his subordinates—Pye and Brown after Pearl Harbor; Fletcher and Spruance at

Midway—but Ghormley remained pessimistic and overly defensive. On the evening of 15 October, after much "anguished consideration," Nimitz brought the idea of relieving Ghormley to his staff. The situation in the South Pacific was deteriorating. The Japanese were about to make another effort to retake Guadalcanal. Ghormley was "not sufficiently bold and aggressive." All the staff members who had seen Ghormley in person voted in favor of his relief.[36]

Nimitz needed a South Pacific commander who could resonate with his aggressive disposition, employ calculated risk, and reinvigorate the offensive. His mind turned to Halsey. Halsey was senior enough, he was an aggressive and inspirational leader, and he was already on his way to the South Pacific. Nimitz quickly made his decision and sent an "eyes only" message to King: "I have under consideration his [Ghormley's] relief by Halsey at earliest practicable time. Request your comment." King's response was a swift "Approved." Nimitz ordered Halsey to assume command in Noumea. The man who had agreed to "go anywhere" would take charge of the maelstrom in the South Pacific.[37]

Nimitz's timing was nearly perfect, both for operations in the theater and morale in the United States. On 16 October, the day that Nimitz chose Halsey, the *New York Herald Tribune* and the *New York Times* published editorials proudly proclaiming the defenders of Guadalcanal would "do all that humanly can be done to stand their ground." Later that day, Secretary Knox held a press conference. When asked whether Guadalcanal could be held, his response betrayed a lack of confidence: "I certainly hope so. I expect so. I don't want to make any predictions, but every man out there, ashore or afloat, will give a good account of himself." That much had been clear to Nimitz during his visit. He was counting on Halsey to harness that energy.[38]

Two days later, Halsey took command. He moved his headquarters ashore and took over buildings vacated by the French high commissioner. Approved by King as a "military necessity," the shift allowed Halsey and his staff the space they needed to develop a clear view of the overall situation. He immediately tried to impose his operating tempo on the Japanese by ordering his two carrier groups—*Hornet*'s TF 17 and *Enterprise*'s TF 16—to rendezvous north of Espiritu Santo and then, combined as TF 61 under Rear Admiral Kinkaid, to make a sweep north of the Santa Cruz Islands. Halsey hoped Kinkaid would appear from an unanticipated direction and ambush the Japanese carrier striking force. Rear Admiral Willis A. Lee's battleship force, TF 64, would remain farther back, ready to intervene in case enemy invasion forces approached Guadalcanal.[39]

On 21 October, Lt. Gen. Thomas Holcomb, the commandant of the Marine Corps, arrived on Guadalcanal to confer with Vandegrift. The two flew back to Noumea the next morning to meet with Halsey, Harmon, and Patch. Halsey asked Vandegrift about the situation on the island. Vandegrift stressed the poor physical condition of his Marines and the need for more material support. He felt another infantry division was necessary to secure the island; Harmon and Patch agreed. The rest of the Americal Division would be ready to move soon. Halsey closed the conference by asking, "Can you hold?" Vandegrift said he could but needed "more active support than I've been getting." According to historian Richard B. Frank, the comment wounded Halsey. He used the opportunity to set a new tone for SOPAC and immediately promised Vandegrift "everything I have."[40]

At Pearl Harbor, Nimitz tried to give Halsey even more. Nimitz's staff found more planes—fifty Army fighters, twenty Navy dive-bombers, and twelve Marine torpedo bombers—that could be sent south, stripping "Navy and Marine squadrons in the Hawaiian Islands to the bone." He warned King that "[n]o other air support can be furnished . . . from Hawaii at this time." But more planes were needed. Attrition was consuming half of Geiger's inventory every ten days. Nimitz also sent another Army infantry division south, further reducing the defenses in and around Hawaii.[41]

By 22 October, the Japanese offensive appeared to be under way. The CINCPAC staff agreed that the enemy was about "to start his long expected all-out attack on Guadalcanal" and that "the next three or four days" would be "critical." Nimitz knew that Halsey had "inferior forces" and would have to rely "on attrition" and "calculated risk." Halsey's mindset resonated with this assessment perfectly; he later wrote to Nimitz, "I had to begin throwing punches almost immediately."[42]

Japanese forces on Guadalcanal had been steadily reinforced and were planning a two-pronged offensive. While one attack drew Vandegrift's reserves to the Matanikau River on his western flank, another would strike from the south. Several IJN task forces supported the operation, ready to fly planes to the newly occupied airfield and ambush any of Halsey's forces that sought to intervene. The offensive along the Matanikau stalled, and when the attack from the south erupted the night of 24 October, Vandegrift correctly perceived it as a greater threat. Initially, his defenses gave way, and it appeared to the Japanese that success was at hand. Ugaki was elated and believed the airfield had been captured. Unfortunately for him and others in the Combined Fleet, Vandegrift's defenders held the Japanese at a place they called "coffin corner."[43]

Misled by premature reports of victory, the IJN task forces, including Vice Admiral Nagumo's striking force with carriers *Shokaku*, *Zuikaku*, and *Zuiho*, rushed south. Five different enemy forces appeared to be converging on Guadalcanal. Halsey issued a succinct order to his task force commanders: "Strike—repeat, strike." Kinkaid obeyed, but he was too far away. The Japanese carriers moved out of range before his planes arrived. Lee swept the waters near Guadalcanal "but failed to make contact."[44]

The following day, 26 October, Kinkaid and Nagumo launched attacks almost simultaneously. *Shokaku* was seriously damaged by a series of bombs, but because IJN damage control had improved since Midway, she survived. Cohesive Japanese carrier strikes overwhelmed *Hornet*'s defenses and hit her with bombs and torpedoes. A second strike hit *Enterprise* with three bombs, but she resumed flight operations quickly and recovered many of *Hornet*'s planes. Kinkaid, with one of his carriers crippled and the other damaged, began to withdraw. A final strike that afternoon doomed *Hornet*. In the meantime, Nagumo realized that the Guadalcanal airfield was still firmly in American hands; unwilling to press further, he withdrew, ending the Battle of the Santa Cruz Islands.

Although the Pacific Fleet was once again down to just one operational carrier, Halsey felt the result validated his aggressive tactics. In a letter to Nimitz on 31 October, he promised not to "send any ship back to Pearl Harbor unless it is absolutely necessary." *Enterprise* would stay in the South Pacific. With repair ship *Vestal* now in SOPAC, Halsey had three vessels that could help repair battle damage; he augmented their crews with Seabees and Army "mechanics, electricians, and welders." However, to mitigate the risk of having just one carrier, Halsey asked if the Royal Navy could loan a carrier from their Eastern Fleet. Nimitz forwarded the request to King, recommending that "this idea be explored to the utmost."[45]

Nimitz immediately recognized that the lull after Santa Cruz was a perfect opportunity to send more reinforcements to Guadalcanal. He told Halsey that the "ground situation [on] Cactus can be turned in our favor only by offensive action." Although Vandegrift's forces had "performed magnificently," they were too few to take the offensive. Now was the time to bring enough reinforcements to "permit offensive operations." Halsey was "in complete agreement." He ordered a new batch of troops to Guadalcanal and covered the movement with Scott's task group. In a personal letter to Nimitz, Halsey explained, "We are not a bit down hearted and we are going to continue to give them hell."[46] The situation in SOPAC had transformed, but Halsey had yet to turn his enthusiasm into victory.

## THE NAVAL BATTLE OF GUADALCANAL

At the start of November, Nimitz's intelligence organization produced another estimate of Japanese capabilities. Recent changes to IJN codes had made it more difficult to track the movements of Japanese ships and air forces, but the analysis revealed that the strategy of attrition was working. Japanese air attacks on Guadalcanal had "slowed down considerably" because of "heavy losses" in planes and pilots. On the ground, the Japanese appeared to have "lost the initiative." However, there was "no indication that the enemy had abandoned plans to recapture" the island, and if they succeeded in doing so, they would most likely extend their "control along the island chain to New Caledonia." Nimitz and his staff concluded that the Japanese would resume their "all-out attack on Guadalcanal in the near future."[47]

Halsey prepared for it. He left Kinkaid in command of his lone carrier group, *Enterprise*'s TF 16. Halsey gave Rear Admiral Callaghan, Ghormley's former chief of staff, command of a new cruiser force, TF 65. On 7 November, Halsey flew to Espiritu Santo and met with Rear Admiral Fitch. Fitch had built up strength at Guadalcanal and kept some planes ready in reserve; he felt it was a good time to be aggressive. Halsey left for Guadalcanal the next day. For Vandegrift, Halsey's visit was a "wonderful breath of fresh air." Halsey was struck by the "gaunt, malaria-ridden bodies" of the men, "their faces lined from what seemed a nightmare of years." After enduring a Japanese destroyer bombardment with them that night, he left the next day, determined not to let them down.[48]

When Halsey returned to Noumea, Nimitz's assessment of the coming Japanese offensive was waiting. They were mounting a "major operation" with a powerful carrier striking force covering a reinforcement convoy. Daily aerial attacks from their bases in the northern Solomons would suppress the airfield on Guadalcanal; another massive battleship bombardment would cripple it. Once the airfield was wrecked, the reinforcement convoy would arrive with enough troops and supplies to overwhelm Vandegrift and his defenders. Nimitz made sure to include a personal message of encouragement: "While this looks like a big punch, I am confident that you with your forces will take their measure."[49]

Halsey reviewed his dispositions with his staff and Kinkaid. Major reinforcements were already on their way to Guadalcanal. Three attack cargo ships escorted by Scott's TG 62.4 arrived 11 November. Callaghan's cruiser force was covering Turner's TF 67; it was bringing about six thousand men and was expected to arrive the next day. Halsey's most powerful striking group was Kinkaid's TF 16, with carrier *Enterprise* and battleships *Washington* and *South Dakota*. Halsey planned to keep *Enterprise* out of danger by operating her south of the Solomons, beyond the reach of Japanese striking forces, but close enough to attack an enemy convoy approaching from Rabaul or the Shortlands. If any Japanese task force made it past Callaghan and Scott, Rear Adm. Lee would take Kinkaid's two battleships and move north to intercept. When Rear Admiral Spruance wrote the CINCPAC action report for the ensuing battle, he summarized the developing situation this way:

> Despite our successes in the skirmishes on Guadalcanal, the situation appeared critical. Our only available carrier was the incompletely repaired *Enterprise*. . . . *Saratoga* was just leaving Pearl Harbor following repairs. . . . It is possible we had superiority in numbers on Guadalcanal but the Japanese were continually landing fresh troops and massing a large assault force to the north. The October battles had achieved some reduction in Japanese warships, but the fleet gathered against us was still far stronger than our available fleet. We were inferior in land-based

as well as carrier aircraft. On 10 November when it became apparent that the Japanese were on the eve of renewing the grand scale attack on Guadalcanal, the situation did not look promising.[50]

The Naval Battle of Guadalcanal began with a large Japanese bombing raid that interrupted the unloading of Turner's transports and damaged Callaghan's flagship, cruiser *San Francisco*. Fitch's B-17s located an approaching Japanese bombardment force commanded by Vice Admiral Abe Hiroaki. Abe's mission was to cripple Henderson Field with his two battleships. He and his superiors had correctly assessed that Turner's transports would withdraw that evening, but they had failed to account for Halsey's determination and Callaghan's resolve. At Halsey's prompting, Turner ordered Callaghan and Scott to return to Savo Sound and stop Abe's powerful formation.

Callaghan assumed command of the combined task force. As Ghormley's chief of staff, Callaghan had participated in the conferences with Nimitz and understood the vital importance of Henderson Field. Now, outnumbered and outgunned, Callaghan had the opportunity to save it. He deliberately sought to turn the ensuing battle into a close-range brawl—a melee in the dark that would give his cruisers and destroyers a chance against the Japanese battleships. When Abe's formation appeared on radar, Callaghan headed straight for it, disrupted its cohesion, and tore it apart. Callaghan's formation disintegrated in the process. He and Scott were both killed, but the plan worked. Abe's bombardment was thwarted. His flagship, battleship *Hiei*, was crippled and scuttled the next day.[51]

Abe's failure to bombard the airfield seriously disrupted Yamamoto's plans. Henderson Field had to be disabled to allow the slow transports of the reinforcement convoy to safely reach Guadalcanal. The Japanese held their transports back and hoped that a cruiser bombardment scheduled for the next night—originally intended to cover the unloading of the transports—would disrupt aerial operations sufficiently to allow them to close. A new bombardment was added to the plan for the night after that; battleship *Kirishima* would finish what the cruisers started, destroy American planes, and allow the transports to safely reach the island. Halsey was unaware of these particulars, but he moved quickly to counter the threat. He ordered Lee to form TF 64, take his battleships north, and "prevent the bombardment of

Guadalcanal." Lee did not arrive in time to challenge the Japanese cruiser bombardment. The attack caused "much concern" at Nimitz's headquarters, but damage was relatively light, and the staff continued "to be optimistic."[52]

The next day, hopeful that the bombardment had rendered Henderson Field inoperable, the Japanese sent their eleven transports toward Guadalcanal. Scout planes sighted the convoy that morning. Halsey ordered Kinkaid to attack while keeping *Enterprise* "about 100 miles" south of the Solomons. Throughout the day, the Japanese convoy was subjected to a series of strikes from *Enterprise*, Guadalcanal, and Espiritu Santo. By that evening, only four transports were still on their way to the island.[53]

That night, as Vice Admiral Kondo Nobutake approached to bombard Henderson Field with battleship *Kirishima*, Lee was waiting for him. Patrol planes had tracked Kondo and intelligence intercepts told Lee to expect him just before midnight. At 2322, Lee reported that he was "engaging [the] enemy." Although three of his four destroyers were sunk and *South Dakota* was damaged by over two dozen hits, Lee won a decisive victory. Patient use of radar-assisted gunfire by his flagship *Washington* sank *Kirishima* and sowed confusion among her escorts. With the airfield secure, Lee turned northwest and headed for the Japanese transports, forcing them to reverse course and delaying their arrival off Guadalcanal. That gave U.S. pilots, Marine artillery, and destroyer *Meade* the opportunity to attack them. Their collective action set fire to the Japanese transports and much of their supplies, ending the Japanese effort to retake the island. Although many specific details had yet to reach Pearl Harbor, Nimitz was confident of the outcome. His staff concluded, "[I]t is certain that TF 67, 64, and 16 inflicted such heavy damage on the enemy that the push was completely broken up."[54]

These various actions—collectively known as the Naval Battle of Guadalcanal—marked an inflection point. It was the last time that Nimitz, Halsey, and the South Pacific Area would confront the Japanese with inferior forces. The new battleship *Indiana*, carrier *Saratoga*, and the Army's 25th Infantry Division were on their way. As these and other reinforcements arrived, Halsey began to assert control of the situation. He provided turkeys for Thanksgiving dinner on Guadalcanal and formed new, more powerful, task forces. He assumed the island would soon be secure and started planning to resume the offensive. By late November, Nimitz declared that "the enemy is in no position to dispute our command of the sea area in the southern Solomons."[55] The struggle for Guadalcanal was not over, but the outcome was no longer in doubt.

As the outlook improved, King asked Nimitz and Halsey who should lead the "next step." Originally, MacArthur was to be responsible for Task Two, but now, Nimitz felt differently. He drafted a response and sent it to Halsey for comment. In it he "strongly" recommended that Task Two "be revised" so that Halsey would "command the forces which will extend control up the Solomons chain." Nimitz expected "the bulk of the Pacific Fleet" to continue to operate in the South Pacific and that "a change of command of these forces which Halsey has welded into a working organization would be most unwise." Nimitz identified Buin, at the southern end of Bougainville, as the next objective; it was the nearest Japanese base with an airfield. Munda, on New Georgia was a possible alternative as the Japanese appeared to be building an airfield there.[56]

Halsey reviewed Nimitz's argument and responded to King directly. "Buin," Halsey said, was the "key" Japanese position in the Solomons, but his forces were insufficient to seize it. To move against Buin, he would need a major naval base at Guadalcanal and Tulagi; he would need to neutralize or seize the Japanese position at Munda; and he would need more planes, surface ships, and transports. Halsey stressed that it was essential to establish firm control over Guadalcanal before anything else. The Japanese had not "abandoned it" and were continuing to send reinforcements. Efforts to consolidate the island were absorbing all of Halsey's attention.[57]

The Battle of Tassafaronga emphasized Halsey's point. On the night of 30 November, TF 67, a mixed force of cruisers and destroyers under the command of Rear Admiral Wright, engaged Japanese destroyers on a resupply mission. Wright relied on his guns while the Japanese attacked with torpedoes; almost all of Wright's cruisers were hit. *Northampton* was sunk; *Minneapolis, New Orleans*, and *Pensacola* were damaged. Despite these losses, Nimitz and his staff viewed the battle positively. Wright "repulsed another push of the enemy and inflicted severe losses," allowing Halsey to "retain command of the sea." They were unaware of how correct they were; none of the supplies carried by the Japanese destroyers reached their soldiers ashore. However, just one Japanese destroyer was lost.[58]

On 3 December, Nimitz's staff estimated that the Japanese were about to make "another major effort," but before it could begin, they reassessed the situation. Getting their supplies to Guadalcanal was increasingly difficult; Turner's ships, in contrast, unloaded with virtual impunity. On 7 December, Ugaki noted that "[t]he enemy sends two or three transports into Guadalcanal daily. . . . So frequent are they that it is rather too much trouble to make note of them." Halsey was winning the logistical contest. On 9 December, Major General Patch relieved Vandegrift. While Patch's forces grew stronger, the Japanese were steadily weakened by combat, malnutrition, and disease. Before the end of the month, they decided to abandon the island and anchor their defense on the new base at Munda.[59]

Nimitz's staff drafted a new "Estimate of the Situation" for December that reflected this fundamental shift; it eschewed the defensive emphasis of previous estimates and focused on the next offensive movement, concluding that the best course of action would be to seize the Shortlands area and then occupy the island of Bougainville. The estimate argued that Halsey should command Task Two, as Nimitz had recommended in his draft message. Nimitz used this estimate and its arguments to prepare for his next meeting with King, scheduled for early December in San Francisco.[60]

## ADJUSTING IN THE ALEUTIANS

Although Nimitz wanted to recapture the western Aleutians, he withdrew forces from the North Pacific to ensure victory in the south. On 24 September, he astutely framed the strategic situation for King. Theobald's ships were wasted in the north; the "current stalemate," Nimitz argued, "has caused the neutralization of . . . considerable naval strength . . . without a corresponding holding or reduction of Japanese naval forces." The Japanese appeared to have abandoned Attu, but raids from Adak had failed to prevent the Japanese from "consolidating and strengthening" their position on Kiska. The only way to push the Japanese out was by direct assault. Since the Marines were already occupied, Nimitz recommended that the Army prepare amphibious forces to seize Kiska.[61]

In October, Nimitz's staff went further and recommended abolishing the Northern Force, withdrawing Theobald, and allowing the Northwest

Sea Frontier and the Army to deal with the Japanese. Nimitz proposed this course of action to King and Theobald on 13 October. The "changing situation," Nimitz argued, necessitated an "adjustment of forces" to "replace losses in SOPAC." He wanted to withdraw heavy cruisers and modern submarines from the North Pacific and leave behind older submarines and patrol planes. Theobald agreed; he felt the "static situation" in the Aleutians could be "maintained with sea frontier forces." Nimitz began to execute this plan. He gained King's approval to replace Theobald's heavy cruisers with the old light cruisers *Detroit* and *Raleigh*, but King was not ready to withdraw Theobald or TF 8.[62]

While these negotiations were under way, the Japanese reassessed their strategy. They had been planning to abandon the Aleutians during the winter and fall back to the Kuriles. However, on 30 September they discovered Theobald's move to Adak. Soon thereafter, they realized that U.S. forces had also occupied the Pribilofs. IGHQ began to fear that the Americans were preparing for "a northern invasion of the homeland." To forestall this possibility, they ordered Vice Admiral Hosogaya to bring additional troops to the Aleutians, reoccupy Attu, and seize nearby Shemya. Hosogaya also prepared to invade Amchitka, an ideal spot for an airfield between Kiska and Adak.

Nimitz made quick adjustments and disrupted Hosogaya's plans. Informed by his intelligence organization that the Japanese planned to reinforce Kiska and seize other islands, Nimitz ordered Theobald to locate the enemy task forces and attack them. In the final days of October, B-24s searched to the west; they missed Hosogaya's forces at Attu and had difficulty observing Kiska through the clouds. An overfly of Shemya failed to locate anything, but Hosogaya's lookouts saw the plane and he feared he had been sighted. After being warned that a U.S. task force was likely in the vicinity—the Japanese had monitored the increased message traffic between Nimitz and Theobald and concluded a task force was at sea—Hosogaya withdrew without landing any forces at Shemya or Amchitka.[63]

Renewed Japanese interest in the Aleutians led Nimitz to revise his assessment. Although NORPAC remained a secondary theater, it was important to get to Amchitka first and keep the Japanese from gaining the upper hand. On 17 November, Nimitz ordered Theobald to "submit a plan . . . for expulsion of [the] Japanese from the Aleutians" that included the "early occupation of Amchitka to deny it to the enemy." Nimitz's instructions were far more aggressive than what Theobald had discussed with his Army counterparts; they wanted to occupy Tanaga, much farther to the east. By 22 November, Nimitz was urging a rapid move to Amchitka because an airfield there would make the Japanese base at Kiska untenable. In his staff's estimate for December, they noted that "plans for this project are underway." Once again, Nimitz called for a decisive move that would put the enemy off balance.[64]

## DECEMBER CONFERENCE WITH KING

Nimitz brought two memoranda to his next meeting with King. One analyzed potential offensive operations in the South Pacific. The other reviewed the situation in the Aleutians. In the Solomons, it was important to build up strength. "It must be remembered," Nimitz wrote, "that Task One was undertaken with the full knowledge . . . that the forces for the accomplishment of Tasks Two and Three were not in sight." Because Halsey lacked a "preponderance of strength," Nimitz argued against assaulting Buin directly. Instead, he recommended a "step-by-step" advance. King would not be pleased; he preferred to advance more boldly, but the network of "mutually supporting" Japanese bases required incremental steps until more forces were available for the South Pacific. At Munda, the enemy airfield was "almost ready." Just 180 miles from Guadalcanal, it could be seized with Halsey's existing forces, and once captured, it would support his continued advance to Bougainville.[65]

In Nimitz's second memorandum, he discussed the Aleutians and linked the fight in the North Pacific to the situation in the south: "It is considered that a careful survey of the Aleutian situation is necessary at this time—not only because of its own aspects, but because of its bearing on future operations in the present major Pacific theater—the Solomons Sea area." Nimitz argued that opportunities had been missed to act more aggressively in the Aleutians. The fighting was in danger of becoming an attritional struggle. Nimitz wanted to avoid that by seizing Amchitka, building an airfield, and using it to blockade the enemy garrisons on Attu and Kiska.[66]

Nimitz and King began their conference on 11 December. Others joined for various sessions, including Kinkaid, McCormick, King's planning officer Rear

Admiral Savvy Cooke, and Captain William M. Fechteler from the Bureau of Personnel (BuPers). The first major topic was the Aleutians. All agreed that Amchitka should be occupied as soon as possible; Kinkaid left the next day to work through the details with DeWitt. King agreed that Tanaga was a waste of effort; he would convince General Marshall and bring the Army around. Once Amchitka was occupied, Kiska would follow. The target date for the recapture of Kiska was set for 1 March 1943. Troops were a major concern. Nimitz thought Kiska would require two divisions trained for amphibious operations. DeWitt appeared to have plenty of men, but too few with the necessary training. King said they would have to make do with "the troops in hand."[67]

Nimitz expressed his displeasure with new intelligence arrangements that gave OPNAV primary responsibility for the Pacific theater. Joseph Rochefort, who had identified Midway as the target of the Combined Fleet's June offensive, had been relieved without Nimitz's knowledge or approval. To their credit, Nimitz and King focused on how to move forward and agreed to foster a shared sense of purpose by using "we" and not "I" in their communications. King wanted to work toward the "ultimate goal" of fostering cohesion through a "joint intelligence agency" that integrated the efforts of all services. ICPOA was a potential model for this approach at the theater level. Within the next year, Nimitz would expand ICPOA's operations to embrace all services and transform it into a joint organization. Until that time, friction between Pearl Harbor and OPNAV continued.[68]

The boundary between MacArthur's SWPAC and Halsey's SOPAC was a problem. It meant that Halsey could not move against Munda without entering MacArthur's theater. Nimitz wanted to know if Halsey was "free to launch an attack on Munda" without MacArthur's interference. If not, any offensive up the Solomons would be unduly delayed. Nimitz felt a new JCS directive was needed to "clarify the situation" and eliminate these concerns. Once it was issued, Halsey could move against Munda and then Buin. After MacArthur secured the north coast of New Guinea and the Papuan Peninsula, the two could advance on Rabaul. Logistics and reinforcements would be crucial. Nimitz wanted to be "kept saturated" with Army and Navy planes. King supported Nimitz but insisted Harmon and Patch request additional planes through the Army's chain of command.[69]

Nimitz and King reviewed several options for an offensive in the Central Pacific. The Marshalls were a logical starting point, but Nimitz feared it "might be the reverse of Midway." He felt a "frontal attack" in the Central Pacific would be less "profitable" than continued pressure in the south. King countered that it was important to advance in large steps and not "nibble." McCormick wanted to advance into the Carolines and seize Truk. Its central position, large anchorage, and extensive facilities would make it an excellent base. Eniwetok was another valuable anchorage that could support operations farther west. Regardless of the initial direction of the offensive, Nimitz and King expected to capture the Marianas after Rabaul and eventually reach the Chinese coast. Both agreed that "the situation must be left fluid" to preserve their options; they would commit to a specific path when the time was right.[70]

As they had in prior meetings, Nimitz and King discussed important personnel decisions. Ghormley would have an opportunity to redeem himself as commander of the Fourteenth Naval District. Capt. Ernest G. Small, who had captained *Salt Lake City* during the Battle of Cape Esperance, would join Nimitz's staff and relieve McCormick, who would go to sea. Rear Adm. Robert C. Giffen and Rear Adm. John F. Shafroth would soon report to Nimitz. Both would go to SOPAC, Giffen as a task force commander and Shafroth as deputy COMSOPAC. Rear Adm. Walden L. Ainsworth—Nimitz's destroyer type commander—was already there. Nimitz had sent him to investigate destroyer repair facilities, and Halsey, apparently at Ainsworth's "instigation," had made him a task force commander. Nimitz said that he would let Halsey get away with it "this time." Nimitz had also accumulated enough evidence to convince King that Theobald had to be relieved. Kinkaid, now busy working out the plans to seize Amchitka with DeWitt, would replace him.[71]

After the conference, King continued to question the lack of progress in the South Pacific. On 31 December, he sent a message that expressed frustration with the "current status of delay, linger, and wait." Nimitz used the opportunity to explain the challenges of tropical combat and ask for reinforcements. Troops had to be identified for amphibious training "now" so that Halsey could take the offensive immediately once the ships and material became available. Nimitz also reminded King of their earlier discussions: "In line with your view expressed at our last conference, I urge that our Pacific effort, which we are impatient to apply in a thorough going offensive, be allocated its proper portion of the nation's strength."[72]

## OFFENSIVE IN THE ALEUTIANS

By early December, Nimitz had lost confidence in Theobald and started working directly with DeWitt. Longer term, Nimitz knew he needed an effective subordinate who could take the offensive in the north. He chose Kinkaid, who had proven himself as a cruiser and carrier task force commander in all the major battles of 1942—Coral Sea, Midway, the Eastern Solomons, and Santa Cruz. Nimitz and King recognized that Kinkaid was aggressive enough to make progress in the Aleutians, and Nimitz was confident Kinkaid could create an effective joint command with Buckner and DeWitt. After intensively studying "the problem of seizing Kiska" with Nimitz's staff, Kinkaid joined him in San Francisco and then planned the Amchitka operation with DeWitt.[73]

While Kinkaid prepared for his new command, Nimitz assumed control of operations in the theater. On 14 December, Rear Admiral McMorris relieved Rear Admiral Smith as head of the North Pacific striking group. McMorris would operate more aggressively, taking his ships far to the west, seeking out Japanese convoys, and augmenting the Army's aerial blockade. The next day, Nimitz ordered Theobald to prepare to occupy Amchitka "at [the] earliest practicable date." After King said the JCS would order the operation if a survey reported it was feasible to construct an airfield on the island, Nimitz told Theobald to create "detailed plans."[74]

In the meantime, Nimitz worked with DeWitt to create a joint vision for upcoming operations in NORPAC and ensure unity of effort. DeWitt responded well; he asked to work out detailed plans directly with Kinkaid and Rear Adm. Francis W. Rockwell, the new commander of the Northern Pacific Amphibious Force, but Nimitz wanted to agree on a high-level concept of operations first. The main disagreement involved assault troops for Kiska. DeWitt planned to use a single division. Nimitz recognized that was inadequate. The best intelligence estimates indicated there were ten thousand enemy troops on the island; two divisions would be required. To work through the disagreement, Nimitz sent Spruance to San Francisco to consult with DeWitt.[75]

On 21 December, a survey team reported that a fighter airstrip could be constructed on Amchitka in "two or three weeks." Nimitz immediately proposed a draft joint directive for the operation: "Objective, occupation of Amchitka at earliest date. Purpose, to immediately deny Amchitka to enemy and utilize it as soon as possible in air operations against enemy forces and Kiska installations. Task, seize and occupy Amchitka and build airfield thereon. . . . Code name of this operation is Crowbar." DeWitt agreed "entirely" with Nimitz's proposal and, with Kinkaid's concurrence, recommended a target date of 5 January. Nimitz issued the joint directive to Theobald and Buckner on 23 December.[76]

Theobald and Buckner were hesitant. They felt it was too risky to land forces on Amchitka with the Japanese barely fifty miles away at Kiska. The enemy could cover that short distance with barges and make a counter-landing. Kinkaid reassured his Army colleagues that the Navy would "do everything possible to prevent enemy action [from] interfering" with the operation. DeWitt used Kinkaid's reassurances to get Buckner to move. Theobald made the necessary arrangements but continued to object. Confident in his choice to relieve Theobald, Nimitz allowed Kinkaid and Rockwell to work through remaining details with DeWitt. Kinkaid relieved Theobald on 4 January.[77]

Foul weather delayed the Amchitka operation for a week. On 12 January, the weather was clear enough to attempt a landing. McMorris, having returned from a sweep to the west, ordered the destroyer *Worden* into Constantine Harbor to land the first contingent. Even in the harbor, the waves were twenty feet high; *Worden* delivered her scouts to the beach, but an unanticipated current pushed her onto a rock on the way out. She was a total loss. Four transports followed her in and landed the rest of the occupation force. Later that day, Kinkaid reported that operations were proceeding on schedule. Despite Japanese bombing raids—they discovered the U.S. presence on 23 January—work on the airfield proceeded rapidly and, on 28 January, the first Army fighters landed on Amchitka. Less than a month later, these planes and their reinforcements had achieved aerial supremacy in the Aleutians.[78]

Nimitz had been correct, both about the value of a quick move to Amchitka and about Kinkaid. His new North Pacific commander demonstrated he could work effectively with the Army and translate Nimitz's vision for aggressive operations into reality. The occupation of Amchitka strengthened the aerial blockade of the Aleutians and made the Japanese decision to hold Attu and Kiska more costly. Historian Brian Garfield, in his detailed study of the Aleutian campaign, explained the change Kinkaid brought to operations in the north: "In many respects he was Admiral Theobald's antithesis. Theobald had been caustic, brainy, inclined to be bitter because his pessimistic side always saw the possible perils of any undertaking. Kinkaid was the opposite. Far from contemplative . . . he made quick decisions, boldly committed everything he had, and bulled ahead tenaciously." Because they shared an offensive mindset and were determined to make the most of the limited forces available, Kinkaid and Nimitz acted harmoniously. With Kinkaid, Nimitz finally had a North Pacific commander whose outlook resonated with his own.[79]

## CONCLUSION

By the end of January 1943, Nimitz and his team had taken control of the war in the Pacific. They had won at Guadalcanal, had broken the stalemate in the North Pacific, and were preparing for the next set of offensives, intent on continuing to push the Japanese back while building up strength for an even more powerful move. It had taken just a year to transform the state of the war. Simultaneously, Nimitz had reconfigured his staff and command structure so that he could lead operations in the Pacific more effectively.

In mid-1942, Nimitz had brought team members onto his staff whose outlook resonated with his aggressive disposition. Victory in the south and progress in the north required extending this concept. Nimitz needed subordinate commanders who could be aggressive and embrace his concept of calculated risk. Nimitz lacked sufficient forces to meet all his obligations; he could not defend Hawaii, win at Guadalcanal, and take the offensive in the Aleutians simultaneously. His skill lay in recognizing that he did not need to. By maintaining Vandegrift's position at Henderson Field, he enmeshed the Japanese in a static, attritional struggle that prevented them from undertaking major offensives elsewhere.

The weakness of the approach was that Nimitz lacked subordinate commanders who could tolerate the necessary level of risk and balance their relative inferiority with aggressive action. Ghormley had reluctantly crafted a vision for a Solomons offensive but discarded it after the initial Japanese reaction to Operation Watchtower led to the battles of Savo Island and the Eastern

Solomons. Ghormley's stance remained fundamentally defensive and kept him from recognizing the centrality of Henderson Field to the fighting at Guadalcanal. Theobald was unable to discern that victory in the Aleutians required an effective joint strategy. With the South Pacific demanding the bulk of Nimitz's naval forces, the Army's planes and men had to provide the striking power in the North Pacific. To effectively harness them, Theobald needed to create a collaborative partnership with Buckner and DeWitt; he failed to do so.

Nimitz addressed these limitations by replacing both commanders. Halsey was an inspired, if desperate, choice for COMSOPAC. He aggressively translated Nimitz's commitment to Guadalcanal into direct action, sending Kinkaid's carriers far to the north before the Battle of Santa Cruz in October and hurling his limited surface action groups into November's night battles. These were costly decisions, but they were necessary to preserve Vandegrift's hold on the island at the height of the campaign. In Halsey, Nimitz had found an inspiring area commander who would exploit opportunities, take risks, and make the most of his limited forces.

Kinkaid was more methodical, but no less aggressive. Although he had yet to prove his full capability by the end of January, it was clear he would collaborate with the Army in a way Theobald could not. Kinkaid would hold the necessary meetings and conferences, use his political acumen to work through differences, and gain support by meeting his commitments. Kinkaid would bring the Army along, and once he was installed as COMNORPAC, Nimitz could begin to withdraw some of his attention from the Aleutians and focus on the broad entirety of the Pacific.

The successful conclusion of the Guadalcanal campaign shifted the balance in the Pacific and made victory for the Allies possible. In 1943, Nimitz and his subordinates would build on the foundation they had created and turn to their next challenge. While the offensives in the north and south gained momentum, Nimitz and Spruance assessed lessons from the war's first year and used them to prepare to harness the industrial might of the United States for a new, powerful offensive, designed to take the war across the Pacific and to the shores of Japan. Their preparations would require another set of reconfigurations and reorientations within Nimitz's command.

Rear Adm. Chester W. Nimitz. This photograph was taken when Nimitz was chief of the Bureau of Navigation and before President Franklin D. Roosevelt asked him to assume command of the Pacific Fleet in the aftermath of the attack on Pearl Harbor. *National Archives: 80-G-K-13455*

In this photograph, Nimitz's plain expression hints at the stress of the first months of the war. It was taken early in 1942, soon after Nimitz assumed command of the Pacific Fleet and before he knew his preliminary raids were forcing the Japanese to react. Pictured with Nimitz are Lt. Gen. Delos C. Emmons, USA, commanding general of the Hawaiian Department (*center*) and Rear Adm. Milo F. Draemel, USN, Nimitz's chief of staff. *Naval History and Heritage Command: NH 62650*

Inspection of Midway - early May '42.
before the action -
C.W. Nimitz

Nimitz inspecting Midway's defenses on 2 May 1942. He left the island confident it could withstand a "moderate attack" but moved quickly to augment its defenses. Midway would soon be the objective of a major Japanese operation; Nimitz used "calculated risk" to thwart their plans and destroy their carrier force. *The Nimitz Education and Research Center at the National Museum of the Pacific War*

Nimitz visits Guadalcanal. In this photo from 30 September 1942, Nimitz is shown with staff officers and local commanders. *Front row, left to right*: Brig. Gen. DeWitt Peck, USMC; Lt. H. Arthur Lamar, USN; Adm. Chester W. Nimitz, USN; Maj. Gen. Alexander A. Vandegrift, USMC; Brig. Gen. Roy S. Geiger, USMC; and Col. Omar T. Pfeiffer, USMC. *Back row, left to right*: Cdr. James P. Compton, USN; Capt. William M. Callaghan, USN; Capt. John R. Redman, USN; Air Commodore Robert V. Goddard, RNZAF; Capt. Ralph A. Ofstie, USN. Note the B-17 in the background.

*Naval History and Heritage Command: NH 62413*

Admiral Nimitz and Admiral Halsey confer on board seaplane tender *Curtiss* in the harbor at Espiritu Santo, 20 January 1943. During this visit to SOPAC, Nimitz urged Halsey to move forward aggressively and capture the Japanese base at Munda on the island of New Georgia. *National Archives: 80-G-34822*

Nimitz, King, and Halsey pictured outside of Nimitz's headquarters on 28 September 1943. King and Halsey were at Pearl Harbor for a conference with Nimitz. They discussed upcoming offensive operations, including the start of the Central Pacific offensive, Operation Galvanic. Each of the admirals signed the photograph. *Naval History and Heritage Command: NH 62645*

Nimitz and several of his key officers are pictured at his headquarters on 14 November 1943, not long after Nimitz introduced his new staff structure. *Left to right*: Vice Adm. William L. Calhoun, Vice Adm. John H. Towers, Adm. Chester W. Nimitz, Vice Adm. Robert L. Ghormley, and Vice Adm. Aubrey W. Fitch. Ghormley was commandant of the Fourteenth Naval District. The others were part of Nimitz's command; Calhoun and Towers were masterful with logistics and administration, respectively. *Naval History and Heritage Command: NH 58032*

Nimitz competes against a sailor in a game of horseshoes while others look on. This photograph may have been taken during the infamous "Texas Picnic" of January 1944, when an estimated 40,000 soldiers, sailors, and Marines relaxed, socialized, and drank beer in Honolulu's largest park. According to eyewitnesses, Nimitz enjoyed it as much as anyone. *Naval History and Heritage Command: NH 58032*

Nimitz regularly visited newly captured islands immediately after they were secured. Here, he is shown at Kwajalein Island after Operation Flintlock on 5 February 1944. *Left to right*: an unidentified officer; Gen. Robert C. Richardson, USA, commander of the Hawaiian Department; Admiral Nimitz; Vice Adm. Richmond K. Turner, USN, commander of the Joint Expeditionary Force; and Vice Adm. Raymond A. Spruance, USN, commander of the Central Pacific Force (*in profile, extreme right*). The two men in the background are unidentified. *Naval History and Heritage Command: NH 62234*

Admiral Nimitz confers with General MacArthur at MacArthur's headquarters in Brisbane, Australia, on 27 March 1944. The nearest objective to MacArthur's pointer is Green Island, which Admiral Halsey had occupied on 15 February. During their conference, MacArthur and Nimitz discussed plans for MacArthur's capture of Hollandia, Operation Reckless. *National Archives: SC 190409*

Nimitz regularly took time for exercise and intentionally built it into his schedule. Here, he is pictured with one of his favorite walking partners, Admiral Spruance. They are striding along the deck of battleship *New Jersey* while at anchor in Majuro Atoll on 8 April 1944. During this visit with Spruance, Nimitz discussed plans for Operation Forager, which would seize the Mariana Islands. *Naval History and Heritage Command: NH 62511*

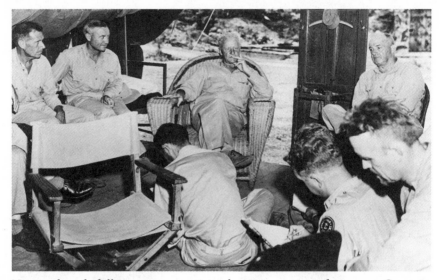

Nimitz thoughtfully answers questions during a press conference on Guam in mid-August 1944, soon after the island was secured. Pictured with Nimitz are, *left to right*: Adm. Raymond A. Spruance, Rear Adm. Forrest P. Sherman, and Lt. Gen. Alexander A. Vandegrift, commandant of the Marine Corps. *Naval History and Heritage Command: NH 62469*

Nimitz and the senior officers of the Fifth Fleet on board Spruance's flagship, cruiser *Indianapolis*, in February 1945 before Operation Detachment, the capture of Iwo Jima. *Left to right*: Adm. Raymond A. Spruance, Vice Adm. Marc A. Mitscher, Fleet Admiral Chester W. Nimitz, and Vice Adm. Willis A. Lee. *Naval History and Heritage Command: NH 49705*

Nimitz maintained a tight feedback loop between strategy and tactics by relying on talented planners who shared his aggressive disposition. Two are pictured with him here, outside of his headquarters on Guam in 1945. Vice Adm. Charles H. McMorris is on the left, and Rear Adm. Forrest P. Sherman is in the center. Together, these three officers planned Nimitz's late-war operations. *Naval History and Heritage Command: NH 62265*

On the cusp of victory, Fleet Admiral Nimitz, Commander in Chief, Pacific Fleet and Pacific Ocean Areas, is pictured in his advanced headquarters on Guam in July 1945. *National Archives: 80-G-K-5976*

# COILING THE SPRING

*He won't be let alone; that is why we must go on with*
*offensive action and hit him wherever we find him.*

—Adm. Chester W. Nimitz[1]

Victory at Guadalcanal gave Nimitz and his Pacific Ocean Areas command the initiative in the Pacific; it was essential to maintain and exploit it. For the first nine months of 1943, he relied on Halsey and Kinkaid to conduct opportunistic offensives and keep the pressure on the Japanese. Halsey worked under General MacArthur's direction and advanced through the Solomons toward Rabaul. Kinkaid isolated and blockaded Japanese positions on Attu and Kiska, preparing them for recapture and threatening to invade Japan through the Kuriles. These capable subordinate commanders helped Nimitz keep the Japanese off balance, allowing him time to adapt and reconfigure his command structure.

While Halsey and Kinkaid advanced, Nimitz and his staff prepared for the long-anticipated Central Pacific offensive. They integrated valuable lessons from the war's first year and introduced new tactics, crafted new approaches for developing plans and doctrine, and reconfigured shipboard organizational structures to process information more effectively. These adaptations helped maximize the combat potential of the Pacific Fleet. To make his Pacific Ocean Areas command more effective, Nimitz introduced a new joint staff that integrated the Army into plans and operations. An entire division of the joint staff was dedicated to logistics; it ensured Nimitz's plans reflected his logistical capabilities. As his staff's planning process became more sophisticated, Nimitz was able to systematically explore alternatives, create options, and provide the JCS with clear recommendations for upcoming operations. Nimitz's increasingly capable planning staff allowed him to initiate the Central Pacific offensive in late 1943 and, once it was under way, helped him "maintain and extend unremitting pressure against Japan."

To succeed, Nimitz had to abandon prewar assumptions about how to organize a Pacific campaign. Overcoming the increasing strength of Japanese defenses required an offensive that was simultaneously rapid, sustained, and overwhelming. At the same time, the JCS' determination to finish the war with "Germany first" meant that the Pacific would receive a fraction of the United States' increasing industrial output. Nimitz's resources were limited and his challenge unprecedented. It has been suggested that the Allies rode a wave of overwhelming material superiority to victory in World War II, but in the Pacific, where supply lines spanned vast distances, industrial power meant little without a logistical organization and planning capability that could concentrate that power at the right time and place. In 1943, Nimitz and his team established the foundation to make that possible.

## INTEGRATING LESSONS AND CHANGING TACTICS

Over the course of 1943, Nimitz, his staff, and his subordinates improved tactics, doctrine, and force structure. These adaptations were crucial to maintaining the initiative during the upcoming offensive. One of the most significant was the introduction of a new shipboard information system, the Combat Information Center (CIC). During the battles of 1942, ship and formation commanders frequently lost situational awareness. New technologies like radar and very high frequency radio sets ought to have conferred a significant tactical advantage. Instead, the new information generated by these technologies overwhelmed commanders; they were unable to keep pace with the battles unfolding around them.

To help improve the situation, Nimitz issued a new tactical bulletin in November 1942. All ships would establish a CIC. The CIC would evaluate all available information, synthesize it, and provide it in an actionable format to the ship's captain and weapons systems. It was a revolutionary solution to the challenge. By specifying the desired outcomes, but leaving his captains free to explore alternatives, Nimitz fostered rapid parallel exploration of potential approaches to organizing CICs. The best solutions were copied and became the basis for training; within six months, situational awareness in combat had significantly improved. By the end of 1943, the CIC had transformed the Navy's approach to battle, especially at night. New technologies, and new practices that exploited them, combined to outpace the IJN's capabilities.[2]

Nimitz increased the effectiveness of the submarine campaign against Japanese shipping by giving it personal attention. He monitored the submarines closely—their successes regularly appeared in the CINCPAC Command Summary—and recognized they were failing to reach their full potential. Starting in early 1943, codebreaking allowed Nimitz and his subordinates to track enemy convoys and position submarines to intercept them. However, the anticipated success did not follow. Intercepted messages revealed that enemy ships believed to have been sunk were making it to port. Submarine captains were reporting premature detonations of their torpedoes; something appeared to be wrong with them.[3]

The new commander, Submarines, Pacific Fleet (COMSUBPAC), Rear Adm. Charles A. Lockwood, suspected a flaw in the torpedo's magnetic exploder. He believed the exploder—designed to be triggered by the slight variation in the Earth's magnetic field generated by the hull of a target ship—was detonating prematurely. Lockwood and Nimitz regularly held "personal conferences" to discuss the submarine campaign. They accumulated evidence about the exploder's flaws, hoping to spur the Bureau of Ordnance (BuOrd) to action. However, before BuOrd could act, the evidence of a problem became overwhelming. On 23 June, Lockwood asked Nimitz for permission to deactivate the magnetic exploders and use contact exploders instead. Nimitz issued the necessary orders the next day; premature detonations ceased to be an issue.[4]

Unfortunately, the contact exploder also regularly failed. Lockwood began a series of experiments to identify the problem and, by early September, had traced the issue to the exploder's firing pin. Lockwood and his team modified torpedoes at Pearl Harbor to solve the problem and, during King's visit in September, recommended that similar changes be introduced to the production process. King and Nimitz immediately approved. With this final problem addressed, Lockwood and his submarines soon became much more effective. In October, new tactics combined with improved weapons when Lockwood—at King's suggestion—introduced "wolf packs," tactical groupings of four to six submarines that coordinated their attacks against enemy convoys.[5]

Additional improvements were made in task force and fleet organization to allow the Pacific Fleet to capitalize on the potential of carrier warfare. Prewar tactics had emphasized single-carrier task forces because, before radar and effective fighter direction techniques, carriers survived by dispersing and remaining hidden. War experience showed that carriers could pool their resources and offer mutual support; radar could detect incoming strikes and vector fighters to intercept. After experimenting with multiple carrier formations in 1942, the Pacific Fleet officially adopted them in 1943. More experiments helped determine the ideal mix of large and light carriers in each task force. This shift to carrier task forces presented a new challenge. During an amphibious operation, carrier task forces could maximize their striking power by dispersing over a wide area and attacking several targets simultaneously. With these tactics, the fleet could overwhelm a large portion of an island group, secure local aerial superiority, and capture multiple objectives. However, if the battleships and cruisers were distributed among those carrier task forces, the fleet would be vulnerable to defeat in detail if the Japanese initiated a major fleet action. The task forces needed to be able to rapidly coalesce if the enemy threatened; to allow the fleet to smoothly transition between distributed carrier task forces and concentrated strength, new tactics and doctrines were required.

King tried to help address the issue at the fleet commander's level by introducing a new numbered fleet system. From March 1943, all fleets had a number. In the Pacific they were odd-numbered—the Third Fleet was in the South Pacific, and the Fifth Fleet in the Central Pacific—and in the Atlantic they were even-numbered. Task force designations derived from fleet numbers, so Central Pacific task forces numbered in the 50s, and South

Pacific ones in the 30s. King expected the fleets to handle some of the coordination previously delegated to task force commanders, thereby allowing task force commanders to better use their staffs and "exercise the full scope of command."[6]

Nimitz's approach was different. Instead of introducing a modified organizational structure, he convened a board to investigate the problem. The board produced the Navy's most important wartime tactical manual, *Current Tactical Orders and Doctrine, U.S. Pacific Fleet, PAC-10*. Issued in June 1943, *PAC-10* established a new foundation for task force doctrine and battle plans. It allowed "forces composed of diverse types, and indoctrinated under different task force commanders, to join at sea on short notice for concerted action . . . without interchanging a mass of special instructions." *PAC-10* provided a set of coherent tactical approaches that could be applied across the fleet. It addressed the needs of carrier warfare and problems with existing tactical doctrine. The fleet could now operate as a distributed network of carrier task forces, dispersing to overwhelm multiple enemy bases and coalescing when powerful surface forces threatened. This revolutionary new model was essential to the success of the Central Pacific offensive.[7]

## IMPROVING LOGISTICS

A new approach to theater-level logistics was also essential. Prewar plans had recognized the need to establish, fortify, and equip advanced bases, but the steady flow of resources and equipment—troops, ammunition, food, fuel, planes, construction material, and all the other vital supplies of modern war—required to secure Guadalcanal was unanticipated. Nimitz explored the problem by sending Rear Admiral Calhoun, his Service Force commander, to assist Halsey in the South Pacific. Halsey and Calhoun used the framework created by the Joint Logistic Plan of July 1942 and adapted as necessary; there were no established procedures to follow.

One of the most significant changes Halsey made was to disaggregate logistical efforts. He allowed the Army to operate more independently and, to ensure base development received the necessary attention, Halsey temporarily moved Captain Carter's base command out from under Rear Adm. Calvin H. Cobb's SOPAC Service Squadron. King was concerned this unconventional step—and the associated disaggregation—was potentially inefficient. In a more well-developed environment, it might have been. In the South Pacific, it was an essential step to becoming more effective. Nimitz let Halsey experiment. The challenges were unprecedented. In December, Halsey explained, "[T]he base situation here is far different from anything I have known. . . . [W]e are building and supplying bases at the same time. . . . There is no situation . . . anywhere else . . . that compares."[8]

At his conference with Nimitz in December 1942, King suggested that the Army's approach to logistics might offer valuable lessons. Halsey was already leveraging it and starting to rely on Army officers for logistical planning. For example, Brig. Gen. Raymond E. S. Williamson ran the port of Noumea and increased the tonnage unloaded from less than 50,000 in November 1942 to more than 210,000 in January 1943, sufficient for a "major campaign." Maj. Gen. Robert G. Breene commanded the Army's Services of Supply in SOPAC and coordinated logistical support for Guadalcanal, building it into a major base. At his headquarters level, Halsey coordinated joint efforts with "informal cooperation" through interservice boards and "harmonious relations" with Major General Harmon. Breene felt the "cordial" approach permitted swift and coordinated action on logistic efforts.[9]

Halsey's success demonstrated that theaters could assume responsibility for logistical plans and organization, a crucial step recommended in a review of the Navy's logistics planning by the firm Booz, Allen, and Hamilton. The review also emphasized what the Guadalcanal offensive had already shown: "Logistic situations and possibilities have not been fully or properly represented . . . in . . . strategic planning. . . . [S]trategic plans may be made that are not logistically feasible, or it may require so long to determine logistic feasibility that the value of strategic planning is seriously impaired."[10] Pushing logistical planning to the theater level was a way to overcome this deficiency.

King and Marshall agreed. They delegated the challenge of developing joint logistic approaches to theater commanders. There was no straightforward solution because the Army—accustomed to supplying relatively static formations—emphasized centralized planning approaches and the Navy focused on ensuring mobility through delegation and decentralization. Rather than impose a single solution, King and Marshall allowed each theater to develop its own approach. Rear Adm. Oscar C. Badger, assistant CNO for Logistics Plans, worked with the Army to draft a "Basic Logistics Plan for Theatres Involving Joint Army and Navy Operations." It built on the principle of unified command and made each theater commander responsible for "all logistics services" in their theater. King and Marshall approved of Badger's proposal, and on 8 March 1943, they issued "Basic Logistical Plan for Command Areas Involving Both Army and Navy Operations." This retroactively validated Halsey's approach and empowered him to run logistics in his area.[11]

Nimitz learned from Halsey's experience, but because he had to integrate two parallel and preexisting logistical planning structures—one for the Army and one for the Navy—Nimitz could not rely on informal cooperation. Accordingly, on 6 April 1943, he issued his own "Basic Logistical Plan" for the Central Pacific. It established a Joint Logistical Board chaired by Calhoun that included Lieutenant General Emmons, commander of the Hawaiian Department, and Vice Admiral Ghormley, commandant of the Fourteenth Naval District.[12] They were supported by a Joint Working Board that executed their decisions. This interim step created a more integrated joint logistical planning process. Nimitz instructed Halsey to adopt a similar approach, so, on 20 May 1943, he established the South Pacific Joint Logistics Board.[13]

Bases were a significant problem. Before the war, the Navy had incorrectly assumed that all the equipment for an advanced base could be packed up, transshipped, and unloaded as a unit, allowing the rapid establishment of a new base. This led to the creation of prepackaged units that contained all the materials required for large bases, small bases, and air bases, called Lions, Cubs, and Acorns, respectively. However, the approach was too coarse-grained. When all the supplies for a base were unloaded simultaneously at a new location, the result was not a rapidly established base, but waste and confusion. Construction equipment and personnel had to be landed only when and as needed so that bases could grow from a steady flow of supplies. When everything arrived at once, important items were lost and material degraded before it could be used. The solution was to manage base materials at a finer level of granularity. To conserve vital supplies, the South Pacific began to use existing Lion and Cub assemblies "as stockpiles" and ship "smaller units" to bases as they could absorb them.[14]

OPNAV supported this approach by creating an inventory of standard components that could be sent to forward areas as needed. This was the "Catalogue of Advanced Base Functional Components," issued by OPNAV's Base Maintenance Division on 15 March 1943. The catalog contained all the functional components necessary to establish an advanced base. Components "could be selected individually, combined, and regrouped with relative ease so that advanced base assemblies could . . . be tailored . . . to the varied and changing requirements of the theaters." This was an extremely important change that made the Navy's logistic system more resilient, flexible, and better adapted to the needs of the Pacific.[15]

## JCS DIRECTS A DUAL OFFENSIVE

In January 1943, Nimitz became convinced the Japanese had abandoned their efforts to retake Guadalcanal and were adopting a defensive posture in the South Pacific. He wanted to continue the offensive to prevent them from consolidating their forces and attacking elsewhere. However, it would take several months to arrange the next series of advances in the Pacific. The existing JCS directive, which gave MacArthur responsibility for Tasks Two and Three, necessitated cooperation and resource sharing between Nimitz and MacArthur; they had to collaborate and agree on a path forward. Unfortunately for Nimitz, MacArthur was predisposed to develop his own plans in isolation and expected Nimitz to conform. To enable Nimitz to act, the JCS would have to issue a new directive allowing the two theater commanders to operate independently.

On 8 January, General Marshall prodded MacArthur, asking for his "detailed plans" and suggesting he meet with Halsey and Nimitz to arrange Task Two. MacArthur initially declined to meet with Nimitz. He was hesitant to take the offensive and argued that without "long preparation and great resources," the effort to retake Rabaul would "certainly fail." Nimitz's staff recommended advancing immediately. They were intent on "continuing our offensive and keeping the pressure on the enemy" to avoid a "stalemate." Existing air bases could cover Halsey's forces as they advanced to nearby objectives like Munda and Rekata Bay. Simultaneous offensives by Halsey and MacArthur would "be mutually supporting" and reduce the need for overwhelming superiority.[16]

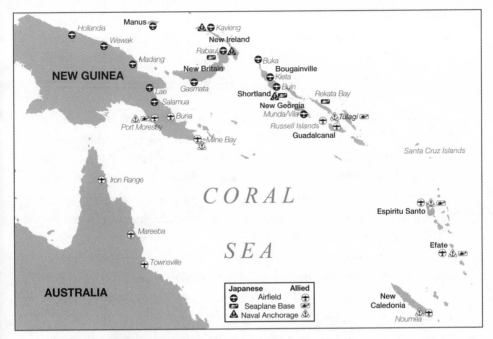

MAP 4. South and Southwest Pacific Operating Areas, March 1943

MacArthur was willing to hold a staff conference to discuss possibilities. Nimitz tentatively agreed, but he wanted to meet with Halsey first. Accordingly, on 14 January, Nimitz headed south with Captain Small, his new head of war plans. Rear Admiral McCain, now chief of BuAer, joined them. At Noumea, they discussed potential offensive operations with Halsey and his staff. Nimitz wanted to know when Halsey could move against Munda. Halsey's war plans officer, Brig. Gen. DeWitt Peck, USMC, anticipated 1 April. Nimitz stressed the importance of "forward movement" and told Halsey to organize everything around it. When Peck suggested seizing Russell Island as an intermediate step, Nimitz and Halsey agreed.[17]

While Nimitz returned to Pearl Harbor, a large enemy striking force gathered at Truk. Halsey thought it was the beginning of another offensive, but Operation Ke was a withdrawal. Over a series of nights, Japanese destroyers evacuated the bulk of their remaining garrison from Guadalcanal while their striking forces provided distant cover. Nimitz was disappointed when cruiser *Chicago* was torpedoed and sunk by enemy bombers, but he was gratified on 9 February when Major General Patch reported "the defeat of the enemy on Guadalcanal."[18]

Like Nimitz, King emphasized the importance of forward movement. In mid-January, he attended the Casablanca Conference, where the Allies agreed to impose "unconditional surrender" on Germany and Japan. Although the principle of "Germany first" was reaffirmed, attendees also resolved to apply "unremitting pressure" in the Pacific. A host of offensives were planned for 1943. The British would reconquer Burma, MacArthur would capture Rabaul, Kinkaid would extract the Japanese from Attu and Kiska, and Nimitz would open "a new drive across the Central Pacific." Burma was especially important; reopening the Burma Road would allow more supplies to flow to Generalissimo Chiang Kai-shek, who was expected to keep the bulk of the IJA's strength occupied in China.[19]

At Casablanca, King presented a potential offensive into the Ellice and Gilbert Islands. After discussing it with the CCS, he urged Nimitz and Halsey to initiate it. King thought it would keep the pressure on the Japanese and overcome MacArthur's indecision by eliminating the need to collaborate with him entirely. Halsey preferred to maintain "all possible pressure" in the South Pacific. Nimitz agreed; an advance into the Gilberts would trigger a "vigorous" enemy reaction and the odds in a major fleet action still favored the Japanese. An advance in the South Pacific would continue to attrit the Japanese while Nimitz built up strength.

King accepted their logic but pressed for simultaneous, mutually supporting offensives to "whipsaw" the Japanese and prevent them from concentrating against any single line of advance. Rather than challenging King directly, Nimitz coached Halsey to emphasize the importance of maintaining the initiative. Halsey recast his argument. He would pin down the Japanese with a "strong offensive." Halsey's new deputy commander, Rear Adm. Theodore S. Wilkinson, had just agreed to details of Task Two at MacArthur's headquarters in Brisbane. The next step, the occupation of the Russell Islands, would occur in just a few days. After that, Halsey would infiltrate troops into

New Georgia and take Munda and Vila. Constant pressure would keep the Japanese focused on the South Pacific.[20]

By the time Nimitz and King met in San Francisco in February, their planning staffs had examined various alternatives. Nimitz's staff rejected the thrust into the Ellice and Gilbert Islands because its objectives were too broadly dispersed; the IJN could concentrate and overwhelm each attacking force in turn. A proposed "Setting Sun Campaign" was also dismissed. It would have seized Chichi Jima, Marcus, and Wake simultaneously in an attempt to force a decisive battle with the Japanese fleet. However, it also would have left Japanese bases in the Marshalls athwart Nimitz's lines of communication, dispersed his striking forces, and invited defeat in detail.

Both staffs agreed that penetrating the Japanese defenses in the Mandated Islands—the Marshall, Caroline, and Marianas Island groups—would be a major undertaking. Nimitz would have to overwhelm a substantial portion of the defensive network and seize "at least two [air]fields simultaneously." Otherwise, the Japanese would use their network of bases to bring overwhelming aerial strength to the threatened area and repulse the attack. Nimitz and King decided that until the Pacific Fleet was stronger, it would focus on "limited operations" rather than a major offensive. However, King urged Nimitz to take "considerable calculated risks" to maintain the initiative. King had argued vehemently for ships, planes, and men for the Pacific. He reminded Nimitz that they "had to be used in order to justify" their presence in the theater. Otherwise, Nimitz might be "ordered to undertake" hasty operations to satisfy the CCS or Allied political leaders. One way to use those forces was to allow Halsey to proceed independently and act opportunistically, which Nimitz and King agreed to do.[21]

King's conference with Nimitz highlighted how the lack of effective coordination in the South and Southwest Pacific was delaying offensive operations. To resolve the issue, the JCS summoned representatives from MacArthur, Nimitz, and Halsey to Washington for the Pacific Military Conference in March 1943. Nimitz took advantage of the fact that those representatives— Major General Sutherland and Major General Kenney from SWPAC and Major General Harmon and Capt. Miles Browning, Halsey's chief of staff, from SOPAC—stopped at Pearl Harbor on their way to Washington.

MacArthur had developed a plan, code-named Elkton, and Sutherland and Kenney shared it with Nimitz and his staff. Elkton broke Tasks Two and Three into five separate phases. The first would seize airfields on New Guinea's Huon Peninsula, the second would capture Munda and other positions in New Georgia, the third would establish airfields on New Britain and Bougainville, the fourth would secure the anchorage at Kavieng, and the fifth would capture Rabaul. MacArthur's plans necessitated delaying Halsey's attack on Munda, now scheduled for 10 April. Nimitz, armed with King's approval for Halsey's offensive, got Sutherland and Kenney to agree to allow Halsey to proceed independently.[22]

In Washington, Spruance and Small represented Nimitz while larger questions were entertained. The Army's assistant chief of staff, Maj. Gen. Thomas T. Handy, argued that all operations should be centralized under MacArthur to drive along the coast of New Guinea and recapture the Philippines. Leahy and King objected. They preferred a "dual drive in which MacArthur and Nimitz 'cooperated' in support of a common goal." This concept became the basis of an agreement reached on 28 March. The JCS decided that Nimitz and MacArthur would lead independent but "mutually supporting" offensives. MacArthur was given "full command of operations in New Guinea and the adjacent islands." Nimitz would command "in other Pacific areas" and have "full responsibility for defeating the Japanese fleet." The arrangement introduced a clear boundary between the two commands and increased their freedom of action.[23]

The JCS issued a new directive based on the Elkton plan; they ordered MacArthur to "prepare for . . . seizure of [the] Bismarck Archipelago." However, Rabaul was left off the list of objectives because the Japanese had steadily reinforced it. Capturing it in 1943 was no longer considered feasible. Instead, the JCS instructed MacArthur to establish airfields on Kiriwina and Woodlark Islands; seize Lae, Salamaua, and western New Britain; and advance through the Solomons to Bougainville. Halsey would remain under Nimitz's command but operate under MacArthur's "general directives" in the Solomons. Unfortunately, by accepting Elkton, the JCS delayed Halsey's advance to Munda.[24]

Nimitz was initially apprehensive that the delay would allow the Japanese to attack in the Central Pacific, so he kept a striking force near Hawaii, but quickly reverted to his habit of concentrating his forces where they could be most effective. In late April, he prepared to send carrier *Victorious*—on loan from the Royal Navy—and battleship *North Carolina* to Halsey. King opposed the move; he wanted Nimitz to be prepared for "prompt powerful reactions" when Kinkaid assaulted Attu on 7 May. King suggested keeping those ships at Hawaii until *Washington* and *Enterprise* returned from the South Pacific for scheduled refits. Nimitz agreed. In the meantime, he began a "radio deception plan" to draw "enemy attention to the Marshalls–Gilberts area" and distract from operations elsewhere.[25]

While Halsey and MacArthur prepared to advance, ICPOA made several important discoveries. On 6 April, they learned that the Japanese were planning Operation I-Go, an aerial offensive against Guadalcanal intended to disrupt Halsey's timetable. Timely warning allowed most of Halsey's ships to withdraw south before the attack. Additional intercepted messages revealed that Admiral Yamamoto, commander in chief of the IJN's Combined Fleet, was at Rabaul, planning to visit Japanese bases in the Solomons. On 14 April, ICPOA decrypted a message with Yamamoto's planned itinerary. Layton quickly realized its importance and delivered the news to Nimitz personally that morning. Nimitz ordered Halsey to mount an ambush. On the 17th, the CINCPAC staff summary recorded, "[I]t seems probable that CinC Combined [Fleet] was shot down." He had been. Vice Admiral Ugaki, who was traveling with Yamamoto, observed the commander in chief's last moments as his plane descended toward "the jungle top with reduced speed, emitting black smoke and flame." Yamamoto's death devastated IJN morale; Admiral Yoshida Zengo, who had served as Navy Minister before the war, called it "an irrecoverable loss." Admiral Koga Mineichi assumed command of the Combined Fleet.[26]

Nimitz's aggressiveness and the new JCS directive created the opportunity for future success. King directed Halsey to confer with MacArthur and determine the "timing of major offensive operations." In mid-April, the two met in Brisbane and, surprisingly, given MacArthur's penchant for self-aggrandizement, discovered they enjoyed working together. MacArthur considered Halsey "a real fighting admiral." Halsey "felt as if the two 'were lifelong friends.'" They revised MacArthur's Elkton plan and created a new draft called Elkton III, which became the basis for Operation Cartwheel, the Allied campaign to isolate and reduce Rabaul. Halsey would invade New Georgia simultaneously with MacArthur's occupation of Kiriwina and Woodlark, planned for 15 May. Delays in preparing MacArthur's amphibious force pushed the operation back to 15 June, but the next offensive steps in the south were finally clear.[27]

## PROGRESS IN THE NORTH

In the Aleutians, Kinkaid's collaborative style became increasingly important. Nimitz and DeWitt had agreed to an aggressive schedule for the recapture of Kiska, but there were insufficient amphibious forces available for the assault. Rather than delay, Kinkaid proposed leapfrogging Kiska and assaulting more lightly defended Attu. At the end of February, he flew to San Francisco to share the idea with DeWitt. Nimitz approved the concept and had Spruance discuss the proposed Attu operation with DeWitt when Spruance passed through San Francisco on the way to the Pacific Military Conference. The JCS "looked with favor" on the proposal, provided the operation could be undertaken with no further reinforcements. By 13 March, Nimitz was confident enough to tell Kinkaid to begin planning for it. Eight days later, Nimitz learned that the Japanese were building an airfield on Attu. That convinced the JCS. They approved the operation and urged it be "undertaken as soon as practicable." The target date was set as 7 May.[28]

McMorris was continuing to blockade Japanese positions by aggressively patrolling with his surface action group. On 26 March, while on a sweep to intercept Japanese transports, McMorris ran into the bulk of Vice Admiral Hosogaya's surface fleet. In the ensuing Battle of the Komandorski Islands, McMorris was outnumbered two-to-one. He fought an aggressive "retiring action" in the hope that Hosogaya's superior strength could be offset by land-based air attack. McMorris achieved his objective of preventing the Japanese reinforcement mission and withdrawing without significant loss when Hosogaya, knowing that American bombers were on their way, withdrew before they could find him. Hosogaya's handling of the battle was criticized and Vice Admiral Kawase Shiro relieved him as commander of the Fifth Fleet and Northern Area Force on 31 March.[29]

After the Battle of the Komandorski Islands, Kinkaid grew apprehensive that the Japanese would reinforce their Fifth Fleet and requested additional forces. Nimitz acted characteristically and sent the last battleships based in Hawaii to support the upcoming Attu operation. Despite Nimitz's action, there were not enough destroyers to meet Kinkaid's needs; Nimitz told him to employ "calculated risk" and reduce the number of destroyers on escort duty to free some for the operation.[30]

Nimitz also urged Kinkaid to move his headquarters closer to the operating area. On 21 March, Kinkaid left the relative comfort of Kodiak and moved to Adak. Buckner and Butler were already there, and when Kinkaid arrived, Buckner suggested that he and Kinkaid create a joint mess so that they and their staffs could share meals. Kinkaid welcomed the idea. Regular interaction between Kinkaid, Buckner, and their two staffs rapidly created shared understanding and fostered a strong friendship.[31]

The foul Aleutian weather forced a small delay, but on 11 May, the Army's 7th Division, commanded by Maj. Gen. Albert E. Brown, landed on Attu. Kinkaid employed a command structure based on the lessons from the South Pacific. He directed the entire operation from Adak, Rockwell commanded the assault forces, and Brown took command of the assault troops once he established himself ashore. Brown's troops struggled against the terrain and Japanese defenders, creating the opportunity for the IJN to intervene. Admiral Koga, fearing a potential thrust into the Kuriles, moved his flagship and a substantial portion of his fleet from Truk to Tokyo Bay. ICPOA observed these moves but was unsure how to interpret them.[32]

On Attu, the beaches grew congested and the attack bogged down. Kinkaid knew that he could not keep the vulnerable transports exposed for long. Japanese submarines were already among his ships. Nimitz became concerned the Japanese would attack in strength. Brown failed to appreciate this context and did not attack aggressively enough. He asked for "immediate reinforcement" and requested heavy equipment to build roads and defenses. Kinkaid was alarmed; he decided to relieve Brown and place Maj. Gen. Eugene M. Landrum in command. DeWitt and Buckner concurred. This kind of interservice collaboration was unimaginable under Theobald, but because Kinkaid had developed effective relationships with the Army generals, his relief of Brown passed without issue. Landrum's forces soon overwhelmed the Japanese defenders, securing Attu and irrevocably undermining the Japanese position in the Aleutians. In June, Kinkaid was promoted to vice admiral.[33]

## MAY CONFERENCE WITH KING

At the end of May, Nimitz flew to San Francisco for another conference with King. They discussed a variety of topics, but two dominated the agenda—personnel and how to initiate "a move into the Marshalls in the late fall" of 1943. The planned British offensive in Burma, Operation Anakim, was no longer feasible, and that freed amphibious forces for a Central Pacific operation.[34]

Nimitz and King focused on the Central Pacific because it was clear that was where the Pacific Fleet would have the necessary "freedom of action" to rapidly advance. Nimitz's Plans Section had grappled with the challenge of how best to attack the Marshalls and produced an "estimate of operations in the Central Pacific." Armed with their analysis, Nimitz argued for occupying a substantial portion of the island group, at least five bases. Capturing positions in the Gilberts would be a good first step; from there, land-based planes could support an attack on the Marshalls. Rear Admiral Cooke, familiar with the planning done in Washington, preferred a "direct assault" upon the atolls of Kwajalein, Wotje, and Maloelap. Air bases on these atolls would allow Nimitz to "attain control of the Marshall Islands" and sever "Japanese lines of communication." However, Cooke agreed that it was important to avoid a "frontal attack." There were many atolls in the Marshalls, and the Japanese could not defend them all equally, a fact that would become more important as planning moved ahead.[35]

The balance of forces would soon favor Nimitz's Pacific Fleet. By the end of September, Nimitz was expected to have five fleet carriers and an equal number of light carriers. To augment their striking power, Nimitz requested two Army Air Force bomb groups. He did not think the Japanese could match this force; intelligence estimates suggested they were reduced to just two large carriers, *Shokaku* and *Zuikaku*. The attritional fighting in the South and Southwest Pacific had consumed many of their planes and pilots. JCS studies of the enemy fuel situation indicated that the Japanese could not "conduct major prolonged offensive operations to the eastward." Nimitz believed they would guard their remaining strength, refuse to "fight on the fringes," and seek a major fleet action only when the Philippines or the China coast were threatened. That had important implications for broader Pacific strategy. If the Japanese fleet withdrew from the perimeter, the Royal Navy's Eastern Fleet could return to Ceylon and pressure the Japanese from the west.[36]

When the subject turned to personnel, Nimitz and King agreed that senior officers who did "not measure up" ought to be removed.[37] One officer they discussed was Captain Browning. In December 1942, Nimitz had recommended that Halsey find a rear admiral to serve as his chief of staff and take care "of most details except those pertaining to operations." While Nimitz felt Browning was an effective operations officer, he did not think Browning was up to this challenge. King and Nimitz discussed their options, and while they made no decision, they agreed to make a change. In July, King ensured that Browning was offered command of the new carrier *Hornet*; Capt. Robert "Mick" Carney became Halsey's new chief of staff and was promoted to rear admiral.[38]

Command arrangements for the Central Pacific were easier to resolve. Nimitz and King quickly agreed that Spruance would lead the upcoming offensive and be promoted to vice admiral. On 30 May, with the conference still ongoing, they informed Spruance of their decision. Spruance had anticipated this and told Nimitz that he wanted Capt. Charles J. Moore as his chief of staff. Nimitz put this to King; it was a sensitive issue because Moore was currently serving on King's staff. King did not welcome the move, but Moore was unhappy in Washington. He leapt at the chance to serve with Spruance and translate his "decisions and ideas into intricate written plans."[39]

In anticipation of the coming offensive, adjustments were made to commands in Hawaii. Captain Small was ready to go to sea. In July, Small's assistant, Capt. James M. Steele, took over Nimitz's War Plans Section and Small assumed command of Cruiser Division Five. At the end of May, Lieutenant General Emmons was relieved by Lt. Gen. Robert C. Richardson. Nimitz and King both felt Richardson would be better disposed to guide the Army's participation in the Central Pacific offensive. Nimitz worked with Richardson to strengthen POA's joint intelligence capabilities. Emmons returned to the United States and, in September, relieved DeWitt as head of the Western Defense Command.[40]

When Nimitz and King turned their attention to ongoing operations, they expressed frustration at the delays in the South Pacific and the way MacArthur had constrained Halsey's assault on New Georgia. MacArthur insisted that it be done without "major forces" because he was afraid that a Japanese counterblow would distract from his efforts to the west. MacArthur wanted Halsey to advance tentatively and incrementally. That precluded a direct assault on Munda. Instead, Halsey would seize a series of intermediate positions and take Munda by advancing overland. Nimitz was anxious because Halsey's plan would risk "valuable" attack transports in a night approach and the Japanese had proven their skill in night aerial torpedo attacks by sinking cruiser *Chicago* in January.[41]

In a dedicated session, Nimitz, King, and other attendees assessed lessons from the assault on Attu. Maj. Gen. Holland M. Smith, USMC, who had trained forces for the assault, felt that the soldiers had failed to press forward aggressively and infiltrate around Japanese strongpoints. The Marines were well practiced at the technique, but more training was required to familiarize Army divisions with it. Capt. Austin K. Doyle, commanding officer of escort carrier *Nassau*, reviewed the utility of escort carriers for amphibious operations. It was the first time an escort carrier had provided close air support and Doyle felt the small carriers were "well suited" for the mission. He recommended operating them in groups of four to ensure enough planes would always be available. Attu also revealed the need to improve intelligence estimates; the number of defenders on Attu was "almost double" what ICPOA had predicted. These lessons—especially the need for better intelligence, more thorough preparation, increased on-call air support, and improved coordination of all arms—would be incorporated into future amphibious operations. To help ensure that they were, Major General Smith returned with Nimitz to Pearl Harbor to begin training amphibious forces for the Central Pacific.[42]

After a brief stop in Pearl Harbor, Nimitz and Smith headed south. Nimitz wanted to meet with Halsey, develop a better sense of his upcoming offensive, and share details from the conference with King. Nimitz was gratified that

Halsey was prepared to attack New Georgia and that the management of logistics and supplies in the South Pacific had improved. To draw attention away from Halsey's attack, Nimitz ordered a B-24 strike against Nauru the night of 28–29 June (east longitude date). In concert with this, Nimitz continued his radio deception efforts. These aggressive measures created the impression that Nimitz was "about to strike in the Eastern Mandates" and freed Halsey's hand to seize New Georgia.[43]

## HALSEY AND KINKAID ADVANCE

Operation Toenails, Halsey's advance on Munda, finally began on 30 June. In the weeks prior, steady attrition in the Solomons and the threat of offensives elsewhere had "whipsawed" Admiral Koga as King had desired. To conserve his strength, Koga pulled his planes back to Rabaul. Anticipating a strike in the Central Pacific, he moved most of his ships to Truk. When Kinkaid attacked Attu, Koga took several of his most powerful units north, to block any offensive through the Kuriles. Nothing opposed Rear Admiral Turner as he approached New Georgia with Maj. Gen. John H. Hester's 43rd Infantry Division. The initial objectives were all quickly captured, setting off the next phase of multidimensional fighting in the Solomons. Halsey kept Nimitz up to date with "daily dope" messages that summarized his progress. It was limited. The effort to reach Munda by advancing overland stalled in the face of fierce Japanese resistance.[44]

Through surface action, Halsey tried to isolate Munda. On the night of 5–6 July, three groups of Japanese destroyers ran afoul of Rear Admiral Ainsworth's TG 36.1. Ainsworth lost cruiser *Helena* to enemy torpedoes but believed he had sunk "all seven [enemy] ships except one or two cripples." A week later, he fought a similar battle. This time, three of Ainsworth's cruisers—*Honolulu*, *St. Louis*, and the Royal New Zealand Navy's *Leander*—were torpedoed and destroyer *Gwin* was sunk. In both battles, Ainsworth lost situational awareness once the shooting started. He hadn't fully accepted the potential of the CIC. The Japanese completed their reinforcement missions on both occasions and suffered losses much lower than Ainsworth estimated.[45]

Destroyer commanders were more successful at embracing the CIC and its potential. Rear Admiral Wilkinson relieved Turner—who began to prepare for the Central Pacific offensive—as commander of the South Pacific Amphibious Force on 15 July. Wilkinson compensated for the loss of cruisers by freeing his destroyer squadrons for independent operations. A few weeks later, one of his destroyer commanders, Cdr. Frederick Moosbrugger, masterfully executed an attack on four Japanese destroyers attempting to deliver reinforcements. Moosbrugger used an approach developed by the brilliant tactician, Cdr. Arleigh A. Burke. Moosbrugger sank three of the Japanese ships and thwarted their reinforcement effort.[46]

In the meantime, additional troops and new leadership improved the situation on the ground. Harmon gave Maj. Gen. Oscar W. Griswold, USA, the XIV Corps commander, control of the forces on New Georgia. Reinforced by the 37th Infantry Division, Griswold captured Munda by 5 August.[47] Halsey quickly advanced to Vella Lavella, landing there on 15 August and bypassing the Japanese base at Vila. By early September, Nimitz's staff was gratified that "operations in the Solomons and New Guinea are proceeding in accordance with plan."[48]

In the Aleutians, Nimitz pushed Kinkaid to recapture Kiska. Kinkaid discussed with DeWitt, who proposed attacking in September, when the weather would be favorable. Nimitz agreed and the JCS approved, but they wanted to attack sooner so that Kinkaid's amphibious forces could come south in time to participate in the Central Pacific offensive. DeWitt drafted a plan and shared it with Nimitz on 27 May. His staff refined it while Nimitz discussed the important details with King in San Francisco. The target date was advanced to 15 August, coincident with Halsey's move to Vella Lavella. Nimitz's revised joint directive was ready by 29 May and approval from the JCS quickly followed. On 22 June, Nimitz and DeWitt issued their joint directive for Operation Cottage. The speed with which Nimitz and DeWitt made their arrangements contrasted markedly with the lack of coordination that had hamstrung Aleutian operations during 1942. Kinkaid's political acumen, Nimitz's facilitation skills, and Nimitz's new reputation—earned through recent victories—were essential to this improvement.[49]

Intelligence gave Nimitz a window into Japanese intentions. He initially planned two raids to distract from Kinkaid's assault. One was a carrier strike against the Japanese picket line east of Tokyo; the other was a powerful attack on Wake Island. When it became clear that the Japanese were unlikely to fight for Kiska, Nimitz abandoned these plans. However, when ICPOA discovered that the Japanese were "shuttling air strength" from bases in the Kuriles south to oppose Halsey's advance, Nimitz acted aggressively to hold Japanese assets in the north. He asked Kinkaid if an air strike on the Japanese base at Paramushiro was "within your capabilities." Kinkaid said it was. Nimitz ordered him to attack whenever the challenging Aleutian weather permitted. The first strike came on 10 July when eight B-25s from Attu bombed Paramushiro Straits through the clouds. Similar harassment strikes took place with varying intensity for the rest of the war.[50]

As the date of the assault approached, Kinkaid continued to blockade and bombard Kiska. The Japanese knew an invasion was coming and prepared to withdraw their garrison. Kawase tried to use submarines, but they were inadequate. On 21 July, he set out from Paramushiro with his cruisers and destroyers. He kept his ships to the south, beyond the range of Kinkaid's searches, and planned to use foul weather to mask his approach. Once within five hundred miles of Kiska, he paused, refueled his destroyers, and waited.[51]

ICPOA alerted Nimitz; he told Kinkaid to expect a Japanese operation. When a patrolling PBY reported a radar contact with "enemy ships" south of Attu, Kinkaid assumed it was a Japanese reinforcement convoy. He ordered his heavy ships to intercept. On the night of 25 July, they encountered a series of radar contacts that maneuvered like enemy ships and "fired [at them] intermittently for more than an hour." Though the radar returns were real, there were no Japanese ships present. After this "Battle of the Pips," Kinkaid's task forces withdrew to refuel. They were out of position when Kawase reached Kiska and evacuated the garrison on the 28th.[52] When Kinkaid's forces landed on 15 August, they encountered no opposition; Kiska was secure by the 19th.

## RAPID PLANNING FOR THE CENTRAL PACIFIC

By mid-1943, as the opportunistic offensives of 1942 began to give way to more deliberate and methodical ones, the Allies introduced a more rigorous approach to planning. Shipping—of all types, but especially amphibious assault shipping—had become a constraint on offensive operations. There was not enough of it; plans for individual theaters had to be integrated into a comprehensive set of global priorities. That integration occurred at the CCS level, but because the Pacific was the responsibility of the United States, the CCS delegated planning in the Pacific to the JCS. Nimitz's planners "engaged in a study of . . . Pacific Operations for 1943–44" and drafted detailed preliminary plans to allow the JCS to understand what was feasible, select between alternatives, and allocate resources appropriately. King hoped that the JCS would make Nimitz responsible "for timing major amphibious operations throughout the Pacific."[53]

To provide the information he and the JCS needed, Nimitz increased the size of his planning staff. His War Plans Section had just seven people, but at the beginning of June 1943 he requested six additional officers. They would come from all the services—Army, Army Air Forces, Marines, and Navy—and make War Plans the first fully joint part of his staff. By the time Captain Steele took over the section on 18 June, the new officers were in place. CCS priorities influenced their work. At the Trident Conference, held in Washington in May, the CCS agreed that Allied Pacific strategy should be "to maintain and extend unremitting pressure against Japan with the purpose of continually reducing her military power and attaining positions from which her ultimate surrender can be forced." The addition of the word "extend" was deliberate; the CCS wanted to accelerate the war and force Japan's unconditional surrender "at the earliest possible date." Because the Central Pacific afforded the greatest potential for rapid maneuver, the JCS focused their attention on it.[54]

On 15 June, they informed MacArthur that they expected to initiate operations in the Central Pacific in mid-November. The JCS instructed him to increase the "tempo of [his] operations" and "urgently" requested an "outline of operations in South and Southwest Pacific areas" with dates they could use for planning. They assumed that if MacArthur and Halsey reached Madang and Buin before November, then assault shipping and other critical resources could be transferred from the South Pacific in time to allow Nimitz's Central Pacific offensive to begin by 15 November. The JCS' desire to accelerate timelines was one reason Halsey leapfrogged to Vella Lavella.[55]

Marshall followed up with specific suggestions for MacArthur. He could accelerate his advance by isolating Rabaul instead of capturing it. Air bases at nearby strongpoints would allow him to blockade the base and prevent the need to assault it directly. Marshall also recommended MacArthur synchronize his offensive movements with Nimitz's. The Japanese would have to choose whether to oppose MacArthur or Nimitz; they could not do both. MacArthur failed to appreciate this broader context and concentrated on his own goals. "Certain" that the IJN would not divert forces to the Central Pacific and that his advance beyond Rabaul would be "opposed by hostile naval elements in full force," MacArthur insisted on capturing Rabaul to provide a naval base for the "major fleet units" that would support him as he advanced "along the north coast of New Guinea."[56]

Marshall and King recognized that the Japanese were ill prepared to oppose advances on multiple fronts simultaneously. Marshall also knew the Japanese were turning Rabaul into a fortress. ICPOA already suspected large numbers of troops were there, but in September, documents captured in the South Pacific revealed how powerful the bastion had become. In December 1942, the Japanese had 51,000 troops at Rabaul. By January 1943, the number had increased to 61,000 and, by February, nearly 80,000 Japanese were guarding the base and its surroundings. MacArthur's intelligence organization had underestimated the strength of Rabaul and was forced to revise its assessments.[57]

Coincident with their message to MacArthur on 15 June, the JCS directed Nimitz to "submit an outline plan for the seizure of the Marshall Islands." Nimitz's planners worked on the problem and, in early July, he sent Captain Steele and Capt. Forrest Sherman to Washington to present the latest draft plan. The JCS approved, and on 20 July, they issued the directive initiating the Central Pacific offensive. The first step would be Operation Galvanic, timed for 15 November. Galvanic would seize Nauru and other positions in the Ellice and Gilbert Islands. Those bases would become a springboard for the attack on the Marshalls, Operation Flintlock, targeted for 1 January 1944. Nimitz was ordered to provide a plan and "detailed estimate of forces required" for Flintlock before 1 September so that the JCS could review it, integrate it with other plans, and issue the necessary directive. By 19 August, Nimitz and his staff had "outline plans" and were forwarding them along.[58]

During these planning efforts, Nimitz and King met again at the end of July. They focused on the organization and training of amphibious forces, the upcoming offensive, progress in the North and South Pacific, flag officer assignments, and Nimitz's staff structure. For parts of their discussions, they were joined by others, including Rear Admiral Turner, Rear Admiral Cooke, Rear Admiral Jacobs, Captain Small, and Captain Steele.[59]

Nimitz and King abolished the Pacific Fleet's amphibious force and created three separate amphibious commands in its place, one each for the North Pacific, Central Pacific, and South Pacific. Each was designated with a number reflecting the fleet it operated under. The South Pacific Amphibious Force, for example, became the III Amphibious Force. The Pacific Amphibious Corps, containing the assault forces for amphibious operations, was restructured to mirror this arrangement and a dedicated corps was created for the Central Pacific with Maj. Gen. Holland Smith in command. Separate organizations were created for the other amphibious forces. King made these changes official on 11 August.[60]

King wanted to begin the Central Pacific offensive "as soon as possible" to justify the resources allocated to Nimitz's theater; King was apprehensive that any delay would be used by the British to "hedge on the recall of ships" from the Atlantic and Mediterranean. Once the offensive began, King wanted to maintain a rapid tempo. He suggested that Nimitz plan overlapping operations, with the next starting before the prior had ended. King hoped the Japanese would oppose the advance with their powerful naval forces at Truk. If a fleet action ensued, the Pacific Fleet would have an opportunity to reduce the IJN's striking power, creating the potential to accelerate the pace of future offensive operations. As they discussed the possibilities, Nimitz and King agreed that the Japanese were more likely to wait and seek a large battle "in the vicinity of the Marianas," but they prepared for an earlier fight.[61]

Nimitz and King criticized MacArthur for not sharing his plans. Even worse, he was holding on to twenty-four merchant ships. With shipping the most important constraint on Allied strategy, MacArthur's unilateral decision to keep these ships in his area caused consternation. Halsey's behavior, in contrast, was praised. He was "rolling up the rear areas" and moving men and material forward to make the most of his limited resources. In their previous conference, King had stressed that Nimitz needed to be prepared to move Halsey and the Third Fleet out of the South Pacific and "wherever" they "might be needed." Now, King pressed the point again. Nimitz had anticipated it and already prepared Halsey for such a move.[62]

North Pacific operations were proceeding well, and Nimitz and King discussed what to do next. Nimitz wanted options; he directed Kinkaid to develop plans for three eventualities: "offensive operations" against Japanese positions, "attrition operations" to wear their forces down, and the "bare necessity to secure [the] Aleutians." Nimitz suspected one of the last two options would be best. He transferred Kinkaid's amphibious ships and many of his combatants to the Central Pacific. DeWitt wanted to keep the offensive going and invade Paramushiro, but the JCS declared it "impracticable before spring 1944." They moved the 7th Infantry Division from the North Pacific to the Central Pacific for Nimitz's offensive. Even though further offensive operations in the north were unlikely, Nimitz directed Kinkaid to "prepare [a] plan for [the] seizure of [the] northern Kuriles" to allow him to act quickly if the opportunity arose.[63]

As usual, Nimitz, King, and Jacobs discussed various personnel topics. They considered whether to replace Rear Adm. Charles A. Pownall, commander of the Central Pacific carrier forces, with Rear Admiral Mitscher. They did not make the change, but their discussion reveals why Nimitz was prepared to take that step so quickly in early 1944. Vice Adm. John H. Hoover was shifted from the Caribbean Sea Frontier to the Pacific. He would become commander of land-based planes and newly occupied bases in the Central Pacific. Nimitz explicitly requested that Captain Sherman remain Towers' chief of staff "as long as possible," undoubtedly because Nimitz had recognized Sherman's talents and wanted to put him in a position where they could be fully employed.[64]

Staff work was becoming increasingly complex and demanding. The traditionally small Navy staffs were a disadvantage in areas like the South Pacific, where effective plans and operations required coordination across many services and functions. Rear Adm. John F. Shafroth, the new deputy COM-SOPAC, wrote a paper emphasizing the difficulty he had finding "adequate officer personnel in the upper grades who are qualified by experience to meet our needs." He cited several examples and noted how the lack of skilled officers was interfering with Halsey's ability to plan and conduct operations.

The problem went beyond Halsey's staff; across the South Pacific there were too few officers to meet the need.[65]

## NIMITZ'S NEW STAFF STRUCTURE

The most important topic Nimitz and King discussed in July was Nimitz's command and staff structure. Earlier in the month, King sent Nimitz a message urging him to establish another layer of staff, separating the work of CINCPAC from CINCPOA:

> Expansion of operations in [the] Pacific will involve [a] large increase of Army ground and air attack units, garrison forces, as well as increased Naval units, particularly in Central Pacific area. This ever widening scale and area of Joint activities will necessitate overall coordination by Commander in Chief Pacific Ocean Areas as distinguished from the purely NavOp [Naval Operations] functions of Commander in Chief, Pacific Fleet. The overall functions will apply . . . both to coordination of the three [Pacific Ocean] areas and to coordination of the activities of the two services. Desire your consideration and comment on establishing differentiation between staff work done for you as Commander in Chief Pacific Ocean Areas and that of Commander in Chief Pacific Fleet and further relationship between the overall command and appropriate Army and Navy commands in the three areas, North, Central, and South Pacific.[66]

King suggested a division of functions and potentially two separate staffs. He did not want a new layer of command. The Army did. General Marshall and his subordinates were pushing Nimitz to give up his responsibilities as a fleet commander so that he could focus wholly on his theater-level responsibilities. They felt this would address two shortcomings; it would establish a clear delineation between the Pacific Fleet and the POA theater, and it would integrate the Army more effectively into Nimitz's plans and operations.

Evidence of these shortcomings came from Brig. Gen. Edmond H. Leavey, USA, and Maj. Gen. LeRoy Lutes, USA, members of the newly created Army Service Forces (ASF). Leavey was sent to Nimitz's staff by Lt. Gen. Brehon B.

Somervell, head of the ASF, to improve joint logistical planning. After touring POA, Leavey reported, "From the logistics and supply standpoint, there seems to be no section and not even an officer on the Commander-in-Chief's staff, charged with supervision . . . of the overall logistics and supply." Leavey felt the best solution would be for Nimitz to establish a General Headquarters (GHQ) along Army lines with a joint staff, a subordinate command for the Pacific Fleet, and a dedicated organization to supervise logistics. Major General Lutes, head of the ASF Operations Directorate, endorsed these views.[67]

General Marshall wrote a memorandum in support. He recommended that Nimitz be elevated to "Supreme Commander of the Pacific Ocean Areas" and Halsey become CINCPAC. To support his argument, Marshall provided summaries of how MacArthur and Gen. Dwight D. Eisenhower had organized their GHQs. Each had established independent naval and air force commands, so that unified command was exercised at the headquarters level through "general coordination and supervision" and a "joint planning staff." This meant that each subordinate service in MacArthur's and Eisenhower's theaters had a significant degree of autonomy to plan and prepare operations. It was clear that the two services had fundamentally different approaches. The Army emphasized a centralized, labor-intensive staff structure while the Navy preferred smaller, more flexible, and more adaptive organizations. Eisenhower had a staff of nine hundred officers; Nimitz had just over one hundred.[68]

Nimitz—and the Navy generally—preferred smaller staffs because they allowed faster sensemaking and more rapid decision-making. Spruance captured this perspective well. He felt that "staffs . . . should be composed of the smallest number of first class" individuals who could do the work. In larger staffs, "a lot of energy" was "expended overcoming internal friction." Ensuring relevant information passed "through the hands of everyone who may have a possible interest in the problem" introduced delay.[69] The effort to be thorough and reduce the risk of not knowing relevant information could introduce a different risk—missing an opportunity because of a delayed decision. The Navy addressed this through delegation and decentralized decision-making. Staffs could simultaneously be small and effective because many essential details were left to subordinate commands. Nimitz operated this way through most of 1943. He kept his staff small by delegating operations in the North and South Pacific to Kinkaid and Halsey. Nimitz provided guidance, oversight, and coordination but refrained from interfering in their decisions so long as they kept consistent pressure on the Japanese.

When POA was established as a joint command, Nimitz integrated the Army into this approach. Instead of establishing a GHQ with subordinate service commands, he decentralized the integration of the services. Nimitz's subordinate commands were not service commands, but joint ones; this was a deliberate decision informed by the Navy's long experience. The goal was effective collaboration and unified direction at lower levels. Nimitz wanted his subordinates to be able to exploit emerging opportunities and respond to Japanese threats without having to rely on a decision from his headquarters. The approach subordinated service autonomy to achieve faster decision-making and more thorough integration at lower levels. Nimitz had intentionally organized for greater flexibility and agility, a fact that King clearly recognized.

However, Leavey and Lutes made an effective criticism. Nimitz's staff had grown in an opportunistic manner without centralized direction. In his search for adaptive capacity and war-winning capability, Nimitz had allowed his staff to grow based on his immediate needs. Without a predefined structure to conform to, some of that growth was now creating friction, redundancy, and waste. It was time to reassess and investigate the potential of a more effective structure.[70]

This was particularly true for logistics. The need to plan future operations in sufficient detail to meet the needs of the JCS convinced Nimitz that the Joint Logistical Board established in April was inadequate. Established patterns of logistical planning within the services were too entrenched. A more comprehensive approach was needed to answer the questions of the JCS and VCNO Horne, who was responsible for arranging Pacific logistical support in the United States. Nimitz recognized "that some Section of the Staff [must] assume responsibility for the movement and assignment" of the increasing quantities of material that was coming to his command. Initially, Nimitz delegated this work to a new "Current Plans Section" within War Plans, but it was insufficient to meet the need.[71]

During the July conference, King and Nimitz agreed changes were necessary, but they refused to create a fleet command under Nimitz. Tactical success in a major fleet action could establish sea control across the Pacific; therefore, the fleet was an arm of strategic decision and was appropriately controlled at the theater level. To integrate the Army more effectively, Nimitz and King agreed to make organizational changes and improve personal relationships. They did not want a fundamental revision of POA command structure. King suggested that Nimitz reorganize his staff, dedicate a portion of it to the Pacific Ocean Areas to further delineate the work of CINCPOA from CINCPAC, and install a deputy commander. These steps would help address the Army's concerns while simultaneously increasing Nimitz's flexibility and adaptive capacity.[72]

Nimitz took this guidance back to Pearl Harbor, consulted with his staff, and created a draft plan; Captain Steele reviewed it with King during a trip to Washington in August, and King gave his approval. On 6 September, Nimitz's Staff Memorandum No. 13–43 introduced the CINCPOA Joint Staff. The new structure was intended to address the Army's criticisms and allow Nimitz and his staff to better prepare for the coming offensive. It followed King's suggestion and created two staffs, one for CINCPOA and one for CINCPAC. Nimitz explained: "In order to more effectively meet the increasing scope and responsibilities of the Commander in Chief, Pacific Ocean Areas, for joint plans and operations and of the Commander in Chief, U.S. Pacific Fleet for Fleet plans and operations, a Joint Staff as well as a Fleet Staff is hereby established." This approach allowed Nimitz to remain close to operations and control the Central Pacific offensive himself, with Spruance his key deputy at sea. As the *CINCPAC/CINCPOA Command History* explained, this was different from the arrangement used in the North and South Pacific.[73]

> CINCPAC could have followed . . . the pattern established in SOPAC and NORPAC, by establishing a "Commander Central Pacific Force and Area" with the task of making all detailed plans for forthcoming operations. Against this however, stood the geography of the Central Pacific. NORPAC and SOPAC operations had been carried out at a great distance from CINCPAC's Headquarters, with

land-masses near at hand to support a large independent staff. Initially at least, Central Pacific operations were close at hand and in a region . . . without facilities for an Area Headquarters. Also . . . Admiral Spruance, in the formative stages of organizing the Central Pacific operations, had frequently emphasized his desire to remain wholly a Task Force Commander, without area responsibilities. Thus the Central Pacific campaign was planned by CINCPAC's own staff and carried out chiefly by Admiral Spruance.[74]

Spruance was an excellent choice for two reasons. First, he had thoroughly studied the challenge of a Pacific campaign while at the Naval War College. During that time, he gained an appreciation for logistics and recognized that logistic planning and operational planning had to be "closely coordinated." In Spruance, Nimitz had a subordinate who could broker that coordination and keep operations synchronized with the logistic support that sustained them. Second, Nimitz could trust Spruance to work well under the unusual command arrangements in the Central Pacific. During the fifteen months they spent together, Nimitz and Spruance developed a tacit understanding of how to employ the increasing size and strength of the Pacific Fleet; Spruance "knew Nimitz's thoughts and desires" for upcoming operations. This implicit knowledge allowed them to blur the lines that separated their two commands and collaborate more effectively during the upcoming offensive.[75]

In POA, there were now three separate staffs: Joint, Fleet, and Army. The deputy CINCPAC was head of the Fleet Staff; the deputy CINCPOA was head of the joint staff. During the July conference, King suggested Cooke as a potential candidate for deputy CINCPAC, but Nimitz chose McMorris, who had returned to the staff after his successes in the North Pacific. Initially, McMorris served as deputy CINCPAC *and* deputy CINCPOA. Vice Adm. John H. Newton became deputy CINCPOA after the next conference with King in September.[76]

The Joint Logistical Board was abolished and replaced by an entirely new division of the joint staff responsible for logistic planning. Nimitz put Brigadier General Leavey in charge of the new division, so he could work on addressing some of his own criticisms. Leavey harnessed wartime lessons

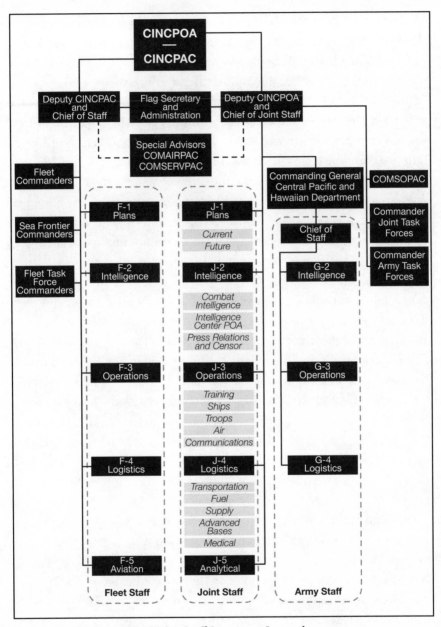

FIGURE 1. CINCPAC/CINCPOA Staff Structure, September 1943

and integrated them with his Service Force experience as well as the latest thinking from Washington. He created a solid foundation for logistical planning that was able to rapidly answer important questions from OPNAV and effectively prepare for the coming offensive.[77]

The planning process changed substantially with the introduction of the joint staff. The War Plans Section became the Plans Division. Two officers responsible for logistics moved into Leavey's division; the others were divided into two planning teams. Each was fully joint and "self-sufficient." Nimitz wanted the capability to accelerate the campaign and "extend unremitting pressure on Japan," so he had the planning teams overlap. As King had recommended, one team would plan an operation while the other "studied plans for the next." Nimitz expected this would allow him to mount operations in quick succession, one immediately after the other.[78]

Nimitz's Plans Division and its two teams worked "through a series of experiments in the late summer and fall of 1943" to determine how best to structure plans for the Central Pacific offensive. The "Joint Staff Study" emerged as the preferred approach. Staff studies had two major parts, an Outline Plan and a Detailed Plan. The Outline Plan was modeled on the Estimate of the Situation, a planning approach the Navy had used and refined for decades. The Detailed Plan provided more specifics and bridged the gap between an operational concept—as expressed in the Outline Plan—and the Operation Plans and Operation Orders issued for each operation. The approach struck a balance; it provided enough detail to allow other staff divisions to review and comment while also being lightweight enough to allow regular revisions of the original concept.[79]

The staff study also met the needs of the JCS. It gave them the necessary information to prioritize the operation and determine whether to proceed. While the JCS was responsible for overall strategy in the Pacific, their decision-making was anchored in the staff studies created by Nimitz's new Planning Division. Studies were the vehicle for translating potential concepts into real operations; they allowed the JCS to entertain options and select the most effective. Once they approved an operation, Nimitz's staff took the Detailed Plan and revised it, condensing the relevant details into an Operation Plan. In parallel with this effort, subordinate echelons used the staff studies as the starting point for their own Operation Plans. This allowed the planning process to be quick because parallel planning could occur across all echelons. Subordinate commands, like Spruance's Central Pacific Force, did not wait for Nimitz's staff to issue an Operation Plan before starting to draft their own. Regular conversations and frequent reviews kept the Operation Plans in sync, allowing the Central Pacific offensive to proceed at a very rapid pace.[80]

Nimitz also introduced a more comprehensive, joint approach to collecting and assessing intelligence. Two issues had kept ICPOA from reaching its full potential. First, it lacked a stable pool of talent and frequently had to rely on other intelligence units for its work. Second, disputes with OPNAV kept the crucial signals intelligence system "awkward and ineffectual." For Nimitz and his staff to get the intelligence they needed, an improved organization was necessary. On 7 September, ICPOA was restructured to become Joint Intelligence Center, Pacific Ocean Areas (JICPOA). Col. Joseph J. Twitty, USA, was placed in command and became assistant chief of staff of intelligence for CINCPAC. Layton remained Nimitz's chief intelligence officer, but his work was now augmented by a much more capable team responsible for "the collection, collation, evaluation, and dissemination of strategic and tactical intelligence." With JICPOA in place, the dispute with OPNAV ended and Pacific intelligence gathering employed a comprehensive, contextually sensitive approach.[81]

## CONCLUSION

With the new staff structure and its supporting components in place, Nimitz and his team completed the work of integrating lessons from the war's first year and anticipating the challenges of the next. The reconfiguration of the Pacific Fleet and the Pacific Ocean Areas maximized their chances of success in the upcoming offensive. New tactical approaches—the CIC and *PAC-10*— had been devised and promulgated. The challenges of the Navy's submarine torpedo had finally been addressed, allowing the thorough destruction of Japanese maritime commerce. The joint staff integrated the Army, created the ability to rapidly plan future operations, and synchronized logistical and operational planning. A new joint intelligence organization, JICPOA, gathered all sources of intelligence and made their findings available to Nimitz, his planners, and his senior commanders, increasing their ability to successfully execute future operations. By the end of September, Nimitz's command was like a coiled spring, ready to release its new and increasingly capable potential against Japanese defenses in the Central Pacific.

This was possible because Nimitz deliberately created space and time to reconfigure, reorient, and absorb the war's lessons. By installing capable subordinates like Halsey and Kinkaid, who resonated with Nimitz's aggressive disposition and maintained pressure on the Japanese, Nimitz created adaptive capacity. He delegated the war to them for much of 1943, and while Kinkaid and Halsey undertook opportunistic offensives to keep the Japanese focused on their flanks, Nimitz regularly probed Japanese defenses in the Central Pacific with bombing raids and radio deception. This allowed Nimitz to maintain the initiative and control the pace of operations despite the Japanese decision to shift to the strategic defensive. Nimitz used the space and time he gained to reconfigure his staff, adjust his command structure, and prepare for the upcoming offensive.

Nimitz's new staff structure was emergent; it was not based on an existing design. It reflected lessons gained during the war and the best advice from a talented group of officers who served with him. Nimitz's insistence that he remain responsible for fleet operations and theater strategy meant that his command staff was much smaller than contemporary Army GHQs or modern organizations of similar scope and complexity. This was a deliberate choice. Rather than a hierarchy of tactics, operations, and strategy, Nimitz kept the most complex of these two disciplines—tactics and strategy—coupled together through his personal oversight. What we describe today as the "Operational Level" of war, Nimitz delegated to experienced administrative and logistic officers—Towers, Leavey, and Calhoun—who discerned the consistent and repeatable aspects of operations and built the necessary logistical infrastructure to support them. That was a complicated endeavor that could be planned and managed using predictable techniques. Nimitz, in contrast, focused on the less predictable elements of the campaign, the actual operations that linked strategy and tactics together in an effort to defeat Japan.

His offensive would unleash the new combat power of the Pacific Ocean Areas against the Gilbert Islands in November and tear through the Japanese defensive network in a series of "storm landings" with unprecedented speed and power. While much of that power was contained in the vast resources produced by the increasing industrial output of the United States, it was the new planning and logistical capabilities of Nimitz's command that ensured those resources were organized and deployed so effectively. Nimitz and his team took the time to learn, adapt, and innovate; the Pacific Fleet that attacked the Mandates shared its core principles and underlying orientation with its prewar predecessor, but the way it acted upon those principles and applied them to the challenge of war was different. The fleet had become more capable, more effective, and better able to meet the challenge of sustaining a modern naval campaign in the vast reaches of the Pacific. It would soon demonstrate that capability.

# UNLEASHING THE
# CAMPAIGN

*Not a coconut tree was left whole. The Japanese had
prepared a magnificent defense and fought to the last.*

—Adm. Chester Nimitz[1]

By the fall of 1943, Nimitz and his team were ready. He initiated the
Central Pacific offensive with Operation Galvanic, the assault on the
Gilbert Islands, that November. It was a stepping-stone for the real
objective: the penetration of the Japanese defensive network in the Marshalls.
The two operations were inextricably linked, and thorough preparation
allowed Nimitz to rapidly fold lessons from one into the next. Clear intelligence and a daring choice of objectives permitted the Pacific Fleet to fully
exploit the maneuverability of its carrier and amphibious forces. Japanese
defenses in the Marshalls were outmaneuvered and quickly collapsed,
overwhelmed by Nimitz's effective planning and the rapid learning of the
Pacific Fleet.

Crumbling Japanese defenses created new opportunities and the potential
for more rapid movement. Nimitz was characteristically aggressive; he moved
quickly to "follow up every advantage." Nimitz's new campaign plan, code-
named Granite, facilitated the exploitation of emerging opportunities by
presenting future operations as options that could be exercised when the time

was right. Nimitz's planners focused their efforts in two directions: inward, to the operations of POA and the subordinate commands that would execute them, and outward, to Admiral King and the JCS, who set Pacific strategy and brokered between the dual offensives in the Central Pacific and Southwest Pacific. Granite served both audiences; it created a common framework for understanding the potential of Nimitz's increasingly powerful command.

As the JCS became more involved, Granite anchored discussions concerning future operations and fostered a comprehensive strategy that balanced the greater mobility of Nimitz's forces with the larger logistical support of MacArthur's Southwest Pacific theater. The JCS allowed the offensives to feed off each other, confronting the Japanese with threats along two axes. Nimitz's bold choices and the shared understanding created by Granite made it possible to accelerate both offensives in early 1944. It was that acceleration, the extension of "unremitting pressure," that put the Japanese off balance and kept them there. Vice Admiral Ugaki compared these "irresistible" offensives to the "raging fire" that swept Tokyo after the 1923 earthquake.[2]

One of the reasons Nimitz was able to operate so effectively was that he and his headquarters sat at the nexus of four different lines of effort. At the highest level, the JCS defined Allied Pacific strategy; within the theater, Nimitz and his planners explored what was possible through detailed investigations of potential offensive operations. Granite provided a conceptual framework that bridged these two lines of effort, ensuring that Nimitz acted in accordance with the JCS' strategic direction and that they accounted for operational realities in their plans and discussions. The other two lines of effort were the offensive operations in the Central and Southwest Pacific. As CINCPOA and CINCPAC, Nimitz exerted a powerful influence on both. Although he was not involved in planning for MacArthur's theater, Nimitz shaped the general's operations by using the Pacific Fleet to "cover" them. The locomotive force behind all major offensive operations in early 1944 was Nimitz's fast carrier task force; it tied the Central Pacific and the Southwest Pacific together and placed Nimitz in a unique position to guide the Allied effort.

This chapter follows all four lines of effort to illustrate how Nimitz used his position to set the course and direction of offensive operations. Nimitz coordinated with MacArthur to time offensive movements, he influenced

JCS decision-making through Granite and conferences with King, he shaped the plans for upcoming Central Pacific operations, and he quickly made sense of newly emerging information and acted with full cognizance of the strategic context. Nimitz used his position at the nexus of these efforts to ensure that the offensive was rapid and successful.

As retired Army general Stanley McChrystal explained in his book, *Team of Teams*, speed of decision-making is constrained by how quickly information can be shared across a network. Because Nimitz was at the center of the network driving the Pacific theater's operations and strategic direction, he and his staff could rapidly identify emerging opportunities, seize them, and deliver strategic outcomes. The Japanese could not keep pace.[3]

## PRELIMINARIES IN THE CENTRAL PACIFIC

Before the offensive, Nimitz undertook a series of preliminary operations to probe Japanese defenses and determine the best way to organize his forces. The Seventh Air Force, based on Oahu, was crucial to that effort. Through much of 1943, it had remained small; Nimitz sent its planes to other areas where they were more urgently needed. Maj. Gen. Willis H. Hale, the Seventh's commander, used his B-24s to strike Wake in January, May, and July. They alternated these attacks with raids on Tarawa and Nauru in the Gilberts. Reconnaissance flights followed the bombers, photographing Japanese installations and gathering important intelligence.

Nimitz wanted to make it easier for Hale to attack targets in the Gilberts and fly reconnaissance missions over the Marshalls. The B-24s were "just short" of being able to reach those islands, so Nimitz occupied Baker Island on 1 September; within two weeks heavy bombers were operating from there.[4] To make it easier to raid the Gilberts, Nimitz seized Nukufetau and Nanomea in the Ellice Islands. Airfield construction on those islands took longer, but Hale's bombers arrived in October and began a steady campaign of attrition against Japanese bases.

Carrier raids covered these operations and gave Nimitz's staff the opportunity to explore new dispositions for multi-carrier task forces. Vice Admiral Towers and his chief of staff, Forrest Sherman, wanted to determine the best tactics for the carriers to use in offensive operations. They followed

|  | STRATEGIC PLANNING | CENTRAL PACIFIC PLANNING | CENTRAL PACIFIC OPERATIONS | SOUTHWEST PACIFIC OPERATIONS |
|---|---|---|---|---|
| AUGUST 1943 | Quadrant Conference |  |  |  |
| SEPTEMBER 1943 | Nimitz and King meet at Pearl Harbor | Nimitz introduces Joint CINCPOA Staff | Nimitz occupies Baker Island, Nukufetau, and Nanomea.<br><br>Carrier raids on Marcus Island and the Gilberts |  |
| OCTOBER 1943 |  | Operation Plan for Galvanic<br><br>Draft plans for Flintlock and Catchpole | Carrier raid on Wake Island | MacArthur captures Finschhafen |
| NOVEMBER 1943 | Sextant Conference |  | Operation Galvanic occupies positions in the Gilbert Islands | Halsey invades Bougainville |
| DECEMBER 1943 |  | Operation Plan for Flintlock<br><br>Granite Plan Drafted |  | MacArthur seizes Cape Gloucester |
| JANUARY 1944 | Nimitz and King meet in San Francisco | Granite Plan Issued<br><br>Pearl Harbor Conference | Operation Flintlock seizes positions in the Marshall Islands |  |
| FEBRUARY 1944 |  |  | Operation Catchpole captures Eniwetok<br><br>Operation Hailstone raids Truk | Halsey occupies Green Island<br><br>MacArthur advances to the Admiralties |
| MARCH 1944 | JCS direct an accelerated advance in both Central and Southwest Pacific | Nimitz and MacArthur meet in Brisbane | Operation Desecrate raids Palau | Halsey occupies Emirau |
| APRIL 1944 |  | Operation Plan for Forager | Carrier raid on Truk | Operation Reckless seizes Hollandia |

TABLE 1. Four Lines of Effort in the Pacific: August 1943–April 1944

events closely when Rear Admiral Pownall's TF 15 attacked Marcus Island on 1 September. The raid showed that three carriers allowed "more effective air defense with fewer fighters per carrier . . . and provided a greater concentration of antiaircraft fire." Pownall gained more experience later that month when he and Hale made a coordinated attack on the Gilberts. They struck Makin, Tarawa, Abemama, and Nauru. Hale's bombers suppressed Japanese airfields to make it easier for the carriers to approach and withdraw unscathed. Planes from *Lexington*, *Princeton*, and *Belleau Wood* struck enemy installations and took oblique photographs of Tarawa, which aided planning for the assault on the atoll.[5]

While Pownall and Hale struck the Gilberts, Nimitz conferred at Pearl Harbor with Spruance, Towers, McMorris, and Sherman. They agreed more experience was needed to work out the best approach to multi-carrier operations. Rear Adm. Alfred E. Montgomery and his chief of staff, Capt. H. S. Duckworth, explored alternatives in a strike on Wake Island in early October. They had three large carriers and three smaller ones. During their approach to Wake and the ensuing strikes on 5 and 6 October, Montgomery and Duckworth experimented using *PAC-10* as a guide. According to Duckworth, "Virtually all the techniques of ship handling for a multi-carrier force which were later used successfully had their origins in this operation."[6] He and Montgomery validated the concepts that Towers and Sherman had developed for handling the new carriers and ensured Spruance's Central Pacific Force was ready.

Nimitz knew the Japanese had concentrated strong naval forces at Truk and thought they might seek a major fleet action. That was exactly what Admiral Koga planned. He believed it was essential to win a decisive victory before the increasing strength of the Pacific Fleet became overwhelming. When Pownall raided the Gilberts in September, Koga sent Vice Admiral Ozawa Jisaburo's Third Fleet, a powerful striking force with three carriers and two battleships, to Eniwetok. JICPOA detected this move but assessed it as a "radio deception plan," not an immediate threat.[7] Koga remained at Truk to await developments, and when the anticipated amphibious operation did not occur, Ozawa returned to Truk on 25 September.

When Montgomery attacked Wake, Koga initially did nothing. The failure of "any major [enemy] ships" to react led Nimitz and his staff to reassess their estimate. However, when Koga's radio intelligence suggested another attack was coming, he sortied with the bulk of the Combined Fleet—six battleships, three carriers, and supporting forces. They moved first to Eniwetok and then took station 250 miles south of Wake. JICPOA recognized that the Japanese were conducting "extensive searches" but failed to detect Koga's movements. When no amphibious assault came, Koga returned to Truk on 26 October. Only then did Nimitz realize that "the main forces of the Japanese Fleet" had left Truk nine days before. He and his staff knew the Japanese were poised to "counter our moves into the Gilberts and Marshalls."[8]

In the meantime, Nimitz was struggling to obtain the necessary shipping and assault forces. The 2nd Marine Division, commanded by Maj. Gen. Julian C. Smith, USMC, and the 27th Infantry Division, under Maj. Gen. Ralph C. Smith, USA, would take part in Galvanic. The 4th Marine Division and the 7th Infantry Division would attack the Marshalls. This left Nimitz one division short of anticipated requirements. He was also short of oilers that could conduct underway refueling. King met that need by providing new, modern oilers for the Pacific. Transports were another major constraint. By early September, the JCS had provided nine additional transports by taking them off the trans-Pacific run for four months. However, King explained it was "essential" that the demand for transports "be kept at a minimum." These constraints, coupled with the demand to "maintain and extend unremitting pressure against Japan," would exert a strong influence on Nimitz's thinking.[9]

## PLANNING AT QUEBEC AND PEARL HARBOR

In August 1943, the CCS met in Quebec at the Quadrant conference. They discussed how to force Japan to surrender unconditionally. The CCS was optimistic that sustained aerial bombardment might force Japan to capitulate. Even if it did not, it would pave the way for invasion by destroying Japanese industrial and military power. Bombers would need bases near the Home Islands, and the ideal location appeared to be the "littoral of the South China Sea," containing Hong Kong, Formosa, and Luzon. The CCS recognized the best way to get there was "straight across the Pacific through the Mandates," suggesting Nimitz's campaign should be the "principal effort." However, the CCS encouraged Nimitz and MacArthur to mount "mutually supporting" offensives to reach Palau and Vogelkop, in western New Guinea, by the end of 1944.[10]

To seize Vogelkop, MacArthur would have to bypass Rabaul and advance along the north coast of New Guinea. The CCS expected him to reach Hollandia by August 1944 and Manokwari by the end of November. After Nimitz struck the Gilberts and Marshalls, he would advance to Ponape in June, seize Truk in September, and capture Palau before the end of the year. Nimitz might also seize the Marianas "in conjunction" with Palau.[11] The CCS felt this pace was too slow because it would not reach the South China Sea until 1946, pushing operations against Japan "into 1947 and perhaps 1948." Accordingly, the CCS directed "intensified study of ways . . . for shortening the war" and recommended bypassing enemy strongpoints. The JCS wanted a Japanese surrender within "12 months after the defeat" of Germany.[12]

The need to accelerate the war dominated planning discussions. On 1 September 1943, after their return from Quadrant, the JCS authorized Nimitz's advance into the Marshalls, designated Operation Flintlock. His target date was 1 January 1944, coincident with MacArthur's planned operations in the South and Southwest Pacific.[13] Later in September, Nimitz and King met again, this time at Pearl Harbor. Other attendees included Cooke, Spruance, Steele, McMorris, Halsey, Carney, and for personnel decisions, Vice Admiral Jacobs. The sessions "began with a general discussion of the Galvanic Operation."

Spruance, Turner, and Holland Smith wanted to seize Makin instead of Nauru. Nauru was heavily defended; the assault would require an entire division and even then "success [was] doubtful." Moreover, Nimitz lacked the transports and cargo ships to attack Tarawa and Nauru simultaneously in divisional strength. Makin was more lightly defended, and it could be seized using the available assault shipping. King and Cooke initially opposed the change. King wanted to advance on a broad front and was concerned that Makin and Tarawa were too close together. Cooke preferred Nauru because it had an operational air base. Eventually, they assented to the change, provided

Nauru could be denied to the Japanese. The JCS followed suit. Nimitz ordered Spruance to revise plans for Galvanic accordingly.[14]

As the discussion moved to the Marshalls, Spruance shared a variety of options and suggested that "it might be advisable to first seize Mili and Jaluit before further operations to the northward." That would mean seizing the Marshalls in two steps. Nimitz and his staff preferred a single move that would capture Wotje, Kwajalein, Maloelap, and Roi. Jaluit and Mili would be bypassed. King also preferred that approach. Before the discussion closed, Nimitz—now aware of the JCS' desire for a rapid pace—agreed to try to take the Marshalls in "one bite . . . as soon as possible."[15]

Progress had been good in the South Pacific, but there was some uncertainty over the next steps. Before the conference, Halsey had revised his plans for Bougainville to accelerate operations. Carney presented the new concept. Halsey would advance to Treasury Island and establish a staging area; then he would bypass Buin-Faisi and seize Empress Augusta Bay in October or November 1943. Airfields there would be ready in time to strike Rabaul in support of MacArthur's capture of Cape Gloucester, anticipated in December 1943. All attendees agreed with this plan; a direct assault on Buin-Faisi "would be too costly." Halsey's timeline was set by MacArthur, who insisted on attacking Bougainville before the end of November to comply with the JCS directive of March 1943. King was concerned that MacArthur was adhering to a six-month-old directive and stressed that they all needed to find ways to accelerate the advance.[16]

After Bougainville, Halsey expected to encircle Rabaul by capturing Kavieng and Manus Island in the Admiralties. Since these positions were beyond the range of his land-based planes, the operation would require carrier support. The conference attendees agreed on a 1 March 1944 target date; Flintlock and Galvanic would be complete by then, allowing Nimitz's carriers to participate.[17] After the conference, Halsey left for Brisbane to confer with MacArthur in person and work out the specifics of upcoming operations.

The North Pacific remained important but was becoming less active after the recapture of Kiska. Vice Admiral Fletcher would take over from Kinkaid. Kinkaid would relieve Carpender as MacArthur's naval commander; it was hoped that Kinkaid's political acumen would allow him to collaborate effectively with the general. The conference attendees discussed the potential of seizing Paramushiro, but that risked becoming "a Kiska in reverse." The threat of invasion seemed much more valuable than actual amphibious operations. Large garrisons were maintained in the north as part of Nimitz's "snow-ball" deception campaign, designed to draw Japanese attention away from the Gilberts and Marshalls by "making it appear that the seizure of Paramushiru [sic] is imminent."[18]

When the topic turned to personnel, King emphasized two points he had made previously. He wanted to ensure younger officers were given opportunities; older officers could be shifted to naval district commands. King also suggested a flat 10 percent reduction in ships' complements to reduce demands for personnel. Nimitz thought such a move would be "dangerous" and recommended "drastic cuts in shore establishments" instead. They failed to reach a decision, but it was apparent that personnel was becoming a significant issue.[19]

Nimitz wanted to ensure he had capable staff and subordinates. He suggested making Vice Admiral Edwards deputy commander, Pacific Ocean Areas. However, King thought Vice Admiral Newton would be better and Newton was ultimately selected. Nimitz and King agreed to promote Charles A. Lockwood, Nimitz's submarine commander, to vice admiral. After King returned to Washington, he made one more personnel change. King instructed Nimitz to replace Captain Steele, head of the Plans Division, with an aviator; the Central Pacific offensive would rely on airpower. Someone familiar with its strengths and limitations needed to be involved in planning it.[20]

## PLANNING GALVANIC AND FLINTLOCK

A well-structured collaborative planning process was essential to the success of the Central Pacific offensive. Nimitz and his staff prepared for Galvanic and Flintlock by working through details in conference; he preferred "vocalizing . . . thoughts before committing them to paper." That meant much of the "planning was done orally" in conversations that allowed Nimitz's team to collectively make sense of their options. To accelerate the process, Nimitz's command echelons crafted their operation plans in parallel; regular conversations kept those plans aligned and maximized the potential of the limited numbers of planes, ships, and men. The schedule was aggressive and there was enormous pressure to succeed. While the industrial output of the United States offered enormous potential, organizing that output and harnessing it was an unprecedented challenge.[21]

Nimitz issued the operation plan for Galvanic on 5 October 1943. It directed Spruance to "gain control of the Gilbert Islands" by capturing Makin, Tarawa, and Abemama. Nauru would be "vigorously denied" to the enemy. The initial draft of the plan gave Spruance a force that could defeat the IJN in surface battle. Spruance would have thirteen battleships—seven old and six new—and just four large and four light carriers. Four escort carriers would provide close air support for the assault forces. D-day was set as 19 November in an effort to ensure tides would be high enough to clear the surrounding reefs. Over the month of October, revisions to the plan augmented Spruance with two additional large carriers.[22]

Galvanic would test the theory that major elements of the fleet would be able to "remain at sea within the forward operations area for extended periods of time." Providing the sustained logistical support that could keep the fleet ready to fight was a major challenge. Tarawa and Makin were more than two thousand miles from Pearl Harbor, the nearest major base. Nimitz tasked Calhoun with developing a mobile logistic capability that would allow the fleet to sustain itself over these vast distances. In preparation for Galvanic, Capt. Herbert M. Scull, Calhoun's chief of staff, established SevRon 4, a mobile supply base, on 1 November. SevRon 4 initially operated from Funafuti in the Ellice Islands. Capt. August H. Gray, the new commander of SevRon 8, kept the fleet fueled using a rotation of oilers. The initial intent was to ensure a rapid pace of the offensive with leapfrogging SevRons, much like the two planning teams in Nimitz's Plans Division. A new SevRon was anticipated for the Marshalls.[23]

Spruance and Turner issued their plans later in October. Turner's northern force would transport the 27th Infantry Division's 165th Regimental Combat Team to Makin; Rear Adm. Harry W. Hill's southern force would bring the 2nd Marine Division to Tarawa. Virtually undefended Abemama would be occupied by a reconnaissance platoon. Spruance arranged his task forces to overwhelm these objectives and maximize his chances of winning a major surface action. He created four carrier groups; two were assigned to cover the assaults on Makin and Tarawa. A Carrier Interceptor Group would attack Jaluit and Mili in the Marshalls and then patrol between them and the Gilberts, ready to intercept any Japanese attacks from the north. The most powerful surface forces were concentrated on Spruance's northern flank, so that he was prepared for battle if the IJN came south from Truk. The Relief Carrier Group was ordered to suppress Nauru and then cover the landing of garrison forces after the main objectives were seized.[24]

Spruance promulgated "general instructions" a few days later. He was concerned about the threat of a fleet engagement. An "equatorial front" was expected to cover the northern Gilberts and make it difficult to detect approaching enemy forces; Turner's Northern Attack Force and the northern carrier groups had to be prepared for an attack by a superior enemy "with little or no warning." Spruance instructed them to remain within "close tactical supporting distance" of each other. If the IJN did appear, Spruance would form a battle line under Rear Admiral Lee and fight a traditional fleet action. Spruance's concept married the best of the fleet's recent lessons—as expressed by the tactical formulations of *PAC-10*—and interwar plans. If the Japanese did not seek battle, Spruance would send Pownall to raid into the Marshalls after Galvanic's objectives were secured. Spruance would let circumstances dictate specific targets, but he expected to strike some combination of "Mille [*sic*], Maloelap, Wotje, [and] Kwajalein." Oblique photos of those atolls would help finalize plans for Flintlock.[25]

While Spruance, Turner, and Pownall developed their plans, Nimitz produced a draft plan for Operation Flintlock, the attack on the Marshalls, and issued it on 6 October. It called for a single operation that would "occupy, defend, and develop Kwajalein, Wotje, and Maloelap." Mili and Jaluit would be bypassed. These objectives made sense, but Nimitz wanted to preserve flexibility. He expected to receive additional assault shipping, which would give him more options. In the operation plan issued six days later, the objectives were left unspecified. Instead, the plan called for seizing "one advanced fleet anchorage and two supporting positions." Although specific targets would be identified in "later directives," some were obvious. Detailed maps of Kwajalein and Wotje were included in the operation plan.[26]

Nimitz's parallel planning structure allowed his staff to look one step ahead. At about the same time that the Flintlock plan was issued, an "outline plan for Catchpole," the seizure of Eniwetok, was ready. Planners were also examining the potential of bypassing Truk and advancing to Saipan and Tinian in the Marianas. The Marianas had become increasingly important because JCS planners recognized that the new Boeing B-29 could bomb Japan from those islands. CCS planners recommended that the Central Pacific offensive skip directly from the Marshalls to the Marianas, optimistically hoping that they might be reached by June 1944.[27]

King was preparing for the Sextant Conference (22–26 November) in Cairo and wanted to ensure JCS and CCS discussions reflected realistic alternatives. In late October, he asked Nimitz for "recommendations concerning sequence, timing, and nature of Pacific Operations for 1944." Nimitz responded with his latest assumptions. Flintlock would quickly follow Galvanic. After that, a "simultaneous" effort would extend Allied control to Eniwetok and Kusaie. "Wake, Ponape, and Truk" would follow in "successive phases." Truk might be bypassed, but Nimitz was not certain that was feasible. After Truk, he would seize Yap and Palau "in a simultaneous operation." Control of the Marshalls was not anticipated "before early February 1944," but experience gained in Galvanic and Flintlock would accelerate later operations and allow "the Mandates to be in our hands by the end of 1944." Nimitz knew this was not fast enough to defeat Japan twelve months after victory in Europe, which at the time was optimistically anticipated in October 1944.[28]

## REDUCING RABAUL

After the September 1943 Pearl Harbor conference, the JCS—at King's urging—prompted MacArthur to maintain "constant pressure" on the Japanese. They let him know that despite the increasing importance of Nimitz's Central Pacific offensive, they wanted to be able to shift resources between theaters to maximize the rate of advance. "The dispositions taken by the Japanese," the JCS informed MacArthur, "will have considerable influence" on the decision as to the main effort in the Pacific. If the Japanese responded aggressively to Nimitz, MacArthur had to be ready to seize the opportunity. The JCS wanted more details about how he might do that; they asked MacArthur to clarify his next steps and develop plans for "re-entry into the Philippines . . . as quickly as possible."[29]

That direction provided the backdrop to Halsey's meeting with MacArthur on 9 and 10 October 1943. They discussed the Pearl Harbor conference, the JCS directive, and their next moves. After seizing Empress Augusta Bay, Halsey would capture Kavieng, supported by Nimitz's Pacific Fleet. MacArthur would land at Cape Gloucester and advance west along the northern coast of New Guinea. They would bypass Rabaul and seize Manus to secure a fleet anchorage. Starting "about 1 May" 1944, MacArthur wanted Nimitz and the Pacific Fleet to guard the northern flank of his advance and "deter" an attack by the Japanese fleet. These concepts were incorporated into MacArthur's latest plan, Reno III, issued on 20 October 1943.[30]

On 1 November, Halsey's forces landed at Empress Augusta Bay. The Japanese sent a powerful surface striking group from Rabaul to attack the landing forces. Rear Adm. A. Stanton Merrill's TF 39 fought them off, sinking an enemy cruiser and destroyer with no major losses to his own ships. The developing threat to Rabaul convinced Koga that the greatest danger was in the south. He sent his carrier squadrons and most of his cruiser forces to Rabaul and gave up on countering Nimitz's advance into the Gilberts and Marshalls. When Halsey realized that IJN forces were heading south, he wired Nimitz to "strongly urge" battleships be sent to the South Pacific. Nimitz embraced calculated risk and declined. Instead, he temporarily assigned one cruiser division and one destroyer division to Halsey. Carpender loaned Halsey two heavy cruisers and four destroyers from the Seventh Fleet. Nimitz felt these, "coupled with [Halsey's] heavy air superiority," would be enough to meet the threat.[31]

He was correct; Halsey had Rear Adm. Frederick Sherman's TF 38, with carrier *Saratoga* and light carrier *Princeton*, attack Rabaul in concert with a raid by Army B-24s on 5 November. The strike damaged most of the newly arrived Japanese cruisers, foiling Koga's plan to disrupt the Bougainville landings. At about the same time, Nimitz and his staff realized that planes from two Japanese carriers were operating from Rabaul. He capitalized on the situation by temporarily assigning Rear Admiral Montgomery's TG 50.3, with carriers *Essex* and *Bunker Hill* and light carrier *Independence*, to

Halsey. Nimitz delayed Operation Galvanic by one day to allow Sherman and Montgomery to strike Rabaul again on 11 November.[32]

Low clouds prevented much damage to enemy ships, but an air battle ensued in the skies above TG 50.3. During furious attacks that afternoon, the "flower of Japan's air strength" tried to cripple Montgomery's carriers; his aviators decimated the attacking Japanese formations. These battles and the others fought in early November severely crippled Koga's carrier wings; half their fighters and over 80 percent of their attack aircraft were destroyed. Koga withdrew the remnants on 12 November. Nimitz and his staff gained confidence from TG 50.3's performance; the new carrier groups were much more effective at defending themselves than the task forces of 1942.[33]

Koga was pressed on two fronts—three if the diversion in the North Pacific is included—and forced to react. He could not oppose advances in the Central Pacific and Southwest Pacific simultaneously. When Halsey moved to Bougainville, Koga shifted his mobile forces to Rabaul, where Nimitz and Halsey engaged them. Crippled by these attacks, the IJN's mobile forces were unavailable when Nimitz moved into the Gilberts. Halsey was free to suppress Rabaul. From his new airfields on Bougainville, fighters fought for aerial dominance over the bastion. The attritional campaign waged through the Solomons had reached its final objective. In the coming weeks, the base would become increasingly untenable as Halsey's aerial attacks intensified.[34]

## GALVANIC

Operation Galvanic was a "high-stakes gamble" that would test "unproven and controversial new doctrines concerning fast carrier operations, mobile logistics, and offensive amphibious warfare."[35] Nimitz and his staff had validated some of these doctrines. The fast carriers had demonstrated their proficiency in attacks on Wake, Marcus, and most recently Rabaul. Mobile logistics had dramatically improved. The greatest uncertainty was amphibious assault against well-prepared enemy defenses. Nimitz's apprehension showed in the final conference he held with Spruance, Turner, and other senior officers before they departed for Galvanic. For nearly an hour, Nimitz shared his perspective on the operation and stressed its importance with a "severity" that "astonished" those accustomed to his more "genial" attitude.

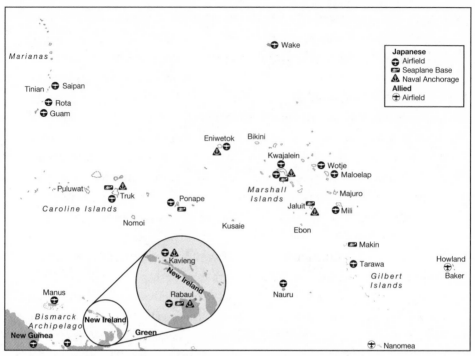

Map 5. Central Pacific Operating Area, November 1943

Nimitz emphasized the importance of working as a team, a joint force that would accomplish the mission together. He said that he would "immediately relieve" any naval officer who failed to give the "required help to the Army." They would succeed together or not at all.[36]

Preliminary strikes by Hale's bombers and Pownall's carriers paved the way for the assault of Turner's V Amphibious Force, which arrived on schedule the morning of 20 November. At Makin, the landing went well, but the 27th Division advanced cautiously. By the end of the day, the division had only seized about half of the atoll's main island. Nimitz had expected more; Holland Smith called the progress "infuriatingly slow." Spruance's northern forces had to linger dangerously close to the Marshalls longer than anticipated because Makin was not "taken" until midday on 23 November.[37]

At Tarawa, the amphibious assault doctrine received its most serious test. The 2nd Marine Division faced the "unbelievably difficult" challenge of Rear Admiral Shibasaki Keiji's thorough preparation and determined defense. An abnormally low tide made it difficult to get to the beach. The Marines might have been pushed off it if Shibasaki had counterattacked, but accurate salvoes from destroyers *Dashiell* and *Ringgold* killed him as he tried to shift his command post. Col. David M. Shoup, commanding the assault, requested that the 2nd Marine Division's reserve be landed. Hill and Maj. Gen. Julian Smith approved. Smith also requested release of the V Amphibious Corps reserve and closed his request with the words, "Issue in doubt."[38]

This message disturbed Nimitz. The defenders of Wake in December 1941 had sent the same words before they were overwhelmed. For a time, Nimitz sat quietly; then he said, "I've sent in there everything we had, and it's plenty. I don't know why we shouldn't succeed." At the end of the day, with the situation gradually improving, Nimitz's staff summary optimistically recorded, "[T]he capture is believed sure." One reason the struggle was so difficult was that JICPOA's estimate of 2,500 defenders was too low; prisoner interrogations revealed that 4,500 Japanese were on Tarawa when the assault began.[39]

The Japanese struck back with planes and submarines. The evening of 20 November, torpedo bombers hit carrier *Independence* in the Southern Carrier Group. The next morning, Towers told Nimitz that the Japanese had found the carrier groups because they had been kept in static positions close to the amphibious objectives. McMorris and Forrest Sherman agreed. They pointed out that the Japanese fleet, which had been the major factor behind Spruance's dispositions, had shown no sign of coming out. Therefore, Towers argued, Nimitz should tell Spruance to give the carrier groups more freedom to maneuver. After the others left, Nimitz and Towers discussed how to improve plans for future operations. Nimitz already knew he needed an aviator to take over his planning efforts; Sherman was a perfect choice. Towers agreed to have Sherman replace Steele as head of Nimitz's planning division. Later that day, Nimitz told Spruance to give the carrier groups "greater freedom of movement."[40]

Galvanic proved the theory upon which the Central Pacific offensive was based. Success at Tarawa and Makin demonstrated that "it was feasible to mount such operations from distant bases and to secure local air superiority with carrier-based aircraft." Other, more specific lessons regarding amphibious operations had "a great influence on the future conduct of the war."[41] Naval gunfire needed to be more thorough and conducted from closer ranges. Aerial bombardment had to be better coordinated. Communications had to improve. Underwater demolition teams needed to scout beaches before the assault. More tracked amphibious vehicles were needed. Lessons from Galvanic fed into plans for Flintlock, increasing the likelihood of success in the Marshalls.[42]

After the assault, as anticipated, Pownall raided the Marshalls with his carrier task force. His primary objective was Kwajalein in the heart of the island group. Pownall was cautious and refused to linger long enough for a second strike, preventing his pilots from destroying a group of Japanese bombers captured in reconnaissance photographs. That evening, as the carriers withdrew, the bombers attacked. Carrier *Lexington* was hit and one of her propeller shafts broken. With *Lexington* and *Independence* out of action, Nimitz would have two fewer carriers for Flintlock than anticipated.[43]

### SEXTANT, FLINTLOCK, AND GRANITE

While Nimitz captured the Gilberts, the CCS met at the Sextant Conference in Cairo. There were two crucial outcomes: Roosevelt, Churchill, and Chiang Kai-shek proclaimed their intent to eradicate the Japanese Empire in the Cairo Declaration, and the CCS transferred responsibility for Allied strategy in the Pacific to the JCS.[44] Before Sextant, it had been "a combined British-American problem"; after Sextant, it was "almost exclusively" an American one.[45]

The JCS agreed that Nimitz and MacArthur would mount mutually supporting offensives. Nimitz's advance was crucial because it promised a "more rapid advance," but the empty ocean that offered mobility was also a disadvantage. The combined might of the nation's increasing land, sea, and airpower could be more effectively employed from the larger land masses in the Southwest Pacific. At Sextant, the CCS created a draft timetable. If Nimitz reached the Marianas in October 1944, long-range B-29s could bomb Japan by the end of the year. Later in 1945, after Nimitz and MacArthur seized a position "in the Formosa-Luzon-China area," the bomber offensive could intensify by using bases in the South China Sea. After Sextant, only two major strategic questions remained: where those bases would be established and whether to invade Japan.[46]

Nimitz used the brief window between Galvanic and Flintlock to adjust his staff organization based on feedback from King and Towers. Nimitz made the main divisions Plans, headed by Forrest Sherman, who replaced Captain Steele on 11 December; Operations, under Capt. Thomas J. Keliher; Intelligence, headed by Army Col. Joseph J. Twitty; and Logistics under Brigadier General Leavey. The Aviation and Analytical Divisions were retained but became less important to daily operations. Colonel Twitty played a dual role, heading both the Intelligence Division and JICPOA. This basic structure remained in place throughout 1944, and it worked so well that in May, the Fleet and Army staffs officially disappeared; Nimitz's CINCPOA Joint Staff took over all responsibilities.[47]

Forrest Sherman recognized that the leapfrogging strategy employed by the Plans Division was not working well. The alternating planning groups lost continuity with each other and failed to share enough information about how one operation would influence the next. Sherman retained the two groups but divided their work differently. He created a Future Plans Section and a Current Plans Section. Each section focused on a specific planning horizon that "enabled one group to concentrate exclusively on strategic planning while the other became thoroughly familiar with the current situation" and supervised "the planning of the various subordinate commands."[48] This clarified responsibilities, increased focus, and delivered improved results.

Flintlock and subsequent operations presented a serious challenge. Nimitz gained approval to delay Flintlock to allow more time to prepare, but King ordered him to attack "as early as possible after 1 January and not later than 31 January 1944." In early November 1943, Nimitz made 17 January the target date. A new operation plan was drafted by 14 December. Although the objectives remained unspecified, Kwajalein, Wotje, and Maloelap—which had been part of plans for months—remained the most likely. Shipping was the most serious constraint; the situation in POA was "critical." Landing craft were also in extremely short supply; sea frontiers and naval districts were ordered to release their combat-ready stocks. These constraints overshadowed the preliminary study of Operation Catchpole. Although it recommended seizing Eniwetok as part of Flintlock or immediately after, there were no assault forces available and no ships to convey them. Catchpole required the 2nd Marine Division and 27th Infantry Division to occupy Eniwetok and Kusaie; before they could do so, they would have to recuperate from their fight in the Gilberts. That meant Catchpole would have to wait until late February, about a month after Flintlock.[49]

More aggressive plans for Flintlock rapidly coalesced as three new pieces of information emerged. JICPOA's intelligence work revealed that Kwajalein was the Japanese "command and control center" for the Marshalls and that it was lightly defended; roughly seven thousand Japanese occupied the entire atoll, with four thousand on Kwajalein Island and the others on Roi-Namur. The Japanese were building up strength elsewhere but not Kwajalein.[50] Pownall's raid showed that Kwajalein Island could support a bomber field, something that was thought impossible before; capturing one was a requirement for a successful operation. Finally, there was the great pressure to advance rapidly; an analysis of the fighting in the Gilberts had revealed the Japanese intended to draw out the war, force high casualties, and trigger a negotiated settlement. In line with this strategy, they had heavily fortified Maloelap and Wotje. Nimitz wanted to avoid another Tarawa and remained focused on taking the Marshalls in "one bite." Available shipping and assault troops limited him to two major objectives. He discussed alternatives with Forrest Sherman and McMorris and decided to assault Kwajalein; its two main islands—Roi-Namur and Kwajalein—would be the two objectives. That would provide the two air bases; virtually undefended Majuro Atoll would provide a "major fleet anchorage." Wotje and Maloelap would be bypassed.[51]

On 14 December 1943, the same day he issued the revised Flintlock plan, Nimitz held a conference with Spruance, Turner, and Holland Smith. Nimitz shared the new information about Kwajalein and asked them where they should strike. All three argued for the "outer islands" of Wotje and Maloelap. Nimitz declared his intention to go to Kwajalein directly. A heated discussion followed. Spruance, Turner, and Smith argued against Nimitz's plan. Turner "raised his voice" and called Nimitz's plan "dangerous and reckless." Nimitz told Turner that if he was unwilling to execute the plan, he could be replaced. This aggressive decision was unusual because Nimitz rarely imposed his view so forcefully on his subordinates. However, it displayed Nimitz's "marvelous combination of tolerance for the opinions of others, wise judgement . . . , and determination to carry things through." Nimitz always emphasized the most important outcome—in this case "to avoid loss of time"—and focused his subordinates upon it. As at Midway eighteen months before, an opportunity had arisen to act extremely aggressively. Nimitz assumed significant risks and made a decision that would radically change the war. On 20 December, Nimitz set the target date for Flintlock as the latest permitted by King's instructions, 31 January 1944.[52]

In mid-December, King sent Cooke to Pearl Harbor to discuss the details of Sextant with Nimitz. King also requested "outline plans" for the next year's offensive operations by 15 January so that the JCS could ensure operations in the Central and Southwest Pacific were integrated. Soon thereafter, on 23 December, the CCS issued a directive encapsulating their new concept. Although Nimitz and MacArthur would advance concurrently and mount "mutually supporting" operations, they recognized that Nimitz's offensive promised "a more rapid advance toward Japan and her vital lines of communication; the earlier acquisition of strategic air bases . . . and, of greatest importance," an increased likelihood of "a decisive engagement with the Japanese Fleet."[53]

This directive integrated with plans that were already under way. Nimitz was working on his Granite Campaign Plan and issued the preliminary draft less than a week later, on 27 December 1943. It presented upcoming operations as a cascading series of offensives that would penetrate the heart of Japanese defenses and take Nimitz's forces to the threshold of the Philippines. In contrast to MacArthur's Reno III, which proposed a linear series of "phases," Granite presented subsidiary operations as options that could be executed earlier or discarded if "favorable developments" permitted.[54] This was deliberate; the Central Pacific route "offered a wide choice of successive objectives." Nimitz and his staff planned to exploit opportunities as they emerged. However, to ensure feasibility and clarify timing, each optional effort was examined in detail.[55]

| OBJECTIVE | TARGET DATE (CCS) DECEMBER 1943 | TARGET DATE (GRANITE DRAFT) DECEMBER 1943 | TARGET DATE (GRANITE PLAN) JANUARY 1944 |
|---|---|---|---|
| Marshalls | 1 – 31 January 1944 | 31 January 1944 | 31 January 1944 |
| Kavieng | 20 March 1944 | 20 March 1944 (coincident with carrier raid on Truk) | n/a |
| Manus, Admiralty Islands | 20 April 1944 | 20 April 1944 | 24 March 1944 (coincident with carrier raid on Truk) |
| Eniwetok | n/a | 1 May 1944 | 1 May 1944 |
| Ponape | 1 May 1944 | n/a | n/a |
| Mortlock | n/a | 1 July 1944 | 1 August 1944 (simultaneous with Truk) |
| Truk | 20 July 1944 | 15 August 1944 | 1 August 1944 |
| Palau | n/a | n/a | 1 August 1944 (alternative to Truk) |
| Marianas | 1 October 1944 | 15 November 1944 | 1 November 1944 |

TABLE 2. Target Dates—CCS, Granite Draft, Granite Plan

The Fifth Fleet would seize Kwajalein and Majuro at the end of January. Halsey planned to occupy Kavieng in March. The Pacific Fleet would cover his operation by undertaking Operation Hailstone, "the largest possible carrier strike on Truk."[56] The following month, Southwest Pacific forces would capture Manus Island, supported by the Pacific Fleet. Operation Catchpole would secure Eniwetok in May; a fleet anchorage there would open a path to Truk. Operations Gymkhana and Roadmaker would follow. Gymkhana would seize Mortlock in July, providing a nearby base for Roadmaker, the assault on Truk in August. The move against Truk was expected to trigger a major battle with the IJN. During Roadmaker, six divisions would assault Truk and its environs; two would still be fighting when Operation Forager, the assault on Guam and Saipan, began in November. A logistic appendix mentioned Operation Stalemate—an attack on Palau—that might be mounted instead of Forager, but given the JCS' emphasis on bombing Japan, that was unlikely. Stalemate was not examined in detail. Ponape, which the CCS had identified as a target, was deliberately omitted. It was "certain to be costly in expenditure of time, forces, and logistic resources." Nimitz planned to bypass it. Although the challenges of Pacific logistics forced Nimitz's timeline to be slower than that of the CCS, bypassing Ponape allowed him to make up some time.[57]

Uncertainty surrounded Gymkhana-Roadmaker, expected to be the longest combat operation in the Central Pacific. Two needs drove the desire to seize Truk. The first was logistics; Nimitz needed a base to support operations west of the Marshalls and Truk appeared to be the most suitable location.[58] The second reason to assault Truk was that it was "the key" to the Japanese "interlocking air base system" in the Central Pacific. Nimitz believed attacking Truk would create "the best opportunity . . . to bring [the] enemy fleet to action."[59] Crippling or destroying the IJN would dramatically accelerate the advance.

## JANUARY 1944 CONFERENCES

In early January, Nimitz and King met in San Francisco. Cooke, Halsey, and Forrest Sherman participated in some of their discussions. Granite provided a framework that grounded the conference and clarified when and how the offensives in the Southwest Pacific and Central Pacific could reinforce each other. Nimitz was using his position as CINCPAC to influence both offensives. His carrier task forces were recognized as the "governing factor" for major offensive operations throughout the Pacific.

Nimitz shared his plans for Hailstone, the upcoming raid on Truk. He hoped to "bring the enemy fleet to action" and "engage them decisively." Spruance would approach from the south, use an equatorial front as cover, and ideally catch the IJN "as unprepared as possible." After the raid, the enemy fleet would withdraw, perhaps to Japan or the Philippines, so it was essential to mount a powerful strike to do as much damage as possible. Cooke agreed. King recognized Hailstone's importance but emphasized that the Marianas were "the key to the Pacific." Sherman suggested "it might be possible to bypass Truk" and move to the Marianas directly after the Marshalls. That would avoid the costs of Gymkhana-Roadmaker and accelerate the advance. If the IJN withdrew its major forces after Hailstone, the only reason to invade Truk would be to secure a forward operating base.[60]

In the South Pacific, Halsey would bypass Kavieng and seize Green Island instead on 15 February. Kavieng was too small for an effective fleet base; the Japanese had prepared a strong defense, and bypassing it meant there was one less operation for the Central Pacific's carriers to support. Sherman explained that each offensive operation would require the carrier forces to "remain [in the area] for approximately three weeks" until airfields ashore were operational; an additional month might be needed for rest and refitting. That meant operations would have to be "about two months apart." Bypassing Kavieng eliminated one of these intervals and allowed the seizure of Manus and Emirau to be advanced by three weeks, to the beginning of April. Manus, not Kavieng, would be MacArthur's fleet base in the Bismarck Archipelago. Nimitz planned to cover the operation with the Truk raid, which meant Catchpole would occur on 1 May, even though Nimitz wanted to do it a month earlier.[61]

The fate of Halsey's forces remained uncertain. Major operations in the South Pacific Area would cease after the Manus-Emirau operation was completed. Halsey and his staff would come to the Central Pacific, but his forces would be reallocated by the JCS. In Reno III, MacArthur optimistically assumed they would all come to him. Nimitz and King expected them to be divided between the Central and Southwest Pacific. King agreed to push for a firm decision after returning to Washington.

Several personnel decisions were made at the January conference. The most important ones involved aviation. After Pownall's lack of aggressiveness during the Marshalls raid, Nimitz consulted with Towers, McMorris, and Sherman. Towers "strongly recommended changes" and suggested Mitscher— currently commanding Fleet Air West Coast—would be a better fit. Sherman agreed. Nimitz and King decided to replace Pownall with Mitscher. To ensure the specialized expertise of aviators was properly used, Nimitz and King also agreed to restructure the command of PACFLT task forces. From now on, every major commander would either be an aviator or have an aviator as chief of staff. Nimitz set an example on his own staff by replacing Vice Admiral Newton with Towers. Towers became deputy CINCPAC and CINCPOA while McMorris became chief of staff, CINCPAC and CINCPOA.[62]

After the conference, Nimitz and his staff revised the Granite draft and issued an official plan. Its goal was to "force the surrender of Japan" by

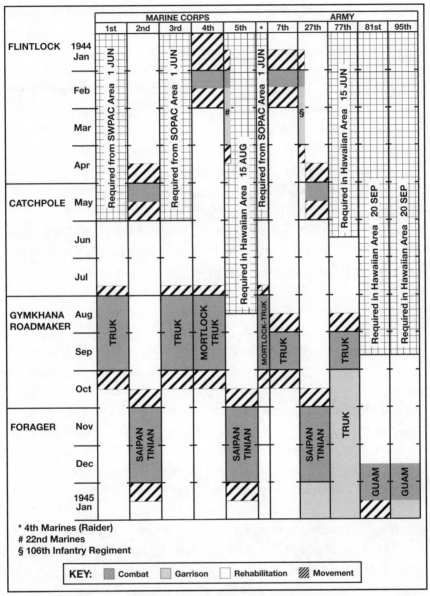

FIGURE 2. Employment of Marine Corps and Army Divisions as Anticipated by the Granite Plan, issued 13 January 1944

"intensive air bombardment, by sea and air blockade, and by invasion if necessary." Granite had three general tasks: to "maintain and extend unremitting pressure against Japan"; to attrit Japanese air, naval forces, and shipping; and to "establish and protect sea and air communications" to newly occupied positions. "Close coordination" was required between the offensives in the Southwest Pacific and Central Pacific to accomplish these goals. Granite remained a flexible "guide to long range planning" that would allow Nimitz to "take any short cut made possible by developments in the situation." Destroying the "Japanese Fleet at an early date" would do that; until it was eliminated or contained, Nimitz's forces had to "maintain maximum readiness" to "bring important enemy naval forces to action."[63]

The new version of Granite refined future operations and examined Operation Stalemate in detail. Presented as an "alternate to Roadmaker," Stalemate would capture Palau to provide "an advanced base in the Western Pacific." If the IJN would not fight for Truk, "considerable expenditure of time, forces, and logistic resources" could be avoided by seizing a base elsewhere. Palau was well positioned to be a western Pacific base; it could support operations in the Southwest Pacific and "dominate the approaches to the Philippines." Bypassing Truk would allow Palau to be seized in August and the Marianas in November. Details for the Marianas were becoming clearer. Operation Forager would occur in two phases. The initial assaults would capture Saipan—"the Japanese command and control center for the Marianas and Palau"—and Tinian. Air bases on those islands would support the subsequent capture of Guam. Once the islands were secured, bases on Saipan and Tinian would "support long range attacks on Japan" by B-29s.[64]

Later in January, as the forces committed to Flintlock approached their objectives, Nimitz met with members of MacArthur and Halsey's staffs at Pearl Harbor. The JCS had ordered Nimitz to "provide cover" for MacArthur's operations "by containing or destroying the Japanese fleet." The two theater commanders interpreted this differently. MacArthur requested a "commitment of carriers" to the Manus operation to provide close cover for his invasion forces. Nimitz planned to raid Truk and provide "strategic support." At the conference, Sutherland, Kenney, and Kinkaid spoke for MacArthur; Carney and Harmon represented Halsey. Nimitz brought key members of his staff. The attendees discussed overall Pacific strategy and upcoming operations. They agreed that bases on the China coast would be necessary to force the surrender of Japan and that the Philippines ought to be an intermediate objective. The best way to get there was through the Southwest Pacific. Palau should be seized to secure the northern flank of MacArthur's advance. Truk ought to be bypassed; the Marianas might be as well. McMorris "had little faith in the effectiveness" of bombing Japan from the Marianas and Nimitz was "skeptical" that bombardment would "force Japan to surrender." Bases closer to the Home Islands were needed to impose a naval blockade and threaten invasion.[65]

It is curious but revealing that Nimitz allowed this wide-ranging discussion knowing the JCS was responsible for strategic direction in the Pacific. He reminded attendees of this fact before the conference closed. Their discussions were the "views of individuals," not official decisions; no commitments had been made; and Granite remained the guide for planning.[66] The evidence suggests that Nimitz drew out the attendees' perspectives for three reasons. He wanted them to feel comfortable expressing their opinions so that Pacific strategy could continue to benefit from their insights; he wanted to make sure the JCS was aware of their perspectives so they could account for them in strategic decisions; and he wanted to foster a collaborative atmosphere so that the attendees could work together more effectively going forward. Nimitz excelled at using conferences to create a climate of open discussion and foster psychological safety, and he apparently did so here.

However, Nimitz's attempt to cultivate increased collaboration through shared understanding backfired. MacArthur was convinced that the conference validated his view that the Southwest Pacific should become the main effort. He pushed for official recognition of the idea by sending Sutherland to Washington to argue his position. King reacted "with fury" at these developments, especially the suggestion that the Marianas might be bypassed. Concentrating forces exclusively along MacArthur's line of advance was "absurd." In a strongly worded letter to Nimitz, King expressed his "indignant dismay" and walked through the logic of capturing the Marianas.[67]

King ensured the Central Pacific was not deprioritized. He used Granite— a clear vision for implementing the CCS' directive—to argue that MacArthur needed to revise Reno III and explain his plans for 1944. Marshall countered that because neither Granite nor Reno III could be executed without additional forces, "the scale and timing of future operations are not clear-cut and cannot be until the JCS inform" MacArthur and Nimitz how well "their requirements can be met." The JCS had directed an advance toward the Formosa-Luzon-China area but had not identified an objective. Marshall and Arnold agreed that "a new directive" was needed to reiterate that responsibility for Pacific Strategy rested with the JCS and to give more specific direction to Nimitz and MacArthur. The clarity provided by the Granite plan and the tension resulting from the Pearl Harbor conference were instrumental in prompting this recognition.[68]

## FLINTLOCK

Spruance issued his plan for Flintlock on 6 January 1944. It capped off years of thought about how to assault the Japanese defensive network in the Marshalls. Tempered by Nimitz's aggressiveness and insistence on concentrated striking power, the plan called for a multidimensional array of carriers, amphibious assault forces, land-based planes, and surface ships to enter the island group, overwhelm enemy defenses, and seize Kwajalein and Majuro. The four carrier groups of Mitscher's TF 58 would maneuver independently of the assault forces, using their mobility to avoid attacks and strike from unanticipated directions. Two assault forces—Turner's Southern Attack Force with the 7th Infantry Division and Rear Adm. Richard L. Conolly's Northern Attack Force with the 4th Marine Division—would seize the major islands of Kwajalein Atoll. Hill's Majuro Attack Group with the 2nd Battalion of the 27th Infantry Division's 106th Infantry Regiment would seize that lightly defended anchorage. The remainder of the 106th, along with the 22nd Marine Regiment, formed the operation's reserve; they would be ready to support the Northern or Southern Attack Force as required.[69]

Nimitz expected to overwhelm Kwajalein's defenders, seize the centerpiece of the Japanese position, and prevent Flintlock from becoming an attritional struggle. To sustain the pace of the offensive, he had to strike opportunistically; he lacked the ability to make a more methodical, steady advance. Facilities in Hawaii had already been "severely taxed" by preparing "less than two divisions . . . for Flintlock and the simultaneous loading of support shipping for Galvanic." Sutherland and other Army critics, who preferred an advance from the Southwest Pacific because of its larger logistical base, had correctly perceived that the Central Pacific would be constrained. Nimitz's base facilities were insufficient to support a large striking force. He had to risk attacking Kwajalein directly—a step that most of his chief subordinates had rejected—to secure the Marshalls in a single operation.[70]

The fight for the Marshalls began long before Mitscher's carriers struck. Immediately after the occupation of Tarawa and Makin, land-based planes began an attritional campaign against targets in the island group. On 14 December 1943, Nimitz ordered Rear Admiral Hoover to intensify these attacks and operate "at [the] maximum rate it is practicable to sustain." The steady campaign of attrition followed by overwhelming carrier strikes worked. The Japanese defensive network was neutralized. On 31 January, when the assaults began, the CINCPAC Summary noted, "Reports indicate that our air attacks both by shore based and carrier-based planes have been very effective and that enemy aircraft in the area have been destroyed or shot down."[71]

It fell to the assault forces to secure the victory. Turner feared that Roi-Namur would be more difficult than Tarawa. It "was more heavily defended" and, proportional to its size, had a larger garrison. However, Conolly was determined to capitalize on Tarawa's lessons. After an intense close-range bombardment, he seized an entrance to the lagoon on the first day. On 1 February, the main assault came from inside the lagoon, avoiding most of the Japanese defenses. On Roi, the Marines captured the island before the end of the day. The fight for Namur was tougher, but the Marines prevailed the next day.[72]

The assault on Kwajalein progressed more slowly. Maj. Gen. Charles H. Corlett, the 7th Division's new commander, used lessons from Tarawa and prepared his soldiers well. Everything went "according to plan" on 31 January. The next day, 1 February, Corlett's men landed on the western end of Kwajalein in a "well-executed amphibious assault." Initial resistance was light, but the soldiers pressed less aggressively than the Marines to the north. It took until the afternoon of the fourth day for Corlett's men to reach the northern tip of the island and overcome the last pockets of organized resistance.[73]

The overwhelming success allowed Nimitz to accelerate the Granite timeline. On 31 January, the same day the amphibious assaults began, Spruance and Turner ordered "detailed photographic coverage of Eniwetok." Nimitz was gratified they were considering the immediate execution of Catchpole. Spruance knew that "enemy surface forces at Truk" were weaker than anticipated and that the balance of risk favored a rapid advance. He quickly made plans to seize Eniwetok and strike Truk. Three of Mitscher's task groups withdrew to Majuro—where the new mobile supply base, SevRon 10, was established under Captain Carter—for "fueling and replacement of ammunition and aircraft in preparation for a carrier . . . strike on . . . Truk." Nimitz's insistence on taking Kwajalein created the opportunity to initiate Catchpole and Hailstone months ahead of schedule.[74]

**OPERATIONS ACCELERATE**

On 10 February, Nimitz ordered the assault on Eniwetok and the long-anticipated carrier raid on Truk. JICPOA interrogators had questioned prisoners on Kwajalein and discovered there were fewer defenders on Eniwetok than anticipated. An immediate attack could "catch the Japanese in a moment of weakness." Flintlock's eight-thousand-man reserve assault force was available. This time, Spruance, Turner, and Holland Smith all agreed with the decision. Nimitz chose 17 February as the date for the operation. Covered by the carriers of TG 58.4, the attack went "according to plan" against "weak opposition." Eniwetok provided a sheltered anchorage that became a valuable fleet base.[75]

While Eniwetok was taken, Spruance and Mitscher raided Truk. The original concept for Hailstone had been a "Pearl Harbor in reverse," a major strike that would "bring [the] enemy fleet to action" and cripple it. Reconnaissance flights in early February suggested the opportunity had been lost. Only limited IJN forces remained at Truk. Admiral Koga, deprived of his cruiser screen and carrier air groups, had decided not to risk his fleet in the Marshalls. Instead, he withdrew his forces to Palau and Japan. Operation Hailstone destroyed Japanese planes and shipping but did not trigger the anticipated fleet battle. At his Makalapa headquarters, Nimitz tracked the progress of the attack through radio intercepts. JICPOA informed him that the Japanese were planning to fly in reinforcements and mount night attacks from Tinian.[76]

Mitscher's control of the air limited Japanese counterattacks, but their planes harassed Mitscher's strikes and sought out his carriers. Torpedo bombers found and hit carrier *Intrepid* that night, forcing her to withdraw to Pearl Harbor. Mitscher, however, made night attacks of his own; a specially trained torpedo squadron from carrier *Enterprise* attacked shipping in Truk lagoon with great success. The next morning, Mitscher made another fighter sweep; "not one Japanese plane rose to contest it." Confident in their success, Spruance and Mitscher ordered their forces to retire at noon on 18 February.[77]

In the meantime, Nimitz and his staff assessed the latest intelligence. The Japanese had not reacted as anticipated. There had been no fleet action and the IJN appeared to have withdrawn. JICPOA believed that the commanders of the IJN's Combined Fleet and Second Fleet had moved to Palau. Weakening aerial attacks suggested that most of the Japanese air strength in the Marshalls and Carolines had been destroyed. Convoys originally bound for the Carolines were being rerouted to Saipan. The Japanese were apparently focusing on their next line of defense, the Marianas and Palau. No major obstacles stood between the Fifth Fleet and the Marianas.[78]

Nimitz was determined to maintain the initiative. The "early execution of Catchpole" and Hailstone made it "possible to speed up" Granite operations even further. He ordered Spruance to send Mitscher to attack the Marianas; Mitscher refueled and took TGs 58.2 and 58.3. His carriers were sighted during the approach, but he fought his way in against "almost continuous" enemy attacks the night of 22–23 February. The next morning, two strikes were made against Saipan and Tinian; a fighter sweep covered Guam; and photographs were taken of Saipan, Tinian, Guam, and Rota. The fighting was lopsided; none of Mitscher's ships were damaged and just six planes were lost. Enemy ships, flushed out by the attacks, were set upon by Pacific Fleet submarines. With photographic intelligence of the Marianas, Nimitz could begin preparing to assault them months ahead of schedule.[79]

When Japanese defenses in the Mandates were shattered, faith in the highest levels of leadership was undermined. Prime Minister Tojo Hideki secured Emperor Hirohito's "consent to a drastic shake-up of the command structure." To strengthen his position in the face of growing criticism, Tojo ousted the chief of the Army General Staff, Field Marshal Sugiyama Hajime, and stepped into his role. Tojo simultaneously served as prime minister, Army minister, and chief of the Army General Staff. Admiral Nagano, chief of the Naval General Staff, was blamed for the defeat. He was pressured to resign by Navy minister Admiral Shimada Shigetaro, who replaced Nagano and served in both roles simultaneously. With Hirohito's permission, Tojo "set aside one of the most hallowed" Japanese military traditions, "the division of power between military command and administration." With his newfound control of government and military command, Tojo emphasized major operations—land offensives on the Asian mainland, and a fleet action in the Marianas—to regain the strategic initiative during 1944.[80]

In the South and Southwest Pacific, MacArthur and Halsey used the collapse of enemy defenses in the Mandates to accelerate their advance. On 15 February 1944, Halsey attacked Green Island on schedule and quickly overwhelmed Japanese resistance. He covered the operation with raids on Rabaul and Kavieng; those attacks encountered little opposition, suggesting that Japanese power in the area was "waning." MacArthur was alert to the possibilities. As late as 22 February, he was still planning to occupy the Admiralty Islands on 1 April, but an intelligence coup accelerated his timeline. In early January, Australian troops found an abandoned trunk buried in a riverbed northwest of Sio on New Guinea's northern coast. The trunk contained the "entire cipher library of the [Japanese] 20th Division." Once returned to Brisbane and analyzed, the material gave the Allies—and especially MacArthur's GHQ—incredible insight into the "IJA's order of battle and operational plans."[81]

MacArthur took advantage. On 25 February, after aerial reconnaissance and decrypted messages suggested the Admiralties were lightly defended, he ordered a risky "reconnaissance in force" with just a few days' preparation. Kinkaid gathered his forces and landed units of the 1st Cavalry Division on Los Negros Island. The initial landing was far too weak to overcome Japanese resistance, but it was enough to secure a beachhead. A steady flow of troops and supplies allowed MacArthur's forces to assume the offensive by 4 March. A month later, on 5 April, Kinkaid informed Nimitz that "Naval Base Manus" had been established, providing a major fleet anchorage in the Southwest Pacific.[82]

## A NEW JCS DIRECTIVE

After the January Pearl Harbor conference, the JCS recognized they would need to provide clearer strategic direction to Nimitz and MacArthur. In early March, they summoned the two to Washington to discuss Pacific strategy. MacArthur explained that he was needed in his theater and sent Sutherland instead. Nimitz came in person and brought Forrest Sherman. The JCS wanted to understand their options so that they could make force allocations and devise a clearer strategy. Granite was Nimitz's effort; MacArthur needed to revise Reno III. He was already doing so. Bolstered by his new insight into Japanese deployments, MacArthur crafted a new, more opportunistic approach. He would "take advantage of enemy weakness" and eliminate "objectives or phases" of his Reno plan. The first phase discarded was the occupation of Hansa Bay. Instead, MacArthur intended to "leap several hundred miles" and take Hollandia on 15 April. The dramatically named Operation Reckless would trap 60,000 Japanese troops and allow MacArthur to break away from "two years of dreadful attrition warfare." It would also permit him to keep pace with Nimitz; on 5 March, MacArthur informed Marshall of these intentions. From Washington, "the New Guinea approach began to look better." Sutherland submitted the official draft of MacArthur's new plan, Reno IV, on 8 March. It anticipated occupying Mindanao by November 1944 and Luzon by March 1945.[83]

Nimitz, Sherman, and other members of Nimitz's staff arrived in Washington just before Reno IV. During discussions on 6 March, it was clear that Truk could be bypassed; Nimitz did not think Japanese naval forces would return to the base. He wanted a definitive decision as to whether to bypass it. If so, the Marianas would be the next objective, although it would also be possible to advance to Palau. Capturing Palau would protect MacArthur's flank and provide a large fleet anchorage.[84]

King approached the question of bypassing Truk indirectly. He was looking for evidence to counter Sutherland's argument that MacArthur's advance should be the primary one in the Pacific. One part of the argument was that the Marianas lacked a fleet base; King felt Eniwetok was suitable. It was, but Sherman said "an anchorage for a large number of ships" was needed, and none was available in the Marianas. King asked Sherman to present the plans for seizing those islands and Truk. When Sherman finished, King asked if MacArthur got everything he asked for, would it still be necessary to neutralize Truk and the Marianas. Nimitz said, "Yes." This is what King needed. He could counter Sutherland by explaining that Nimitz's offensive, if it advanced to the Marianas and neutralized Truk, would cover "the flanks of . . . [the] Southwest Pacific advance" and allow MacArthur to make his leap to Hollandia. In a choice between the Marianas and Palau, it was clear that the JCS would prefer the Marianas because it would allow B-29s to begin bombing Japan.[85]

The discussions in Washington resolved the confusion from the Pearl Harbor sessions, highlighted the emerging opportunities in the Pacific, and led to a new JCS directive. On 12 March, they declared that the "most feasible approach" to Luzon or Formosa was by occupying the line connecting the Marianas, Carolines, and Palau. While Nimitz prepared for those moves, the offensive would accelerate in the Southwest Pacific. Plans to occupy Kavieng were cancelled. Rabaul would be neutralized by a "minimum commitment of forces." MacArthur was free to make his bold leap to Hollandia, "covered" by Nimitz's carriers. Heavy bombers based at Hollandia would strike Palau and neutralize western New Guinea. Nimitz's forces would bypass Truk and invade the Marianas in June and Palau in September. From the Marianas, operations would commence against "Japanese sea routes" and the enemy "homeland." Palau would become a massive base, the "forward staging area for the support of operations against Mindanao, Formosa, and China."[86]

MacArthur's advance to the Philippines was approved. He would seize Mindanao on 15 November "to reduce and contain Japanese forces . . . preparatory to a further advance to Formosa either directly or via Luzon." The JCS preferred the direct path to Formosa because it would accelerate the advance, but they left the question open. Nimitz was responsible for planning Formosa and MacArthur for Luzon. The JCS emphasized both of their offensives and split Halsey's South Pacific forces between them. The JCS set the target date for Luzon or Formosa as 15 February 1945. If Formosa was attacked directly, Luzon would be bypassed; otherwise, Formosa would follow Luzon. The JCS demanded "outline operation plans" from MacArthur and Nimitz at the "earliest practicable date."[87]

MacArthur immediately cancelled his plans for Kavieng and ordered Halsey to "seize, occupy, and defend" Emirau instead. Halsey had anticipated the order; he set the target date for Emirau as 20 March. Old battleships mounted a diversion by shelling Kavieng and nearby airfields while Marines landed on Emirau. An air base was operational there by early May, ensuring an effective blockade of Rabaul and helping to neutralize Truk.[88]

In collaboration with Spruance, who had flown to Pearl Harbor on 14 March, Nimitz devised a plan—Operation Desecrate—to suppress Japanese bases and provide distant support for Southwest Pacific operations. Starting about 1 April, Nimitz's carriers would launch "all out simultaneous" attacks on Palau, Yap, and Woleai. These attacks would be followed by raids on Truk and Satawan. Nimitz's land-based planes would suppress Truk in concert with these efforts, but for such a deep incursion into enemy territory, he needed more help. Nimitz asked MacArthur to use his land-based planes to search ahead of the carrier groups, bombard enemy bases in the Bismarcks and along the coast of New Guinea, and neutralize Woleai while the carriers attacked Truk. Nimitz issued orders for the operation on 18 March and set the target date for the strike on Palau as 1 April.[89]

MacArthur still wanted more direct support from Nimitz's carriers. He asked that in addition to Nimitz's plan for distant support, the carriers attack Hollandia and Wakde Island for three straight days before, during, and immediately after the landings. Hollandia was within range of Kenney's strike aircraft, but it was too distant for a sustained campaign guaranteed to neutralize enemy airfields. In exchange, MacArthur agreed to "render all practicable assistance to the operations of the fleet." On 23 March, Nimitz, Forrest Sherman, and other staff members departed for Brisbane to meet with MacArthur and work out the details. In their discussions, Kenney promised to wear down enemy air at Hollandia, smoothing the way for Nimitz's carrier strikes. The schedule was tight. When MacArthur pushed the Hollandia operation to 22 April, the JCS considered it "acceptable" provided the operation was not delayed further. MacArthur was temporarily using

South Pacific assault shipping that had to be transferred to "CINCPOA control by 5 May" in order to meet the schedule for the Marianas.[90]

## UNREMITTING PRESSURE

The new JCS directive gave Nimitz clarity of direction and freed him to mount a pair of wide-ranging offensive sweeps into Japanese territory in March and April 1944. These incursions exposed the weakness of Japanese defenses, covered MacArthur's advance to Hollandia, and ensured that the Pacific Fleet retained the initiative. The first was Operation Desecrate, the powerful raid on Palau; like the strike on Truk in February, it was designed to cripple IJN fleet units and "exploit every opportunity to seek a decisive fleet action."[91]

The attack caught Koga off guard. He had withdrawn to Palau, regrouped, and formulated a new plan for decisive battle, Operation Z. Issued on 8 March, it anticipated a combined land, sea, and aerial contest in the Philippine Sea. Troops from Manchuria would reinforce garrisons in the Marianas and Carolines, Koga would concentrate "all the naval strength that Japan could muster," and he would defeat Nimitz's forces during the next amphibious operation, creating the opportunity for a negotiated peace. When Nimitz issued his directive for Operation Forager on 28 March, the stage was set for a major fleet action, but before Koga could take advantage of it, Spruance and the Fifth Fleet descended on Palau. The carrier task groups were sighted during the approach, so to maximize the potential of surprise, Spruance pushed ahead and advanced the date of the attack from 1 April to 30 March.[92]

Throughout the day and for part of the next, the planes of TF 58 struck the Japanese base. Decidedly different from Pownall's tentative hit-and-run raid into the Marshalls the previous December, Desecrate was a sustained effort to destroy Japanese naval and airpower. Planes dropped mines to trap ships in the harbor while others tried to sink them with bombs and torpedoes. Japanese aircraft were destroyed on the ground and in the air. Yap was also attacked, and on their way back to Majuro, the carriers struck Woleai, south of Guam. Vice Admiral Ugaki, who had assumed command of the First Battleship Division, recorded his anger at the "insolent attitude" of the Americans, who were "doing whatever they like and completely disregarding us."[93]

Nimitz was not "disregarding" the Japanese. He was deliberately trying to disrupt their plans and operations. Although the attack on Palau sank relatively few ships, it had significant ramifications. Admiral Koga and his chief of staff, Vice Admiral Fukudome Shigeru, attempted to escape the impending raid by flying out in a pair of seaplanes. They hoped to reach Saipan via Davao, in the Philippines. Koga's plane was lost in a storm and never seen again. Fukudome's was forced down near Cebu. He was captured by Philippine guerillas and although he was eventually freed, the plans for Operation Z were seized and handed over to U.S. forces. Once it was certain Koga was lost, Admiral Toyoda Soemu assumed command of the Combined Fleet on 15 April.[94]

TF 58 returned to Majuro on 6 April. Nimitz and Sherman arrived soon thereafter to confer with Spruance and Mitscher; they finalized plans for Operation Reckless and discussed Operation Forager. Seven days later, Mitscher was on his way to Hollandia with TF 58. His plan employed three of the carrier groups, with a total of five large carriers, seven smaller ones, and six fast battleships. Vice Admiral Lee was ready to form a powerful battle line if the IJN chose to interfere. With Koga lost and their command structure in disarray, they did not.[95]

The carrier groups distributed their efforts and overwhelmed Japanese airfields at Hollandia, Wakde, Sawar, and Humboldt Bay starting the day before the landings. On 22 April, MacArthur's forces came ashore as planned. "Negligible enemy resistance and . . . the absence of suitable targets" led Mitscher to put his planes on standby the following day. The operation progressed quickly and "most favorably" against "only minor opposition." Tadji airfield, near Aitape, was operating American fighters within just a few days. By 27 April, Operation Reckless was "virtually completed." All the airfields around Hollandia had been seized. They would be operational in less than a month. MacArthur's successful gamble changed the dynamics of the war in the Southwest Pacific.[96]

## CONCLUSION

The Central Pacific offensive began with a pair of operations, Galvanic and Flintlock, that were linked and followed each other in sequence. After that, the preconceived script ended, and the options of the Granite plan came to the fore. What followed appears to have been a linear series of operations, conducted in a logical sequence, but each operation was an option executed when circumstances were right. Once they recognized that success in the Marshalls allowed them to accelerate the advance, Nimitz and his subordinates departed from existing assumptions and moved quickly to seize emerging opportunities. They captured Eniwetok and raided Truk, the anchor of Japanese defenses in the Carolines. These bold moves forced the Japanese to withdraw to their next line of defense, accelerated the progress of the war, and allowed the JCS to take the shortcuts they had been looking for. They authorized MacArthur's leap to Hollandia and ordered Nimitz to bypass Truk and advance to the Marianas. Japanese defenses were pushed back thousands of miles in less than four months.

Multiple factors led to that success. One of the most important was the aggressive approach Nimitz took with Flintlock. Once more under enormous pressure—from King and the JCS to accelerate the offensive, from shipping constraints that restricted his amphibious assault capacity, and from his subordinates who were less tolerant of risk—Nimitz took it upon himself to clarify the way forward and make a bold decision. Confident in his intelligence estimates and the increasing capabilities of his forces, he chose to strike at Kwajalein and seize the Marshalls in a single operation. Success has obscured the aggressive nature of this decision and its importance; without it, Japanese defenses would not have collapsed so quickly and the opportunity to shorten the war would have been lost.

Another factor was the dual offensive. Admiral Koga had correctly anticipated that the Central Pacific offensive would begin in the fall of 1943 and was waiting to counterattack; when Nimitz's carrier forces raided, Koga moved his forces to strike, but the anticipated amphibious assault did not come. Halsey's advance to Bougainville changed Koga's calculus; the threat to Rabaul was too great to ignore. Koga sent his cruisers and carrier planes south, where they were quickly spent. When Spruance and Turner moved into the Gilberts, Koga was no longer in position to oppose them.

Finally, Nimitz's position at the nexus of the lines of effort that controlled strategy and operations in the Pacific allowed him to quickly translate emerging battlefield opportunities into strategic success. The structure of communication and decision-making networks in the Pacific meant that Nimitz's headquarters was able to keep abreast of the JCS' strategic vision, translate them into plans for the Central Pacific, and then execute operations in the Central and Southwest Pacific that delivered on the JCS' intentions. Because Nimitz was both a theater and a fleet commander, there were no handoffs and no intermediate layers. This was why he and King insisted that there not be a GHQ in the Central Pacific; the structure they established allowed for more rapid sensemaking. Nimitz's opportunistic moves in early 1944 were directly attributable to this decision.

During those operations, Nimitz displayed inspirational leadership that created opportunities for his subordinates to excel. He delegated extensively, but when major decisions called for his authority or expertise, he took in the best advice available and acted decisively. With responsibility resting on his shoulders, he then invited his subordinates to cocreate positive outcomes through dialogue and conversation. Leadership for Nimitz was not a position of authority but an "emergent, interactive dynamic" that created new possibilities. Professor Mary Uhl-Bien and her colleagues have investigated the characteristics of this interactive approach and coined it "Complexity Leadership." The interactive patterns they describe repeatedly manifested in Nimitz's style and behavior. Those patterns were especially important in late 1943 and early 1944 at the start of the Central Pacific offensive, when outcomes were most uncertain and the pressure for success extremely high.[97]

Because of the synergistic relationship between the offensives in the Central Pacific and the Southwest Pacific, Nimitz's leadership enabled rapid success in both theaters. As TF 58 swept through the Japanese defensive network "like a raging fire," the Japanese struggled to gain enough space and time to mount an effective response. This made the advance to Hollandia possible, isolated Truk, and freed the carrier forces to raid far to the west. The attack on Palau disrupted Koga's attempt to prepare for a decisive battle and led to his death. Toyoda would also struggle to prepare a counterblow. By maintaining and extending "unremitting pressure," Nimitz and the Pacific Fleet retained the initiative and kept the IJN from regrouping for their long-anticipated decisive battle.[98]

While Nimitz and his subordinates prepared to win a fleet engagement, they did not rely on success in decisive battle to win the war; instead, they emphasized a flexible campaign strategy expressed in the Granite plan. Nimitz's advance used battles to seize islands and capture anchorages, but his focus was on stringing together a series of operations that allowed him to retain the initiative and prevent the IJN from planning and executing a major counterblow. Ugaki described the impact in his diary, noting that "the enemy has made one onslaught after another in a successive wave of decisive battles." As a result, the IJN was unable to effectively resist.[99] In the ensuing months, Nimitz's greatest challenge would be working with his staff, superiors, and subordinates to maintain that operational tempo as he tried to seize the Marianas-Carolines-Palau line.

# MAINTAINING TEMPO

*Maintain and extend unremitting pressure against Japan.*
—Granite Campaign Plan[1]

T he Central Pacific offensive required a rapid operational tempo to succeed. A fast pace achieved two crucial goals. First, at the operational level, it kept the Japanese off balance and prevented them from mounting an effective defense. They had created a powerful network of bases in the Central Pacific designed to slow the advance, attrit Nimitz's fleet, and when the time was right, secure their war aims in a decisive battle; Nimitz wanted to prevent that by moving quickly. A fast pace also served Allied strategy; the JCS recognized that American citizens would eventually lose enthusiasm for war and "might not" be willing to push for "the final objective—unconditional surrender." Nimitz knew this, and so he consistently provided options to the JCS in their "continuing search for shortcuts." In 1944, the pressure on Nimitz to find ways to accelerate the war was acute.[2]

He had to balance this pressure against operational constraints and the capabilities of his growing forces. Galvanic had proven the new tactics for the fast carrier groups and the new doctrines for amphibious assault, but success in the offensive's initial operations did not guarantee success in an extended campaign. Serious limitations remained. Between its powerful strikes, the Pacific Fleet had to rest, recuperate, and rearm; that required advanced bases and a logistic system that could maintain the fleet in forward areas. While logistical capabilities were improving, the challenge of maintaining a *constant* fleet presence in forward operating areas had yet to be solved.

Fortunately for Nimitz, although the Japanese recognized the importance of slowing the offensive, their senior military leaders could not agree how to do it. An Imperial Headquarters Conference in September 1943 revealed the fundamental disagreement: the IJN planned to fight at the outer limits of Japanese territory, while the IJA emphasized an "absolute defense zone" containing the Kuriles, Bonins, Philippines, Marianas, and Palau. Emperor Hirohito "tacitly approved" the IJN's approach "while not rejecting the army's insistence on contraction." Nimitz and MacArthur's offensives in early 1944 resolved the debate. Prime Minister Tojo aligned Japanese strategy with the IJA's view. IJA divisions were sent from China and Korea to the Central Pacific to reinforce the absolute defense zone.[3]

These reinforcements made the next phase of Nimitz's offensive more challenging. In the Gilberts and Marshalls, he had relied on limited Japanese resistance and a bold choice of objectives to overwhelm enemy defenses and quickly move forward. By mid-1944, the Japanese had prepared for a decisive battle on air, land, and sea. With their resistance strengthening, Nimitz had to adapt, adjust, and find alternative means to maintain the offensive's momentum. The success of his offensive became even more important when Japanese offensives in China and Burma gave them the initiative on the Asian continent.

Nimitz and his planners relied on rapid sensemaking to identify emerging opportunities. Nimitz deliberately maintained short feedback loops between operational planning and tactical outcomes. That allowed him to make three crucial decisions in mid-1944 that accelerated the advance and made the most of his limited resources. First, once Nimitz realized that the Japanese had strengthened their contracted defensive perimeter, he revised plans for Palau. Second, when carrier strikes in the Philippines exposed apparent Japanese weakness, Nimitz quickly recommended that he and MacArthur advance to Leyte months ahead of schedule. Third, when planning revealed that the resources of POA were insufficient to capture Formosa, Nimitz and his staff identified alternative objectives. Nimitz's effective planning ability allowed him to expose opportunities and maintain the momentum of the offensive. The Pacific Fleet's growing material strength was crucial, but Nimitz's decision-making ability is what allowed him to overcome increasingly determined Japanese resistance.

## MAY CONFERENCE WITH KING

In early May 1944, Nimitz, King, Cooke, Halsey, Sherman, and Jacobs met in San Francisco. They discussed upcoming operations and the constraints that would govern them. The immediate future was already set—Nimitz's forces would occupy the Marianas and Palau—but beyond that the course of the offensive was uncertain. Nimitz and King, focused on the need to seize a position in the South China Sea, anticipated a JCS directive to occupy Formosa and positions on the Asian mainland. They discussed how best to achieve this within the limitations of manpower and logistics.

Unfortunately for Nimitz's plans, there were too few men to meet the needs of the Army and Navy. In January, Marshall told Nimitz that the impending invasion of Europe would become the primary draw on the Army's manpower and that POA had to maximize efficiency "of each individual man." The Navy faced an absolute limit of 2,610,000 enlisted men and, as the fleet continued to grow, King anticipated shortages of nearly half a million men in 1944 and 1945. At the May conference, Jacobs, head of BuPers, told Nimitz that he had to work within these limitations. King would "not ask for more men until all other personnel reduction possibilities have been exhausted." However, Nimitz, King, and Jacobs were unwilling to make use of all available manpower; they refused to recruit Hawaiians or Puerto Ricans, for example.[4]

Logistics was another challenge. As the Pacific Fleet moved farther from its bases, more fuel, aircraft, ammunition, and supplies had to be shipped to the forward areas. For example, "approximately twenty-five" escort carriers were needed to ferry planes to TF 58 and keep its carriers equipped with combat aircraft. The fast carrier groups also required massive quantities of fuel. Cooke and Nimitz hoped it would soon be possible to get fuel from the

East Indies. A forward base would reduce the complexity of the challenge. Palau was expected to be that base and serve as the "forward staging area" for assaults on the Philippines, Formosa, the China coast, and if necessary, Japan.[5]

Nimitz shared his staff's latest understanding of upcoming operations, encapsulated in a new version of Granite, issued as a draft on 6 May. Operation Forager, the assault on the Marianas, had been advanced to 15 June. Nimitz now expected to attack Saipan and Guam simultaneously. Saipan would provide an air base and Guam a local harbor. The invasion of Tinian would follow. Nimitz, King, and the other attendees felt it was "unlikely" the IJN would contest Forager. Assuming the capture of the Marianas was "not unduly protracted" and the necessary shipping became available, Operation Stalemate, the capture of Palau, would occur on 8 September. It envisioned three phases: the capture of Peleliu, the occupation of Babelthuap, and the seizure of Malakal Harbor to provide a secure anchorage for the fleet. Ulithi would also be occupied and Yap neutralized. King felt Stalemate was more likely to draw out the Japanese fleet. By that time, Halsey—who participated in these discussions—would be commanding the Central Pacific forces.[6]

After these operations, King wanted to strike Japan. In September 1943, he began to consider a large carrier raid—with enough strength to attack Tokyo directly—and worked through the concept with BuAer. During the May 1944 conference, King ordered Nimitz to prepare plans for the raid, designated Operation Hotfoot. King stopped short of committing the Pacific Fleet to it, but he made clear that he wanted it done.[7]

While Nimitz captured the Marianas and Palau, MacArthur would advance "westward along the coast of New Guinea" and then toward the Philippines. He was expected to assault Mindanao on 15 November. Nimitz planned to cover MacArthur's attack with the fast carriers and assumed the general would need "assault shipping from the Pacific Fleet" for the operation. Although not yet approved, conference attendees anticipated Operation Causeway, the assault on Formosa, would follow. Luzon was a possible alternative. Both operations remained tentatively scheduled for 15 February 1945.[8]

Causeway would require the equivalent of twelve divisions organized into four corps, nearly all of Nimitz's combat troops. He planned to seize all of Formosa and a fleet anchorage in the Pescadores. Cooke reflected the

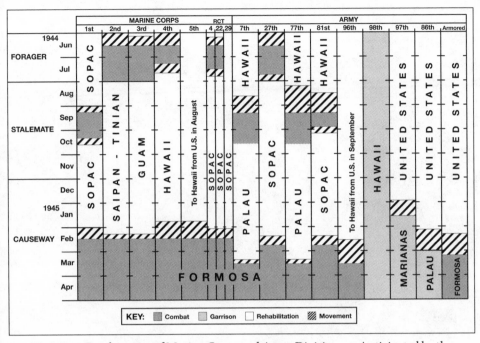

FIGURE 3. Employment of Marine Corps and Army Divisions as Anticipated by the Granite II Draft Plan, issued 6 May 1944

optimism of Washington planners by saying if the war in Europe ended in 1944, it would be important to "get to China before 1945." Weather off Formosa would be favorable in November and December, so Cooke urged an accelerated pace to reach Formosa before the end of 1944. Perhaps then Nimitz could attack with just seven divisions because the Japanese would have less time to prepare their defenses. However, the IJA's substantial forces on the continent would make any operation that close to China challenging.[9]

The course of the offensive after Formosa was uncertain. Nimitz expected to leapfrog up the China coast the way MacArthur had advanced along the northern shore of New Guinea. "Chinese manpower"—an expected total of ninety divisions—would tie down Japanese forces and allow the Pacific Fleet to move up the coast to Shanghai, cutting Japan off from the mainland.

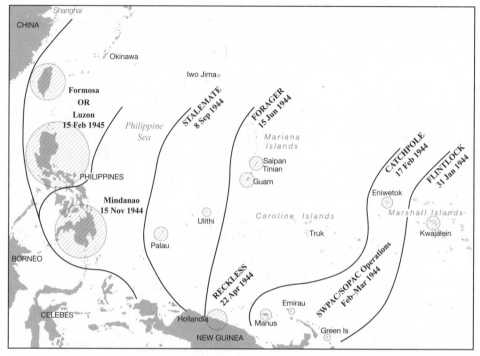

MAP 6. Major Operations of the Granite II Draft Plan, issued 6 May 1944

Once the Home Islands were isolated, blockade and aerial bombardment would cripple the Japanese war effort. If necessary, an invasion of Kyushu would follow.[10]

At the conference, King presented proposed administrative changes intended to allow greater flexibility in amphibious operations. He wanted to reorganize the Pacific Fleet's amphibious forces and introduce another modular layer, the amphibious group. The six groups could then be moved individually between amphibious forces as necessary to support upcoming operations. This increasing flexibility and modularity paralleled that of the carrier forces; King made the necessary changes official by early June.[11]

Nimitz and King also prompted the creation of a new Army command structure in the Pacific. After their conference, Richardson became responsible for almost all Army forces in POA, including the South Pacific, Hawaii, and the new forward area. The Alaskan Department was excluded. A similar consolidation occurred with the Army Air Forces, which were placed under Lt. Gen. Millard F. Harmon, deputy commander of the Twentieth Air Force. Harmon was under Richardson's command for "logistics and administration," but Nimitz's approach to unified command remained in place. Except for the Twentieth Air Force, Nimitz retained "operational control" of Army units in POA. This change ensured that Nimitz, Harmon, and Richardson had responsibility for nearly identical geographic areas and could collaborate more effectively. When they agreed they needed a new Army headquarters for Causeway, Lieutenant General Buckner was chosen to command it.[12]

## GRANITE II AND LOGISTICS

Logistics were a major constraint on Nimitz's operations, but the solutions devised by his subordinates, especially Calhoun's Service Force, allowed the Pacific Fleet to maintain an unprecedented rate of advance throughout the campaign. The SevRons were crucial to this effort. They built upon decades of experience with mobile fleet support.[13]

SevRon 8, an administrative command based at Pearl Harbor, was given cognizance over oil and lubricants in 1942. It met the needs of the relatively small task forces employed that year, but the Central Pacific offensive required mobile bases in the forward area. The first of these was SevRon 4, established at Funafuti in the Ellice Islands in November 1943. It supported Galvanic and Flintlock, validating the concept and helping to identify necessary improvements. In mid-January 1944, SevRon 10 was created to address them.

Originally, SevRon 10 was intended to parallel SevRon 4 and the two were expected to leapfrog each other as the fleet advanced. However, SevRon 10 became an improved version, designed to "furnish logistic support, including general stores, provisions, fuel, ammunition, maintenance, repair, salvage, and such other services" at an advanced fleet anchorage. Its commander— initially Captain Carter, who had worked with Halsey in SOPAC—acted as Calhoun's agent in the forward area, accomplishing Service Force tasks required by the operations of Spruance's Fifth Fleet and Halsey's Third Fleet.[14]

| SHIP TYPE | FLINTLOCK (GRANITE DRAFT OF DECEMBER 1943) | FORAGER (GRANITE PLAN OF JANUARY 1944) | STALEMATE (GRANITE II DRAFT OF MAY 1944) | CAUSEWAY (GRANITE II PLAN OF JUNE 1944) |
|---|---|---|---|---|
| Battleship | 6 | 8 | 8 | 8 |
| Fleet Carrier | 6 | 8 | 8 | 11 |
| Light Carrier | 6 | 8 | 8 | 7 |
| Heavy Cruiser | 12 | 14 | 9 | 11 |
| Light Cruiser | 6 | 14 | 16 | 17 |
| Old Battleship | 7 | 9 | 8 | 8 |
| Escort Carrier | 8 | 24 | 20 | 41 |
| Destroyer | 91 | 120 | 144 | 180 |
| Destroyer Escort | 23 | 30 | 30 | 42 |
| Oilers | n/a | n/a | 21 | 32 |
| Amphibious Force Command Ships | 1 | 3 | 3 | 7 |
| Transports | 63 | 128 | 75 | 177 |
| Landing Ships | 108 | 201 | 245 | 432 |

TABLE 3. Growth of Naval and Amphibious Forces in the Granite Campaign Plan

SevRon 10 initially operated from Majuro in the Marshalls, absorbing the ships of SevRon 4 that were already there. From Majuro, SevRon 10 supported Catchpole, Hailstone, and Forager. In June 1944, anticipating the struggle for the Marianas, the squadron moved to Eniwetok and operated there until September. SevRon 10 arrived at Ulithi soon after the atoll was captured on 23 September. It would remain based there until April 1945. Additional service units were located at Manus.

The SevRons and the capabilities they provided were essential to Nimitz's revised campaign plan, Granite II, officially issued in early June, on the eve of Operation Forager. Granite II remained a "guide to long range planning," but now contained just three operations, Forager, Stalemate, and Causeway. Most of the changes between May's draft and June's official version involved

Causeway. The operation was reduced in scope. Instead of seizing all of Formosa, Nimitz now planned to occupy just the southern portion of the island and secure port facilities by capturing Amoy on the Chinese coast. These changes reduced the forces required for Causeway from twelve divisions to just nine, reflecting the two major constraints governing Nimitz's operations: logistics and manpower. There was not enough shipping to support twelve divisions during a lengthy campaign and the Army needed more divisions in Europe.[15]

Causeway involved two major phases. In the first, two amphibious corps would capture Formosa's southwestern coastal plain, securing sites for airfields. Twelve hundred planes were expected to base on the island, including B-29s, which would begin attacking Japan as soon as possible. Twenty days after the initial landings, a third amphibious corps would initiate the second phase by seizing Amoy. Amoy would become an "advanced fleet base," allowing the Pacific Fleet to "sever Japanese sea communication between the Empire and the Philippines, Malaya, and the Netherlands East Indies." The fleet would then advance north "along the coast of China" toward Japan.[16]

Even though the number of potential future operations was limited, Nimitz remained intent on accelerating the offensive and stressed the need to take advantage of "any short cut made possible by developments in the situation." The JCS also wanted to move faster. On 13 June, they asked MacArthur and Nimitz about "the possibilities of expediting the Pacific Campaign." They presented three potential options: accelerating previously planned operations, cancelling them and advancing to Formosa directly, or bypassing existing objectives and choosing new ones, including "Japan proper." They asked MacArthur and Nimitz for their views.[17]

MacArthur said it was not feasible "to advance target dates for scheduled operations" and argued a direct attack against Formosa was "unsound." He felt it made more sense to occupy Luzon, which could then become a base for operations against Formosa. MacArthur also opposed attacking Japan directly, because there was only enough shipping in the Pacific to lift about seven divisions—fewer than Nimitz's latest plans for Causeway—and therefore any assault force would be too small. "Even with unlimited shipping," MacArthur argued, "I do not believe a direct assault without air support

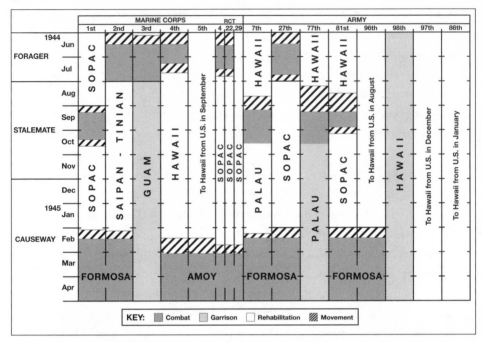

FIGURE 4. Employment of Marine Corps and Army Divisions as Anticipated by the Granite II Plan, issued 3 June 1944

can possibly succeed." He remained focused on his desire to recapture the Philippines, because of the "national obligation" to liberate them and the "military considerations" he outlined.[18]

Nimitz was more flexible; he felt that a rapid advance to Formosa was possible if Japanese airpower on Luzon was neutralized or if the Pacific Fleet won a major victory at sea. Nimitz did not address the question of a "long jump" to Japan, but his silence on the question suggested he would be open to it if the right circumstances arose.[19]

## FORAGER AND A-GO

Nimitz's Operation Plan No. 3-44 was issued on 23 April; it called for establishing bases in the Marianas from which to "initiate the bombing of Japan." Spruance's Fifth Fleet would execute the operation. Land-based planes from the Central, South, and Southwest Pacific would isolate the objectives by attacking Palau, Truk, and other Japanese bases. Mitscher's carriers would achieve aerial supremacy in the Marianas, cut them off from Japan by raiding Iwo Jima and Chichi Jima, and cover the assault forces. Turner's amphibious force would deliver Lt. Gen. H. M. Smith's V Amphibious Corps to Saipan, the headquarters of the IJA's 31st Army, on 15 June. The timing of subsequent amphibious assaults remained flexible. Major General Geiger's III Amphibious Corps would seize Guam on W-Day, tentatively set as 18 June. Smith's troops would capture Tinian on J-Day, after regrouping from the fighting on Saipan.[20]

POA plans assumed enemy garrisons in the Marianas would be "heavily reinforced" but failed to appreciate the extent of Japanese efforts. From January to early June, about 45,000 troops were sent to the islands, including two additional IJA divisions. Lockwood's submarines attacked the reinforcement convoys, but most of these troops arrived at their destinations.[21] JICPOA significantly underestimated Saipan's garrison. Smith expected only 15,000 to 17,600 defenders; there were about 30,000. They were intent on delaying the assault long enough to allow Vice Admiral Ozawa's First Mobile Force and the Base Air Force to defeat Spruance's Fifth Fleet.[22]

Before the operation, King reviewed Spruance's anticipated dispositions and expressed concerns. He worried the Fifth Fleet would risk defeat in detail when two of Mitscher's carrier groups raided Iwo Jima and Chichi Jima. If the Japanese reacted quickly to the assault on Saipan, they could strike with roughly equal strength when the carrier forces were separated and the amphibious forces were tied down with landing operations. Even more concerning was the "disparity in cruiser strength." King felt the Japanese might make a nocturnal "cruiser-borne torpedo attack." He asked Nimitz for his thoughts.[23]

Nimitz was confident in Spruance's plans. The two of them had "given extensive consideration" to the question of fleet action; "destruction of the enemy fleet" was their "primary objective." Nimitz said the possibility of enemy interference with the amphibious operation was "both hoped for and provided against." If the Japanese sought battle, Spruance would adjust the timing of the raids on Iwo Jima and Chichi Jima to concentrate the fleet in time. Before the Hollandia operation in April, Mitscher and Lee had developed six different battle plans that covered everything from major action to independent destroyer attacks. Nimitz referenced these plans and promised that Spruance, Mitscher, and Lee would be prepared for battle and "destroy [the] enemy fleet if it gives us this opportunity."[24]

While Nimitz planned Forager, MacArthur continued to advance. He hoped to seize Halmahera when Nimitz invaded Palau in September, so that the Pacific Fleet's carriers could cover both operations. Along the way, MacArthur planned to capture Wakde-Sarmi, Biak, and an airfield site "on the coast of the Vogelkop" in May, June, and August, respectively. As he learned more about "weak and disorganized" Japanese defenses, MacArthur accelerated his timeline. He bypassed Sarmi, his forces landed at Wakde on 17 May, and they assaulted Biak on 27 May. MacArthur's intelligence organization assumed only 5,000 to 7,000 troops defended the island, but more than 12,000 Japanese offered "strong resistance" from well-prepared positions. They foiled MacArthur's attempt to get Biak's airfields operational in time to support Forager.[25]

Fortunately for MacArthur, siloed planning disrupted the Japanese response. The IJA had contracted their defensive perimeter and expected Biak to fall, but the IJN felt it was crucial to hold the island. Biak's air bases were essential to Operation A-Go, Admiral Toyoda's plan for "all-out battle near Palau." When Toyoda issued his plan on 3 May, he assumed Biak would remain in Japanese hands and that its bases would ensure aerial superiority over the seas to the north. When Nimitz made diversionary strikes on Marcus and Wake in preparation for Forager, Toyoda correctly perceived that they signaled the start of a major operation. On 20 May, he issued the order to execute Operation A-Go. Ozawa's First Mobile Force prepared to sail from Tawi-Tawi and IJN planes deployed to the battle area. Preparations proceeded apace until MacArthur's forces landed. The Japanese quickly realized that if Biak was lost, A-Go would become "impracticable." Toyoda ordered a counter-landing, Operation Kon. In the meantime, preparations for A-Go continued.[26]

These dual preparations confused Nimitz's view of Japanese intentions. JICPOA intercepted Toyoda's "urgent order" to his striking forces and anticipated they would move toward Palau. In the meantime, Japanese planes were rushing "to western New Guinea." The enemy was clearly preparing for a major operation, but its focus was uncertain. After two Biak counter-landings were forced to turn back, Ozawa suggested that a more powerful attempt might draw out the Pacific Fleet and trigger A-Go. Toyoda agreed; he assigned Ugaki's First Battleship Division, with battleships *Yamato* and *Musashi*, to Kon the next day. JICPOA detected this rearrangement of the IJN's order of battle and on 11 June, Nimitz alerted subordinate commands that a force resembling the First Battleship Division had been observed moving south from Tawi-Tawi.[27]

Forager began the same day. Prompted by the "extent of enemy air searches" and concerned TF 58 would be discovered, Spruance attacked the Marianas a day early. Toyoda realized that the opportunity for A-Go was at hand. He "temporarily" suspended Operation Kon, recalled Ugaki, and ordered all IJN aircraft in New Guinea to advance to Palau. Initially, Nimitz remained unaware of these moves, but on 13 June submarine *Redfin* observed Ozawa's departure from Tawi-Tawi. Nimitz marked the movement on his operations plot. Intercepted message traffic suggested the IJN would seek battle. The next day, Layton confirmed that the IJN's plan for decisive battle was in effect. Accordingly, Nimitz ordered Lockwood to position his submarines "to intercept Japanese fleet units" and provide early warning of their movements. Spruance estimated that the enemy forces might "assemble and be within striking distance" by the 17th. That gave him time to attack Iwo Jima and Chichi Jima as planned; he detached TG 58.1 and TG 58.4 under Rear Adm. Joseph J. Clark to "carry out scheduled strikes." If the IJN continued to advance, Spruance would recall them and concentrate his carrier groups.[28]

Mitscher and his staff "prepared for an aggressive, hard hitting battle." They expected the Japanese to approach from the southwest. Although there was a possibility that the enemy could detach "a small, high speed carrier unit" to attack the invasion forces, they did not think the risk was worth "serious consideration." The invasion force, with its old battleships and escort carriers, could defend itself. It was essential, therefore, to move west, "engage the major portion of the Japanese fleet" as soon as possible, and strike the first blow. However, Spruance's view was very different. His instructions for TF 58 emphasized the need to "protect the joint expeditionary force" and keep it from having to fight "a prolonged engagement."[29]

On 15 June, the Saipan landings occurred on schedule. As anticipated, the Japanese adopted a layered defense, combining static defenses around the beaches with mobile forces in the interior. They offered "considerable opposition." Smith committed all his Marine reserves and brought 20,000 men ashore the first day. To Spruance, the situation looked good enough to designate W-Day as 18 June; Nimitz and his staff were pleased with the progress, but appearances were misleading. The next day, Smith realized "a long and vicious fight was in prospect." He and Spruance agreed to land the V Amphibious Corps reserve, the 27th Infantry Division. That would accelerate progress on Saipan and get the soldiers out of the transports, reducing the risk of casualties at sea if the IJN attacked.[30]

Reports from submarines showed the Japanese were still approaching. *Haddo* entered Tawi-Tawi and found it empty. *Flying Fish* sighted a "large task force" headed east from San Bernardino Strait; that was Ozawa. *Seahorse* observed Ugaki's task force on radar, heading northeast from a position about two hundred miles east-southeast of Surigao Strait. Coastwatchers in the Philippines substantiated these contacts. Nimitz informed subordinate commanders that the Japanese would likely be in position to strike the Fifth Fleet on 17 June.[31]

Spruance adjusted his plans. He ordered TG 58.1 and TG 58.4 to make just one day of strikes on Iwo Jima and Chichi Jima and then return, so that TF 58 would be concentrated by the 17th. Clark advanced his schedule and attacked on the 15th and 16th before heading south for the rendezvous. Off Saipan, Spruance conferred with Turner, Mitscher, and other subordinates. They agreed to indefinitely postpone W-Day, withdraw the fast carriers from ground support missions, and augment TF 58 with cruisers and destroyers from the invasion forces. Before returning to his flagship, Spruance promised Turner that he would "try to keep the Japanese off your neck."[32]

Despite their discussions, Mitscher and Spruance lacked a shared understanding of how to fight the battle. Mitscher and his staff were predisposed to be very aggressive. From their extensive experience in carrier operations, they knew it was essential to strike first. Spruance and his team were more methodical. Spruance focused on the need to protect the amphibious forces and the logistical infrastructure—the amphibious shipping especially—necessary for the campaign. These differences had not been reconciled and would lead the two admirals to interpret evolving circumstances very differently.

Nimitz was partially responsible for this. At Midway, he had created the conditions for victory by using his best intelligence to position his subordinates appropriately and leaving the tactics of the engagement to them. Now, he had told Spruance to protect the amphibious force *and* simultaneously destroy the Japanese fleet. Nimitz felt bold execution of the second mission—by embracing calculated risk—would accomplish the first, but Spruance sought to balance the two.

## BATTLE OF THE PHILIPPINE SEA

On 17 June, Mitscher signaled his concept of operations to Spruance. Mitscher requested permission to separate Lee's battle line from the carrier groups and form it into TG 58.7 so that it would be "ready for immediate action against enemy surface forces." Mitscher also recommended heading west that night and gaining a position from which he could flank the approaching enemy. He wanted to rendezvous with TG 58.1 and 58.4 and place the Japanese downwind, so that in the morning TF 58 could close the range while launching strikes. Mitscher hoped to engage Ozawa far to the west and keep him away from the invasion forces off Saipan.[33]

Spruance responded to Mitscher's concept by issuing his own battle plan. Spruance intended to knock out the enemy carriers, slow the enemy battleships, and then "destroy [the] enemy fleet" with TG 58.7. Spruance seemingly gave Mitscher leeway to fight as he saw fit: "Desire you proceed at your discretion, selecting dispositions and movements best calculated to meet the enemy under most advantageous condition. I shall issue general directives when necessary and leave details to you and Admiral Lee." However, Mitscher interpreted this to mean that Spruance would ultimately control the battle through his "general directives." Rather than risk having his orders countermanded, Mitscher decided to submit his ideas to Spruance first. This constrained Mitscher's initiative and undermined Spruance's ability to maximize the potential of his forces. Nimitz would not have been pleased; he revealed his focus on fleet action by telling Spruance, "We count on you to make victory decisive."[34]

Submarine *Cavalla* provided the best intelligence of Japanese movements. Early on 17 June, she sighted a group of two oilers but was unable to maintain contact. That evening, she found a new enemy formation of "fifteen or more large combatant ships" 810 miles west of Guam. The ships zigzagged to make torpedo attacks more difficult and headed east at nearly twenty knots. *Cavalla* lost contact at dawn after making another sighting report.[35]

This information was interpreted very differently by Spruance and Mitscher. Spruance conferred with Captain Moore, his chief of staff, and based on the report of just fifteen ships, concluded the Japanese were operating in multiple groups. They had done so before, and it was reasonable to assume they would again. Additional evidence was provided by captured documents that discussed using multiple formations to feint and strike from unanticipated directions. Focused on the need to cover the amphibious groups, and aware that TF 58 had been located, Spruance was concerned that an unseen Japanese force was "coming in around one of our flanks." Mitscher reacted very differently. *Cavalla*'s fix meant that "the Japanese were right on schedule." If they kept coming, an afternoon search would sight them; if both sides wanted to close and fight, "a night surface action was quite possible."[36]

Mitscher was ready for it, but deferred to Lee and asked him, "Do you desire night engagement?" Commo. Arleigh Burke, Mitscher's chief of staff, who had demonstrated the effectiveness of the Navy's night battle tactics in the Solomons, expected a positive answer, but Lee responded with an emphatic negative: "Do not, repeat, not believe we should seek night engagement." He explained that the advantages of radar would be "more than offset by difficulties of communications and lack of training in fleet tactics at night." Lee had fought and won a night battle off Guadalcanal in November 1942 and knew how chaotic and confused they could be. He did not want to risk a close-range duel in the dark.[37]

Spruance reacted to this exchange by reasserting control over TF 58. He informed Mitscher and Lee that "TF 58 must cover Saipan and our forces engaged in that operation." Mitscher's aggressive suggestion may have reminded Spruance of Midway, when Mitscher had sent *Hornet*'s air group in the direction of a Japanese carrier group that was presumed to be present but did not exist. Spruance did not want to miss the Japanese this time. He planned to advance west during the day and retire eastward at night "to reduce [the] possibility of [the] enemy passing us during darkness." Mitscher's aggressive plans were curtailed; TF 58 would wait for the Japanese to initiate contact. Back at Pearl Harbor, Towers pointed out Spruance's positioning was problematic. Ozawa could strike with impunity by remaining far to the west, out of range of Mitscher's strikes, and use Guam and Rota as bases for his planes. As they flew back and forth between his carriers and the Marianas, Ozawa's planes could attack TF 58 on each pass. Towers urged Nimitz to order Spruance to move farther west; Nimitz refused to overrule the commander on the scene, but he had McMorris inform Spruance of the risk.[38]

At 2200 on 18 June, TF 58 was headed east per Spruance's instructions. Less than an hour later, Nimitz sent out a dispatch alerting his commanders that a radio direction-finding fix placed Ozawa in a position roughly 585 miles west of Saipan. As at Midway, Nimitz tried to provide essential information and help his subordinates make effective decisions. The fix put Ozawa 355 miles west-southwest of TF 58, too far away for a strike. If the two forces maintained their relative positions during the night, which Mitscher believed likely, he would be unable to attack that morning. He wanted to head west and seek action; Mitscher told Burke, "It might be a hell of a battle for a while, but I think we can win it." Burke composed a succinct message for Spruance that suggested a reversal of course to put TF 58 in "ideal striking distance of 200 to 150 miles at 0500."[39]

Over the next hour, Spruance's decision to assume responsibility for the tactical handling of TF 58 cost him the opportunity for a decisive victory. Focused on the danger to his amphibious forces, Spruance overruled the advice of his staff and discounted the perspective of Mitscher and his team. Spruance weighed Nimitz's dispatch against a message submarine *Stingray* sent to Lockwood. *Stingray*'s message was garbled and Lockwood asked her to retransmit. Spruance assumed *Stingray* was trying to send a contact report and the Japanese were jamming it. He estimated the submarine's position to be about 175 miles east-southeast of Nimitz's direction-finding fix; in actuality, the submarine was fighting a fire. There were no enemy ships near *Stingray*. Since direction-finding was susceptible to errors of one hundred miles or so, it was not an unreasonable conclusion. It was also possible, Spruance told his staff, the Japanese were operating in two groups and had forces in both locations; the situation was too uncertain to say for sure. Spruance told Mitscher, "Change proposed does not appear advisable." If enemy ships were where Spruance thought they were, they would be within range in the morning.[40]

Unfortunately, Spruance was incorrect. The Japanese were in a single formation, and Nimitz's direction-finding fix was a better approximation of their position. Two factors influenced Spruance's erroneous conclusion. First, he was focused on covering the invasion forces and interpreted information accordingly. Second, Spruance was occupied with the direct control of TF 58; he devoted too little attention to his role as a fleet commander, leaving him unprepared to create the conditions—and take the risks—necessary to trigger the decisive battle Nimitz anticipated.

On 19 June, Mitscher launched searches at 0200 and 0530 but found no contacts. During the day, Spruance ordered TF 58 to head west-southwest, but the frequent course changes required by flight operations meant that the formation was generally heading east. By 1000, the first of "four massive raids" was visible on TF 58 radars. Mitscher quickly launched a "searching and striking force" in an effort "to locate and attack [the] enemy carriers." It found nothing; the Japanese were still too far away. He also launched all available fighter planes. TF 58's ships and pilots consistently intercepted incoming strikes and shot down Japanese planes before they could make coordinated attacks on Mitscher's ships. Most of the attacks came against Lee's TG 58.7. The Japanese lost more than three hundred planes.[41]

Lockwood's submarines were the first to find Ozawa's force. COMSUBPAC had placed four boats in a square based on Nimitz's direction-finding fix. At about 0910, *Albacore* torpedoed Ozawa's flagship *Taiho*. A single hit ruptured an aviation gasoline tank and spread combustible fumes. *Cavalla* had more immediate success; she torpedoed and sank carrier *Shokaku*. Soon thereafter, the fumes onboard *Taiho* ignited a terrific explosion that left her burning uncontrollably and sinking. Ozawa transferred his flag to cruiser *Haguro*.[42]

Mitscher remained ignorant of Ozawa's specific location throughout 19 June. The submarines and a PB4Y sent contact reports, but the enemy remained out of reach of his searches. That evening, Spruance told Mitscher, "Desire to attack enemy tomorrow if we know his position with sufficient accuracy," and ordered an advance to the west. Mitscher detached TG 58.4 to keep enemy airfields on Guam and Rota suppressed and moved west at twenty-three knots. Ozawa completed his air operations earlier and had a head start.[43]

Spruance sent Nimitz a summary of the day's action that revealed TF 58's failure to strike the enemy carriers. Tension erupted as some members of Nimitz's staff argued that Spruance had lost a great opportunity by keeping TF 58 too close to the beachhead. "Strong evidence" suggested the enemy fleet was retiring; the chance of a decisive battle appeared to be lost. However, Ozawa had not committed to a withdrawal. The limited communication facilities of *Haguro* kept him ignorant of his severe losses in planes and aircrew. He planned to refuel and renew his attacks. After shifting his flag to carrier *Zuikaku*, he gained a clearer sense of his options and delayed his next attack until the 21st.[44]

Navy search planes found nothing the night of 19 June. Mitscher launched a fruitless morning search at 0525 and continued west. Spruance vacillated between determined pursuit and remaining close to the Marianas. About 0800, he shared his latest estimate and told Mitscher that he wanted to push searches "far to the westward." However, if the enemy fleet could not be found, Spruance expected that "further pursuit" would be "unprofitable." By the early afternoon, Spruance had reconsidered and told Mitscher that he "would like to continue pursuit of enemy to northwestward tonight" if there was a chance to strike the enemy.[45]

A little over an hour later, Mitscher's search planes sighted the Japanese ships. At 1553, he launched a "full deck load" strike, fully aware it meant night landings for his pilots. He told Spruance that losses and fatigue from this long-range effort would probably prevent a follow-up attack the next morning. Mitscher hoped to inflict enough damage for Lee's battle line to close during the night and sink survivors in the morning, obviating the need for additional air strikes. Spruance appreciated the situation better. When Mitscher asked permission to send Lee ahead; the Fifth Fleet commander refused, arguing that TF 58 "should be kept tactically concentrated." A quick review of the plot showed why. It would be impossible for Lee to bring his ships into range by morning.[46]

Mitscher's strike mortally wounded two oilers, sank carrier *Hiyo*, and damaged carriers *Zuikaku*, *Junyo*, and *Chiyoda*. Most of Ozawa's remaining planes were lost. Mitscher's planes returned in the darkness; many landed in the water, out of fuel. Others returned to the wrong carriers. To facilitate recovery and retrieve as many pilots from the water as possible, Mitscher maintained a low speed and turned on his carriers' lights. The confused recovery operations meant there would be no chance to catch Ozawa, who was now intent on retiring. Searchers found the Japanese again the next morning, and another strike was launched at dawn, but it failed to reach the target; Ozawa had gained too much distance. Spruance was "keenly disappointed."[47]

## COHESION DESPITE CONTROVERSY

The Battle of the Philippine Sea triggered a dispute that threatened to undermine the cohesion of Nimitz's command. In his comments on the battle, Nimitz emphasized that Spruance had to protect the amphibious forces and foreshadowed an argument made more authoritatively by Capt. Wayne Hughes decades later. "There was never much chance of a fleet gunnery action" and the air action was most crucial by 1944. "The Japanese," Nimitz argued, "had their air power wiped out while still at long range" and, having exhausted their offensive power, "there was then nothing for them to do but retreat." Spruance had clearly won an important victory, and Nimitz channeled the frustration of Towers and other aviators—who were "disgusted at Spruance for missing his chance to destroy the Japanese fleet"—toward winning the war.[48]

Nimitz recognized that "winning the day of battle is not enough." Victory in a fleet action was desirable, but a secondary goal. The campaign, and the accelerated application of "unremitting pressure," was how the war would be won. In the months they spent working together, Nimitz imparted this understanding to Spruance, who was one of the "few" who could appreciate the "magnitude and complexity" required to orchestrate the amphibious operations that were the campaign's centerpiece. Spruance's stance west of Guam kept him from winning a decisive battle but preserved Nimitz's amphibious shipping and ensured that the campaign could retain its momentum.[49]

However, Nimitz was clearly disappointed. He had stressed the need to win a fleet action and promised King his forces would be prepared. Victory in a major naval battle would have eliminated the IJN as a threat and accelerated future operations. The possibility of a speedy advance to Formosa, or even a direct leap to Japan, as the JCS had suggested just a few days before, had slipped away. Nimitz did not want to miss a future opportunity. Plans for upcoming operations would include new guidance for the fast carrier task forces: "In case opportunity for destruction of major portion of the enemy fleet offers or can be created, such destruction becomes the primary task." There would be no question of the objective the next time the IJN came out to fight.[50]

A more fractious dispute erupted during the fighting on Saipan. Holland Smith, already disappointed with the 27th Division's performance on Makin, believed that its commander, Maj. Gen. Ralph Smith, lacked the necessary "offensive spirit" to ensure victory. Friction between the two men gradually increased until the morning of 23 June, when a three-division attack kicked off. The 27th failed to attack on time and its slow progress in the center of the line "uncovered the flanks" of the neighboring Marine divisions. The effort stalled. Holland Smith convinced Turner that it was time to relieve Ralph Smith and the two of them went to Spruance, who approved.[51]

It was a justifiable decision. However, the event triggered a "Smith vs. Smith" controversy and created significant tension between the Army and Navy. Lieutenant General Richardson convened a board to investigate. King felt Richardson's board was insubordinate, but Nimitz allowed it; he wanted to resolve the controversy within POA. However, in August and September, articles appeared in *Life* and *Time* magazines that were critical of the 27th Division. The "irresponsible reporting" undermined the "mutual interest, respect, and cooperation . . . essential to joint operations." Nimitz wanted to issue an official statement expressing confidence in the 27th Division, but King and Marshall agreed not to fuel controversy with any additional public statements. Nimitz took the same approach he had with Spruance's handling of TF 58. He emphasized to his subordinates that they were all one team and had to work together to win the war.[52]

Teamwork was essential to overcome Japanese resistance in the Marianas. They failed to win at sea, but on the ground, they disrupted Nimitz's plans.

When Holland Smith committed his corps reserve on Saipan, Spruance agreed to hold the III Amphibious Corps ready for employment there if necessary. That meant more assault forces would have to be brought forward to keep to the timetable. Nimitz allocated the 77th Infantry Division to Forager on 18 June. The 77th had been planned for Stalemate, so another division would have to be found to keep that operation's target date. Nimitz asked King to send the 96th Infantry Division to Oahu as soon as possible. In the meantime, Nimitz pushed his subordinates to make progress.[53]

Soldiers and Marines advanced slowly on Saipan throughout June, delaying the assault on Guam. Finally, on 3 July, the assault forces seemed to have gained the upper hand. Spruance held a conference with his subordinate commanders and they agreed that the 77th Division needed to be in place before W-Day to serve as a reserve for the III Amphibious Corps. They tentatively set W-Day for the date of the 77th's anticipated arrival, 25 July.[54]

Nimitz responded that this delay was "unacceptable" because it would slow the "entire campaign," not just in POA, but SWPAC as well. Nimitz asked Spruance to "reexamine the question" and suggested having W-Day to coincide with the arrival of the 77th Division's first regimental combat team. After discussing with his commanders, Spruance said that if they had to proceed with only one regimental combat team then the decision would need to be made "by higher authority," a clear indication that they lacked confidence in the idea. Nimitz acquiesced, but the timing of the division's movement made the question irrelevant. Spruance set W-Day as 21 July, the day the first regimental combat team of the 77th Division arrived; the rest of the division was in position the following day.[55]

Organized resistance on Saipan ceased on 9 July. The assault on Guam followed on the 21st. After a series of Japanese counterattacks, Japanese resistance on Guam ended completely by 10 August. Rear Admiral Hill and the assault forces of the V Amphibious Corps, now under command of Maj. Gen. Harry Schmidt, attacked Tinian on 24 July. They outmaneuvered enemy defenses by attacking over small northern beaches, and by 1 August, organized resistance on Tinian had ceased; the rapid success of the assault "epitomized the fusion of innovative planning and violent execution" that was the hallmark of POA amphibious operations.[56]

Forager had succeeded. The loss of "impregnable" Saipan collapsed Japan's "absolute defense zone." Emperor Hirohito, "personally disappointed with the state of the war," withdrew support for his prime minister; Tojo's cabinet collapsed on 18 July. A new cabinet was formed under General Koiso Kuniaki. He was committed to continuing the war and set out to "arm virtually the entire nation." IGHQ discarded the "absolute defensive zone" strategy and in its place adopted the Sho (Victory) plan, which anticipated a decisive battle in one of four areas, the Philippines, Formosa and the Ryukyus, southern and central Japan, or northern Japan and the Kuriles. If Allied forces entered one of these zones, "the imperial army and navy would hurl their entire might against the invaders in a decisive battle."[57]

## JULY 1944 CONFERENCES

The strong Japanese resistance on Saipan led Nimitz to make his first major revision to his plans for 1944. He sent King a detailed message on 4 July that summarized his new concept. Increasing enemy strength—the Palau garrison had apparently grown from 9,000 men to 40,000 since February—necessitated a revision of Stalemate. Nimitz planned to conserve his strength and preserve momentum by capturing just Angaur, Peleliu, Yap, and Ulithi. The rest of the Japanese garrison would be isolated and bypassed. The revised plan would quickly secure Palau and keep Nimitz's strike forces ready to help MacArthur, who was now expected to seize Morotai (instead of Halmahera) in September, Sarangani Bay on Mindanao in October, and Leyte in November. Leyte was expected to require "practically all" covering forces and assault shipping from both theaters, but air bases on the island would deliver "air supremacy in the Philippines." Nimitz had become favorably disposed to combine his forces with MacArthur's because of increasing Japanese resistance. He wanted to concentrate and exploit the full extent of potential combat power to maintain the offensive.[58]

King and the JCS approved Nimitz's changes to Stalemate. The two admirals discussed the implications when they met later in July at Pearl Harbor. Nimitz's new assessment was the centerpiece of a "review of Pacific strategy in light of recent experience." King was apprehensive about the impact on Operation Causeway. The more limited set of objectives for Palau meant that it could not be a major base. Where would the forces for Causeway stage from? King did not want it to be Luzon, because that would delay the advance to Formosa. He argued that the existing facilities at Eniwetok combined with a buildup in the Marianas would suffice. It was important to keep moving forward.[59]

Towers, who was very familiar with the logistical support of the fleet, argued that "bases presently and prospectively available" could support Stalemate and "subsequent operations in the Southwest Pacific" but that they were "not adequate to support" operations beyond Formosa. Even if Causeway was successful, that would not resolve the issue, because bases at Amoy and Formosa would require "considerable development." The fleet could get to Formosa, but there the offensive would stall. Nimitz still hoped to advance up the Chinese coast to Shanghai, but he lacked the necessary logistical support. Additional bases would be needed for operations against Japan.[60]

King reiterated his desire to execute Operation Hotfoot. A quick review of upcoming operations made it clear that the carrier attack on Japan was impossible before late January 1945. King accepted that but ordered Nimitz to "draw up plans" in case circumstances changed. King also wanted to know if it was feasible to occupy Chichi Jima and Iwo Jima immediately after Stalemate. Towers supported the idea; airfields there would augment bombing raids from the Marianas. Sherman felt the effort would be a distraction from the "decisive operations" of Leyte and Formosa. He also believed Chichi Jima and Iwo Jima were extremely vulnerable to raids, regardless of who held them. If U.S. forces occupied them, Sherman expected "considerable plane losses" from Japanese attacks; if left in Japanese hands, they could be a "sink hole" for enemy aircraft.[61]

Logistics and manpower remained important constraints. In addition to supporting offensive operations and building advanced bases, Nimitz had to create air bases for B-29 bomb groups in the Marianas. Initially, four bomb groups would base there, but eventually the islands were expected to support twelve. King wanted the buildup to proceed, but not at the cost of offensive operations. He was unwilling to delay Stalemate or Causeway to get more than four B-29 groups operational. King had asked for more enlisted personnel to allow all projected ships to be adequately crewed—and President

Roosevelt would authorize an increase to 3,389,000 enlisted naval personnel later in July—but King stressed that even with this increase, it was "urgent" to conserve enlisted personnel.[62]

King shared recommendations from Vice Admiral McCain, the deputy CNO (Air). McCain wanted more fighters on the large carriers and he suggested two approaches. One was to replace all the SB2C dive-bombers with fighters in half the carrier groups, giving those groups eighty-four fighters and eighteen torpedo planes. The other was to equip each carrier group with sixty fighters, eighteen dive-bombers, and eighteen torpedo planes. Nimitz deferred to the aviators because of their "wider range of experience." Forrest Sherman and Towers preferred the latter arrangement, but with slightly fewer fighters. They recommended fifty-two fighters, twenty-four dive-bombers, and eighteen torpedo planes. King directed Nimitz to send a formal recommendation to this effect.[63]

As usual, King leaned heavily on Nimitz's talent for managing personnel and identifying the right billets for senior officers. They agreed that McCain would leave OPNAV and alternate command of the Pacific Fleet's carrier task forces with Mitscher. Nimitz and King planned to rotate Halsey and Spruance as fleet commanders. Mitscher would team with Spruance and McCain with Halsey.[64]

After their conference, Nimitz and King flew to Saipan and met with Spruance. Spruance had thoughts about Causeway. He wanted to capture bases in the Philippines first. Spruance and Turner felt Philippine harbors would be essential to the assault on Formosa because the harbor facilities in the Marianas were inadequate. As an alternative to Causeway, Spruance suggested seizing Okinawa and Iwo Jima. They were smaller, closer to Japan, and would allow Nimitz to maintain his offensive's momentum.[65]

Later in July, President Roosevelt came to Hawaii to personally review details of Pacific strategy with MacArthur and Nimitz. Roosevelt forbade the JCS to come along, so Marshall, Arnold, and King were excluded. Leahy attended, but as personal chief of staff to Roosevelt, not as a member of the JCS. Before departing, Leahy conferred with the JCS to absorb their perspectives on Pacific strategy and make sure he could represent their views. He was convinced that Japan had effectively been beaten. However, Leahy was unsure how to avoid the invasion of Japan, which he considered "unnecessary," because the planners of the joint staff and the War Department were advocating for it.[66]

Ostensibly, the central question of the conference was the JCS' deferred decision regarding whether Luzon or Formosa would be the next major objective. However, because Nimitz had adjusted his plans and was seeking ways to accelerate the advance by using his forces together with MacArthur's, there was less disagreement than is generally assumed. MacArthur was true to form and argued forcefully for an advance through the Philippines to Luzon. Nimitz advocated for Formosa, but willingly conceded the merits of MacArthur's arguments. One of the most compelling was MacArthur's insistence that abandonment of the Philippines and its people would "substantiate Japanese propaganda that Americans were unwilling to fight for their friends."[67]

As the discussions continued, Leahy was "surprised" at how easily—"away from the politically charged atmosphere of Washington"—the theater commanders came to an understanding. Both focused on "the weaker points in the Japanese defenses" and the need to capture positions that would make an invasion of Japan "unnecessary." Nimitz and MacArthur intended to seize Mindanao and Leyte. From there, U.S. forces could cut the Japanese off from the resource-rich areas to the south and impose a strangling blockade. This gave Leahy what he needed. Not only would this line of advance accelerate the end of the war, it would render an invasion unnecessary. Although Leahy, Roosevelt, and his Pacific commanders had reached an understanding, the JCS still disagreed on the best way forward. King continued to believe that occupying Formosa was essential; he argued it ought to be seized *in addition* to Luzon. Marshall disagreed. Their dispute continued until Nimitz forced a decision in September.[68]

## NEXT STEPS

While Nimitz seized the Marianas, MacArthur advanced in New Guinea. On 2 July, his forces landed unopposed at Noemfoor Island, effectively closing the entrance to Geelvink Bay and cutting off the Japanese at Sarmi. To forestall his next move, the Japanese prepared an "elaborate defense system" at Manokwari on the western end of Geelvink Bay. On 30 July, MacArthur outflanked their position by moving to Sansapor, further along the coast. He announced that the capture of Sansapor rendered "the enemy base at Manokwari, the pivot of the defenses of the Vogelkop Peninsula . . . bypassed and useless." An estimated 15,000 Japanese troops had been cut off. MacArthur's effective use of intelligence allowed him to outmaneuver the Japanese and attack where they were weakest. The coastal islands and rugged terrain of New Guinea gave MacArthur options for maneuver that Nimitz lacked in the Central Pacific.[69]

With New Guinea in hand, MacArthur turned his attention to Mindanao. He needed to capture intermediate positions to allow his land-based planes to support the occupation of Sarangani Bay near the southern tip of the island. Initially, he planned to take Halmahera next, but after MacArthur's planners discussed the operation with Nimitz's staff, they revised their plans. Halmahera was defended by roughly 40,000 troops. Morotai, which appeared to be lightly defended, was a better option. MacArthur issued his warning order for Morotai on 21 July; he planned to seize the southern portion of the island and establish a base that would support operations against the Philippines. The Morotai assault was timed to coincide with Stalemate so that the Pacific Fleet's carriers could support both operations.[70]

After Morotai, MacArthur planned to capture Salebaboe Island in the Talaud group on 15 October. He requested a very specific strike plan from Halsey's Third Fleet with attacks on Mindanao and Leyte starting 14 October and ending on the 21st. Nimitz agreed to provide support but refused to constrain Halsey with a precise schedule. Instead, he asked MacArthur to share more details so that Halsey could determine how to best employ the fleet. Nimitz was intent on retaining the flexibility of his carrier striking force. "Except where local coordination necessitates," Nimitz told MacArthur, "consider it advisable [to] avoid precise schedules in long range planning Fast Carrier operations."[71]

In the Central Pacific, Nimitz maintained steady pressure on Japanese positions with his land-based planes and carriers. Major General Hale advanced his headquarters to Saipan in mid-August. His planes attacked Iwo Jima, Chichi Jima, Palau, Yap, and other targets with increasing intensity as Stalemate approached. Long-range bombers from MacArthur's theater also took part in these raids. Consistent air strikes destroyed planes and cratered runways, reducing Japanese air strength. The carriers augmented these raids with intense attacks. On 25 July, TF 58, less TG 58.4, struck Yap, Palau, and Ulithi. The planes destroyed enemy aircraft and took reconnaissance photographs to prepare for the assault. After refueling, TG 58.2 retired to Eniwetok while TG 58.1 and TG 58.3 struck Iwo Jima and Chichi Jima. TG 38.4 struck those islands again at the end of August, destroying "all airborne enemy planes."[72]

## JCS APPROVES THE PHILIPPINES

While no definitive decision had been made regarding Formosa, the island remained a crucial objective in the minds of Nimitz, King, and many others. Prior to their last conference, King had forwarded Nimitz a series of questions about his latest Causeway study from the JCS planners. What would happen, they wanted to know, if MacArthur's planes were unable to "effectively reduce and contain" Japanese air strength on Luzon? What if the Fourteenth Air Force could not provide "direct support" from its air bases in China? Would the northern portion of Formosa and the Pescadores be occupied? If so, when, and what forces would be required?[73]

Nimitz did not respond immediately because he was preoccupied with the July conferences and revising plans for Stalemate. When Nimitz did respond, he explained his current plan. He would not capture the Pescadores unless they were substituted for Amoy; he only needed one fleet base. Nimitz did not believe it was worth capturing all of Formosa as that would require 208,000 additional troops and thirty-five cargo ships every month to support them. Instead, Nimitz wanted to move "rapidly into more advanced positions." He expressed "doubt" that Causeway would succeed if Japanese air strength on Luzon could not be overcome; MacArthur had to suppress enemy airpower throughout the Philippines. If the Fourteenth Air Force could not support Causeway, MacArthur's efforts were even more vital. The fast carriers would augment these efforts and help clear a path to Formosa by attacking the Ryukyus and Japan, but it was essential to secure a position in the Philippines, as discussed during the July conference with Roosevelt and envisioned in MacArthur's latest Reno V plan.[74]

Forrest Sherman had been working with MacArthur's planners to determine how best to invade the Philippines and suppress Luzon. After addressing "certain weaknesses" in the Reno plan, they agreed on a way forward. At the end of July, MacArthur set target dates of 15 November for Mindanao—Operation King I—and 20 December for Leyte—Operation King II. Leyte would provide airfields in the central Philippines, making it easier to reach Luzon and reduce Japanese air strength there before Causeway. However, the timing of these operations meant Causeway would slip. Nimitz informed King.[75]

The JCS planners were not pleased. They reminded MacArthur and Nimitz's planners that the "primary objective" of the Pacific campaign, as outlined in March, was to capture Formosa at the "earliest practicable date." Airfields on Leyte and Mindanao were necessary prerequisites, but because weather conditions made early March the "latest practicable date" for Causeway, Leyte had to be invaded earlier to allow at least three months to overcome Japanese airpower in the Philippines. The JCS planners asked what could be done to accelerate the Leyte operation and initiate it by 15 November. They suggested "bypassing objectives," such as Talaud or Sarangani Bay, or "compressing intervals between presently contemplated operations." If Nimitz and MacArthur did that, they could make a combined effort against northern Mindanao and Leyte simultaneously. Nimitz made no immediate changes, but the pressure to advance more quickly influenced his future decisions.[76]

In August, Nimitz gave Spruance overall command of Causeway. Turner would command the amphibious operation and Buckner the expeditionary force. As their staffs began to examine the operation more closely, additional concerns arose. Richardson felt it was essential to capture all of Formosa. The IJA's recent Ichigo offensive in China had demonstrated the "huge gap between the theoretical strength of the Chinese forces" and their actual capability. Richardson and other Army officers had no doubt that the Japanese would ferry reinforcements from China to Formosa and make "strong counterattacks." Without consulting Nimitz, Richardson asked the War Department for a second Army Corps to support operations on Formosa.[77]

Nimitz was disappointed in Richardson but remained intent on fostering a collaborative planning environment. Nimitz explicitly welcomed Richardson's criticism but asked that he voice his concerns directly so that any necessary changes could be incorporated into existing plans. Nimitz also reminded Richardson that extensive discussion was under way regarding future operations. The choice between occupying northern Formosa or moving rapidly to more advanced positions would "depend on the strategic situation." In the meantime, Granite II remained the "basis for acquiring and preparing forces." Subordinate commands like Richardson's ought to adhere to it.[78]

In August the JCS asked Nimitz to take reconnaissance photographs of the Bonins and Ryukyus "as soon as possible." He was willing but increasingly concerned about the lack of a definitive JCS directive for upcoming operations. Nimitz urged King to eliminate the uncertainty and optimistically presented the case for Causeway. It would follow Leyte "as closely . . . as movement and preparations of forces will permit" and secure a position in the South China Sea before the 1945 typhoon season. Nimitz disputed the contention that the entire island had to be occupied. Bougainville, New Britain, and New Guinea had all been partially seized; Formosa would be similar. Nimitz was confident he could secure his objectives with "minimum force," just 250,000 troops. Occupying the entire island would require nearly twice that. Nimitz requested a "firm directive" approving the advance to Formosa with a target date of 15 February to allow preparations to proceed "with a minimum of uncertainty."[79]

The JCS refused to commit to Causeway. King supported the operation and Marshall felt it was strategically desirable, but Leahy believed concentrating on the Philippines would be less costly. Army planners supported his view. They argued Causeway would tie down so many troops, landing craft, and planes that no further advance would be possible until November 1945. Nimitz recognized time was running out. In another message to King, he said that "without a firm directive . . . for operations . . . in the first quarter of . . . 1945, the forces required [for Causeway] will not be assembled and prepared in time."[80] To help resolve the issue, Nimitz sent Forrest Sherman and other staff members to Washington.

Their discussions with the JCS promoted a new directive on 9 September 1944. MacArthur was ordered to "occupy the Leyte-Surigao Area" on 20 December and then "seize and develop bases . . . in the Central Philippines necessary to . . . support a further advance" either directly to Formosa or to Luzon. The target date for Formosa was set as 1 March; for Luzon, it was 20

February. This allowed detailed planning and preparations to start, but the JCS clearly indicated that the efforts would not be simultaneous; one would be chosen, and they specified that "a firm decision as to whether Luzon will be occupied before Formosa will be made later." One of the factors in that decision was the war in Europe. Marshall was optimistic that Germany would be defeated that fall, freeing additional troops and resources for Causeway. In the meantime, Nimitz and MacArthur began to prepare for both operations.[81]

## SEPTEMBER 1944

In early August, Nimitz prepared Halsey to relieve Spruance and assume command of the Pacific Fleet's striking forces and forward operating area. Nimitz visited Spruance at Guam on 10–11 August and shared his intentions. Halsey would take over on 26 August. In his instructions to Halsey, Nimitz provided his plans for Stalemate, guidance for supporting MacArthur's operations, and Granite II. Nimitz augmented this material with personal letters, but he never achieved the same level of tacit understanding with Halsey that he had with Spruance. Halsey was forced to assume Spruance's role and operate in the Central Pacific's unusual command structure without the implicit knowledge Spruance possessed. Ultimately, this deficiency would create friction, but Halsey and Nimitz collaborated well initially. Nimitz encouraged Halsey's initiative by asking him to "submit recommendations" for "feasible and desirable" offensive operations. If there was any possibility to accelerate the advance, Nimitz wanted to know about it.[82]

Nimitz's Operation Plan No. 6-44 covered the Stalemate operation and instructed Halsey to "gain and maintain control of the eastern approaches to the Philippines and the Formosa-China Coast area" by capturing Peleliu, Angaur, Yap, and Ulithi. Even though this plan was more limited than his original concept, Nimitz still provided two corps, one for each phase. The first would begin on 15 September; Geiger's III Amphibious Corps, with the 1st Marine Division and 81st Infantry Division, would occupy Peleliu and Angaur. Each of those islands would become an advanced air base capable of supporting heavy bombers (B-24s) and long-range reconnaissance aircraft (PB4Ys). In the second phase, Maj. Gen. John R. Hodge's XXIV Army Corps with the 7th and 96th Infantry Divisions would capture Yap and Ulithi beginning on 4 October. The 77th Infantry Division and 5th Marine Division were in distant reserve.[83]

Although Nimitz expected Halsey to support the amphibious operations, he included new guidance regarding fleet action: "[I]n case opportunity for destruction of [a] major portion of the enemy fleet offers or can be created, such destruction becomes the primary task." Halsey emphasized this point throughout his instructions. He told his subordinates to "utilize every opportunity which may be presented or created to destroy major portions of the enemy fleet," and expressed his intention to "*seek out and destroy* any enemy naval force within range." This perspective reflected Halsey's aggressive disposition and aligned closely with Mitscher's.[84]

As Stalemate approached, Halsey stressed the importance of readiness. He noted "unmistakable signs of wear in the ships and in the personnel of the Fleet" and planned to devote "early and serious attention" to "maintenance and upkeep." Ulithi would be a valuable prize in that respect; it would provide a secure anchorage for rest and recuperation and, once based there, the Third Fleet could counter any Japanese effort to oppose the upcoming assault on the Philippines. Halsey was intent on being ready for such a contingency; he set an example with his own staff. While at sea, they conducted daily drills and occupied themselves with "strategic and tactical battle problems." In a letter to Nimitz, Halsey promised that the Third Fleet would be "fully prepared to take maximum advantage of any opportunities" in a fight with the Japanese.[85]

Stalemate began with the typical series of aerial attacks. B-24s bombed Peleliu and Angaur to prepare for Halsey's arrival. The fast carriers of TF 38—renumbered because it was now part of the Third Fleet—struck Palau, Yap, and Ulithi. Japanese strength appeared to be waning; Rear Adm. Ralph E. Davison, commanding TG 38.4, reported, "[N]o enemy interception was encountered, no enemy airborne planes were observed, no operational aircraft were on the ground, and the two damaged airfields at Yap had not been repaired."[86]

Halsey took his three other carrier groups ahead and struck Mindanao on 9 September. The Japanese appeared equally weak in the Philippines. Just six enemy planes were seen in the air and all were shot down. Halsey reacted with his characteristic aggressiveness. To cover the Morotai operation, he distributed his carrier groups to attack Leyte, Cebu, Negros, and Luzon simultaneously. Nimitz had anticipated the enemy might be weak but was concerned Halsey was going too far; it was "preferable," Nimitz reminded him, to make strikes against the Philippines with "at least three carrier task groups within tactical support distance." That had been Halsey's original concept, but he revised his plan to take advantage of Japanese weakness. Nimitz dealt with the stress caused by Halsey's decision by firing "thousands of rounds" on the pistol range.[87]

In the meantime, MacArthur wanted firm arrangements for the Talaud operation, planned for 15 October, and asked Nimitz for permission to communicate with Halsey directly. Nimitz told MacArthur that he was free to communicate with Halsey, but Nimitz also emphasized the importance of keeping the carrier task forces "free to strike the enemy fleet and air forces wherever they may be." Imposing specific schedules for amphibious operations limited the carriers' flexibility and "freedom of action." Nimitz wanted MacArthur to rely on escort carriers and land-based planes for "direct support," freeing Halsey to operate more strategically and opportunistically. Nimitz also wanted to keep the carrier forces from becoming exhausted during upcoming operations, which were expected to "extend almost continuously over a four-month period." Halsey would need flexibility to determine how best to rotate the carrier groups out of combat for rest. To clarify how Nimitz and MacArthur could best synchronize their efforts, Nimitz recommended "a conference of planning staffs" at Pearl Harbor.[88]

Nimitz's suggestion was overtaken by events. Halsey's three days of carrier strikes triggered an "air slugging match" that apparently destroyed Japanese air strength in the central Philippines. It was "unbelievable and fantastic." Halsey felt the central Philippines were "wide open" and, in line with Nimitz's instructions, recommended initiating the Leyte operation "immediately." Halsey recommended bypassing Palau because it did not "offer opportunities for destruction of enemy forces commensurate with delay and effort involved." Only the anchorage at Ulithi was needed.[89]

Nimitz was not ready to abandon Stalemate, but he adjusted it again. Nimitz ordered Halsey to carry out its first phase—Peleliu and Angaur— and occupy Ulithi. Yap could be neutralized from Guam and Peleliu. The Yap assault forces—the XXIV Corps with the 7th, 77th, and 96th Infantry

Divisions—would then be "available to exploit favorable developments in the Philippines." Nimitz asked MacArthur for his views. He was at sea with the Morotai assault forces and observing radio silence. Sutherland responded for him and said that MacArthur had provided for advancing the Leyte operation, so diverting the Yap assault forces made sense, but Sutherland wanted "further information" before agreeing to a "direct movement against Leyte."[90]

Nimitz went to the JCS. He told King that the neutralization of Palau and capture of Ulithi was "essential" and that "it would not be feasible" to reorient plans as rapidly as Halsey suggested. Nimitz expected the capture of Ulithi, Peleliu, and Angaur would support the occupation of the Philippines as well as advances toward Luzon, Formosa, and the China coast. However, the apparent collapse of "enemy air forces in the Philippines" was "even greater" than expected and Nimitz boldly recommended accelerating the offensive by using the Yap force to "assist in an early movement into Leyte." If MacArthur was not ready, the force could seize Iwo Jima instead while the fast carriers raided Japan.[91]

Nimitz's message reached the JCS while they were in Quebec for the Octagon Conference. Marshall radioed MacArthur for his views, but he was still at sea. Sutherland gathered other members of the CINCSWPAC staff; they felt that if they declined to advance to Leyte immediately, they would implicitly endorse an advance to Formosa in favor of Luzon. That was unacceptable. Sutherland responded in MacArthur's name and told Marshall that intermediate operations would be dropped. Based on Nimitz's recommendation and MacArthur's apparent concurrence, the JCS approved Halsey's concept. Nimitz's flexible strategy of treating future operations as options to be executed when the time and conditions were right had created the opportunity to "advance the progress of the war . . . by many months." It was "speed, flexibility, cooperation, and control at its best."[92]

MacArthur cancelled his preceding operations and set the date for King II, the assault on Leyte, as 20 October. There were many details to sort out. MacArthur reached out to Nimitz to coordinate planning with division and corps commanders, Forrest Sherman left to confer with MacArthur at Hollandia, and Halsey looked to confer with MacArthur as well. Nimitz prepared to release his amphibious assault forces to Kinkaid.[93]

In the meantime, the 1st Marine Division landed on Peleliu on 15 September. Progress was slow as the Marines fought through "prepared defenses organized in depth" and "stiff" Japanese resistance. After the lessons of Biak and Saipan, the Japanese had adjusted their tactics. They recognized it was impossible to defeat an American amphibious operation. Instead, they prepared *fukkaku* positions, "formidable defensive strongholds," with reinforcing fields of fire that could slow the advance, inflict as many casualties as possible, and demonstrate their resolve. By making "the Americans pay the maximum price in blood for every yard," they hoped to prolong the war, task American patience, and force a negotiated peace.[94]

Two days after the assault on Peleliu, the 81st Infantry Division landed on Angaur. They overcame most resistance by 20 September, but it took another month to extract the Japanese defenders from their caves in the northwest corner of the island. While fighting on Angaur continued, two regiments of the 81st Division relieved the 1st Marine Division, which had succeeded in cutting the island off from reinforcement but was exhausted from fighting in Peleliu's Umurbrogol Mountains. Eugene B. Sledge, who fought there, remembered it as "an alien, unearthly, surrealistic nightmare" unlike any "other battlefield described on earth." Major General Geiger called the battle for Peleliu the "toughest in the entire Pacific war." Fighting within the steep ridges did not end until 27 November.[95]

Nimitz's determination to overrule Halsey's recommendation and proceed with the assaults on Peleliu and Angaur has been called "a terrible operational decision" that "did little to nothing to contribute to U.S. strategic goals." Nimitz made that decision for the same reason Toyoda ordered counterlandings on Biak, to secure airfields that could dominate the Philippine Sea. Nimitz followed established patterns. The Central Pacific offensive used networked air bases to suppress Japanese-held islands and augment the operations of the fleet; Nimitz felt air bases on Peleliu and Angaur were "essential" to neutralize Palau, protect MacArthur's flank as he advanced to the Philippines, and cover the fast carrier task forces. Seizing Ulithi alone would not accomplish those goals. However, with hindsight that choice may have been the better one. The rapid move to Leyte was about to isolate Palau and cut it off from reinforcement. Peleliu was strongly defended, and in late August, intelligence estimates had revealed that there were twice as many Japanese defenders there than originally anticipated (10,700 instead of 5,000). Given the increasing constraints on Nimitz's manpower, the 1st Marine Division and the 81st Infantry Division could have been used more advantageously elsewhere. Nimitz justified their struggle by arguing that the air bases on Peleliu and Angaur secured his lines of communication, completed the isolation of Truk, and freed his striking forces for "long range offensive sweeps" toward the Philippines, Formosa, and the Ryukyus. Nimitz had the means to accomplish those goals without committing two divisions to the unearthly nightmare in the Umurbrogol.[96]

## CAUSEWAY'S END

Nimitz knew that MacArthur was arguing persuasively for an invasion of Luzon. The "recent successes of our land-based and carrier-based air operations in . . . [the] Philippines," MacArthur told Marshall, "point clearly to the feasibility of proceeding directly from . . . Leyte to the main assault against . . . Luzon." MacArthur expected to assault the island on 20 December 1944 and, to get his forces there, MacArthur would need the support of the Pacific Fleet's striking forces and amphibious ships. But securing Luzon would, MacArthur argued, make the capture of Formosa "unnecessary," and create the potential for a "direct move" against Kyushu.[97] In a letter to Halsey on 24 September, Nimitz acknowledged the merit of these arguments. It was "almost certain," he said, that MacArthur "will be ordered to conduct his Luzon operation in December."[98]

That would mean the end of Causeway, but by September, Nimitz felt the invasion of Formosa was no longer feasible. His planners knew it exceeded his logistic capabilities. Fortunately, there were alternatives. In July, Spruance had suggested assaulting Okinawa and Iwo Jima instead. He reinforced this point when he returned to Pearl Harbor in August. The day after the new JCS directive, Nimitz asked his subordinates for their thoughts on occupying Okinawa and Iwo Jima rather than Formosa. Their response was favorable. Twelve days later, Nimitz recommended this course of action to King. It was a major topic at their conference in September.[99]

When Nimitz and King met, the agenda was very similar to their prior conference. They discussed personnel, future operations, and logistics. For parts of their discussions, Nimitz and King were joined by Forrest Sherman, Spruance, Cooke, Fitch, and Jacobs. The centerpiece of the operational discussions was the decision to advance the target date for Leyte and its potential impact on Causeway. JCS planners had studied Causeway in detail and, like Nimitz, concluded it was infeasible. There were too few Army service troops and insufficient shipping. Unless Germany surrendered very soon, the resources would not be available in time. Sherman noted that even if resources were available and a directive issued "immediately," the earliest the operation could occur was March 1945. Transferring MacArthur's forces to Nimitz would make no appreciable difference. The conclusion was clear. "Formosa," King said, "might have to be bypassed." Nimitz had deftly used the evidence accumulated by his subordinates to help King understand that Causeway was no longer the best way forward.[100]

The discussion quickly turned to alternatives. King suggested assaulting Kyushu instead of Luzon, a bold leap that appeared even less feasible than Causeway, but Nimitz had prepared a thorough recommendation. In the July meeting with MacArthur and Roosevelt, MacArthur had explained that he would be unable to advance "through the Philippines from Leyte [to Lingayen Gulf on Luzon] by shore-to-shore operations." He would need the assistance of the Pacific Fleet. Since Nimitz lacked the capacity to take Formosa, he felt "the best way to keep pressure on the Japanese was . . . to support the Lingayen Gulf operation proposed by MacArthur and to take Nanpo Shoto and Nansei Shoto with POA forces." Now, he recommended this course to King. Iwo Jima (in the Nanpo Shoto island group) and Okinawa (in the Nansei Shoto island group) would be Nimitz's next objectives, with tentative dates of 20 January and 1 March respectively.[101]

King asked what had changed since July, when Iwo Jima was considered a liability. Sherman explained Nimitz's new concept. Carrier strikes would "eliminate the [Japanese] air in Formosa," just as Halsey had already done in the Philippines. A raid on the Home Islands—Operation Hotfoot—would occur 5 November, further reducing Japanese airpower. Two divisions would quickly seize Iwo Jima and construction personnel would turn it into an air base. With Japanese planes on Formosa "neutralized by carrier strikes assisted by shore-based air from Luzon," Nimitz would take Okinawa. From there, he still hoped to secure a base on the Chinese coast, capture Shanghai, and open the Yangtze River to naval operations.[102]

King was uncertain of the value of Iwo Jima if Okinawa was also captured. Nimitz explained that airfields on Iwo Jima would provide fighter escort for the B-29s, which the Army Air Force was "anxious to obtain." Cooke suggested that a rapid buildup of planes on the island would allow U.S. forces to steadily attrit Japanese airpower. Sherman agreed; "[T]his operation," he said, "will set up a place where we can wear them down continuously." King asked how Nimitz's forces would react if the Japanese fleet opposed the operation. Nimitz "hoped" they would because that "would give us the opportunity we have been waiting for." The increasing size and striking power of the Pacific Fleet—especially its air arm—gave Nimitz confidence the Japanese "will be destroyed if they attack."[103]

Nimitz planned to have Halsey command the fleet's striking forces during operations in the Philippines—the capture of Leyte and Luzon—while Spruance would take over for Iwo Jima and Okinawa. King asked about alternatives and suggested a divided command for Luzon, with Spruance in charge of supporting MacArthur and Halsey "standing by for the Japanese Fleet." King also suggested having Halsey under Spruance for Iwo Jima and Okinawa. King had recognized their strengths. Spruance was methodical, precise, and well suited for commanding fleet operations; Halsey seemed to be better suited to aggressively pursue the Japanese fleet with the carrier task forces. The point was not lost on Nimitz, but he was unwilling to entertain King's suggestion. Nimitz felt it was better to give each fleet commander regular rest and time to prepare for upcoming operations.[104]

The conference then turned to other topics. The Marianas were becoming a major base. The first B-29 airfield on Saipan was operational; the second was expected to be ready by 3 October. Airfields on Guam and Tinian would follow. Unloading capacity was growing. Guam and Saipan could already support roughly ten thousand tons each day from existing berths; Tinian would approach that capacity by the end of January. There were no protected anchorages nearby, but Nimitz pointed out that the limited danger from Japanese submarines meant that the "open anchorage at Saipan" could be used, meaning "no other anchorages will be required." This lessened the impact of not developing a major base at Palau.[105]

By 3 October, Nimitz and his staff members were back in Pearl Harbor. That same day, the JCS issued their final decision on Formosa. They directed MacArthur to move against Luzon on 20 December. Once there, he would develop bases "to support further advances" and assist Nimitz's move to Okinawa. Nimitz would support MacArthur's move to Luzon, capture Iwo Jima in January 1945, and then occupy Okinawa in March. Nimitz's recommendations had become the official strategy in the Pacific.[106]

## CONCLUSION

Between May and October 1944, Nimitz initiated two large amphibious operations, provoked a major battle with the Japanese fleet, and prompted three crucial decisions that shaped Pacific strategy. The first was the reduced set of objectives for Stalemate, intended to allow his forces to continue to rapidly advance despite increasing Japanese resistance; the second was the decision to advance to Leyte in October, months ahead of schedule; and the last was the abandonment of Operation Causeway in favor of more feasible efforts, the capture of Iwo Jima and Okinawa. Nimitz was able to provoke these decisions because of his unique position at the center of strategic and operational decision-making in the Pacific and because of the sensemaking capabilities of his staff.

As the structure of that staff changed over the preceding months, Nimitz preserved his ability to focus on operations by segregating that work from administrative functions. In 1942, he had done this by delegating administrative work to his chief of staff, Rear Admiral Draemel. Nimitz maintained that division as the staff grew and reorganized. When Vice Admiral Newton became deputy CINCPAC-CINCPOA in December 1943, he was responsible for "logistics, administration, and Pacific Ocean Areas," while McMorris, as chief of staff, focused on "plans, operations, and staff coordination." Nimitz followed this pattern throughout the war. His chief planner was a close, trusted collaborator who helped him run the war, while competent administrators managed logistical support. It was an effective reaction to "the complex type of war" fought in the Pacific.[107]

Towers fit into this model when he became Nimitz's chief of staff and deputy CINCPAC-CINCPOA. Towers, a proven and able administrator, kept the fleet running while Nimitz and McMorris focused on operations. Forrest Sherman assisted them; on 23 March 1944, Sherman became deputy chief of staff and assumed responsibility for coordinating the Plans and Operations Divisions, including "all planning activities of Staff divisions which affect combat operations." The four of them—Nimitz, Towers, McMorris, and Sherman—became the core of planning and operations for POA. Although they regularly disagreed with each other and even with Nimitz, he facilitated their discussions and ensured that the dialog remained productive. Nimitz used their disagreements to draw out alternative ideas and identify his best options. That is one reason why he was able to quickly identify emerging opportunities and act on them.[108]

Nimitz's approach was an alternative to today's standard hierarchy of strategy, operations, and tactics. Once Nimitz was made commander, Pacific Ocean Areas, he had a dual role, serving as both CINCPOA and CINCPAC. His decision to remain in both roles has been criticized. Naval War College professor Milan Vego assessed Nimitz's position as "both a theater-strategic and an operational commander" as problematic.[109] However, Nimitz and King felt it was the correct choice because it allowed Nimitz to integrate strategic directives from the JCS with the tactical efforts—the plans, operations, and orders—required to achieve them. By not installing a separate fleet or operational level command, Nimitz kept the feedback loop between planning and operating short and focused. That is another reason Nimitz was able to quickly identify emerging opportunities. Nimitz delegated what we today call "operations" to administrative commanders like Towers. Instead of a hierarchy, Nimitz created an integrated triangle; strategy and tactics were closely and directly linked. Operations supported them both without becoming the interface between them.

This organizational structure gave Nimitz the ability to rapidly detect changing circumstances and take advantage of them. His staff organization was the key to a sensemaking capability that maintained and extended "unremitting pressure" on the Japanese and blended the best qualities of prewar strategies—the speed of the "through ticket" with the methodical advance that relied on advanced bases. However, as effective as Nimitz's staff structure was, he had failed to ensure his fighting forces were similarly well equipped. As the Battle of the Philippine Sea showed, fleet commanders at sea could overstep their authority and stifle the initiative of their subordinates. That is how Spruance missed the opportunity for a decisive victory. It remained to be seen if Halsey would behave differently. When the Third Fleet covered MacArthur's assault on Leyte, Halsey and Nimitz would have an opportunity to demonstrate how well they had absorbed the lessons of the Battle of the Philippine Sea.

# SEEKING DECISION

*In case opportunity for destruction of major portion of the enemy fleet offers or can be created, such destruction becomes the primary task.*

—CINCPOA Operation Plan No. 6-44[1]

Nimitz's recommendations had accelerated offensive operations once again. In the Philippines, he would combine forces with MacArthur. However, Japanese weakness proved illusory; they committed themselves to a decisive battle for Leyte. Determined resistance and bad weather kept MacArthur from building up his air strength as anticipated and disrupted the timing of upcoming operations. To triumph in the lengthy campaign of attrition, Nimitz's carriers supported Philippine operations extensively; they nearly exhausted themselves. The effort was made more challenging by the Japanese introduction of kamikaze tactics; suicide planes struck in small groups and exploited the weaknesses of the Navy's aerial defense systems. Many ships were damaged or sunk.

In the face of these difficulties, Nimitz struggled to maintain the aggressive schedule adopted in October 1944. Five major operations were expected to follow in quick succession—Leyte, Mindoro, Luzon, Iwo Jima, and Okinawa. Japanese resistance upset the operational tempo and made it challenging to give the carrier forces enough time to rest. Halsey's aggressive disposition exacerbated the challenge. His resolute determination to come to grips with the enemy had helped restore the morale of the Pacific Fleet and brought victory at Guadalcanal, but now, it threatened the ability of the carrier forces to sustain the offensive.

Nimitz was similarly aggressive, but unlike Halsey, he tempered his personal drive and built an effective organization. Halsey relied much more on his individual initiative. During World War I, Halsey had served as the model for Peter Macfarlane's "Captain Bradshaw" of the *Saturday Evening Post*. Bradshaw was "a boyish-spirited, insuppressible hellion of the sea" who "handle[d] his ship with . . . dash and reckless daring."[2] So was Halsey. Armed with Nimitz's new guidance that the "primary task" of the carrier forces was the "destruction" of the enemy fleet, Halsey looked for opportunities to turn tactical success into strategic victory.[3] Unlike Spruance, who understood that the campaign was paramount, Halsey devoted insufficient attention to long-term success. Halsey's challenge was exacerbated by the unusual command structure of the Central Pacific. Nimitz had placed him in a role designed for Spruance, one that relied on common understanding and a series of implicit assumptions developed over the many hours Nimitz and Spruance spent together. Halsey lacked that common understanding. As a result, his actions diverged from Nimitz's expectations, and Nimitz felt compelled to oversee Halsey's plans and operations in detail to ensure the offensive's continued momentum.

Nimitz had to take a similar approach with MacArthur. Like Halsey, the general was overly focused on near-term success, especially in the Philippines, which he felt duty-bound to liberate. The key difference was that, for MacArthur, command was an egocentric exercise, not a collaborative endeavor. He consistently subordinated operations that were not his own. Nimitz had to broker the misalignment between his plans, MacArthur's, and those of the JCS to ensure a coherent and sustained offensive. Nimitz was able to do this through regular conferences, honest assessments, and the flexibility of his increasingly large and powerful command. Nimitz's skill combined with logistical improvements and detailed planning to allow the Pacific Fleet to maintain an exhausting operational tempo and apply "unremitting pressure" in the face of Japan's best efforts.

## PLANNING: OCTOBER 1944

The October 1944 JCS directive resolved Nimitz's uncertainty about the sequence and timing of upcoming operations. The assault on Leyte would occur later in the month. Afterward, MacArthur would retain the Pacific Fleet's amphibious forces and advance to Luzon in December. In between these operations, the fast carriers would raid Japan. In January 1945, Nimitz would assault Iwo Jima and then, in March, advance to Okinawa. The JCS directive triggered a series of planning efforts as Nimitz and his staff refined their schedule for the next six months. It was extremely aggressive and reflected the optimistic promise of a rapid advance against waning Japanese resistance.

Nimitz's Induction Joint Staff Study outlined how to support Operation Mike, MacArthur's assault on Luzon. Planes from new air bases on Leyte and Mindoro, "together with previous carrier attacks," would reduce Japanese airpower on Luzon. The Seventh Fleet's escort carriers would provide direct support to the amphibious operation, freeing the fast carriers to make deep offensive sweeps "throughout the Western Pacific." Hotfoot was one such sweep. Nimitz hoped it would "force an engagement with the enemy fleet and destroy" it.[4] Even if it failed to do so, these deep sweeps were expected to isolate Luzon and cut it off from reinforcement. During MacArthur's amphibious landings in Lingayen Gulf, one fast carrier group would provide direct support while the others attacked enemy shipping "along the Southeast China coast." Timing was crucial; the carriers had to withdraw from Mike in time to rest before Detachment, anticipated to begin on 20 January.[5]

Detachment—the capture of Iwo Jima—would secure a position "from which we can engage the enemy in the Empire itself." Fighter planes from there could escort B-29s based in the Marianas. Two Marine divisions were expected to defeat Iwo Jima's estimated 13,000 defenders so quickly that the first of its three airfields would be operational within a week. The Iceberg Joint Staff Study emphasized the tight timing between the Iwo Jima and Okinawa operations and the dependencies that linked them. Luzon and Iwo Jima both had to be secured in time for fire support ships, escort carriers, and amphibious shipping to participate in the assault on Okinawa, scheduled for 1 March.[6]

| OPERATION NAME | OBJECTIVE | ANTICIPATED DATE | ACTUAL DATE |
|---|---|---|---|
| King II (Insurgent) | Leyte | 20 October 1944 | 20 October 1944 |
| Hotfoot | Raid Japan | 10 November 1944 | Deferred |
| Love | Mindoro | 5 December 1944 | 15 December 1944 |
| Mike (Induction) | Luzon (Lingayen Gulf) | 20 December 1944 | 9 January 1945 |
| Detachment | Iwo Jima | 20 January 1945 | 19 February 1945 |
| Iceberg | Okinawa | 1 March 1945 | 1 April 1945 |

TABLE 4. Upcoming Pacific Operations as Conceived in October 1944

Nimitz's plans optimistically assumed the "weakness of Japanese aviation in their forward areas" would allow "rapid advances." However, after the fall of the Marianas, the Japanese had adopted the Sho plan, first issued on 24 July 1944. Sho had four variants, each with a different "decisive battle area." Sho-1 would be fought in the Philippines, Sho-2 around Formosa and the Ryukyus, Sho-3 in south and central Japan, and Sho-4 around Hokkaido and the Kuriles. When Sho was triggered, "all available Japanese sea, air, and ground forces would be quickly concentrated to destroy the enemy forces." Halsey's incursion in the Philippines encountered limited resistance, not because the Japanese were on the edge of defeat, but because they were holding back for a major battle. Instead of weakening, the Japanese were preserving their strength.[7]

Losses suffered by the Combined Fleet's Mobile Force put Admiral Toyoda in a difficult position; he "lacked both the carriers and the well-trained pilots to fight a major battle."[8] However, he believed the IJN had to commit itself to the defense of the Philippines because loss of the archipelago would cut Japan off from its sources of fuel oil and bring the fleet to a standstill. He planned to capitalize on the strength of his surface forces—the Second Fleet at Lingga Roads and the Fifth Fleet in the Inland Sea—and renamed them the First and Second Diversionary Attack Forces, respectively.

Toyoda's plans, like Nimitz's, were overly optimistic. Sho-1, the battle plan for the Philippines, assumed that the IJN's Mobile Force would serve as bait and draw the U.S. carrier forces north, away from the decisive action.

Land-based planes would make up for the IJN's deficiency in carrier aircraft and cover the First Diversionary Attack Force as it divided and executed a pincer movement, falling upon the unprotected U.S. amphibious forces and destroying them. Timing was crucial. The attack had to catch the amphibious forces while they were still unloading.

## LEYTE PRELIMINARIES

As Halsey prepared for Leyte, he doubted the Japanese would seriously contest MacArthur's advance to the Philippines. Instead, he focused on Hotfoot and the fleet battle he expected to initiate and win. Halsey's plans for Leyte mirrored the Insurgent study; he would raid Okinawa, Formosa, and Luzon with his four carrier groups. Between attacks, he would retire for fuel. During the amphibious operation, Halsey would support MacArthur with just two carrier groups, allowing his carriers to rotate between the Philippines and Ulithi for regular rest and replenishment. They would be ready for Hotfoot as soon as King II ended. Anticipating this, Nimitz issued his warning order for Hotfoot on 7 October; Halsey planned to strike Japan on 11 November.[9]

Halsey confidently explained to Nimitz that he would attempt to draw out the enemy fleet, use submarines to ambush their task groups, and employ "tactics which will bring air, surface, and submarine weapons to bear." Interwar exercises had shown the value of coordinated strikes by planes, surface ships, and submarines; Halsey hoped to exploit these lessons. He would "deny the enemy a chance to outrange" his forces and avoid a repeat of Philippine Sea by "moving smartly" toward the enemy carriers once they were sighted. To maximize his chances of success, Halsey asked Nimitz for control of the Pacific Fleet's submarines, emphasizing that his goal was "the same as yours—to completely annihilate the Japanese fleet if the opportunity offers."[10]

Nimitz approved Halsey's outline but refused to release control of the submarines. In addition to fleet support, they had to provide lifeguard duties for downed flyers, destroy enemy shipping, and perform strategic reconnaissance. In his response to Halsey, Nimitz explained that he could arrange the submarines more effectively because "the information available to me . . . is often more complete and usually more recent than is the information available to you." However, to guarantee that, Nimitz needed regular updates. He asked Halsey to keep him informed and chided the Third Fleet commander for not providing timely details of his 24 September strike on Coron Bay in the Philippines. Nimitz acknowledged that Halsey needed to take advantage of opportunities but stressed the importance of sharing information "as fully and as early as the situation permits." Their exchange highlights the challenges they had developing an implicit understanding of how to employ the Pacific Fleet's striking forces.[11]

However, both agreed that it was important to locate and destroy the Japanese fleet. Halsey convinced MacArthur to agree that the carrier forces would operate in distant support of Leyte and remain free to pursue the enemy. Close cover of the landing beaches would be provided by the escort carriers loaned to Kinkaid's Seventh Fleet. Halsey wanted a passage opened through Surigao Strait to allow him to strike Japanese forces if they were sighted in the South China Sea. Nimitz felt this was a step too far; he forbade Halsey to transit the strait without express permission.[12]

Additional details of the Leyte operation were worked out in conferences between Sherman and MacArthur's planners. The basic outline was straightforward; Nimitz loaned the XXIV Corps—the 7th, 77th, and 96th Infantry Divisions—and his amphibious forces to MacArthur and Kinkaid's Seventh Fleet. Kinkaid would transport Lt. Gen. Walter Krueger's Sixth Army, with the XXIV Corps and the X Corps—the 1st Cavalry Division and 24th and 32nd Infantry Divisions—to Leyte where they would occupy the island and establish airfields for Kenney's Southwest Pacific Air Forces. The Seventh Air Force, operating from Angaur, would neutralize Japanese bases in southern Luzon. Kenney's Fifth and Thirteenth Air Forces would neutralize Mindanao. MacArthur expected to rapidly transfer his land-based planes to Leyte and keep moving forward.[13]

The operation began with Halsey's carrier strike on the Ryukyus on 10 October. The attacks caught Toyoda in Formosa, on his way back from an inspection trip to the Philippines. He recognized Halsey's attacks as the precursor to a major operation. His staff did as well; Toyoda's chief of staff, Rear Admiral Kusaka Ryunosuke ordered the Sixth Base Air Force "to attack and destroy the enemy." He also issued preparatory orders for Sho-1 and Sho-2, anticipating an assault against the Philippines or Formosa.[14]

Halsey refueled on the 11th before initiating a three-day effort to knock out Japanese air strength on Formosa. Almost fourteen hundred sorties were flown by TF 38 on 12 October. Vice Admiral Fukudome, now commanding the Sixth Base Air Force, expressed his frustration with the "indomitable enemy formation."[15] On the 13th, Mitscher's pilots flew almost one thousand sorties. That evening, the Japanese hit cruiser *Canberra* with a torpedo; carrier *Franklin* barely avoided another. The following day, Halsey made just one strike as he prepared to withdraw. The B-29s of the XX Bomber Command covered his retirement with an attack that "pulverized" Takao.[16]

The strikes on Formosa cost the Japanese some five hundred aircraft. Yet, they claimed to have sunk ten American carriers, two battleships, three cruisers, and a destroyer in exchange. Toyoda hoped he was on the verge of a great victory. He ordered Vice Admiral Shima Kiyohide's Second Diversionary Attack Force to "annihilate" the enemy remnants. JICPOA intercepted these instructions and Nimitz informed Halsey of the opportunity. Halsey used the damaged *Canberra*—and cruiser *Houston* after she was also torpedoed—as bait and disposed his forces for fleet action. He told Kinkaid that "until further notice" he would not be able to support Leyte.[17]

Nimitz tried to locate Japanese fleet units. He arranged his submarines to intercept enemy forces approaching Halsey from the north; he asked the Twentieth Air Force to make a maximum effort against Formosa; he had searches flown over the South China Sea to locate the First Diversionary Attack Force if it sortied. However, the opportunity for a fleet action passed when Shima, after being attacked by Mitscher's carrier planes on 16 October, concluded that it was best to withdraw.[18]

**THE BATTLE OF LEYTE GULF**

The amphibious operation at Leyte began according to plan, and on 20 October, MacArthur reported that "all landings . . . were made on schedule and with extremely light losses."[19] That same day, Nimitz estimated that the IJN had two main ship concentrations, one in Japan and one at Singapore, and told Halsey that they would sortie in force. Nimitz's intelligence was incorrect regarding the specific composition of these forces, but his assessment that they were about to move was accurate. By the time he alerted Halsey, the

IJN was already at sea. Prompted by Kinkaid's preliminary landings on the islands at the entrance to Leyte Gulf, Kusaka issued the order for Sho-1 on 18 October. Vice Admiral Kurita Takeo's First Diversionary Attack Force headed to Brunei Bay, Shima's Second Diversionary Attack Force moved south, and Vice Admiral Ozawa's Mobile Force departed Japan.[20]

The details of the ensuing Battle of Leyte Gulf have been thoroughly examined elsewhere; a summary will highlight the most relevant details for Nimitz's command decisions. As Kurita's First Diversionary Attack Force approached the Philippines, it was located and attacked by submarines *Dace* and *Darter* on 23 October. Halsey, who had sent two of his task groups to Ulithi to rearm, recalled TG 38.4 and arranged it, along with TG 38.2 and TG 38.3, east of the Philippines to search for and attack approaching enemy forces. They sighted Kurita's forces the next day. Kurita was executing Sho-1's pincer movement and had separated into a "Southern Force" and "Center Force." Halsey's planes attacked them both. Since the Center Force transiting the Sibuyan Sea was the greater threat, Halsey concentrated his groups against it, left the Southern Force to Kinkaid, and recalled TG 38.1. Kinkaid had Rear Adm. Jesse B. Oldendorf ambush the Southern Force that night in the Battle of Surigao Strait. In the meantime, Halsey's planes forced Kurita's Center Force to turn back before it could exit San Bernardino Strait. Assuming the threat from that direction had been eliminated, Halsey set off that evening to pursue a third enemy force newly sighted that afternoon. This "Northern Force" was Ozawa's Mobile Force, Toyoda's decoy. Halsey took the entire Third Fleet north, leaving the northern flank of Leyte Gulf unguarded. During the night, Kurita reversed course again, exited San Bernardino Strait, and appeared off Samar the next morning. He fought with Kinkaid's escort carrier task units while Halsey struck Ozawa off Cape Engaño. When the desperate plight of the escort carriers became apparent, Halsey divided his forces and sent major units south, but before they could arrive off Samar, Kurita withdrew, bringing the battle to an end.[21]

Leyte Gulf was the opportunity Nimitz had been seeking; the IJN came out in force prepared to give battle. Halsey and Kinkaid won a significant victory, but had Halsey made more effective use of available information, that victory might have been overwhelming. His first mistake was assuming—despite

Nimitz's warning that the IJN was going to sortie in force—the Japanese would not fight for the Philippines. In Halsey's instructions for Stalemate, he had explained that they were "most likely to employ hit and run tactics" and were "not likely to close for decisive surface action" unless aerial attacks had damaged his forces. After the Japanese refused to seek battle off Formosa, Halsey's faith in these assumptions was reinforced. He did not believe the IJN would risk major fleet units. Instead, Halsey felt the greatest threat to the Leyte operation would be nocturnal resupply and interdiction missions like those in the Solomons during 1942 and 1943. This belief kept him focused on future offensive action, like Hotfoot, rather than the battle developing around him.[22]

On 21 October, Halsey revealed his assumptions in a message suggesting that he would take the Third Fleet through the Philippines to seek out and attack Japanese ships in the South China Sea. Nimitz was "alarmed" at the prospect. He told Halsey to remain in position to cover MacArthur and Kinkaid and not move through the Philippines "without orders from me." MacArthur concurred. King even asked Halsey to clarify his intentions. Halsey said he was looking for ways to achieve his primary mission: to "destroy enemy naval and air forces" and to seek an opportunity to defeat a "major portion of the enemy fleet."[23]

Halsey failed to realize that opportunity was coming to him. As late as 23 October, after the First Diversionary Attack Force had been sighted approaching the Philippines, Halsey still did not appreciate a major battle was looming. He recalled TG 38.4 but allowed his other carrier group to continue to Ulithi.[24] By this time, Kinkaid, who had also initially assumed the Japanese were unlikely to seek battle, had revised his views. There was "a possibility," he said, "of a raid in force" on Leyte Gulf. Kinkaid was preparing for major action. Halsey remained wedded to his existing assumption that the Japanese would not seek battle.[25]

Once it became clear that the IJN had committed to battle, Halsey remained fixated on his battle plan and failed to adapt it to developing circumstances. He planned to concentrate the entire Third Fleet, "seek the enemy[,] and attempt to bring about a decisive engagement."[26] However, the Japanese were once again operating in multiple formations. Between the Center Force and the Southern Force, the Center Force was obviously the greater threat, so it made sense when Halsey concentrated against it and left the Southern Force to Kinkaid. However, once the Northern Force appeared, Halsey had to choose whether to concentrate against it or to divide and engage both the Center Force and Northern Force. He followed his battle plan and concentrated; he does not appear to have seriously entertained the possibility of two separate actions.

Yet, the evidence suggests it would have led to a better outcome. Nimitz assumed Halsey was seeking separate actions and his subordinates argued for it. When Halsey issued a preparatory order to form Vice Admiral Lee's battle line, TF 34, on the afternoon of 24 October, Nimitz interpreted it to mean that Halsey had detached Lee from the carriers and left him to guard the exit to San Bernardino Strait. Kinkaid thought the same. But Halsey had not done so. After he issued his order to concentrate the carrier groups and head north that evening, a sighting report was received indicating the Center Force had turned around and was heading for Leyte Gulf once more. Rear Adm. Gerald F. Bogan started working on a plan to send TG 38.3 and TG 38.4 north while TG 38.2 and TF 34 guarded the strait, but he abandoned it after receiving a curt dismissal from Halsey's staff. Lee was convinced the Northern Force was a decoy and Kurita's Center Force was the real threat. He explained this to Halsey before they headed north. After the Center Force was seen heading east, Lee sent another message; neither triggered any action. Mitscher, like Nimitz and Kinkaid, assumed that Halsey's orders would lead to two separate engagements, one with TF 34 off San Bernardino Strait and another with the remaining forces of TF 38 farther north. Once Mitscher's chief of staff, Commodore Burke, realized that this was not the case, he woke Mitscher and urged him to press Halsey to pursue an alternative. Mitscher, having been overruled by Spruance at Philippine Sea, was reluctant to speak up again. He told Burke, "If he [Halsey] wants my advice, he'll ask for it."[27]

Halsey and his staff failed to entertain these viable alternatives. Unlike when he commanded from shore, at sea on board battleship *New Jersey*, Halsey devoted insufficient attention to his role as a fleet commander and became overly focused on tactical outcomes. He failed to develop a command system that could consistently and reliably use the initiative of his subordinates to translate his will into action. Halsey's close-knit staff rejected alternative ideas and allowed him to ignore unanticipated information. While his superiors and subordinates identified alternative courses of action that would have led to better outcomes, Halsey and his staff dismissed them.[28]

This challenge was not lost on Nimitz. When Kinkaid signaled on the morning of 25 October that fast battleships were "urgently needed" at Leyte Gulf, Nimitz took the unusual step of asking Halsey, "Where is TF 34?" To make enemy decryption more complicated, brief messages like this received "padding," nonsense phrases at the start and end of the transmission. Padding was separated from the message by double letters and "should" have been deleted after decryption. However, on board Halsey's flagship *New Jersey*, the padding at the end of the message was not removed. The message given to Halsey read, "Where is Task Force Thirty-Four RR the World Wonders." He assumed the padding after "RR" was part of the message and that Nimitz was not just asking for the location of Lee's surface action group, but implying it was in the wrong place. Halsey was livid. It took him over an hour to calm himself sufficiently to respond and head south to assist Kinkaid.[29]

After the battle, Halsey summarized his perspective to prevent "misunderstanding." He justified his pursuit of the Northern Force by invoking Spruance's tactics at Philippine Sea and arguing that it would have been "childish" to keep his force off San Bernardino Strait where enemy carrier planes could attack it with impunity. Halsey never seriously considered dividing his forces. Nimitz assessed the battle differently; in a letter to King, he confessed that it "never occurred" to him that Halsey would leave San Bernardino Strait unguarded, a clear example of Nimitz's failure to achieve sufficient shared understanding with his Third Fleet commander. Nimitz regretted that Halsey did not leave the fast battleships off Samar, where they could have engaged Kurita's forces. However, a significant victory had been won; "practically every major combatant enemy ship was either sunk or damaged" at Leyte Gulf. Nimitz issued an official communiqué on 29 October that claimed, "[T]he Japanese Fleet has been decisively defeated."[30]

## THE FIGHT FOR LEYTE

Despite the failure of the IJN to achieve its objectives, the Japanese resolved to fight a "decisive battle" on Leyte, giving Nimitz and MacArthur the opportunity to wage an attritional struggle that—much as Nimitz had anticipated—maximized the potential of their combined naval and air forces. However, increasing Japanese resistance disrupted Nimitz's aggressive timeline. Suicidal kamikaze attacks improved Japanese efforts to contest fleet and amphibious operations, Japanese reinforcements delayed MacArthur's ability to secure Leyte, and steady rains fouled the newly captured airfields and kept them from becoming fully operational. Halsey was forced to keep the carriers within supporting distance of the Philippines to ensure victory at Leyte.

In an effort the War Department called "extraordinary," the Japanese flew hundreds of planes to the Philippines and "virtually recovered control of the air." These planes made repeated attacks on Kinkaid's forces. Escort carriers, destroyers, merchant ships, and auxiliaries were hit by conventional and suicide attacks. Japanese bombs left the airfield at Tacloban a "cratered mess." The undeveloped state of Leyte's airfields exacerbated the situation. Sherman inspected them and reported on 4 November that, except for Tacloban, they were "disappointing." It would take at least two weeks longer than anticipated to get them into operation. Halsey's carriers would have to shoulder the burden in the meantime. MacArthur's subordinates—Sutherland, Kenney, and Kinkaid—believed a delay in the assault on Luzon was "inevitable."[31]

In concert with this aerial offensive, the IJA steadily reinforced Leyte. The newly appointed commander of the Fourteenth Area Army, Lieutenant General Yamashita Tomoyuki, had planned to anchor his defense on Luzon, but inflated claims of success by the IJN led Yamashita's superiors to conclude that the U.S. troops on Leyte were largely isolated and ripe for annihilation. Seven Japanese divisions were sent to Leyte in a series of convoys through Ormoc Bay. JICPOA alerted Nimitz to this effort by 1 November, but MacArthur's intelligence chief, Maj. Gen. Charles A. Willoughby, thought the Japanese were evacuating. He did not believe they would fight for the island. MacArthur reflected Willoughby's assessment by suggesting the operation was almost over on 2 November. His confidence was misplaced. A lengthy struggle ensued as Krueger's Sixth Army fought their way to Ormoc.[32]

As Halsey's carriers fought for aerial superiority, a series of attacks in late October damaged carriers *Intrepid* and *Franklin*; light carrier *Belleau Wood* was also hit. Halsey withdrew TF 38 to Ulithi to regroup and reorganize. Nimitz had McCain—who had been learning on the job as commander of TG 38.1—relieve Mitscher so that he could rest and plan upcoming operations with Spruance. Halsey returned to the Philippines and executed operation "pulverize," intended to overwhelm Japanese airpower on Luzon. He destroyed many planes, but in exchange carrier *Lexington* was struck by a kamikaze. Halsey recommended using the fast carriers to support MacArthur and attrit their forces. Nimitz agreed with Halsey's assessment but stressed the importance of keeping the carriers "in [a] state of material readiness, not only for current operations, but to carry on throughout the war." No new carriers would join the fleet before February 1945. In the meantime, Halsey had to preserve what he had. Nimitz deferred Hotfoot "indefinitely" to allow the carriers to remain in the Philippines.[33]

Plans for other operations were also at risk. MacArthur insisted that the enemy's "strong fight" for the Philippines necessitated an "immediate attack" on Luzon; he wanted to keep the target dates of 5 December for Mindoro and 20 December for Lingayen Gulf. Nimitz supported attacking "as soon as possible" but the carriers needed "at least ten days and preferably two weeks" between operations to rest and reprovision. The strength of enemy opposition and delays getting the Leyte airfields operational meant the carriers had been operating "almost without interruption for an unduly long period." They needed an "extended period of upkeep and rest." Even if Nimitz and MacArthur held to the dates for Mindoro and Luzon, future operations would have to be delayed. Nimitz requested approval to postpone Detachment and Iceberg by two weeks. King approved; the new dates were 3 February and 15 March, respectively.[34]

As Halsey continued to aggressively attack, the stress of the high operational tempo led to friction with Nimitz. Nimitz reminded Halsey of the importance of "adequate time" for rest and regular maintenance.[35] On 20 November, Halsey once more suggested taking the Third Fleet through the Philippines and asked for proactive approval to transit Luzon Straits and attack enemy naval forces in the China Sea. Nimitz refused. The risk was too great; seizing Mindoro was necessary to control that route through the Philippines and, by passing into the China Sea, Halsey would make rest and reprovisioning at

Ulithi even more difficult. Nimitz repeated his "insistence on a preparatory period for upkeep, replenishment, rest, and reorganization" and told Halsey to not make any commitments regarding Mindoro without his approval.[36]

On 24 November, Halsey ignored these instructions and issued his operation order for Mindoro, committing TF 38 to support MacArthur's assault. At the time, Nimitz was in conference with King at San Francisco; the two had discussed Halsey's situation and agreed changes to his staff were necessary. Perhaps prompted by that discussion, Nimitz responded with an uncharacteristically stern admonishment; he told Halsey that he was providing insufficient time for his forces at anchor. Nimitz ordered him to "immediately reduce [the] carrier groups operating against the Philippines to two" and keep the other two in reserve until the Mindoro operation. Nimitz showed his frustration and displeasure by demanding an explicit acknowledgment of these instructions. King threw his weight behind them by immediately concurring. Both were unaware that Halsey had already started rotating his carrier groups; the day before he had issued instructions to keep two at sea and two at Ulithi.[37]

When Halsey replied to Nimitz, he finally and explicitly recognized the implications of his sustained operations. Because the current schedule would provide only three days of rest between the Mindoro and Luzon operations, Halsey recommended delaying Luzon to give the carriers fifteen consecutive days "without commitment." Recent damage to his carriers made this rest period even more essential.[38]

In the meantime, as Nimitz's staff summary noted, "[T]he land action on Leyte has apparently turned in our favor." The 32nd Infantry Division had broken through enemy defenses and the 11th Airborne Division had landed, relieving the 7th Infantry Division. MacArthur reported that enemy opposition was "steadily decreasing" and he moved his headquarters to the island. Soon thereafter, Kinkaid made an amphibious landing in Ormoc Bay, cutting off the Japanese from reinforcement.[39]

Leyte triggered the attritional struggle Nimitz anticipated, but the pace of operations and ferocity of the Japanese response overtaxed his striking forces. Although it was clear that Krueger and Kinkaid would soon seize control of the island, Halsey—by focusing on tactical success—had lost sight of the broader context of the campaign. If he continued to maintain his operational tempo, the assaults on Iwo Jima and Okinawa might be delayed further. This concern was foremost in Nimitz's mind as he and MacArthur prepared for the next phase of operations in the Philippines, the advances to Mindoro and Luzon.

## JOINT LOGISTICS

Success at Leyte and in the operations that followed would not have been possible without an effective joint logistical approach. According to the Army's history of World War II logistics and strategy, "[I]n the Central Pacific joint logistics reached their highest point of development." Nimitz achieved this by effectively balancing centralized planning and decentralized execution, an approach that reflected his style of command. Nimitz maintained the existing—and separate—logistical and procurement systems for the Army and Navy but ensured a unified approach to logistics within his theater. His staff at Pearl Harbor managed logistic arrangements with each service and "exercised general supervision" of the entire effort, allowing commanders within the theater to focus on the specific needs of their operations.[40]

Major offensive operations were divided into three phases: the assault, the land operation, and garrison duty. Brigadier General Leavey's logistics section developed a system of "automatic supply" that anticipated the needs of each phase and proactively sent the necessary material forward. Specific requirements were derived through consultation with service representatives. Control points were established in rear areas, first at Eniwetok and later at Saipan, where shipping could be held if operations proceeded more slowly than anticipated, preventing any buildup in the operating area. There was waste in the system—the POA was considered "far too generous" in its allocation of supplies—but the extra capacity was deliberate. It provided economies in other, more crucial, areas. When it came to shipping, for example, the Central Pacific was extremely efficient. Turnaround times were short and congestion largely absent. Spare capacity was also essential to sustaining the rapid pace of the offensive. Leavey's system provided enough slack to effectively couple the complex, unpredictable nature of offensive operations with the systematic planning required for efficient movement of supplies and other vital resources.[41]

MacArthur, in contrast, relied on "centralized planning and direction at the top." He did not establish unified and coherent requirements across his theater. The result was poor coordination and extreme inefficiency, especially with shipping. MacArthur had not "appreciated the lessons" of the Guadalcanal campaign, so the backlog of shipping that developed at Noumea in the fall of 1942 was consistently replicated as MacArthur advanced. It followed him to Milne Bay, Finschhafen, and Hollandia. When he moved to Leyte, a backlog developed there. On 5 December 1944, there were 221 vessels in the harbor, on their way there, or waiting to begin their move to the island. The "critical shipping situation" confronting the Allies in the fall of 1944 was exacerbated by two major factors: the shortage of port facilities in Europe and MacArthur's command.[42]

To solve these problems, the JCS issued a new directive on 9 December based on the Joint Military Transportation Committee's recommendations. The JCS pointed to the "inability of the theaters to discharge and release ships promptly" as the major issue, and therefore, prohibited "the use of ocean-going ships for storage," ordered that shipping schedules factor in port unloading capacity, forbade the partial unloading of ships, and recommended the designation of "a single theater agency for the control of shipping." In January 1945, the JCS added a penalty; any ships held in theater for more than thirty days would count against established quotas. These steps helped ameliorate the crisis.[43]

Another crisis was brewing with service troops. As South Pacific bases were shut down, MacArthur expected to receive the service troops that came available. However, because there was no major Central Pacific base, Nimitz was using the South Pacific as a staging area and needed those service troops to support his efforts. If MacArthur could create staging areas in the Philippines for Nimitz, he could transfer the South Pacific service troops to MacArthur. Forrest Sherman and Leavey visited Hollandia in early November to work out the details.[44]

The result was the FILBAS (Philippine basing) Agreement, which "temporarily" resolved the controversy and established the Philippines as the "main base for the final campaign against Japan." Under its terms, MacArthur agreed to provide support for the XXIV Corps during the Leyte operation and then handle its rehabilitation and staging for Okinawa. MacArthur's command would also establish staging facilities for three additional POA corps—nine divisions—and bases for the Pacific Fleet. All facilities were expected to be ready by May 1945. In exchange, Nimitz would transfer control of Army service units in the South Pacific. The JCS approved FILBAS on 5 December.[45]

In the meantime, Nimitz's team created a new organization to give the carrier striking forces sustained operational capability. Up to this point, they had operated in distinct pulses, after which they withdrew for rearmament and replenishment. In October 1944, Vice Admiral Calhoun sought to change this by introducing a "fully mobile logistic support organization" that could replenish and rearm the fleet in the combat zone. Existing service squadrons operated from advanced bases or brought easily transferrable supplies, like fuel and aircraft, to the fleet. Calhoun envisioned a new organization—SevRon 6—that would become part of the fleet and provide all the "fuel, food, ammunition, airplanes," and other necessary supplies while "*at sea*." Spruance immediately recognized the potential; he felt SevRon 6 would be "essential" for upcoming operations like the assault on Okinawa. Nimitz agreed. When he discussed the concept with King in November, they selected Rear Adm. Donald B. Beary to command the new squadron. It was officially established on 5 December 1944.[46]

The establishment of SevRon 6 made underway supply and replenishment an integral part of fleet operations and dramatically increased its ability to sustain operations.[47] At the same time, the new squadron also enhanced the fleet's adaptability. By becoming part of the fleet, the squadron was an interface that abstracted fleet organization and the specific requirements of logistical delivery from underlying support structures in the rear areas. As the fleet organization changed, SevRon 6 could change with it. The carefully crafted logistical systems outside of the combat zone would be unaffected.[48]

## MINDORO AND LUZON

With Leyte secure, MacArthur sought to quickly advance to Mindoro and then Luzon. He steadily increased his air strength, but delays in achieving aerial superiority meant that Halsey's carriers would have to support the Mindoro assault. The plan called for Kinkaid's escort carriers to provide close cover of the amphibious forces while Halsey suppressed Japanese airfields on Luzon before, during, and immediately after the landings. MacArthur also wanted Halsey to remain on call for several days, ready to strike emergency targets.[49]

In the meantime, on 21 November 1944, Nimitz issued his operation plan for supporting the assault on Luzon. It recognized that IJN surface forces were now less of a threat and tried to keep Halsey's aggressive tendencies in check by eliminating the language that made destruction of the enemy fleet a primary task. After exchanging messages about the Luzon operation with Nimitz, Halsey suggested to MacArthur that the assault be delayed by ten days to allow the carrier forces more time to rest between Mindoro and Luzon. Halsey wanted his pilots fresh for the challenge of cutting Luzon off from Formosa and the Ryukyus and then neutralizing enemy airpower on Luzon itself.[50]

Nimitz did not think Halsey's request went far enough. He asked MacArthur to delay the Mindoro operation to give the carriers time to rest and allow shore-based planes to be "established in strength." The Third Fleet was dominant in the Philippine Sea, Nimitz explained, and "enemy naval forces" were "incapable of interfering effectively" with Leyte or the Mindoro operation. The danger was "severe attacks from enemy aircraft." The Japanese were "capable of operating [planes] effectively from Luzon, the Visayas, and from Mindoro." The fast carriers could suppress them, but the "unprecedented" need to cover Leyte for so long meant that more time was needed "for rest, upkeep, and logistic replenishment." MacArthur agreed. On 30 November, he revised the dates for Mindoro and Luzon to 15 December and 9 January, respectively.[51]

Nimitz immediately told King that Detachment and Iceberg would have to be pushed back as well to allow the carriers to recuperate after Luzon. Nimitz recommended new dates of 19 February for Iwo Jima and 1 April for Okinawa. King and the JCS approved. The determined effort to contest the invasion of the Philippines had bought the Japanese a month of additional preparation.[52]

Nimitz authorized the Third Fleet's support of Mindoro on 7 December. He was concerned because he did not feel MacArthur's planes had "sufficient strength . . . to ensure safe passage of Kinkaid's Expeditionary Force from Leyte to Mindoro." Nimitz told Halsey he would have to make up the difference. Halsey's assessment was similar. To minimize the kamikaze threat, he and McCain planned to use their increased fighter strength to maintain a "continuous day and night" combat air patrol over enemy airfields on Luzon. Nimitz was also apprehensive that Halsey might chase Japanese surface forces into the China Sea; he ordered him not to do so without specific authorization or "unless in hot pursuit" of valuable enemy units.[53]

The combat air patrol over Luzon—called the "big blue blanket"—worked "perfectly."[54] Starting on 14 December, the day before the landings, and continuing for the next two, it kept the threat to Kinkaid's assault forces to a minimum. They were still subjected to attacks, but most came from airfields on islands to the south. Aside from a few kamikaze strikes, the assault was largely unmolested. Unloading was smooth and the assault shipping departed twenty-four hours ahead of schedule.

Halsey withdrew to fuel while MacArthur prepared a reinforcement convoy. To cover it, he requested additional strikes on 19 December. Halsey tried to deliver them, but a typhoon overwhelmed his fleet. Task groups encountered "mountainous" seas and wind gusts over one hundred knots. Three destroyers capsized. Three light carriers—*Monterey*, *Cowpens*, and *San Jacinto*—were damaged. *Monterey* had to be sent to the West Coast; the others were repaired at Ulithi by SevRon 10. Halsey gathered his ships and tried to strike Luzon on 21 December, but the typhoon arrived ahead of him and rendered air operations impossible; he retired to Ulithi.[55]

On 19 December, Nimitz was promoted to Fleet Admiral. For Christmas, he visited Ulithi, and after observing the damage, Nimitz called the typhoon "the greatest uncompensated loss" the Navy had suffered since the Battle of Savo Island. A court of inquiry found Halsey responsible for "errors in judgement" due to "stress of war operations and . . . a commendable desire to meet military requirements."[56] Nimitz provided his own assessment. In February 1945, he summarized his thoughts in a letter to the fleet and stressed that effective command was a collaborative activity anchored in personal initiative; all levels of command had a duty to look out for the safety of their ships and sailors. Individual commanding officers were responsible for their ships, but each senior officer had "to think in terms of the smallest ships and most inexperienced commanding officer under him." Personal judgment was essential, because "in bad weather, as in most other situations, safety and fatal hazard are not separated by any sharp boundary line, but shade gradually from one into the other." The risk of a gradual slide into danger meant that proactive preparation was essential. Nimitz's implication was that Halsey had cut the line too fine.[57]

In the meantime, Lockwood's submarines had mitigated the threat of Japanese striking forces and helped isolate the Philippines. They sank a battleship and two carriers and damaged a third carrier in late November and early December. Despite these successes, the remnants of the Second Diversionary Attack Force bombarded the Mindoro beachhead the night of 26 December. Kinkaid's surface action group did not arrive in time to stop it, but aerial attacks and a PT-boat torpedo sank destroyer *Kiyoshimo*. The rest of the force retired, apparently to Camranh Bay.[58]

After visiting Leyte to confer with MacArthur and finalize preparations for Luzon, Nimitz returned to Ulithi. There, on 28 December, he discussed the situation with Halsey; an enemy force with battleships and "one or more carriers" was expected to be in the South China Sea during the Luzon operation. Nimitz explained that destroying this force would "effectively accomplish the covering and *supporting* task assigned the Third Fleet," so he ordered Halsey to enter the South China Sea and attack these Japanese ships after the amphibious assault. Once they had been destroyed, Halsey was to withdraw "expeditiously" and return to a position east of the Philippines.[59]

Halsey and McCain sortied on 30 December and initiated their next series of strikes by attacking Formosa on 3 January. Poor weather cancelled flights that afternoon as well as those planned for the following day. Skies were clearer over the Philippines. The first of Kinkaid's groups—Oldendorf's bombardment and covering forces—were attacked by kamikazes as they transited the Sulu Sea. Two escort carriers, two battleships, and two cruisers were hit, along with several destroyers and other small ships. Oldendorf felt his escort carriers were "entirely inadequate" and that he needed "considerably more air support." Kinkaid asked Halsey for additional raids on Luzon and the Lingayen area.[60]

After fueling on 5 January 1945, Halsey tried to employ "blanket" tactics on the 6th, but poor weather allowed Japanese planes to slip through TF 38's patrols. When the weather cleared the next day, McCain's coverage of Japanese airfields was much more effective, but on 8 January, TF 38 had to fuel once more and additional kamikazes got through. By that time, Kinkaid's second group—the amphibious assault forces—was in range. Two more escort carriers and an attack transport were hit.[61]

Nimitz was concerned and once more sought to bring Halsey's behavior into line with his expectations. Nimitz wanted Halsey to operate at the appropriate level for a fleet commander, take responsibility for managing "requests for major changes in employment of [the] fast carrier task forces," and provide specific recommendations. Nimitz asked Halsey to assess whether the shore-based air forces and escort carriers could protect the amphibious forces. Halsey recommended more strikes on Formosa to prevent Japanese planes from reaching Luzon; MacArthur agreed. Nimitz was gratified, approved Halsey's plans, and told him to seize "any favorable opportunity to destroy enemy heavy ships." TF 38 struck Formosa on 9 January. Kinkaid's amphibious forces landed the Sixth Army on Luzon the same day. By that point, the Japanese had too few planes on Luzon to make effective attacks.[62]

With his obligations to MacArthur fulfilled, Halsey passed through Luzon Strait and entered the China Sea, intent on destroying the enemy thought to be at Camranh Bay. He launched a predawn search of the area on 12 January and pushed a fast battleship force ahead to sink Japanese ships that attempted to flee, but the major targets—battleship carriers *Ise* and *Hyuga*—had left for Lingga Roads, south of Singapore. Halsey and McCain attacked coastal shipping instead, sinking forty-four ships totaling more than 132,000 tons and temporarily severing Japanese supply routes.[63]

Kinkaid feared that the remaining Japanese surface forces at Singapore and in Japan could combine and attack his ships in Lingayen Gulf. Nimitz and King discussed how best to position TF 38 to counter any potential threat. King suggested placing the Third Fleet west of Luzon Strait; there, it could counter any approaching Japanese force, whether it came from the north or the south. Nimitz ordered Halsey to arrange his forces accordingly.[64] Halsey, fueling west of Luzon, was already there.

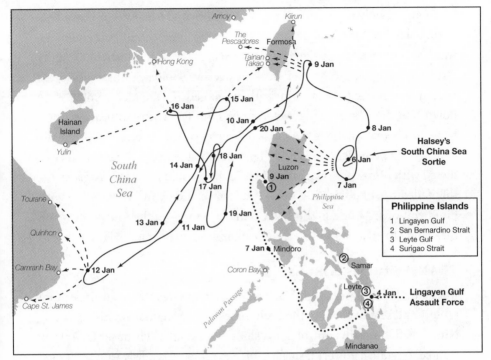

MAP 7. Philippine Operations of January 1945 and Admiral Halsey's Sortie into the South China Sea

After attacking southern Formosa, Hong Kong, and Hainan, Halsey assessed that further operations in the China Sea would not be worthwhile. He proposed to move east of the Formosa-Luzon line. From there, he could cover Lingayen Gulf, attack Okinawa, and conduct photoreconnaissance for Iceberg. Nimitz approved and convinced King that the increasing "enemy air strength in Formosa and Okinawa" ought to become the primary target, not Japanese fleet units. Halsey transited Luzon Strait the night of 20–21 January and prepared to strike Formosa the next day. The attack left airdromes and industrial areas of Takao "burning furiously." In exchange, carriers *Ticonderoga* and *Hancock* and light carrier *Langley* were damaged.[65] On 22 January, Halsey attacked Okinawa and took photographs of the island.

Though steady progress was made on Luzon and MacArthur moved his headquarters to Manila, fighting on the island continued until the end of the war. The prolonged campaign revealed the Japanese commitment to a lengthy attritional struggle. Rather than seeking decisive combat, Yamashita's forces tried to maximize U.S. casualties. They succeeded; extended combat wore down Krueger's formations. MacArthur's limited ability to process intelligence information made the situation worse. He interpreted developments through his preconceptions and "ignored intelligence estimates that conflicted with his operational plan." MacArthur would not allow assessments that failed to align with his "self-styled sense of destiny" to interfere with his operations. Although this had occurred before—at the Admiralties and Biak—on Luzon it had a more significant impact on operational timetables.[66]

## TRANSFERRING FORCES

By combining his forces with MacArthur's, Nimitz was able to advance more rapidly and secure bases in the Philippines. However, to meet his schedule, Nimitz had to regain control of his ships and assault divisions. MacArthur wanted to retain a powerful surface force to protect his newly won positions; Nimitz had to negotiate with him to get his old battleships back. The situation with combat troops was more straightforward, but it was comingled with service troops. The FILBAS Agreement had set the stage for MacArthur to rehabilitate Nimitz's XXIV Corps and provide a staging area for POA forces, but those careful arrangements began to fall apart because of the shortage of service troops in the Pacific.

The XXIV Corps was crucial to Nimitz's plans for Iceberg, especially after the 86th and 97th Infantry Divisions were sent to Europe instead of POA. On 6 January, Nimitz asked when XXIV Corps could be relieved from combat operations and start to recuperate. MacArthur responded that the corps and its component divisions—the 7th, 77th, and 96th—would be out of combat by early February. That was not soon enough; after conferring with Richardson, Buckner, and Hodge, Nimitz sent a lengthy dispatch to MacArthur asking him to free the entire corps from any duties and transfer it to Buckner's Tenth Army. Buckner expected the transfer to be delayed and postpone Iceberg. Spruance noted that, because of the close timing of

Iceberg and Detachment, "any delay" would also impact Iwo Jima. That was unacceptable. Nimitz stuck to the dates and ensured that the XXIV Corps was ready. However, because of delays receiving replacements, it would be short by about three thousand men. Richardson asked MacArthur to make up the difference.[67]

The shortage of Army service troops was impossible to resolve. As early as November 1944, Nimitz had recognized the issue; the shortfall for Iceberg was expected to be more than 20,000. He prioritized "the prosecution of the war in forward areas" and stripped rear areas of infrastructure support. Under FILBAS, Nimitz would transfer Army service troops from the South Pacific to MacArthur in exchange for staging areas for three corps of assault troops. Japanese resistance kept MacArthur from establishing the necessary facilities in time and Nimitz refused to divert his resources from "the momentum of the Central Pacific Campaign." As the FILBAS Agreement broke down, Nimitz relied on his own logistical infrastructure to continue the advance and insisted on keeping the service troops necessary to support it.[68]

Nimitz needed the Pacific Fleet's old battleships for gunfire support off Iwo Jima and expected them to be released ten days after the Lingayen landings, but MacArthur wanted to keep them to protect the Lingayen beachhead. Nimitz agreed that it was necessary to cover Lingayen until the "enemy units which threaten it are destroyed" or shore-based planes were established in force on Luzon. Nimitz hoped Halsey's sortie into the South China Sea would remove the threat; when it did not, he proposed a compromise. Four old battleships would remain with Kinkaid and protect Lingayen from IJN forces at Singapore. Nimitz would augment his Iwo Jima bombardment with the modern fast battleships. Spruance's strikes on Japan before Detachment would prevent any Japanese forces in the Empire from threatening MacArthur. Together, these steps would "ensure" the safety of Lingayen and allow Detachment to occur "close to [the] scheduled date." King approved, but MacArthur did not. He felt that four battleships were insufficient and requested six.[69]

In response, Nimitz argued that maintaining a force in the Philippines "capable of meeting all the heavy ships left in the Japanese fleet" would prevent major offensive operations in the Pacific indefinitely. The best way to protect the Philippines was "to proceed with offensive operations against Japan." Halsey agreed and told MacArthur that it was important to advance quickly because the Japanese were strengthening their defenses in the Ryukyus. After these explanations and Nimitz's offer of two heavy cruisers instead of two battleships, MacArthur was satisfied. He released the battleships in early February.[70]

## ADVANCED CINCPAC-CINCPOA HEADQUARTERS

Nimitz felt it was important to move his headquarters forward, to put him closer to the Pacific Fleet's operational area and allow him to oversee upcoming amphibious operations. Nimitz identified Guam as the best location for an advanced headquarters and planning for the move began in August 1944. He and key members of his staff arrived there on 17 January 1945 and established the CINCPAC-CINCPOA Advanced Operating Headquarters.[71]

The way Nimitz divided his staff between administrative and operational functions made the move easier. Towers, ever the capable administrator, remained at the official headquarters at Pearl Harbor to oversee the administrative and logistical work. Nimitz and those portions of the staff focused on plans, and operations moved to the advanced headquarters. Some functions—intelligence, communications, and personnel—were divided between both locations. This created some challenges; the division of intelligence work, for example, meant JICPOA had to transfer analysts to a new organization, the Advanced Intelligence Center (AIC), at Guam. When the transfer occurred, it left JICPOA without enough experienced personnel at a critical time. Preparations for Iwo Jima suffered as a result.[72]

In parallel with the move to the advanced headquarters, Nimitz reorganized part of his staff. In December 1944, the Current Plans Section, with responsibility "for the movement and assignment of . . . forces," shifted from the Plans Division to the Operations Division. This was logical because the work of Current Plans aligned with the mission of the Operations Division, which became the "assignment, training, and movement of all forces." The head of the Operations Division became assistant chief of staff for Operations. Because of Nimitz's habit of conducting operations through, first, the War Plans Section, and then the Plans Division, the Operations Division had never reached its full potential. Now, with Forrest Sherman overseeing both Plans and Operations, Nimitz was comfortable shifting to a more standard approach, one driven less by personalities. At the advanced headquarters, Sherman, McMorris, and Nimitz were the driving force of POA's late-war operations.[73]

## THE BRITISH PACIFIC FLEET

As the challenges associated with applying "unremitting pressure" increased, Nimitz looked for additional ways to sustain his momentum. He followed closely as the Royal Navy's Eastern Fleet began offensive operations in 1944 and the British prepared to enter the Pacific in strength. Their initial efforts concentrated on the Netherlands East Indies and the Malay Barrier. When carrier *Saratoga* was loaned to the British in May 1944, she participated in an attack on Surabaya. In late July, the British struck Sabang off the northern tip of Sumatra. Nimitz recognized that the Royal Navy could augment his own efforts in the Pacific and believed—as he had said during a conference at Noumea in late 1942—"[I]f we can't use our allies, we are G… D… fools."[74]

By the time of the Octagon Conference in September 1944, it was clear that if the Royal Navy was to play a significant role against Japan, it would need to establish a larger presence in the Pacific and cooperate more formally with Nimitz's Pacific Fleet. The CCS agreed that "the British Fleet should participate in the main operations against Japan." King—aware of the logistical challenges involved—insisted that the British Fleet must be "balanced and self-supporting" to keep it from increasing the burden on Nimitz and his logistical infrastructure.[75]

The British anticipated beginning major operations with their Pacific Fleet in January 1945. Admiral Bruce A. Fraser, RN, who had assumed command of the Eastern Fleet in August, was selected to lead the effort. First Sea Lord Admiral Andrew B. Cunningham, RN, suggested that Nimitz and Fraser meet in December to work through detailed arrangements. In preparation, Nimitz and King discussed British participation during their November conference. King emphasized that Fraser's command was administrative and "not operational." Fraser would report to King, who would then issue directives controlling the employment of the British Pacific Fleet. King urged Nimitz to emphasize to

Fraser the importance of keeping the British fleet "self-supporting." Nimitz promised to keep his discussions with Fraser "exploratory" and "make no commitments" beyond those King had already approved.[76]

During their conference, Nimitz and Fraser agreed on command relationships and issued a memorandum of understanding. It echoed Nimitz's discussions with King. Fraser would maintain "administrative command" over his forces, but when they operated with the Pacific Fleet, Nimitz would exercise "operational control." The British forces would "operate as a carrier task force under" one of Nimitz's fleet commanders or carrier task force commanders. Fraser agreed to be responsible for his own logistical support and supply but he would be free to use American anchorages. The first combined operation—joining Fraser's and Nimitz's forces together—was expected to be Iceberg.[77]

King insisted that Fraser first report to him before beginning operations with Nimitz. King was very specific that "allocations of his [Fraser's] forces . . . will result from directives issued by me and implemented by you [Nimitz] in the same manner as US Fleet matters are handled." Fraser reported to King for duty on 15 January. Although Nimitz, Fraser, and Spruance had worked through important concepts for British participation in Iceberg, King did not immediately assign Fraser to Nimitz. When Nimitz inquired about it, King responded that he intended to keep "operational allocation of [the] British Pacific Fleet" in his own hands; he wanted Nimitz to officially request the British force and justify the request by including "reasons why you need such units."[78]

On 1 February, Nimitz officially requested the British Pacific Fleet's participation in Iceberg. He explained to King that while the British force was "not absolutely necessary," it would "expedite [the] campaign," allow more "complete neutralization of [the] enemy air force," and reduce losses. Nimitz expected the British to strike Japanese positions in Sakishima Gunto, south of Okinawa. King responded that the British would not be available for the first phase of the operation. Nimitz and Fraser put their plans on hold. Fraser reached out to Nimitz for help, confessing that he found it "a little difficult to understand what is happening." Fraser was trying to plan for Iceberg and bring his fleet into action, but he was uncertain how to do so.[79]

With the operational future of the British Pacific Fleet uncertain, Nimitz worked through basing arrangements. Fraser's fleet, even if it was self-supporting, would need a sheltered anchorage and facilities ashore. Manus, given its proximity to Australia and its size, seemed the best choice. King underappreciated the complexity of coordinating detailed arrangements and delegated them to Nimitz, who worked with MacArthur and Kinkaid. They agreed to allow Fraser to use Manus, but MacArthur was clear that his command accepted "no obligation for additional construction." By the end of February, all uncertainty had been resolved. The British mobile base would be at Manus.[80]

Getting the British to participate in Iceberg was more difficult. Nimitz tried to understand King's position and asked for clarity about how Fraser's ships would be employed. King insisted on reserving the right to determine when and how the British Pacific Fleet would be used. He was unwilling to commit them to Iceberg without a firm decision from the JCS regarding future operations. He expected that decision by the middle of March. When it came, King finally assigned Fraser to Nimitz. Fraser had Vice Admiral Henry Bernard Rawlings, RN, report to Nimitz "for duty in operations connected with Iceberg." Rawlings told Nimitz "with a feeling of great pride and pleasure" that his forces would be ready to sail on 17 March.[81]

## DETACHMENT

While MacArthur's forces continued fighting on Luzon, Nimitz brought his offensive to the threshold of Japan. He issued his operation plan for Detachment on 25 November 1944. Spruance's Fifth Fleet would conduct the operation. Mitscher's fast carriers would raid Japan, isolate Iwo Jima, and destroy Japanese "production facilities." Turner's amphibious force would bring three Marine divisions of Major General Schmidt's V Amphibious Corps to Iwo Jima; the 4th and 5th divisions would make the assault while the 3rd remained in floating reserve. The heavy bombers of the Twentieth Air Force would assist by striking "aircraft, manufacturing, and repair installations" in Japan.[82]

Detachment's initial target date had been 20 January, but by the time Nimitz issued his operation plan, the date had been delayed to 3 February;

it would be delayed once more to 19 February. The extra month allowed Lieutenant General Kuribayashi Tadamichi, charged with the defense of Iwo Jima, to improve his fortifications. He was doing his best to execute the new Japanese strategy. Issued on 20 January 1945, Japan's "Outline of Army and Navy Operations" identified Japan as the location of the final battle. Outlying positions—Iwo Jima, Okinawa, Formosa, Shanghai, and the Korean coast—were key strongpoints. According to the strategy, Kuribayashi's goal was to conduct "an intense war of attrition," shatter enemy morale, and "delay the invasion of the Home Islands." He prepared extensively, creating a network of caves, tunnels, and mutually supporting defensive positions.[83]

Nimitz's analysts underestimated the extent of these preparations. Detailed photographs were not available until late January; once they were, they were examined by relatively inexperienced JICPOA analysts who failed to notice what Kuribayashi had done. The size of his force was also underestimated; initially, only 13,000 Japanese were believed to be on the island. Before the assault, this number was revised upward to 20,000, still short of Kuribayashi's actual strength of about 23,000. The impact of these assessments was magnified by the erroneous belief that the Japanese would mount a "beach-oriented defense" rather than a steady campaign of attrition over the entire island. The full implications of the *fukkaku* defenses encountered at Peleliu had yet to be recognized.[84]

Spruance relieved Halsey at midnight on 26 January and Mitscher took over the fast carriers. For two weeks, the striking forces rested at Ulithi while Mitscher reorganized TF 58 into five task groups. To shatter enemy defenses and pave the way for the Marines, Spruance requested a concentrated bombardment by shore-based planes in the weeks leading up to the assault. These attacks continued a pattern that began weeks before; 26 January was the fiftieth consecutive day that Seventh Air Force B-24s had attacked Iwo Jima.[85]

As TF 58 approached Japan, an "offensive screen" of PB4Ys kept it hidden by clearing the seas and skies ahead. The carriers struck the Tokyo area as planned on 16 and 17 February. Rough weather meant "extremely difficult flying conditions over the task force" but allowed Mitscher's planes to approach "completely undetected." They attacked aircraft factories and airfields, claiming nearly five hundred enemy aircraft destroyed. All Japanese attempts to counterattack were intercepted over TF 58's destroyer picket line and broken up. Worsening weather prevented the strike on 18 February and, except for damage to a few destroyers, Spruance retired unscathed.[86]

On 19 February, the Iwo Jima landings took place on schedule, following three days of intense and coordinated air and naval bombardment. Battleships and cruisers closed to within two thousand yards of the shore, B-29s attacked Tokyo, and carrier planes struck island strongpoints. Turner reported that the "initial landing waves met slight opposition," but Kuribayashi quickly brought artillery and mortar fire down on the beaches. On the left flank, the 5th Marine Division advanced and successfully reached the opposite shore of the island; they swung their front toward Mount Suribachi to the south.[87]

Kuribayashi subjected the Marines to a withering fire that historian Samuel Eliot Morison likened to "a relentless desert storm, from which there was no shelter, day or night." Nimitz's command summary recorded that Japanese "defenses were expertly planned and fanatically defended. All emplacements, including block houses, pillboxes, and caves, were mutually supporting and built of concrete." Pinned to the beaches supporting the Marines, Spruance's ships were attacked by small groups of planes. Carrier *Saratoga* was hit and escort carrier *Bismarck Sea* was sunk. Progress ashore was slow, but on 23 February, the 5th Marine Division reached the summit of Suribachi and "at 1035 the [national] ensign was raised on the rim of the crater," a moment captured by Joe Rosenthal's famous photograph.[88]

Japanese resistance once more threatened to disrupt Nimitz's careful timetable. The 3rd Marine Division came ashore to augment the 4th and 5th as they advanced north. With no reserves left to the V Amphibious Corps, Nimitz made the 2nd Marine Division available. It was already allocated to Iceberg, but it was important to ensure the quick success of Detachment. Spruance pointed out that the fierce Japanese resistance and the slow pace of unloading might keep the Iwo Jima airfields from becoming operational as soon as planned. If so, Nimitz would have to choose. Either he could keep the fleet off Iwo Jima to provide air cover for the Marines and construction troops, or he could meet the target date for Iceberg. He could not do both.[89]

While Nimitz considered his options, Spruance prepared another carrier raid on Japan. Anticipated to begin on 24 February with two days of attacks on Tokyo, Operation Jamboree called for strikes on Nagoya, Koke, Kyushu, and Okinawa before ending on 4 March. Nimitz was worried about timing; Spruance's plan would allow just seven days at anchor before Iceberg. Spruance, potentially anticipating a delay because of the slow progress at Iwo Jima, agreed that it was "too ambitious" unless Iceberg was "delayed for other reasons." He adjusted his plans to provide more time at Ulithi. Poor weather limited the effectiveness of the Jamboree attacks.[90]

In the meantime, Nimitz's faith in the Marines and his determination to take a calculated risk were rewarded. The three divisions advanced steadily and, by 26 February, had made "noticeable gains," seizing Iwo Jima's second airfield and the nearby high ground. From their front lines, they could now "observe the entire northern half of the island." Progress came at a high cost; companies shrank from their allocated 250 men down to a few dozen effectives. Division commanders pulled motor transport, artillery, and service troops into the fighting to augment their infantry formations. But Iceberg would not be delayed. By 6 March, Army fighter planes had arrived to take over covering duties and free the fleet. Nimitz released the 2nd Marine Division and, on 16 March, organized resistance on Iwo Jima ended. Nimitz expressed his gratitude to the Marines with his famous remark that among them "uncommon valor was a common virtue."[91]

## CONCLUSION

The six months of fighting from October 1944 to March 1945 arguably demonstrated that Japan's defeat was inevitable. Nimitz and MacArthur seized on the apparent weakness of the Japanese in the Philippines to accelerate their timeline. The choice of Leyte as their initial objective bypassed Japanese strength on Mindanao and allowed the combined might of the Southwest and Central Pacific forces to win a major naval battle and attrit Japanese air and land strength. However, decisive victory was elusive.

Nimitz had done his best to work with MacArthur and through Halsey to maintain the offensive's momentum and overcome Japanese resistance. Halsey had demonstrated his limitations. Effective staff organizations translate command from an individual exercise to a collective responsibility. Nimitz had created such a staff, and the success of the Central Pacific offensive had relied upon it; Halsey had failed. Halsey filtered his decision-making through a small group of trusted staff officers; their "pronounced cliques" revealed Halsey as "a poor manager of men" who "paid too little attention to . . . the human capital closest to him."[92] It cost him the opportunity for a more decisive victory at Leyte Gulf and complicated ensuing operations in the Philippines.

Nimitz's challenges with Halsey had also demonstrated the weakness of Nimitz's command structure in the Central Pacific. Halsey was working in a model developed specifically for Spruance, one that used tacit knowledge to allow Nimitz and Spruance to blur the lines between fleet and operational command and thereby accelerate decision-making. Halsey lacked this implicit understanding. During the Philippine operations, he was operating with a different set of assumptions, and that created friction between him and Nimitz. The two had to repeatedly renegotiate the boundaries of their respective commands and, through that process, develop the shared understanding necessary to be effective.

With MacArthur, Nimitz faced similar challenges. Overly reliant on his own council, MacArthur devoted insufficient attention to intelligence estimates of Japanese strength on Luzon, leading to unanticipated delays. Prioritizing his own theater above all others, MacArthur threatened to delay Nimitz's progress further by retaining Pacific Fleet ships and combat formations past the time they were needed. Nimitz deftly resolved the dispute, relying once again on in-person conversations and talented subordinates to broker compromises. By February 1945, he was ready to begin offensive operations within his theater once more.

The Japanese recognized that loss of the Philippines would cut off the Home Islands from resources to the south but refused to concede. Instead, they consolidated their defenses and resolved to fight a series of costly delaying actions to exact a terrible cost in American lives. Yamashita's tactics on Luzon fit perfectly into this strategy; he used terrain and maneuver to inflict unanticipated casualties on Krueger's forces. Kuribayashi, forced to fight in a much smaller area, arguably executed the strategy even more effectively at Iwo Jima.

Nimitz knew there were limits to the nation's endurance, so he continued to emphasize forward movement and "unremitting pressure." As Japanese defenses contracted, time became more important than ever. With victory looming in Europe, American political leaders feared that the nation's citizens would not support a protracted campaign with high casualties. Nimitz looked to strangle Japan, cut it off from Asia, and force it to submit through blockade and bombardment. Such an approach would be less costly than an invasion and remained feasible despite serious constraints in shipping and manpower. However, in the war's last months, the JCS would emphasize an alternative approach, invasion.

# ACHIEVING VICTORY

*Japanese forces have so far not surrendered in appreciable numbers and
cannot be destroyed without our incurring numerous casualties.*

—Adm. Chester W. Nimitz[1]

In the spring of 1945, Nimitz's forces executed Operation Iceberg, assaulting
Okinawa and nearby islands in the Ryukyus. The Japanese, recognizing
that an assault on the Home Islands was looming, fought an aggressive
delaying action with massed kamikaze attacks at sea and *fukkaku* defenses
ashore. As the fighting intensified, Nimitz looked for ways to continue to
maintain pressure despite increasing logistic and manpower constraints. He
sought to tighten the blockade of Japan and reduce its capacity to wage war.
Accordingly, he planned Operation Longtom, the capture of the Chusan
Archipelago, to secure a base from which planes could interdict Japanese
supplies in Korea and the Sea of Japan.

The JCS focused on an alternative strategy. After the CCS agreed that Japan
would be defeated by "invading and seizing objectives in . . . [its] industrial
heart," the JCS prepared for amphibious operations that would overwhelm
Japan's ability to resist and bring the war to a swift conclusion.[2] MacArthur
planned a pair of assaults, one on southern Kyushu and the other in central
Honshu. Air bases in the Ryukyus would support the first of these, Operation

Olympic. Bases captured on Kyushu would, in turn, support Operation Coronet, which would seek a decision on the Tokyo Plain. MacArthur assumed victory there would end the war. In May 1945, after considering alternatives, the JCS issued a directive anticipating Olympic would occur in November.

Nimitz planned accordingly, but both he and King viewed the execution of the operation as optional, to be undertaken only if necessary. If the Japanese could be forced to surrender through other means, the invasion would be cancelled. Accordingly, Nimitz continued to focus on isolating Japan. His efforts were made more difficult by the JCS decision to introduce a new Pacific command structure. The decentralized joint approach that Nimitz had used in POA was discarded. Instead, the JCS mandated an organization that mirrored MacArthur's centralized approach, with each service controlling its own forces, and joint action coordinated by a centralized GHQ. In the final months of the war, the JCS ordered MacArthur and Nimitz to assume responsibility, respectively, for all Army and Navy forces in the theater. The JCS then became the GHQ for the Pacific.

Nimitz struggled under this framework as he attempted to apply unremitting pressure and simultaneously coordinate invasion planning with MacArthur. Their negotiations exposed fundamental differences in how to command, delegate responsibility, and ensure coordinated joint action. To work through these challenges, Nimitz used his staff to rapidly make sense of the developing situation. The costly battle for Okinawa led him to revise his understanding of the conflict as the Japanese prepared for a final battle on their home shore.

## PLANNING ICEBERG AND LONGTOM

In late 1944, Nimitz considered potential operations after Iceberg and felt the Chusan Archipelago, along the Chinese coast just south of Shanghai, was a viable objective. King had been giving "considerable thought" to the same area.[3] In mid-November, Spruance officially suggested capturing the archipelago and the Ningpo Peninsula. Chusan had several advantages. A base there would control the mouth of the Yangtze River, support aerial attacks on "the most important parts of China, . . . Korea, and western Japan," and establish communications with Chinese forces. The Japanese did not seem to hold the area in strength, so Spruance believed the limited resources of Nimitz's theater would be sufficient to capture it.[4]

Nimitz included the concept in a November 1944 estimate of "Future Operations." Although he anticipated that Okinawa would "occupy all the resources available . . . for some months," Nimitz wanted early approval from the JCS for the next operation so that he could move forward without delay once he was ready. Nimitz outlined the Chusan operation—Operation Longtom—for King and recommended that the JCS issue a directive for it with a target date of 20 August 1945.[5]

Nimitz believed Longtom would be the best way to use his limited forces to maintain pressure on the Japanese. He expected it to improve the effectiveness of the blockade and "cut lines of communication between the Empire and Japanese forces operating in China." Because Longtom could be mounted without "redeployment of forces from Europe," it could take place very soon after Iceberg with the means at hand. Nimitz acknowledged that an assault on mainland China risked an "extensive campaign" against IJA forces; he hoped to avoid it by limiting his objectives. Even so, substantial garrison forces were required to mitigate the risk of a Japanese counterattack, which would leave fewer troops available for the invasion of Japan.[6]

In their November 1944 conference, Nimitz and King discussed Longtom. King "favored" the operation, but it would have to occur before August 1945. At the Octagon Conference, the CCS had agreed to assault Kyushu in mid-September and Honshu in mid-December. King suggested mounting Longtom in July to allow enough time between it and the Kyushu operation. Forrest Sherman argued that the CCS' timelines were unrealistic. It would take "from four to five months" to build up the necessary air strength on Okinawa and start to reduce Japanese airpower on Kyushu. With Iceberg currently planned for mid-March, a mid-September target date for Kyushu would give insufficient time to gain control of the air. King steered the conversation back to Longtom. If it was scheduled for August, the JCS would have to choose between it and Kyushu. The implication was clear; unless Longtom could be advanced, it would be deferred.[7]

In January, Nimitz revised his plans. In addition to seizing Chusan-Ningpo, he also wanted to capture a position in Kiaochow Bay to "control the Yellow

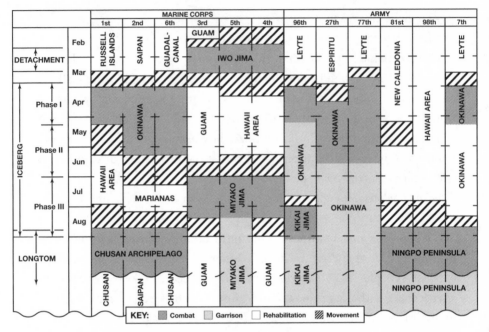

FIGURE 5. Tentative Employment of Divisions in Pacific Ocean Areas as of 1 March 1945

Sea," interdict Japanese communications along the Korean Peninsula, and extend the aerial blockade into the Sea of Japan. Nimitz reiterated his goal of destroying "the Japanese will and ability to resist" through blockade and "ever increasing" attacks by air and naval forces. He wanted to seize locations that would achieve this while accelerating progress and keeping U.S. casualties low. "All our experience in fighting the Japanese," Nimitz argued, had demonstrated that an invasion of Japan would "incur enormous casualties."[8] The JCS did not approve Longtom, but they did order photoreconnaissance of the objective area.[9]

In the meantime, Nimitz refined his plans for Iceberg. The staff study had envisioned three phases. Phase one would capture southern Okinawa and an anchorage at Kerama Retto; phase two would seize the northern part of Okinawa and Ie Shima; and phase three would occupy other unspecified

| | ICEBERG OBJECTIVES | TARGET DATE |
|---|---|---|
| Phase One | Southern Okinawa and Kerama Retto | 1 April |
| Phase Two | Ie Shima and northern Okinawa | 1 May |
| Phase Three | Miyako Jima (Phase Three C) | 1 July |
| | Kikai Jima (Phase Three D) | 15 August |

TABLE 5. Target Dates for Phases of Operation Iceberg

islands. In December 1944, the target date for phase one had been pushed to 1 April. On 3 January 1945, Nimitz set the target date for phase two as 1 May. Later he designated Miyako Jima in the Sakishima group, southwest of Okinawa, and Kikai Jima in the Amami group, northeast of Okinawa, as major objectives of phase three. On 17 January, the JCS officially approved Nimitz's "general concept" for Iceberg as a "necessary course of action to ensure security and adequate support for further advances." They still did not approve Longtom, but they allowed Nimitz to continue planning it.[10]

Nimitz planned to leapfrog his amphibious forces. The three Marine divisions—the 3rd, 4th, and 5th—of the V Amphibious Corps were fighting at Iwo Jima; the III Amphibious Corps—the 1st, 2nd, and 6th Marine Divisions—and four Army divisions were preparing for Okinawa. Nimitz hoped to accelerate Iceberg's phase three by using the V Amphibious Corps to seize Miyako Jima in July.[11] The 96th Infantry Division would seize Kikai Jima in August. Later that month, the III Amphibious Corps and three Army divisions—the 81st, 98th, and 7th—would execute Longtom.[12]

Iceberg, Longtom, and the potential invasion of Japan were on the agenda when Nimitz and Forrest Sherman visited Washington in early March to present their latest plans to the JCS. Nimitz recognized that his carrier forces would have to maintain "highly vulnerable positions" well within the range of Japanese planes on southern Kyushu as they supported Iceberg, so he insisted that Buckner's Tenth Army move quickly and decisively once ashore. The JCS, recently returned from the Yalta Conference, felt the last major strategic decisions had been made for the war in Europe and prepared to give operations in the Pacific "closer scrutiny."[13]

## THE BOMBING CAMPAIGN

In late 1944 and early 1945, the bombing of Japan from the Marianas intensified. General Arnold, chief of the Army Air Forces, planned a campaign that he expected to win the war and justify the creation of an independent air service. Accordingly, he oversaw the Twentieth Air Force's operations himself and refused to allow its B-29s to be placed under Nimitz except during emergencies. Arnold's subordinate, Brig. Gen. Haywood S. Hansell, commanded the XXI Bomber Command in the Marianas. Beginning on 24 November 1944, his bombers executed a high-altitude, daylight precision bombing campaign against the Japanese military industry. However, the powerful winds of the jet stream—previously an undiscovered phenomenon—and cloud cover made it impossible to bomb accurately. Nearly a month went by before Hansell made his "first reasonably successful attack." Arnold directed Hansell to change tactics and execute a "full-scale" incendiary attack on Nagoya.[14]

Hansell objected and directed his B-29s to attack the nearby Mitsubishi Aircraft Plant, not the city. Arnold wanted the city to burn; he knew that Japanese buildings were particularly vulnerable to fire. New incendiary munitions had been developed to create "intense and uncontrollable blazes" and destroy manufacturing facilities, along with the homes of workers and their families. As Hansell continued to attempt precision bombing—his last mission on 19 January 1945 destroyed the Kawasaki aircraft plant at Akashi—XXI Bomber Command's new commander, Maj. Gen. Curtis E. LeMay, arrived in the Marianas. Unlike Hansell, he had no objections to burning down Japanese cities.[15]

On 4 February, LeMay attacked Kobe with incendiaries. Fires burned well into the evening, but damage was limited. On 25 February, during a raid to support Spruance's assault on Iwo Jima, the B-29s were forced by clouds to bomb by radar. Bombardiers selected a target easily distinguishable on their radar screens, the Sumida River in Tokyo. More than two hundred planes dropped loads that were nearly all incendiaries; roughly one square mile of the city was leveled by fire, a result that "exceeded all expectations."[16]

This surprising outcome spurred LeMay to find a way to use XXI Bomber Command to deliver decisive results. He had his planes attack from lower altitudes, allowing them to avoid the jet stream, carry larger bomb loads, and put less strain on their engines. The threat of enemy fighters and antiaircraft fire was reduced by attacking at night; the B-29s traded defensive weapons and gunners for more bombs. Radar allowed the planes to bomb through the clouds so long as targets could be clearly identified. On the night of 9 March, LeMay trialed his new tactics and sent 325 B-29s of XXI Bomber Command to Tokyo.

Nimitz's summary dryly observed that "results achieved were excellent."[17] The incendiaries produced a firestorm that consumed vast areas of Tokyo. Historian Rich Frank summarized the devastation: "By the time the all clear sounded at 2:37 a.m., March 10, the raid had lasted approximately two hours and forty minutes. Across nearly sixteen square miles of Tokyo there was a 'burned empty prairie,' filled with 'a sort of underbrush of roasted sheet-metal and reddish-blackish iron and heavy shards of gray tile.' . . . virtually no human structure remained upright and recognizable."[18] Many thousands died. A contemporary intercepted message put the toll at "about 100,000," a rough figure that is generally accepted today.[19]

The Tokyo raid inaugurated LeMay's campaign of firebombing against Japanese cities. Periodically, his bombers were pulled away to support Operation Iceberg, but starting in March 1945 and running through June, six of the seven largest Japanese cities were subjected to repeated attack. Kyoto, the fourth largest, was spared because of its historical significance as an ancient imperial capital. Tokyo, Osaka, Nagoya, Yokohama, Kobe, and Kawasaki burned. More than half of Tokyo, a little more than fifty-six square miles, was destroyed. The other cities suffered varying degrees of devastation, losing anywhere from 25 percent to 68 percent of their area to fire.[20]

On 27 March, in concert with these efforts, Nimitz had LeMay initiate a "concerted aerial mining campaign" to prevent Japan from importing food and raw materials and to disrupt maritime traffic in the Inland Sea. Aware of the vulnerability of Japanese shipping to mines, the JCS approved the effort as a high priority. It was the largest aerial mining campaign ever undertaken and its code name—Operation Starvation—revealed its intent. The first phase supported the Okinawa operation by closing Shimonoseki Straits and dropping mines in Kure Harbor.[21]

Four additional phases followed. By the end of phase five, the B-29s and Pacific Fleet submarines had totally blockaded Japan. Across the whole mining campaign, more than 13,000 mines were laid, and 670 ships were damaged or sunk—including 65 warships—representing almost 1.4 million tons. Together with the ongoing submarine campaign, Operation Starvation devastated Japanese commerce. At the start of the war, Japan had a little over 6 million tons of merchant shipping; by the beginning of 1945, despite additions totaling over 3 million tons, only a little over 2.5 million tons were left. Mines reduced that by more than 50 percent. By late summer, very little food was coming to Japan from the mainland. The movement of troops and material within Japan was severely curtailed and the Japanese became increasingly dependent on their railway system. When it was unable to meet demands, a "raw material famine" collapsed Japanese industry. Starvation for the Japanese people was sure to follow.[22]

## ICEBERG BEGINS

Operation Iceberg was expected to be a three-phase operation to capture Okinawa, "establish . . . control of the approaches to the East China Sea," and "initiate a close sea and air blockade of Japan." Nimitz issued his operation plan on 31 December 1944; Spruance released his three days later. Their target date was 1 April.[23] Spruance expected violent Japanese aerial attacks—an "all out blow"—on his naval forces. Mitscher's assessment was similar. To mitigate the risk, Spruance directed Mitscher to make a surprise attack on Kyushu at the start of the operation and destroy as many Japanese planes on the ground as possible. Spruance also anticipated enemy surface forces would attack; his instructions reflected the lessons of Philippine Sea and Leyte Gulf and stressed that the "paramount task" of the carrier force was to cover the amphibious operation.[24]

As the target date approached, increasing Japanese resistance at Iwo Jima led Nimitz to modify his plans for Iceberg. In mid-February, he cancelled parts "A" and "B" of phase three, the capture of Daito Shima and Kume Jima. Later in the month, Nimitz issued his warning order for part "C" of phase three, the assault on Miyako Jima, planned for 1 July. However, as the fighting on Iwo Jima sapped the strength of the V Amphibious Corps, Nimitz swapped the order of parts "C" and "D" of phase three. To "maintain the momentum of [the] campaign" and allow the Marines to rest, Kikai Jima would be captured first. On 2 March, Nimitz asked Spruance to designate a commander for Kikai Jima so that "detailed preparations" could begin.[25]

Iceberg required Nimitz to coordinate multiple Pacific commands. The British Pacific Fleet, designated TF 57, would neutralize Japanese airfields in Sakishima Gunto. XXI Bomber Command, which Nimitz was authorized to use to "ensure" the operation's success, would make a "maximum" effort against Honshu in March and then switch to air installations and cities on Kyushu. MacArthur's planes would strike Formosa. Seventh Fleet PB4Ys would sweep the skies in advance of the amphibious forces as they approached Okinawa from Leyte. Nimitz's PB4Ys would screen TF 58 the same way when it refueled and rearmed. Other patrol planes would interdict Japanese shipping along the China coast.[26]

Mitscher sortied with TF 58 from Ulithi on 14 March, fueled, and then planned to make his surprise attack on Kyushu on 18 March. However, TF 58 was "shadowed continuously" by enemy planes the night before. The Japanese dispersed their planes and Mitscher's fighter sweeps encountered only minor opposition. Though only a few "aggressive and determined" Japanese aircraft attacked the carriers, *Yorktown*, *Enterprise*, and *Intrepid* were damaged.[27]

The next day, after aerial photos revealed "major fleet units in the Inland Sea," Mitscher sent his planes to attack them. Japanese planes struck back aggressively. Carriers *Franklin* and *Wasp* were hit. *Wasp* resumed flight operations, but *Franklin* suffered crippling fires. On 20 March, with Japanese attacks continuing, Mitscher withdrew and rendezvoused with SevRon 6, the logistic support group, which refueled, reprovisioned, and replenished his ships with ammunition. *Franklin*, *Wasp*, and *Enterprise* departed for Ulithi and the remainder of TF 58 was reorganized into three carrier groups. Plans were adjusted so that two would always be on station off Okinawa.[28]

TF 58 started attacking Okinawa on 23 March. No Japanese aerial opposition was encountered, leading Mitscher to conclude that his strikes on Kyushu had "interfered with enemy air operations to a greater extent than had been hoped for." Spruance was less sanguine. On the evening of 27 March, he asked Mitscher to make it look like another strike on Kyushu was impending, to draw Japanese planes away from Okinawa. Mitscher sent more fighter sweeps over Kyushu on 29 March.[29]

Three days before, the amphibious assault on Kerama Retto, a small group of islands west of Okinawa, began. After its capture, Kerama Retto provided a safe anchorage for the work of SevRon 10. The assault on Okinawa followed on 1 April. From Nimitz's headquarters on Guam, the situation appeared to be developing favorably. The landing beaches on the western shore of the island "were rapidly secured, and the advance inland commenced against light opposition." Two nearby airfields were seized before midday and advance elements reached the east coast of the island on 2 April, eleven days ahead of schedule. The Marines of Geiger's III Amphibious Corps headed north while Maj. Gen. John R. Hodge's XXIV Corps turned south. In the meantime, Spruance's flagship *Indianapolis* had been hit, forcing him to shift his flag to battleship *New Mexico*.[30]

The "initial successes and light ground opposition" made Nimitz and his subordinates optimistic. Turner told Nimitz, "I may be crazy, but it looks like the Japanese have quit the war, at least in this section." Nimitz jokingly responded, "Delete all after 'crazy.'" He wanted to seize the opportunity to advance more rapidly. Nimitz told his subordinates to "keep their plans and preparations as flexible as possible." He asked Spruance to explore how to rapidly conclude Iceberg and then initiate Longtom. Spruance conferred with Turner and Buckner. They did not recommend advancing north to Kikai Jima until air bases were established on Okinawa. Miyako Jima should be assaulted first. The 4th and 5th Marine Divisions had been exhausted by the fight for Iwo Jima, so to ensure the early capture of Miyako Jima, Geiger suggested using his III Amphibious Corps. They might be ready as early as 1 June. Kikai Jima could follow on 15 August. Nimitz was apprehensive there might not be enough assault troops for Longtom and he considered confining it to the Chusan Archipelago. Spruance felt the forces in POA were adequate for the entire operation.[31]

The hope that Iceberg would complete ahead of schedule evaporated as the 7th and 96th Divisions ran into well-prepared Japanese positions in southern Okinawa. Conforming to the new defensive doctrine issued on 20 January, Lieutenant General Ushijima Mitsuru had prepared his Thirty-Second

Army for "a campaign of attrition" that would "undermine enemy morale" and "delay the final assault on Japan." Ushijima created a series of *fukkaku* positions anchored on three ridge lines running across the island. Each line employed "complex cave defenses and tunnel systems" comparable to the defenses of Iwo Jima. JICPOA had missed these extensive preparations and underestimated the number of Japanese defenders. A March estimate predicted 75,000, but Ushijima had just shy of 115,000 men, 50 percent more than anticipated. Attempts to advance against the first ridge line triggered "exceptionally difficult fighting."[32] By 12 April, Buckner had committed the XXIV Corps reserve, the 27th Division, to try to break through.

While progress on the ground slowed, the Japanese unleashed a series of massed kamikaze attacks, called *kikusui* (floating chrysanthemums). The first began with "very heavy enemy air attacks" the afternoon of 6 April. Turner estimated that 182 Japanese planes attacked in twenty-two groups. Planes from TF 58—which had reorganized into four task groups—shot down many of the attackers, but seventeen different ships were hit. Screening vessels bore the brunt of the attacks. Turner's radar picket destroyers, arranged in a series of stations around Okinawa, allowed incoming strikes to be detected and intercepted, but the isolated pickets were regularly attacked. Two of them were sunk on 6 April and two more damaged the following day.[33]

In coordination with the first *kikusui*, the IJN sent a surface striking force toward Okinawa. Battleship *Yamato*, cruiser *Yahagi*, and escorting destroyers avoided the mines in Shimonoseki Strait and took a more exposed route. Nimitz's submarines sighted them the evening of 6 April. Turner stationed the old battleships in a blocking position while Mitscher concentrated TF 58. The next morning, the fast carriers launched a 380-plane strike; they sank *Yamato*, *Yahagi*, and four of the destroyers. A kamikaze struck carrier *Hancock* in exchange.[34]

To better understand the situation at Okinawa, Nimitz sent Forrest Sherman to the island. Japanese planes were attacking day and night. Suicide boats and swimmers were trying to damage Turner's amphibious ships. The fighting in southern Okinawa resembled trench warfare and progressed at similar speed. Nimitz assessed these details and shared his thoughts with King. The earliest that Japanese resistance was likely to be overcome was mid-May, and that was "optimistic." More destroyers were needed to make up for the losses among the pickets. Before advancing north—to Kikai Jima—Nimitz would have to significantly reduce the number of Japanese suicide planes. He wanted to start that as soon as possible, so he asked Spruance to establish sufficient planes ashore to allow TF 58 to start operating offensively.[35] In the meantime, the Japanese initiated their next major kamikaze attack, striking battleship *Missouri*, carrier *Enterprise*, and destroyer *Kidd* in TF 58 as well as eleven ships in Turner's amphibious force.

Nimitz considered having XXI Bomber Command bomb Japanese defenses on Okinawa to break the stalemate. Spruance recommended "obliteration attacks" on the Kyushu airfields instead. The B-29s tried to strike airfields around Kanoya on 8 April but were forced to divert because of weather. After the second *kikusui*, Spruance briefly freed Mitscher of his support obligations. TF 58 planes attacked southern Kyushu on 15 and 16 April. After the carrier planes departed, P-51s from Iwo Jima attacked Kanoya, but poor visibility limited their effectiveness. A follow-up strike by B-29s the next day hit six airfields. Nimitz believed it interrupted the third *kikusui* operation, which had begun the day before.[36]

As kamikaze attacks continued, Spruance called for "all available means" to prevent them. Nimitz ordered the Twentieth Air Force to attack Japanese airfields every day, weather permitting. The *kikusui* operations did not stop; the fourth began on 27 April. The Pacific Fleet had lost more than forty ships damaged or sunk since 18 March. Nimitz asked King to transfer destroyers from the Atlantic Fleet to make up for the "severe attrition" among the pickets.[37]

Despite intense Japanese attacks, limited resistance in northern Okinawa allowed Nimitz to accelerate part of his schedule. Turner and Buckner advanced the date for Ie Shima to 16 April, and that morning, the 77th Infantry Division went ashore and captured the island's airfields. On 13 April, Nimitz issued his warning order for the assault on Miyako Jima; he expected Geiger's III Amphibious Corps to capture the island in mid-June.[38] In the meantime, Hodge broke through the first of Ushijima's defensive lines and prepared to assault the second, anchored on the ancient capital of Shuri.

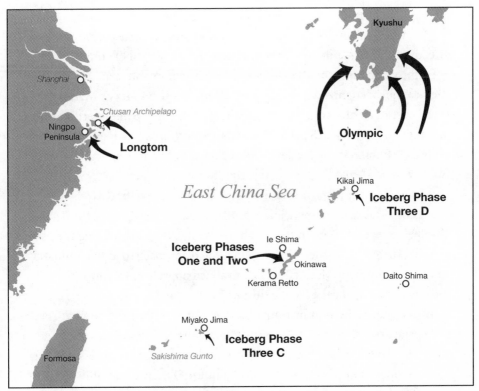

MAP 8. Offensive Operations Planned and Executed in the East China Sea during 1945

## PLANNING FOR INVASION

By the spring of 1945, the Army's planners had been preparing to invade Japan for over a year. "Only invasion," they contended, "could assure Japan's collapse." Blockade and bombardment were insufficient.[39] Marshall was convinced of the need to invade and led the CCS to agree that the Allies would end the war by "seizing objectives in the industrial heart of Japan."[40] By April 1945, it appeared to be the best way to impose unconditional surrender. Planners assumed the invasion would require thirty-six divisions. Blockade would offer little economy as it would require a sustained force of twenty-eight divisions and might not deliver success for "several years."[41] In the meantime, there would be a "constant stream" of casualties.[42] On 3 April, the JCS issued a preparatory directive for the assault on southern Kyushu, code-named Olympic.

At the same time, the JCS introduced a new command structure for the Pacific. They recognized it was impossible to choose Nimitz or MacArthur as the overall theater commander; neither was willing to be subordinate to the other. Instead, the JCS made MacArthur and Nimitz equals and exercised unified command at the JCS level. Admiral Leahy felt the implications were "somewhat academic," but there were significant consequences.[43] MacArthur was designated commander in chief, U.S. Army Forces, Pacific (CINCAFPAC) and Nimitz was made responsible for "all U.S. Naval resources in the Pacific Theater" except for those in the Southeast Pacific. By consolidating the two services, the JCS discarded Nimitz's integrated approach to joint command and replaced it with MacArthur's centralized approach. In effect, the JCS became the GHQ for the Pacific theater.[44]

This increased the administrative burden on MacArthur and Nimitz. They had to start transferring forces to consolidate the services while simultaneously planning for the invasion of Japan and ensuring the success of their ongoing operations. Even though the fight for Okinawa was at its height, Nimitz began planning for Olympic. He and King agreed that Spruance and Halsey would serve in the roles for which they were "best qualified." Spruance would lead the amphibious phase of Olympic while Halsey commanded the Pacific Fleet's striking forces. This would create a more explicit structure and eliminate the friction Nimitz and Halsey had experienced in the Philippines, but to allow detailed planning to begin, Spruance had to be extracted from Iceberg "as soon as practicable." King suggested having Halsey relieve Spruance about 1 May so that Halsey could execute Longtom while Spruance prepared for Olympic.[45]

Nimitz suggested to MacArthur that they meet to discuss the JCS directive and its implications. MacArthur declined; it was "impossible" for him to leave his headquarters. Sutherland, Kenney, and Major General Stephen J. Chamberlin, MacArthur's head of operations, came to Guam instead and conferred with Nimitz, McMorris, and Forrest Sherman. Nimitz expected the conference to focus on the details of forthcoming operations and treat the transfer of forces as a secondary priority. Sutherland had other ideas; he explained MacArthur's desire to take command—administratively and operationally—of all Army forces in the Pacific "as soon as possible." MacArthur also wanted control of the Ryukyus because it was the logical "axis of advance into Japan." When Sutherland insisted that these transfers were essential because unified command was "an unworkable 'shibboleth,'" Nimitz felt he went too far. Nimitz explained how unified command had "gotten us through our period of adversity," facilitated the advance across the Pacific, and was "essential to the efficient conduct of war." He insisted on retaining control of Army units defending "important shore positions" and refused to assume responsibility for any naval forces in the Southwest Pacific currently involved in active operations. Sutherland and Nimitz refused to compromise and the conference broke down. When he was informed of the difficulties, King backed Nimitz's perspective.[46]

The new command structure and the breakdown of this conference introduced a dynamic with noteworthy parallels to the initial North Pacific command under Rear Admiral Theobald. Nimitz tried to work with MacArthur to expedite invasion planning, but the two commanders failed to find common ground. Instead of resolving his differences with MacArthur, Nimitz used his relationship with King to escalate his concerns and push his disputes with MacArthur to the JCS level, especially once he learned MacArthur was doing the same. The crucial difference between Nimitz in 1945 and Theobald in 1942 is that Theobald's superiors regularly and consistently insisted that he collaborate more effectively with his peers in the Army. The JCS, on the other hand, was willing to broker MacArthur's disagreements with Nimitz, in large part because it was politically unacceptable to relieve either one after the significant victories they had won. Nevertheless, it is curious that Nimitz allowed himself to adopt a pattern of behavior similar to one he had criticized.

Nimitz hoped that he and MacArthur could agree to immediately transfer administrative control of Army and Navy units and then shift operational control as rapidly as ongoing operations and the needs of base defense would allow. If they could agree to that, Nimitz argued, then they could move ahead with "planning and conducting" the invasion. MacArthur disagreed. He reiterated that he needed "greater control of Army resources in the Pacific" first. He was ready to pass "full control of the Seventh Fleet" to Nimitz "at any time" and expected Nimitz to reciprocate by transferring the Army units in POA. Nimitz refused. Their different perspectives reflected their views of joint command. MacArthur believed centralized control of each service was a vital prerequisite; Nimitz felt unified command of each operation was essential for success.[47]

Although the JCS had ordered planning for Olympic, there was still uncertainty about executing it. In mid-April, in preparation for JCS deliberations, Marshall asked MacArthur for his views. In his framing of the question, Marshall revealed his preference; he felt additional encirclement operations—like Longtom—would incur "high losses" and fail to bring the war to a quick conclusion. MacArthur agreed. Only invasion would "permit application of [the] full power of our combined forces . . . on the decisive objective." He urged the JCS to authorize invasion and supported his argument by contending that Japanese strength had been significantly reduced. Their air force, for example, was making "uncoordinated suicidal attacks" and "diminishing rapidly." U.S. air bases in the Ryukyus would destroy the few enemy planes that remained.[48]

King forwarded the messages from this exchange to Nimitz and asked for his comment. Nimitz replied on 28 April and included MacArthur in his response. At this time Nimitz supported invading Kyushu as soon as possible; however, control of the sea—now virtually assured—and the air was a prerequisite. The fighting at Okinawa had demonstrated the strength of Japanese airpower; it would have to be reduced before an invasion could succeed. Nimitz expected that air bases on Okinawa would accelerate the destruction of the enemy air force and that airfields on Kikai Jima would cover the invasion forces. That meant shipping, logistics, and assault troops were the most important questions to resolve before invading Kyushu. Nimitz could provide an amphibious corps of Marines; the Army would need to provide the rest of the assault forces. If they were ready in time and if the Army could provide adequate shipping and supplies for them, then Olympic could take place before the end of the year. If that was not feasible, Nimitz recommended executing Longtom instead and then quickly mounting follow-on "operations to control the Korea Strait." Nimitz closed his message with a warning not to underestimate Japanese capabilities. He and MacArthur had overcome many "ill-fed and poorly supplied [Japanese] units." Those in Japan were likely to be better equipped and far stronger.[49]

Nimitz continued to push for an arrangement that would allow invasion planning to proceed. He knew it was essential to visit MacArthur and work out the details, so, in mid-May, Nimitz and Forrest Sherman met with MacArthur and his staff in Manila. MacArthur shared his draft campaign plan, code-named Downfall. Nimitz felt it was too broad—it covered both Olympic and Coronet—and would be "tedious" to maintain, and he disagreed with some of its concepts, such as MacArthur's intention to assume control of the Ryukyus. However, Nimitz felt that he and MacArthur had reached "general agreement as to tactical and strategic concepts" for the invasion and that they could begin to plan independently. Nimitz would control the naval and amphibious operations, and MacArthur the ground campaign. In preparation, Nimitz agreed to help MacArthur establish Kenney's command, now designated the Far East Air Forces, in the Ryukyus and transfer the Seventh Air Force to Kenney's control.[50]

However, in the summary of the conference he sent to Marshall, MacArthur noted that the agreement did not "entirely" represent the views of his headquarters. The issue was Nimitz's control of the amphibious phase. Marshall asked MacArthur if he should "control the amphibious assault through the appropriate naval commander." This gave MacArthur the opening he needed. He was "emphatic" that he should.[51] MacArthur immediately began undermining his agreement with Nimitz, explaining that they had "basic differences" regarding "responsibilities and command structure." MacArthur wanted to control everything and exercise command through independent, subordinate land, air, and naval commanders. Nimitz planned to employ the approach used in prior POA operations, with a naval officer commanding the amphibious phase and an Army commander assuming responsibility once the assault forces were established ashore. These contrasting visions of jointness—MacArthur emphasizing centralization and Nimitz advocating for delegation—represented a "fundamental" difference. MacArthur wanted the JCS to resolve them.[52]

Nimitz was taken aback. He tried to explain to MacArthur that the JCS expected them to merge the best aspects of their collective experience; the most effective way to do that would be to have MacArthur command the land campaign while Nimitz led the naval and amphibious efforts. Experience had shown that "operations of large naval forces" had to be coordinated from a "well-equipped command position ashore" by an officer with the "complete flexibility" to adjust dispositions and "meet a constantly changing strategic and tactical situation." Nimitz could do that, but not if his forces were subject to MacArthur's control.[53]

Marshall agreed with MacArthur that the JCS had to resolve the issue, inhibiting Nimitz's ability to seek common ground with MacArthur at the theater level. The JCS met on 25 May and issued a new directive, setting the target date for Olympic as 1 November 1945. Because the "land campaign" was paramount, MacArthur was given "primary responsibility" for the entire operation including the amphibious assault. He planned to invade Kyushu with nine divisions in three corps plus an airborne division. MacArthur would keep another four divisions in reserve. Against this, the Japanese were expected to defend Kyushu with only eight divisions. Nimitz deferred Longtom and prepared to conduct supporting naval operations. By resolving the controversy this way, the JCS made it clear that they were now the GHQ for the Pacific theater and established a precedent. If there was a disagreement between Nimitz and MacArthur, the JCS was willing to step in and resolve it.[54]

By this time, Nimitz had changed his attitude toward invasion and sent King a detailed analysis of his new perspective. It is worth quoting at length. Nimitz was still drawing on his effective sensemaking apparatus—which had absorbed lessons from Peleliu, Iwo Jima, and Okinawa—and it helped him recognize the following:

> [W]here Japanese troops occupy prepared defenses and have adequate supplies they constitute a competent fighting force against which the best of our troops even with air support and naval gunfire support . . . can advance only slowly. Japanese forces have so far not surrendered in appreciable numbers and cannot be destroyed without our incurring numerous casualties. It would be unrealistic to expect that such obvious objectives as southern Kyushu and the Tokyo Plain will not be as well defended as Okinawa. Although our troops for the invasion of

Japan should be in the best of condition many of the divisions planned to be employed in Olympic are still fighting on Okinawa and in the Philippines.[55]

Fighting for Okinawa was terrible and protracted. U.S. forces were sustaining significant losses on land and at sea. Nimitz knew an invasion would increase these losses dramatically. He now preferred a strategy of blockade. The Twentieth Air Force was destroying Japanese cities and increasing the intensity of its attacks. The carriers, once freed from their defensive role, would achieve "the complete destruction of Japanese industry and shipping." Nimitz felt the "long range interests of the U[nited] S[tates] will be better served if we continue during 1945 to isolate Japan and to destroy Japanese forces and resources by naval and air attack." Historian Rich Frank recognized that Nimitz's revised opinion gave King "the power to halt the invasion." If the senior Pacific naval commander no longer supported it, the invasion would not proceed.[56]

## ICEBERG ENDS

While the JCS debated whether to invade Japan, Nimitz remained focused on forward movement. One of Iceberg's main objectives was to secure airfields. For example, six wings of B-29s were expected to base in the Ryukyus, three on Okinawa, two on Miyako Jima, and one on Ie Shima. Buckner, cognizant of Nimitz's desire to accelerate progress, suggested in early April that Okinawa might support many more planes than originally anticipated, obviating the need to invade Miyako Jima and getting more planes into action faster. Nimitz asked Spruance for his thoughts, stressing that it was a matter "of the greatest urgency." Spruance agreed with Buckner. On 22 April, Nimitz left for Okinawa to judge for himself. His subordinates were correct; there were suitable sites on Okinawa and Ie Shima for all the required airfields. Nimitz abandoned his plans for Miyako Jima and decided to use the III Amphibious Corps to accelerate victory on Okinawa.[57]

The fight for the island remained intense. Buckner and Hodge tried to make progress by rotating the 96th and 27th Divisions to the rear and replacing them with the 77th Division and the 1st Marine Division, but Ushijima's defenses held. With progress on Okinawa stalled, the Japanese launched their fifth and sixth *kikusui* operations on 3 May and 10 May; the count of damaged and sunken ships grew. Nimitz became concerned the situation on Okinawa was "unsatisfactory." He sent a private message to Spruance suggesting Buckner might have "an inadequate appreciation" of the need to accelerate airfield construction and release the fast carriers from covering operations. If Spruance agreed, Nimitz authorized him to "take corrective action." In other words, Spruance could relieve Buckner if necessary. In his response, Spruance reassured Nimitz. Airfield construction had initially emphasized the need to prepare for B-29s, but now fighters were the focus. Buckner was pressuring the enemy ashore; he and Hodge hoped to capture the island "toward [the] end of May."[58]

Publicly, Nimitz showed none of these doubts. In the face of increasing adversity, he emphasized his team's unity and his support for his subordinates. When the *New York Herald Tribune* published an article about "ultraconservative" tactics on Okinawa, Nimitz held a press conference praising the Army's tactics. He called Buckner's effort a "magnificent performance." Other admirals and Navy Secretary Forrestal—who had become secretary after the death of Frank Knox in April 1944—buttressed this view. These expressions of confidence diffused a potential controversy and allowed Nimitz to remain focused on bringing the operation to a successful conclusion.[59]

Nimitz issued his warning order for Kikai Jima on 6 May and set the date of the assault to 15 July. The order triggered a rapid exchange of messages as Nimitz's subordinates shared their thoughts about future objectives. Turner and Buckner acknowledged that the 2nd Marine Division could support the operation, but they felt it was more important to consolidate their position at Okinawa by occupying Kume Jima, just to the west. Spruance agreed. He thought Kikai Jima would be "unnecessary and unprofitable." Nimitz was unconvinced.[60]

Later in May, he asked several of his subordinates whether Kikai Jima should be seized to secure air bases for Olympic. Only those not involved in Iceberg were in favor of the operation. Conolly thought it was "essential" to reduce enemy air strength. Halsey agreed and added that airfields on Kikai Jima would provide cover for the naval assault forces. Spruance, Turner,

Hill, and Towers disagreed; they did not think it was worth the cost and that developing Okinawa would be a better investment. Spruance summed up their views succinctly: "Believe value of position . . . will not be commensurate with its cost for occupation and development. Recommend operation be cancelled." On 1 June, Nimitz told King he was suspending the Kikai Jima operation indefinitely so that the fleet would be free to undertake "offensive naval operations" more quickly. MacArthur concurred.[61]

In the meantime, the situation on Okinawa was gradually improving. After repulsing a Japanese counterattack, Hodge pushed south in early May with four divisions abreast; he seemed to be gaining the upper hand. On 18 May, Buckner assumed command ashore, officially ending the amphibious phase. A few days before, Nimitz released the Twentieth Air Force from its support of Okinawa, but the fleet remained in place and continued to endure intense kamikaze attacks. In the span of three days, Mitscher shifted his flag twice as his flagships *Bunker Hill* and *Enterprise* were hit. The seventh and eighth *kikusui* operations began on 23 and 27 May, respectively.[62]

Nimitz continued to be concerned about airfields. He stressed to Buckner the importance of developing the ones on Okinawa and Ie Shima "with the utmost speed." Nimitz also suggested that "one or more" senior officers might need to be replaced to make more rapid progress. He was giving Buckner a chance to address any deficiencies without an official reprimand. Buckner did not think changes were necessary. He assumed "full responsibility" and initiated "corrective action" to ensure the construction program would meet the needs of Olympic. Buckner argued that relieving any of his officers would only delay things further, but he was willing to take that step if Nimitz insisted. Nimitz deferred to Buckner's judgment.[63]

It took another month—and two more *kikusui* operations—to secure Okinawa. Geiger signaled the end of organized resistance on 21 June. Buckner did not live to see it; he was killed by an artillery barrage when observing the front line on the 18th. There were many other casualties; the Tenth Army suffered more than 7,600 killed or missing in action and nearly 32,000 wounded. Thirty ships had been sunk and 368 damaged during the campaign. More than 4,900 sailors were killed or missing; 4,824 were wounded. Navy and Marine Corps losses at Okinawa were 17 percent "of all the casualties sustained by those services for the whole war."[64] These figures showed what an invasion of the Home Islands might bring.

## THE POTENTIAL COST OF INVASION

On 12 April, President Roosevelt died and Harry S. Truman became president. After the surrender of Germany on 8 May, Truman was confronted with the complex question of whether to invade Japan. The JCS agreed to prepare for invasion, but King was not sure it was the best course and Leahy was opposed. Truman had been an artillery officer in World War I and had a visceral experience of combat. When he called the JCS, Forrestal, and Secretary of War Henry L. Stimson together to review invasion plans on 18 June, Truman was most concerned about casualties. He requested two sets of timelines and casualty estimates, one for those associated with an "invasion of Japan proper" and one for a campaign of "isolation, blockade, and bombardment."[65]

After the invasion of Europe and the Marianas in June 1944, American casualties had surged. Combat deaths had averaged well below 10,000 each month prior to that but were now closer to 15,000 every month and sometimes, as in March 1945, exceeded 20,000. With Okinawa captured and Germany defeated, casualty rates were expected to decrease before climbing again with the invasion of Japan. Truman wanted to know how large this increase might be and how long it would last.[66]

To answer this question, MacArthur, Nimitz, and planners in Washington provided estimated casualty figures. Nimitz's were comprehensive whereas MacArthur's focused on just ground forces and some air units. Nimitz predicted 49,000 total casualties for the first thirty days of Olympic; the figures for an entire campaign would have been much higher. MacArthur arrived at 105,050 for a campaign of ninety days. The Joint Staff Planners projected 193,500 casualties for Olympic and Coronet combined. The formulas they used and assumptions they made are uncertain, but available information suggested casualties could be much higher. Decades later, historian Richard Frank used the surgeon general of the Army's casualty rates from prior Pacific campaigns to estimate 514,072 casualties for Olympic and 687,933 for Coronet; these numbers were just for the assault forces involved in a ninety-day campaign.[67] The variability of these figures demonstrates the challenge confronting the JCS as the scheduled date for the invasion of Japan approached.

During the meeting on 18 June, Marshall presented a strong case for invasion. He emphasized Japanese weakness, described the IJN as "completely powerless," and suggested an invasion would be the best way to indicate "the firmness of our resolution" to impose unconditional surrender. He reinforced his case by reading a message from MacArthur that emphasized the "decisive effect" Operation Olympic was expected to have. Marshall approached the question of casualties indirectly, arguing that experience in the Pacific varied so much that it was "wrong to give any estimate." Instead, Marshall used known casualties from prior operations—Leyte (17,000), Luzon (31,000), Iwo Jima (20,000), and Okinawa (41,700)—as reference points. He also offered the first thirty days of the Normandy campaign, which had resulted in 42,000 casualties, as a potential comparison. Marshall contended that "the first thirty days in Kyushu should not exceed the price we have paid for Luzon." Leahy noted that the casualties at Okinawa had been "35 percent" of the troops employed; he thought that might be a way to arrive at a casualty estimate for Kyushu, but King highlighted the differences between the operations. Okinawa's small size forced Buckner into frontal assaults. On Kyushu, King expected the three simultaneous assaults would create separate fronts and the larger land mass would allow "much more room to maneuver." He suggested casualty rates "would lie somewhere between" Luzon and Okinawa. Marshall successfully steered the conversation to his main point, which was that, regardless of casualty figures, the invasion of Kyushu was the "best solution under the circumstances" for ending the war as rapidly as possible. The rest of the JCS agreed, although King astutely observed that while it was important to let preparations go forward, they could always be stopped if circumstances changed. He was prescient, because the consensus rested on the assumption that just eight Japanese divisions, with a total of 350,000 troops, would be defending Kyushu.[68]

Leahy successfully introduced the idea of approaching the end of the war differently, perhaps by modifying—or clarifying—the concept of "unconditional surrender." He feared that insistence on unconditional surrender would make the Japanese "desperate," encourage them to fight more tenaciously, and increase Allied casualties. In addition to this risk, unconditional surrender might make it more difficult to govern postwar Japan. The way surrender had been imposed on Germany had led to unanticipated difficulties, in large part because of the collapse of German governmental authority. Truman, his cabinet members, and the JCS wanted to manage the defeat of Japan more effectively. In May, Under Secretary of State Joseph Grew, who had served as ambassador to Japan before the war and had some familiarity with its government, suggested tempering the concept of unconditional surrender by allowing the emperor to remain in place, at least until a military occupation was established and the question of a future Japanese government could be examined more carefully.[69]

The morning before the meeting with the JCS, Grew gave Truman a draft statement modifying the concept of unconditional surrender. Grew was optimistic that it would give support to Japanese who wished to end the war. Truman was open to the idea but felt that any major revision of Allied terms needed to be a product of the upcoming Potsdam conference. That gave Secretary of War Stimson, who also favored being more deliberate about the meaning of unconditional surrender, an opportunity to merge his ideas with Grew's in a draft submitted to Truman on 2 July.

At Potsdam, the Japanese emperor was recognized as vital to the process of Japanese surrender. The CCS feared that even a successful invasion of Japan would not guarantee the capitulation of Japanese garrisons outside of it. Marshall hoped that keeping the emperor in place would ensure the surrender of such garrisons; accordingly, he recommended not removing the emperor "prior to the termination of hostilities." After further discussion on this point, the JCS proposed the following language for inclusion in the Potsdam Declaration: "Subject to suitable guarantees against further acts of aggression, the Japanese people will be free to choose their own form of government."[70] The official declaration issued on 26 July included similar wording.

The declaration was insufficient to convince the Japanese to entertain Allied terms. Japanese media promptly conveyed their government's rejection of the declaration. Simultaneously, behind the scenes, Japanese diplomats worked to secure a negotiated peace through the Soviet Union on more favorable terms. Intercepted messages suggested that these peace feelers lacked the sanction of Japanese military leaders responsible for the nation's strategy. There was no reason to believe the Japanese government was willing to capitulate. All the evidence indicated they preferred to fight a decisive battle in Japan.

Further intelligence analysis revealed their logic. When Truman met with the JCS in June, just four Japanese divisions appeared to be defending Kyushu. That this number might double to eight before the invasion was a reasonable assumption, but over the summer, JICPOA and Major General Willoughby, MacArthur's intelligence chief, realized that the Japanese were strengthening Kyushu beyond all expectations. By 9 July, estimates of Japanese forces on the island had already reached 350,000. Later that month, a new series of Japanese divisions was identified, and by early August, Japanese strength on Kyushu was estimated to be 560,000 troops in thirteen divisions. By October, this was expected to grow to 600,000, nearly equal to the 766,700 assault troops planned for Olympic. The actual number of defenders was even greater; the Japanese had readied 900,000 troops to defend Kyushu. No matter how casualty figures for Olympic were estimated, they were sure to be "unacceptable."[71]

At the same time, despite the vigorous effort to destroy Japan's aircraft industry, the threat of kamikazes increased. Photographs of Japanese airfields compiled in the first week of July revealed more than eight thousand planes, the vast majority of which were suitable for suicide missions. Nimitz's headquarters estimated in August that there were more than ten thousand Japanese aircraft available in the Home Islands to oppose invasion.[72] The viability of the invasion was now in serious doubt; the Japanese had used the time purchased by the lengthy struggle at Okinawa to prepare an unanticipated defense.

## STRANGLING JAPAN

With the fight for Okinawa over, Nimitz unleashed the striking forces of the Pacific Fleet against Japan. After taking over from Spruance and Mitscher on 26 May, Halsey and McCain struck Kyushu on 2 and 3 June. Nimitz ordered them to make a follow-up strike on the 8th, but the Third Fleet ran into another typhoon.[73] Heavy seas tore off cruiser *Pittsburgh*'s bow and collapsed the forward flight decks of carriers *Hornet* and *Bennington*. A court of inquiry concluded that Halsey had "primary responsibility" for the damage and recommended "serious consideration" be given to reassigning him. Forrestal entertained the idea but concluded that relieving Halsey would boost Japanese morale; he remained Nimitz's Third Fleet commander.[74] TG 38.4, which suffered relatively little damage from the storm, struck Kyushu as instructed on 8 June. Afterward, TF 38 withdrew to rest.

As Halsey prepared to resume his attacks, Nimitz emphasized the importance of destroying the last remaining Japanese battleships and cruisers. While these ships could not win a major battle, they were still a threat to convoys and supply lines. Eliminating that threat would free more destroyers to screen Halsey's carriers and give TF 38 greater flexibility. Halsey only had enough destroyers to operate three carrier groups and not four. He hoped to increase his striking power by integrating Rawlings' British carrier task force into TF 38, but Nimitz recognized that it was politically important to maintain the independence of Rawlings' command. Nimitz ordered Halsey to have Rawlings operate independently, striking targets suitable for the Royal Navy's capabilities.[75]

Halsey initiated his carrier strikes on 10 July with a raid on the Tokyo area. Enemy opposition was negligible, but McCain's pilots saw well-concealed Japanese planes dispersed over dozens of airfields. Photographic analysis suggested the Japanese were preserving their aerial strength to oppose the coming invasion. Halsey had more success against Japanese ships. On 18 July, TF 38 pilots attacked battleship *Nagato* at Yokosuka. Two rounds of strikes—on 24 and 28 July—struck the Kure-Kobe area. They set battleship *Haruna* ablaze and sank battleship carriers *Ise* and *Hyuga* and two cruisers. Save for coastal forces and suicide craft, the IJN was effectively destroyed.[76]

Halsey also cut off Japanese industries on Honshu from their supply of coal. Rail ferries brought an average of 160,000 metric tons of coal from Hokkaido to Honshu each year.[77] Nimitz told Halsey to destroy the ferries. On 14 and 15 July, planes from TF 38 struck northern Honshu and Hokkaido, damaging shipping and docks, destroying dozens of locomotives in nearby railyards, and sinking eight of the twelve rail ferries. The other four were so badly damaged they were inoperable. Coal shipments to Honshu fell dramatically. The destruction of the ferries was "the most devastating single strategic-bombing success of all the campaigns against Japan."[78]

Halsey sustained his attacks throughout July and into August by relying on SevRon 6, the logistic support group, which performed the largest at-sea replenishment operation of the war on 21 and 22 July. TF 38 received 6,369 tons of ammunition, 379,157 barrels of fuel oil, 1,635 tons of stores and provisions, 99 replacement aircraft, and 412 replacement personnel. This kind of logistic support—where a major striking force took on fuel, ammunition, and supplies at sea outside of a port—was unimaginable at the start of the war. It was a dramatic demonstration of how the Pacific Fleet's logistical capacity had grown over the past three years and the potential unlocked by the new SevRon 6.[79]

## ENDGAME

Early August was a time of increasing tension as Nimitz prepared for the invasion of Kyushu. He had issued his warning order for Olympic on 30 June and expected Halsey—after some additional strikes—to withdraw and prepare for the assault. In the meantime, Truman elected to "make a profound psychological impression" on the Japanese people in an effort to undermine their will "to continue the war." Nimitz's staff summary for 6 August recorded that the president "announced that Hiroshima was bombed . . . by an atomic bomb with explosive power equal to 20,000 tons of TNT." It destroyed 60 percent of the city. A second bomb was dropped on Nagasaki on 9 August. That same day, the Soviet Union invaded Manchuria. These events allowed Nimitz to avoid one of his most severe challenges of the entire war.[80]

The JCS was aware of the recent intelligence showing the Japanese buildup on Kyushu and were concerned. On August 7, Marshall asked MacArthur for his thoughts. Marshall wanted to know if MacArthur thought Olympic was still feasible in the face of increasing Japanese strength, now thought to number 560,000 defenders and thousands of suicide planes. Marshall thought it was possible the Japanese were engaged in a deception campaign, so he wanted MacArthur's "personal estimate" of Japanese capabilities on

Kyushu. Marshall also asked MacArthur to assess "alternative objectives," such as the Tokyo Plain, the target for Operation Coronet.[81]

MacArthur responded with a lengthy dispatch. He was "certain" that Japanese air strength was "greatly exaggerated" and cited Halsey's strikes as evidence that Japanese airpower had been decisively diminished. MacArthur confidently compared Kyushu with Luzon:

> The situation repeats that of the Philippine campaigns. Prior to the invasion of Luzon, reports were received of the concentration of air both on Luzon and on Formosa. An erroneous estimate of widely dispersed planes being held back for the eventuality of landings was repeatedly made. I . . . doubt the often repeated reports that large numbers of aircraft are still being manufactured in Japan. As to the movement of ground forces, the Japanese are reported as trying to concentrate in the few areas in which landings can be effected from Tokyo southward, and it is possible that some strength may have been drawn from areas of northern Honshu. I do not credit, however, the heavy strengths reported to you in southern Kyushu.[82]

MacArthur cited his experience "throughout the Southwest Pacific" to falsely claim that whenever intelligence sources "pointed to greatly increased enemy forces," these reports had been "erroneous." He believed the Japanese were engaged in a massive deception campaign. Even if the Japanese had been able to build up their strength, MacArthur insisted that Kenney's air forces would destroy their planes and weaken their ground forces prior to Olympic. The plan was "sound," should proceed, and would be "successful."[83]

MacArthur's assessment was incorrect and disingenuous. The evidence from Southwest Pacific campaigns showed that MacArthur and his intelligence organization consistently underestimated the strength of opposing forces; Luzon and Biak were clear examples. In August 1945, the stakes were much higher, but MacArthur was determined to lead the greatest amphibious operation in history. As historian Edward Drea put it, "egotistical ambition" overwhelmed thorough and thoughtful analysis.[84]

Other officers and cabinet members recognized this weakness of MacArthur's. It became clear to Nimitz as he tried—without success—to collaboratively plan for Olympic. Now, it was clear to Navy Secretary Forrestal as well. On 8 August, he wrote to Truman to request that a different commander be selected to lead the invasion of Japan, someone more collaborative who could provide the necessary "common direction and command."[85]

King sought to provoke a more direct confrontation. He had occupied the middle ground in the JCS' strategy, allowing invasion planning to proceed while also intensifying blockade and bombardment. This approach preserved options, but King was convinced invasion was no longer the best course. He forwarded the messages from Marshall's exchange with MacArthur to Nimitz and asked for his comments. King told Nimitz to include MacArthur on his response, intentionally forcing the issue on the latest intelligence estimates and expecting to draw Nimitz and MacArthur's differing assessments into the open. King knew he was about to force an interservice confrontation, but he was confident the president and the JCS would place great stock in Nimitz's opinion.[86]

Nimitz could be trusted to present an honest assessment of Japanese capabilities. King knew that he had voiced opposition to the invasion in May. It was unlikely that Nimitz would support it now that the Japanese were in an even stronger position. Nimitz had also been absorbing and assessing lessons from prior campaigns. JICPOA was working on a study of Japanese defensive fortifications on Peleliu. Drafted too late for the assaults on Iwo Jima and Okinawa, the report contained lessons that would be useful in an invasion of Japan. Surprised by the shift to *fukkaku* defenses in late 1944, "shocked" by the sophisticated fortifications of Iwo Jima, and deceived by Japanese preparations at Okinawa, Nimitz and his planners recognized "the enemy had become smarter and more deadly." They reassessed the likely cost of an invasion accordingly and were prepared to recommend against it.[87]

King likely understood this and was deliberately calling on the prestige and authority Nimitz had accrued with his capable performance throughout the war. Roosevelt had known Nimitz's strengths—his ability to collaborate effectively, to forge a team, and to be consistently forthright—when he selected him to lead the Pacific Fleet in December 1941. Over the past three and a half years, Nimitz had lived up to the faith Roosevelt placed in him. Now, King looked to capitalize on those same strengths and force a final decision regarding Olympic, potentially saving thousands of lives. There is no question that Nimitz would have provided his honest assessment of the situation, but before he could respond, the end of the war obviated the need to resolve the dispute.

When the Soviet Union struck, the IJA resolved to fight on, but Emperor Hirohito had lost faith in their ability to continue the war. The decision to modify "unconditional surrender" proved extremely important. Allowing the emperor to retain authority gave Japan's leaders a way to end the war and preserve the *kokutai*, the national polity centered on the imperial house. Not all members of the cabinet agreed it was time to seek peace, but at a Supreme War Leadership Council meeting the night of 9 August, the emperor overruled the disagreement in his cabinet and sanctioned Allied surrender terms by claiming that if he did not act "the Japanese race would perish."[88]

The next day, King sent Nimitz a fateful message: "This is a peace warning." Intercepted communications had revealed Japanese intentions. Four days later, King told Nimitz to suspend attack operations.[89] When it became clear that the Japanese would surrender, Nimitz sent the following message to his command:

> With the termination of hostilities against Japan it is incumbent on all officers to conduct themselves with dignity and decorum in their treatment of the Japanese and their public utterances in connection with the Japanese. The Japanese are still the same nation which initiated the war by a treacherous attack on the Pacific Fleet and which has subjected our brothers in arms who became prisoners to torture, starvation, and murder. However, the use of insulting epithets in connection with the Japanese as a race or as individuals does not now become the officers of the United States Navy. Officers of the Pacific Fleet will take steps to require of all personnel under their command a high standard of conduct in this matter. Neither familiarity and open forgiveness nor abuse and vituperation should be permitted.[90]

With this statement of expectations, Nimitz began to transition his forces to peacetime and helped inaugurate a new relationship with the Japanese people.

## CONCLUSION

During the final months of the war, Nimitz, in the face of increasing difficulties and major command disruptions, maintained his sensemaking capability. Nimitz used it to increase pressure on the Japanese, adjust plans for Iceberg to conserve strength and accelerate progress, and alter his stance on invasion when it became clear that circumstances had changed. Although there was ultimately no need for Nimitz to respond to King's gambit and trigger a direct confrontation over the intelligence regarding Olympic, there is no doubt that Nimitz would have been able to offer clear and effective advice to the JCS and President Truman.

Lloyd Mustin recalled Nimitz's sensemaking capabilities in his oral history. Regarding the struggle against the kamikazes, Mustin said, "I thought there was a beautiful coherence observable between everything we knew or thought we knew, or saw or thought we saw, out in the frontlines . . . , and the way things were understood at Admiral Nimitz's headquarters."[91] As this chapter has shown, Mustin's sentiment applied equally well to operational planning as it did to the fight against Japanese suicide planes. Nimitz kept close to the challenges of his command and remained aware of newly emerging trends.

Nimitz was able to do this because he recognized that command was a collaborative activity, a complex endeavor that relied on effective personal relationships to draw out ideas and make sense of new opportunities. He regularly adopted the suggestions of subordinates—like Spruance's idea for Longtom—and integrated them into his own plans. That made them more likely to offer their ideas and voice their opinions, as with the debate over whether to invade Kikai Jima. This capability ensured Nimitz's command was able to make important decisions rapidly using the best available information.

Unified command was an essential part of this approach. When the JCS introduced a new command structure in the Pacific, they ignored these lessons and made coordination and collaboration slower and more tedious. In July 1945, for example, Halsey had to request supporting strikes from land-based air commands through Nimitz, resulting in a lengthy series of messages before any action was taken.[92] A year before, Spruance, as the Fifth Fleet commander, had exercised control over his supporting land-based planes and issued the necessary orders himself. By centralizing control of each service—the Navy under Nimitz and the Army under MacArthur—the JCS slowed decision-making and disrupted the sensemaking capability that Nimitz had refined during the preceding years.

The significant impact of this restructuring has largely been ignored, because by the time it was introduced, the war was almost over. Its largest influence was on preparations for an invasion that never occurred. Although the execution of Olympic was becoming less likely because of increasing Japanese strength on Kyushu, if the invasion had gone forward, it would have revealed the weaknesses of the Pacific's new command structure. Fortunately, the invasion was ultimately unnecessary.

When the instruments of surrender were signed on 2 September 1945, it was no accident that the ceremony took place on battleship *Missouri*, a ship of the Pacific Fleet, with Nimitz representing the armed forces of the United States. His campaign had swept across the Pacific, destroyed Japanese naval power, and brought the war to Japanese shores. While these efforts alone were not sufficient to win the war, they were crucial. Nimitz's leadership, command structure, and disciplined approach to risk had created the potential for Allied victory.

# CONCLUSION

*The tougher the going the calmer he [Nimitz] got. . . .*
*I don't think anyone ever served his country with more*
*distinction or under more difficult circumstances.*
—Former Secretary of the Navy Charles S. Thomas[1]

D uring World War II, Admiral Nimitz's leadership brought coherence to the Pacific Fleet in the aftermath of Pearl Harbor, earned the trust of his superiors and subordinates, created an effective theater-level organization, and executed the Central Pacific offensive, an opportunistic campaign that rapidly exploited new information to bring war to the shores of Japan and create the conditions for victory. Nimitz foreshadowed how he would fight in his Naval War College tactical thesis from 1923. His four "main and unchanging principles of warfare" emphasized employing the "utmost energy," concentrating superior strength at the decisive point, avoiding the "loss of time," and following up "every advantage." Evidence of these principles recurs throughout Nimitz's command in the Pacific. They are a useful frame for Nimitz's efforts, but while they explain how he fought, they are insufficient for understanding his most decisive influence, his approach to leadership.[2]

Nimitz's leadership combined a series of valuable elements: collaborative sensemaking, decentralized execution, an emergent process I call "organizational unfolding," continual reorientation, and the relentless pursuit of options. The paragraphs that follow will demonstrate how Nimitz combined these elements with his "principles of warfare" to create what I term "strategic artistry," a dynamic approach to strategic planning and execution that delivered rapid success in the Pacific.

## COLLABORATIVE SENSEMAKING

Nimitz recognized leadership as "a complex interactive dynamic" that emerges from patterns of interaction between leaders and subordinates. To be successful, he knew that he had to foster a collaborative environment and create the necessary conditions for him to lead. The Navy's traditional mechanism for strengthening relationships and fostering shared understanding was the conference. The "conference method," as taught at the Naval War College, emphasized conferences as tools for collaborative problem solving and collective sensemaking. Nimitz conformed to this pattern. His regular morning conferences served two purposes. They ensured that Nimitz and his core staff understood the latest intelligence; at the same time, the conferences created opportunity for dialog. Nimitz and his team "made sense" of the war by exchanging perspectives and exposing their disagreements. Nimitz's regular conferences with Admiral King served a similar purpose.[3]

Nimitz's conferences with new commanding officers were different, but no less important. Their objective was to create an initial personal relationship between the fleet commander and his subordinates. Nimitz wanted to get the measure of these new officers and, at the same time, demonstrate his interest in them and their commands' success. Nimitz welcomed them into the Pacific Fleet by sharing details of upcoming operations, creating a personal connection, and establishing a foundation for trust and shared commitment. These conferences were very deliberate and had a profound impact.[4]

In these various conferences, Nimitz displayed his skill at creating an atmosphere of "active open-mindedness" by cultivating psychological safety. He welcomed debate and proved his respect for new ideas by regularly incorporating them into his decision-making. Spruance's suggestions—to attack the Chusan Archipelago and to substitute Iwo Jima and Okinawa for Formosa—are excellent examples. According to Harvard professor Amy C. Edmondson, the purpose of open debate like this is to "provide the lead decision-maker with alternative perspectives to help him or her figure out the best outcome."[5] This is exactly what Nimitz encouraged, and he did it with his subordinates, his peers—like MacArthur and DeWitt—and his superiors—like King and the JCS.

However, psychological safety requires more than open-mindedness. It also requires establishing constraints and setting boundaries of acceptable behavior.[6] Nimitz skillfully did this during his conferences with Vice Admiral Ghormley in the fall of 1942. Arguably, Nimitz was even more effective during his conference with Rear Admiral Fletcher immediately before the Battle of Midway. Nimitz and King were not satisfied with how Fletcher had handled his forces at the Battle of Coral Sea. Nimitz shared that fact with Fletcher and used it to set expectations and clarify standards of performance. At the same time, Nimitz framed the upcoming challenge, presenting it in such a way that Fletcher could, and did, rise to it. Although the specific details of the conversation were not recorded, Nimitz almost certainly displayed a talented mix of humility, inquisitiveness, and open-mindedness to achieve these outcomes.[7]

## DECENTRALIZED EXECUTION

Nimitz fostered collaborative sensemaking deliberately. He emphasized the relentless pursuit of optionality and stressed rapid decision-making so that his forces could seize and maintain the initiative. This had been one of the Navy's core tactical heuristics during the interwar period. Nimitz employed it at the operational and strategic levels. Cybernetician W. Ross Ashby's Law of Requisite Variety is a useful frame for understanding why Nimitz's approach was so effective. Ashby's Law holds that "the variety of stimuli impinging on a system must be countered by the variety of responses that the system can muster."[8] In other words, to remain stable and effective, a system must be able to respond to a wide variety of circumstances, and it must be able to do so quickly.

Naval officers like Nimitz had an intuitive understanding of the challenge of Ashby's Law. Because it was impossible to proactively identify all the challenges a ship or a fleet would face, they delegated authority and fostered the individual initiative of subordinate commanders. Nimitz capitalized on this "pluralistic decentralization."[9] When he assumed command of the Pacific Ocean Areas, instead of creating a joint organization modeled on the Army's GHQ concept, Nimitz decentralized the integration of the services and created a modular structure with joint commands at the lowest levels. By pushing authority down to the point where new information was emerging, Nimitz adopted an approach well suited to the challenge of war in the Pacific.

MacArthur's approach was fundamentally different. While he allowed subordinates to exercise their initiative, his organizational structure centralized authority and forced collaboration between the services to go through his GHQ. This slowed decision-making and led to less effective outcomes, as Halsey learned when he tried to coordinate land-based air strikes with his carrier attacks in July 1945. MacArthur's approach was well suited to "complicated" problems that could be decomposed and executed in a linear fashion.[10] It was not suitable for the complex challenge Nimitz confronted in the Pacific. He needed decentralized structures that would permit faster decision-making and allow him and his subordinate commanders to seize fleeting opportunities.

This approach remains effective today. For example, when he was commanding the Joint Special Operations Task Force in Iraq in the early 2000s, Gen. Stanley McChrystal recognized that he needed to act quickly on newly emerging information. Like Nimitz, he required a greater variety of potential responses. Accordingly, McChrystal fostered shared understanding and pushed authority down. McChrystal expected this would lead to faster decision-making. He was surprised that it also led to better decisions.[11] McChrystal's frank admission shows that he was learning lessons that the Navy's early twentieth-century officers intuitively understood. Their "dislike for centralized authority" was rooted in the knowledge that it could not keep pace with the dynamics of modern naval war. Better outcomes required fostering decentralized execution.[12]

## ORGANIZATIONAL UNFOLDING

When organizations possess structures to deal with these kinds of complexities, they can address challenging problems more successfully. To avoid being overwhelmed by what Ashby called "stimuli," the people in organizations classify and filter inputs so that they can respond to them most effectively. One way to do this is with organizational structure: fire departments respond to fires, police departments respond to crimes, and emergency medical technicians respond to health-related issues. If you call 911, the operator classifies your emergency and alerts the appropriate organization. For this process to work, incoming stimuli must be defined and "coded" so that they can be routed appropriately. Nimitz regularly refined his organizational structure and "codification" strategies to improve the responsiveness of his command.

The most effective structures, both organizational or physical, naturally "unfold" from their surroundings; they harmonize with them and build on them, enhancing their positive qualities and dampening their negative ones. To create good structure is to make choices that resonate with established strengths and make desired outcomes more likely.[13] The evolution of Nimitz's staff structure reflects this insight. He deliberately enhanced existing predispositions and established patterns, building on the strengths of his staff.

Initially, Nimitz focused on his War Plans Section and its leaders— McMorris and McCormick—because they shared his aggressive disposition and desire to strike back at the Japanese. Rear Admiral Draemel was more methodical and less aggressive. As chief of staff, Draemel headed the Operations Section and managed more routine maneuvers, like convoys and their routing. By separating the work this way, Nimitz filtered the work of his combat forces, which required an aggressive opportunistic approach to succeed, from his logistical planners, who sought predictability and greater consistency. Nimitz's organizational structure allowed him to focus his inevitably limited attention on creating the conditions for tactical and strategic success with his war planners.

As this structure unfolded, strategy, operations, and tactics were not arranged in a hierarchy, but a triangle. Nimitz kept strategy and tactics closely linked by rapid feedback loops. He gave them his personal attention so that the tactical handling of his forces could deliver strategic results. The work of supplying and equipping his forces was left to talented subordinates like Towers, Leavey, and Calhoun. In his 1923 thesis, Nimitz presaged this approach. He quoted Rear Adm. Bradley Fiske, USN (Ret.), who argued that "there is no sharp dividing line" between strategy and tactics and "the main difference" between them is "that the strategist sees with the eye of the mind, while the tactician sees with the actual eye of the body."[14]

With logistics delegated to others, Nimitz—and his subordinates in the Pacific Fleet—were free to "see" with both of Fiske's "eyes" and rapidly take advantage of tactical opportunities to create strategically advantageous outcomes. The foregoing chapters provide notable examples, such as: destroying the *Kido Butai* at Midway, recognizing that the decisive struggle in late 1942 was at Guadalcanal, seizing the opportunity to shoot down Admiral Yamamoto's plane in April 1943, advancing directly to Kwajalein in January 1944, and deciding to capture Leyte in October 1944. Without the filtering provided by Nimitz's organizational structure, it is questionable whether he would have been able to take advantage of these opportunities so quickly and effectively. That is why both King and Nimitz insisted that he remain CINCPAC as well as CINCPOA, to keep tactics and strategy closely coupled and allow him to "see" with both "eyes."

However, Nimitz's approach worked best when it could build upon implicit assumptions and shared understanding developed through personal relationships. The contrast between Spruance and Halsey is instructive in this regard. Nimitz's approach worked well when Spruance was in command of the Central Pacific forces because the two had spent months together preparing for the upcoming offensive. That allowed them to collaborate smoothly and effectively as they accelerated the advance through Japanese-held positions. Halsey lacked the benefit of a similar relationship with Nimitz; the two exchanged plans, views, and letters, but never reached the same level of common understanding. The friction between Halsey and Nimitz during the Philippine campaign is evidence of this weakness and highlights the limitations of Nimitz's approach.

## CONTINUAL REORIENTATION

As Nimitz and his subordinates learned more about how best to prosecute the war, they regularly revised their codification strategies for incoming stimuli. For example, as carrier task forces changed from single-carrier formations to multi-carrier units, the way of describing them changed. Single-carrier task forces were often identified by the name of their carrier, like *Lexington, Enterprise,* or *Yorktown.* This would have been burdensome once multi-carrier task forces were adopted; accordingly, the practice was abandoned. Multi-carrier formations were consistently referred to by their number (e.g., TG 38.3); the specific carriers within them were less important than their overall capabilities.

By grouping similar things together, codification strategies introduce abstraction. The term "task force," for example, is an abstraction, but a very useful one. A "carrier task force" describes a force that has at least one carrier; for most purposes, this is sufficient even though we've said nothing about the carriers themselves, like how many there are, how large they are, or the number of aircraft they carry. Once the Pacific Fleet settled on a standard approach to organizing carrier task forces, Nimitz's staff officers could refer to them by their number. They didn't have to specify which carriers were in each task force; that made it easier to plan their movement, supply, and use.[15]

However, codification strategies must strike a balance. They can facilitate rapid communication within and between organizations, but there is always a tradeoff between the efficiency of communication and its effectiveness. The best strategies allow for a rapid transfer of information without sacrificing essential details. They also provide mechanisms for decomposing abstraction layers so that, for example, the higher-level codification strategies used by operational planners can feed into more detailed tactical plans. Many organizations struggle with balancing these trade-offs, but as Nimitz and his subordinates demonstrated, finding the appropriate balance can deliver a strategic advantage.[16]

Several times during the war, they adjusted their codification strategies. For example, the approach used for advanced bases had to be altered when the prewar concept of prepackaged bases—Lions, Cubs, and Acorns—proved inadequate. The solution was a new level of abstraction contained in the "Catalogue of Advanced Base Functional Components" of March 1943. Doctrinal development also had to change. The prewar approach that relied on decentralization was replaced by the more modular and flexible standard vocabulary encapsulated in *PAC-10,* issued in June 1943. For operational planning, a new system of codification and abstraction had to be created, leading to the Joint Staff Study in the fall of 1943. All these adjustments were essential to the success of the Central Pacific offensive. To determine how best to make these changes, Nimitz drew upon the variety of thinking within his command to examine alternatives and identify options. Prominent organizational analysts have identified this ability to regularly "recode" and reorient as a major strength.[17]

Nimitz fostered this organizational strength. He was fortunate that the Navy of the early twentieth century deliberately increased its potential for creative approaches by encouraging diversity of experience. In contrast to today, officers in the interwar period were not channeled into a particular specialty early in their career. Although they all received training in commanding ships and their crews, from that foundation officers could explore alternatives, developing diverse experiences in different platforms like submarines, aircraft, and surface ships. Specializations did exist—Nimitz was an expert in diesel engines early in his career—but the nature of the Navy's personnel system helped ensure these specializations augmented and diversified what was primarily a pool of generalists.[18]

Nimitz capitalized on the diverse experience of his staff with his collaborative approach. They innovated not just with new codification strategies but also with their staff and command structure. The broad revision of Nimitz's staff in September 1943 and the introduction of a new division dedicated to logistics is an excellent example. However, there were many other more subtle adjustments, like the introduction of ICPOA in June 1942, the decision to make the War Plans Section fully joint in June 1943, and the consolidation of the Plans and Operations Divisions under Forrest Sherman in December 1944.

In this way, Nimitz's organization addressed what historian Williamson Murray termed "the essential component in military effectiveness," namely "how quickly and competently a military organization can adapt to the actual conditions that it confronts."[19] Nimitz and his staff regularly reconfigured force and command structures to make them a better fit for their operating context. They learned to do this quickly and efficiently, because in the Pacific, the pressure to accelerate the war and bring it to a successful conclusion was acute.

To make this process effective, Nimitz deliberately created space and time to consider alternatives. The introduction of the shore-based type commands, the initial reorganization of the Pacific Fleet, and the way he delegated operations to Kinkaid and Halsey are examples of this. The way Nimitz arranged his personal schedule is another. Long walks, challenging swims, games of horseshoes, and time spent on the pistol range helped him relax and allowed his brain to subconsciously work through the challenges of war. These activities created the "slack" necessary to make sense of new information, reflect on what it meant, and devise new approaches to take advantage of it. As managers and commanders today know all too well, the discipline required to build slack time into a schedule is extremely difficult to achieve and maintain.[20]

Having time to think allowed Nimitz to keep his organizational structure aligned with the emerging nature of the war and how he wanted to fight it. As Frank Hoffman of the National Defense University has observed, Nimitz's command developed and maintained significant organizational learning capacity, even as the scope of Pacific operations grew from 1942 through much of 1945. Hoffman defined this capacity as "the aggregate ability of a military organization to recognize and respond to performance gaps generated by campaign pressures, unexpected adversary actions, or unanticipated aspects of the operating environment via adaptation or innovation."[21] This ability was rooted in the organizational tools—collaborative sensemaking, decentralized execution, and regular revision of coding strategies—described here. They allowed Nimitz to execute his concept of a trans-Pacific campaign with unparalleled rapidity, melding both major prewar strategies—the "through ticket" and the more methodical "cautionary" approach—to maintain and extend "unremitting pressure" on the Japanese.[22]

## RELENTLESS PURSUIT OF OPTIONS

Nimitz decentralized authority, filtered information through his command structure, and regularly reoriented because he continually sought to create advantage and accelerate the progress of the war. Nimitz and his staff understood something that more contemporary analysts have also recognized: the future—how the current context unfolds through time—can be shaped through deliberate action. By intelligently assessing potential outcomes and acting decisively, Nimitz and his subordinates increased their options, broadening their "cloud of . . . possibilities."[23] They brought the future into closer agreement with their own dispositions, making it easier for them to recognize and gain advantage. In domains dominated by emergent, experiential knowledge, such as warfare, Professor Max Boisot has argued that "we ourselves create the right answers by enacting them, thus converting a possible or plausible prospect into a probable or an actual one."[24] The victory at Midway, where Nimitz converted opportunity into decisive victory, is an excellent example of this process in action.

Nimitz emphasized "calculated risk" because he expected to maximize his future options by concentrating superior force at the decisive point. He was willing to sacrifice the potential of greater certainty in the present to increase his chances of imposing his will on the Japanese in the future. That meant time was arguably Nimitz's most valuable commodity; he embraced the perspective expressed by then–CNO Rear Adm. William S. Benson in 1917: "Time is everything, never waste it, keep ahead of it, deny it to the enemy."[25] Nimitz consistently used time to his advantage, capitalizing on the short feedback loop he maintained between strategy and tactics to act quickly and keep the Japanese off balance. He consistently imposed his desired orientation upon them. The early offensive at Guadalcanal in August 1942, the bypassing of Kiska in May 1943, the quick advance to Eniwetok in February 1944, and the carrier raid on Palau the following month are all excellent examples.

By doing this, Nimitz deliberately avoided what historian Martin van Creveld called "the quest for certainty," the effort of military organizations to deal with the inherent complexity of war by introducing more sophisticated information processing mechanisms. According to van Creveld, this invariably leads to more negative outcomes. As additional staff members are added "to cope with the flood of information," the problem of coordinating the various parts of the staff and their subordinate forces increases. "With each new well-defined procedure or formal language," van Creveld argued, "the gain in reliability and precision was offset by a decline in the informal communications, redundancy, and flexibility that are indispensable for the generation of ideas."[26]

To prevent this, Nimitz kept his staff small for much of the war. Unlike the organizations van Creveld criticized—which sought to understand all the relevant variables and manage the uncertainty "out" of combat—Nimitz assumed that his command decisions would always include varying degrees of risk and uncertainty. There were too many variables and nuances to account for them all exhaustively.

Instead, Nimitz reflected the Navy's established preferences. Navy officers tried to couple delegation with centralized direction through flexible structures, like the conference method and collective sensemaking. Small staffs were essential to this process, because the conference method would not work as well with a larger staff. However, Nimitz ultimately recognized that a small staff would be unable to manage the logistical and operational processes required by the fighting in the Pacific. Therefore, he integrated the best of the Navy's approach—small staffs for rapid, collaborative sensemaking—with the Army's—well-structured, centralized management for thorough operational planning. Nimitz's POA Joint Staff, introduced in September 1943, was the result. It took advantage of everything Nimitz had learned to that point and provided an organizational structure that harnessed the positive qualities of both approaches.

However, there were flaws. Nimitz's comfort with uncertainty and habit of delegation worked well during the first part of the Central Pacific offensive, but his failure to clearly set expectations about how to handle an encounter with the Japanese fleet led to friction between Spruance and Mitscher at the Battle of the Philippine Sea. As a result, they missed an opportunity to deal the Japanese a more decisive blow. Once Halsey assumed command, the situation worsened. At sea once more, he defaulted to task force command, operated at too low a level, and surrounded himself with an ineffective staff. As a result, Halsey missed his chance to inflict an overwhelming defeat on the Japanese because he would not divide the Third Fleet at the Battle of Leyte Gulf. Fortunately, by that time, the striking power of Nimitz's fleet was sufficient to absorb the error and still triumph.

Nimitz's collaborative approach was an asset in the Pacific; he used it to foster shared understanding and work through potential conflicts. However, it proved a hindrance when he was promoted to CNO after the war. Nimitz was too willing to compromise with the Army and Air Force in the "roles and missions" debate in order to avoid the sort of public disputes that he felt would undermine the standing of the military services. He lacked the political acumen that King had brought to the role. The limitations of Nimitz's leadership style had begun to show in the latter months of World War II. When he tried to prepare for the invasion of Kyushu with MacArthur, Nimitz continued to emphasize collaboration and failed to adjust his stance to the new command structure introduced by the JCS. Whether Nimitz could have been more effective is debatable, given MacArthur's penchant to escalate issues to Marshall and the JCS. However, what is certain is that Nimitz's collaborative style was inadequate for securing the best interests of the Navy in a struggle with adversarial peers. It worked through the summer of 1945 but is not universally applicable.[27]

## STRATEGIC ARTISTRY

The preceding chapters have described how Nimitz combined his principles of war with his leadership approaches, such as collective sensemaking, the relentless pursuit of options, and organizational flexibility. Where greater centralization was required, such as with logistical planning for the Central Pacific offensive, Nimitz introduced it. Where delegation was essential, as with the conduct of battles and execution of operations, Nimitz embraced it. Where a personal touch and informal communications were necessary, as in his many conversations with Admiral King and occasional conferences with MacArthur, Nimitz displayed deftness and subtlety. The emphasis on a holistic view—victory in the Pacific through a sustained campaign against the Empire of Japan—gave Nimitz the anchor he needed to adjust his organizational structure to adapt and evolve to best fit the circumstances of the moment.

Nimitz's campaign had to *flow*. A true assessment of his accomplishments must account for this point. Timing, movement, and opportunity all came together in a series of integrated flows. One flow planned operations, another provided the logistical sustenance for them, and the last flow was the offensive itself, the execution of operations that overwhelmed the Japanese and swept their fleet from the seas.[28] While MacArthur often focused on defending or besieging static positions—Port Moresby, Rabaul, and the Philippines—Nimitz emphasized flexible maneuverability to maintain "unremitting pressure" on the enemy. The CINCPAC/CINCPOA staff, the organization of Nimitz's command structure, and his process for developing and issuing orders to subordinates all emphasized the need for flexibility in service of a sustained campaign that flowed around and over enemy strongholds on the way to blockading and bombarding Japan's Home Islands. Shared understanding and collective sensemaking facilitated that flexibility, as did the concise format of operation plans. Those for Galvanic, Flintlock, Detachment, and Iceberg were just five pages; Forager was only three.

The speed with which Nimitz and his staff were able to conceive, plan, and execute operations undermines an established narrative of the Pacific War. We often think of Allied victory as inevitable because of the industrial might of the United States. This view reinforces arguments Sutherland and MacArthur repeatedly made when they contended that the Southwest Pacific should be the main line of advance. For them, overcoming static Japanese positions and destroying Japanese forces were the primary means of ensuring victory. Nimitz, in contrast, emphasized speed and maneuver. His goal was not to destroy Japanese fighting strength, but to isolate the source of that strength. Nimitz treated future operations as options and executed them in rapid sequence to keep the Japanese off balance, prevent them from regrouping, and limit their ability to learn and adapt. This kept U.S. forces from getting bogged down and undermined the Japanese strategy of securing a negotiated peace through excessive American casualties.

To sustain his rapid pace, Nimitz had to act with the "artistic sensibility" historian Jon Sumida described in his study of Alfred Thayer Mahan. When confronted with "difficult, complex, and unpredictable" challenges, Nimitz focused on creating a "flowing series of possibilities"—a collection of options—rather than a rigid, preconceived plan.[29] This allowed him to approach strategy in the way proposed by UCLA management professor Richard Rumelt, who argued that "good strategy must have an *entrepreneurial* component" and that strategists must be willing to dive "into the murky waters of induction, analogy, judgment, and insight."[30] Nimitz did this, and his emphasis on timing and speed helped ensure that his judgments and insights were ultimately more correct than those of his opponents.

Nimitz's strategy won the war, but most histories impose a retrospective coherence—historian Samuel Eliot Morison's *History of United States Naval*

*Operations in World War II* is an excellent example—that makes Nimitz's operations seem linear and predictable, rather than the series of options that they truly were. This has helped the more static perspective expressed by MacArthur's view dominate our sense of the war in the Pacific. It is time to reassess. We must acknowledge how the core characteristics of Nimitz's command structure were essential to victory. Without Nimitz's sensemaking capabilities, relentless pursuit of options, and sustained operational tempo, the war in the Pacific would have been quite different. The offensive that flowed across the Pacific, neutralized enemy strongpoints, and brought the war to the shores of Japan was a result of Nimitz's command structure.

That structure was emergent; it was not based on a preconceived design or preexisting structure. Nimitz's command structure was a result of, as Clausewitz framed it, a struggle of reactive wholes, tempered by Nimitz's characteristic approach to leadership. Nimitz's accomplishments provide a window into how organizations—military ones specifically, and other types more generally—adapt, reorient, and reconfigure themselves to achieve greater effectiveness.[31] As the foregoing chapters have shown, Nimitz was able to perform "as close to perfection as human limitations permit" because of the collaborative environment he fostered, the trust he created, and the sense of unity he brought to the Pacific Fleet and the Pacific Ocean Areas.[32] It is an example that is worthy of study and emulation.

# Notes

## INTRODUCTION

1. Williamson Murray, *War, Strategy, and Military Effectiveness* (New York: Cambridge University Press, 2011), 3–4.
2. Thomas E. Ricks, "George Washington, William T. Sherman and Viking Marauders," *New York Times*, 9 November 2018.
3. Mary Uhl-Bien et al., "Complexity Leadership Theory: Shifting Leadership from the Industrial Age to the Modern Era," *The Leadership Quarterly* 18 (2007): 298–318.
4. Matteo Mossio et al., "Emergence, Closure and Inter-Level Causation in Biological Systems," *Erkenntnis* 78 (2013): 153–78.
5. Uhl-Bien et al., "Complexity Leadership Theory."
6. Uhl-Bien et al., "Complexity Leadership Theory."
7. Cathal J. Nolan, *The Allure of Battle: A History of How Wars Have Been Won and Lost* (New York: Oxford University Press, 2017), 579.
8. Murray, *War, Strategy, and Military Effectiveness*, 16.
9. Vice Adm. Lloyd M. Mustin, *The Reminiscences of Vice Admiral Lloyd M. Mustin*, interviewed by John T. Mason Jr. (Annapolis, Md.: U.S. Naval Institute, 2003), 1:177–91.
10. Mustin, *Reminiscences*, 1:191, 2:1192–93.
11. Mustin, *Reminiscences*, 1:148–50; E. B. Potter, *Nimitz* (Annapolis, Md.: Naval Institute Press, 1976), 158.
12. Arthur Meier Schlesinger, *The Cycles of American History* (Boston: Houghton Mifflin, 1986), 422.
13. Trent Hone, *Learning War: The Evolution of Fighting Doctrine in the U.S. Navy, 1898–1945* (Annapolis, Md.: Naval Institute Press, 2018), 122–62.
14. Frans P. B. Osinga, *Science, Strategy, and War: The Strategic Theory of John Boyd* (New York: Routledge, 2007), 236–37.
15. Keith Sawyer, *Group Genius: The Creative Power of Collaboration*, rev. ed. (New York: Basic Books, 2017), xii.
16. This concept emerged from conversations with Chris Matts, Alicia Juarrero, Marc Burgauer, and Sue Borchardt.
17. David D. Woods, "The Theory of Graceful Extensibility: Basic Rules that Govern Adaptive Systems," *Environment Systems and Decisions* (2018).
18. Amy Edmondson, *The Fearless Organization: Creating Psychological Safety in the Workplace for Learning, Innovation, and Growth* (Hoboken, N.J.: Wiley, 2019), xv.

19. Ryan Grauer, *Commanding Military Power* (Cambridge: Cambridge University Press, 2016), 3–4.

20. Osinga, *Science, Strategy, and War*, 10, 235, 237.

21. Carl von Clausewitz, *On War*, trans. and ed. Michael Howard and Peter Paret, indexed ed. (Princeton, N.J.: Princeton University Press, 1984), 1:90, 95 and 2:149. Emphasis in original.

22. Osinga, *Science, Strategy, and War*, 9.

23. Jon Tetsuro Sumida, *Inventing Grand Strategy and Teaching Command: The Classic Works of Alfred Thayer Mahan Reconsidered* (Washington, D.C.: Woodrow Wilson Center Press, 1997), xiii–xiv.

24. Osinga, *Science, Strategy, and War*, 9.

25. Jon Tetsuro Sumida, *Decoding Clausewitz: A New Approach to* On War (Lawrence: University Press of Kansas, 2008), 180.

26. Fletcher Pratt, *Fleet Against Japan* (New York: Harper & Brothers, 1946), 36–37; Bradley A. Fiske, *The Navy as a Fighting Machine*, 2nd ed. (New York: Charles Scribner's Sons, 1918; repr., Annapolis, Md.: Naval Institute Press, 1988), 221.

## PROLOGUE

1. "Nimitz Diary," 24 December 1941, *Papers of Fleet Admiral Chester W. Nimitz, USN* [hereafter: *Nimitz Papers*], Manuscript Collection 505, Naval History and Heritage Command Operational Archives, Washington, D.C.

2. *Recollections of Fleet Admiral Chester W. Nimitz as Given by Admirals Drake, Fife & Layton and Captain Lamar* [hereafter: *Recollections DFLL*] (Annapolis, Md.: U.S. Naval Institute, 1970), Lamar-2; Potter, *Nimitz*, 13.

3. "Damage to Ships of the Pacific Fleet resulting from Enemy Attacks at Pearl Harbor, 7 December 1942," Commander-in-Chief, United States Pacific Fleet, 12 December 1941.

4. "Nimitz Diary," 20 December 1941, *Nimitz Papers*.

5. "Nimitz Diary," 24 December 1941, *Nimitz Papers*; Potter, *Nimitz*, 15.

## CHAPTER 1. ASSUMING COMMAND

1. Abrams et al. v. United States, 316, U.S. 616 (1919), Dissent of Justice Holmes, 630.

2. "Nimitz Diary," 26 December 1941, *Nimitz Papers*; John B. Lundstrom, *Black Shoe Carrier Admiral* (Annapolis, Md.: Naval Institute Press, 2006), 45; Potter, *Nimitz*, 16.

3. Hone, *Learning War*, 122–62.

4. Edward S. Miller, *War Plan Orange: The U.S. Strategy to Defeat Japan: 1897–1945* (Annapolis, Md.: Naval Institute Press, 1991), 77–149.

5. Hone, *Learning War*, 122–62; Capt. Wayne P. Hughes Jr., USN (Ret.) and Rear Adm. Robert P. Girrier, USN (Ret.), *Fleet Tactics and Naval Operations*, 3rd ed. (Annapolis, Md.: Naval Institute Press, 2018).

6. *Sound Military Decision, including the Estimate of the Situation and the Formulation of Directives* (Newport, R.I.: Naval War College, 1938); Hone, *Learning War*, 104–6.

7. Edward S. Miller, "Kimmel's Hidden Agenda," *Military History Quarterly* 4, no. 1 (1991): 36–43.

8. Miller, "Kimmel's Hidden Agenda"; Miller, *War Plan Orange*, 274.

9. *WPPac-46*, Commander-in-Chief, U.S. Pacific Fleet, 21 July 1941.

10. Miller, "Kimmel's Hidden Agenda"; Miller, *War Plan Orange*, 286–312; *WPPac-46*; Trent Hone, "The Evolution of Fleet Tactical Doctrine in the U.S. Navy, 1922–1941," *Journal of Military History* 67, no. 4 (October 2003): 1107–48.

11. Meir Finkel, *On Flexibility: Recovery from Technological and Doctrinal Surprise on the Battlefield* (Stanford, Calif.: Stanford Security Studies, 2011).

12. David D. Woods, "Four Concepts for Resilience and the Implications for the Guture of Resilience Engineering," *Reliability Engineering and System Safety* 141 (2015): 5–9.

13. Mark R. Peattie, *Sunburst: The Rise of Japanese Naval Air Power, 1909–1941* (Annapolis, Md.: Naval Institute Press, 2001), 168; Samuel Eliot Morison, *History of the United States Naval Operations in World War II*, 15 vols. (1962; repr., Boston: Little, Brown, 1984), 3:80–146.

14. Peattie, *Sunburst*, 151–52; Jonathan Parshall and Anthony Tully, *Shattered Sword: The Untold Story of the Battle of Midway* (Washington, D.C.: Potomac Books, 2005), 15.

15. Quoted in Osinga, *Science, Strategy, and War*, 101.

16. Yukiko Koshiro, *Imperial Eclipse: Japan's Strategic Thinking about Continental Asia before August 1945* (Ithaca and London: Cornell University Press, 2013), 60–61; Nolan, *The Allure of Battle*, 519, 536; John Keegan, *The Mask of Command* (New York: Penguin Books, 1988), 330; Parshall and Tully, *Shattered Sword*, 73–77.

17. Herbert P. Bix, *Hirohito and the Making of Modern Japan* (New York: Harper Collins, 2000), 413.

18. Rear Adm. Edwin T. Layton, USN (Ret.), et al., *"And I Was There": Pearl Harbor and Midway—Breaking the Secrets* (Annapolis, Md.: Naval Institute Press, 1985), 353.

19. Campaign Plan No. 2-R5, 10 December 1941, *Command Summary of Fleet Admiral Chester W. Nimitz, USN*, Nimitz "Graybook" [hereafter: "Graybook"], 1:22–26.

20. CINCPAC Operation Order No. 40-41, 13 December 1941, CINCPAC Operation Order No. 39-41, 15 December 1941, CINCPAC Operation Order No. 41-41, 15 December 1941, *World War II Plans, Orders, and Related Documents* [hereafter: *Plans and Orders*], Record Group 38, Records of the Office of the Chief of Naval Operations, National Archives, Washington, D.C.; Lundstrom, *Black Shoe*, 19.

21. OPNAV 152149, December 1941, "Graybook," 1:50; B. Mitchell Simpson III, *Admiral Harold R. Stark: Architect of Victory* (Columbia: University of South Carolina Press, 1989), 116; Potter, *Nimitz*, 9.

22. CINCPAC 152301, OPNAV 160050, December 1941, "Graybook," 1:50–51.

23. Layton et al., *"And I Was There,"* 339.

24. CINCPAC Operation Order No. 42-41, 18 December 1941, *Plans and Orders*; Lundstrom, *Black Shoe*, 31–36.

25. Gregory J. W. Urwin, *Facing Fearful Odds: The Siege of Wake Island* (Lincoln: University of Nebraska Press, 1997), 516; 22 December 1941, "Graybook," 1:69; "Estimate by Admiral Pye as to action re enemy investing Wake–0700–December 22, 1941," "Graybook," 1:77–78.

26. "Estimate of Captain McMorris as to action regarding enemy investing Wake 0800 Dec. 22," "Graybook," 1:79–81.

27. "Decision by Admiral Draemel as to action regarding enemy investing Wake 0700–22 December," "Graybook," 1:82. Emphasis in original.

28. Morison, *History,* 3:248; Lundstrom, *Black Shoe,* 40; Urwin, *Facing Fearful Odds,* 518–19.

29. Adah-Marie R. Miller, "Fleet Admiral Chester W. Nimitz, U.S.N., A Speculative Study (A Psycho-Biographical Quest for Qualities of Leadership)," (master's thesis, University of Texas, August 1962), 64; Pratt, *Fleet Against Japan,* 46.

30. Potter, *Nimitz,* 4, 9.

31. Paolo E. Coletta, ed., *American Secretaries of the Navy.* Vol. 1, *1775–1913* (Annapolis, Md.: Naval Institute Press, 1980), 445–46; Potter, *Nimitz,* 52–53.

32. Potter, *Nimitz,* 3, 52–53; Edward J. Marolda, ed., *FDR and the U.S. Navy* (New York: St. Martin's Press, 1998), 164.

33. Cdr. Chester W. Nimitz, "Thesis on Tactics," 28 April 1923, *Student Papers,* Record Group 13, Naval War College Archives, Newport, R.I.

34. COMINCH 301701, December 1941, "Graybook," 1:121.

35. COMINCH 301740, December 1941, "Graybook," 1:121.

36. OPNAV 170115, December 1941, "Graybook," 1:70.

37. "Nimitz Diary," 28 December 1941, *Nimitz Papers.*

38. "Notes on Conversation with Fleet Admiral Chester Nimitz at 101 Washington Street, Newport, R.I., 5:30 to 6:30 p.m.," 13 October 1961, *Papers of Rear Adm. Henry E. Eccles, USN,* Manuscript Collection 52, Naval War College Archives, Newport, R.I.

39. Layton et al., *"And I Was There,"* 353.

40. *Recollections DFLL,* Drake-5.

41. COMCRUSCOFOR 052310, January 1942, *Commander-in-Chief, Pacific and U.S. Pacific Fleets, Microfilmed Incoming and Outgoing Dispatches and Chronological Message Traffic, 1940–45* [hereafter: *Messages*], Record Group 313, *Records of Naval Operating Forces,* Entry (A1) 125, National Archives, Washington, D.C.; Lundstrom, *Black Shoe,* 52, 54.

42. Miller, "Fleet Admiral," 71–75; Potter, *Nimitz,* 222–23; Pratt, *Fleet Against Japan,* 49–50; Layton et al., *"And I Was There,"* 356–57.

43. Anita Williams Woolley et al., "Collective Intelligence and Group Performance," *Current Directions in Psychological Science* 24 (6): 420–24; Anita Williams Woolley et al., "Evidence for a Collective Intelligence Factor in the Performance of Human Groups," *Science* 330 (29 October 2010): 686–88.

44. Miller, "Fleet Admiral," 87.

45. Amy Edmondson, "Psychological Safety and Learning Behavior in Work Teams," *Administrative Science Quarterly* 44, no. 2 (June 1999): 350–83.

46. Finkel, *On Flexibility,* 55–56.

47. *Recollections DFLL,* Drake-5.

48. COMINCH 021718, January 1942, *Messages.* Emphasis in original.

49. "Offensive Employment of Carrier Group Task Force," 25 December 1941, "Employment of Carrier Task Forces in January," 2 January 1942, "Graybook," 1:115, 123–35.

50. "Notes on Conversation with Fleet Admiral Chester Nimitz at 101 Washington Street, Newport, R.I., 5:30 to 6:30 p.m.," 13 October 1961.

51. "Notes on Conversation with Fleet Admiral Chester Nimitz"; "Additional Considerations re Samoa Reinforcement Operation," 8 January 1942, "Graybook," 1:143–53; Lundstrom, *Black Shoe*, 56–57.

52. CINCPAC Operation Plan No. 4-42, 9 January 1942, *Plans and Orders.*

53. ACNB 1206Z/9, OPNAV 072251, COM14 090505, Naval Attaché Melbourne 130640, CINCPAC 090445, January 1942, *Messages.*

54. CINCPAC 102157, 140411, COMTASKUNIT 7.6.6 141717, COM14 10000, 110159, 130045, 160001, January 1942, *Messages.*

55. COMINCH 202150, CINCPAC 212217, *Messages*; 21–23 January 1942, "Graybook," 1:158–59, 179–83.

56. CINCPAC 220055, January 1942, "Graybook," 1:180; CTF8 221825, January 1942, *Messages.*

57. COM14 270333, COMINCH 271945, January 1942, *Messages.*

58. ACNB 0918Z/23, January 1942, *Messages*; CINCPAC 280311, January 1942, "Graybook," 1:193; Lundstrom, *Black Shoe*, 59–63.

59. Matome Ugaki, *Fading Victory: The Diary of Admiral Matome Ugaki, 1941–1945*, ed. Donald M. Goldstein and Katherine V. Dillon, trans. Masataka Chihaya (Annapolis, Md.: Naval Institute Press, 2008), 83; *Outline of Operations of the Navy's South Seas Force*, Japanese Monograph No. 139, July 1949 (Japanese Research Division, Military History Section, Headquarters, United States Army Forces, Far East), 9.

60. Ugaki, *Fading Victory*, 82–83; Willem Remmelink, trans., *The Operations of the Navy in the Dutch East Indies and the Bay of Bengal* (Leiden: Leiden University Press, 2018), 212; H. P. Willmott, *Empires in the Balance: Japanese and Allied Pacific Strategies to April 1942* (Annapolis, Md.: Naval Institute Press, 1982), 286; H. P. Willmott, *The Barrier and the Javelin: Japanese and Allied Pacific Strategies February to June 1942* (Annapolis, Md.: Naval Institute Press, 1983), 56; Lundstrom, *Black Shoe*, 70; Layton translation of *Senshi Sosho, Volume 85*, "Naval Operations in Home Waters," *Papers of Rear Adm. Edwin T. Layton, USN* [hereafter: *Layton Papers*], Manuscript Collection 69, Naval War College Archives, Newport, R.I.

61. COM14 112023, February 1942, *Messages.*

62. Thomas Alexander Hughes, *Admiral Bill Halsey: A Naval Life* (Cambridge, Mass.: Harvard University Press, 2016), 161; "Tokyo Loss Heavy," *New York Times*, 13 February 1942.

63. Robert Artigiani, "Chaos and Constitutionalism: Toward a Post Modern Theory of Social Evolution," *World Futures* 34 (1992): 131–56.

64. CINCPAC 070245, January 1942, *Messages.*

65. Operation Plan No. R5-1, "Graybook," 1:198–202.

66. Quoted in David Epstein, *Range: Why Generalists Triumph in a Specialized World* (New York: Riverhead Books, 2019), 163–64.

67. "Nimitz Diary," 28 December 1941, *Nimitz Papers.*

## CHAPTER 2. CREATING OPPORTUNITIES

1. "Nimitz Diary," 22 March 1942, *Nimitz Papers*.

2. Simpson, *Admiral Harold R. Stark*, 124; Wesley Frank Craven and James Lea Cate, *The Army Air Forces in World War II*, 7 vols. (1958; repr., Washington, D.C.: Office of Air Force History, 1983), 1:237–39, 252–53.

3. Rear Adm. Julius Augustus Furer, *Administration of the Navy Department in World War II* (Washington, D.C.: Naval History Division, 1959), 651; Craven and Cate, *The Army Air Forces*, 1:253–54; Thomas B. Buell, *Master of Sea Power: A Biography of Fleet Admiral Ernest J. King* (Boston: Little, Brown, 1980), 164–65.

4. Simpson, *Admiral Harold R. Stark*, 126, 128–29.

5. Buell, *Master of Sea Power*, 168.

6. Henry H. Adams, *Witness to Power: The Life of Fleet Admiral William D. Leahy* (Annapolis, Md.: Naval Institute Press, 1985), 170.

7. Marolda, *FDR*, 165.

8. Richard B. Frank, "Picking Winners," *Naval History Magazine* 25, no. 3 (June 2011): 24–32.

9. Frank, "Picking Winners."

10. Frank, "Picking Winners."

11. COMINCH 241740, CINCPAC 282117, January 1942, "Graybook," 1:185, 197; Lundstrom, *Black Shoe*, 73.

12. RDO Canberra 0956Z/27, 26 January 1942, *Messages*; 28 January 1942, "Graybook," 1:194.

13. COMINCH 311606, January 1942, COMINCH 061513, 062352, February 1942, "Briefed Estimate of the Situation," 5 February 1942, 8 February 1942, "Graybook," 1:205, 211, 220–21, 227–39; CINCPAC War Diary, 5 February 1942; Craven and Cate, *The Army Air Forces*, 1:413; Lundstrom, *Black Shoe*, 74.

14. "Nimitz Diary," 22 March 1942, *Nimitz Papers*.

15. "Briefed Estimate of the Situation," 5 February 1942, "Graybook," 1:227–239.

16. 7 February 1942, "Briefed Estimate of the Situation," 5 February 1942, COMINCH 191400, CINCPAC 210523, March 1942, "Graybook," 1:210, 227–39, 311, 314.

17. 7 February 1942, "Graybook," 1:210. King appears to have been operating with the approval of Knox. See Lundstrom, *Black Shoe*, 49, 103; Clark G. Reynolds, *Admiral John H. Towers: The Struggle for Naval Air Supremacy* (Annapolis, Md.: Naval Institute Press, 1991), 440.

18. COM14 112023, 11 February 1942, *Messages*; SRH-278, War Diary, Combat Intelligence Unit (Pacific–1942), 12 March 1942, *Layton Papers*; 9–10 February 1942, "Graybook," 1:211–12.

19. CINCPAC Operation Order No. 15-42, *Plans and Orders*, Box 20; 11–12 February 1942, "Graybook," 1:213–14; Lundstrom, *Black Shoe*, 76.

20. Lundstrom, *Black Shoe*, 77; Layton et al., *"And I Was There,"* 367–69.

21. CINCLANT 053 of January 21, 1941, Quoted in Buell, *Master of Sea Power*, Appendix I.

22. 15 February 1942, "Graybook," 1:216.

23. CINCPAC 160301, February 1942, *Messages*; 15 February 1942, "Graybook," 1:216.

24. COMINCH 122200, COMANZAC 140336, 140338, 140340, 140344, February 1942, "Graybook," 1:222–24; Lundstrom, *Black Shoe*, 76; Craven and Cate, *The Army Air Forces*, 1:243.

25. COMANZAC 140538, 150244, COMINCH 141835, February 1942, "Graybook," 1:224–25; 13–15 February 1942, I:215–16; Lundstrom, *Black Shoe*, 76; John B. Lundstrom, *The First Team: Pacific Naval Air Combat from Pearl Harbor to Midway* (Annapolis, Md.: Naval Institute Press, 1984), 77–78.

26. CINCPAC 181711, February 1942, *Messages*.

27. *Secret Information Bulletin No. 1: Battle Experience from Pearl Harbor to Midway, December 1941 to June 1942, Including Makin Island Raid 17–18 August* (United States Fleet, Headquarters of the Commander in Chief, 15 February 1943), 4-2.

28. CINCPAC 241943, February 1942, *Messages*; 19, 23 February 1942, COMTASKFOR 11 200237, 200753, 232214, February 1942, "Graybook," 1:240, 243, 250, 253; Lundstrom, *Black Shoe*, 79–80; Lundstrom, *First Team*, 83–110.

29. 23–25 February 1942, 4–5 March 1942, "Graybook," 1:244–45, 262–63; Lundstrom, *Black Shoe*, 77; CINCPAC 240105, 250249, February 1942, *Messages*; Lundstrom, *First Team*, 111–19; Ugaki, *Fading Victory*, 101; Steven Bullard, trans., *Japanese Army Operations in the South Pacific Area: New Britain and Papua Campaigns, 1942–43* (Canberra, Australia: Australian War Memorial, 2007), 72; Remmelink, *Operations of the Navy*, 601–2.

30. COMANZAC 250100, 250430, February 1942, *Messages*; 24 February 1942, CINCPAC 251209, COMTASKFOR 11 260458, February 1942, "Graybook," 1:244, 254–55; Lundstrom, *Black Shoe*, 80; Bullard, *Japanese Army Operations*, 46; Milan Vego, *Major Fleet-versus-Fleet Operations in the Pacific War, 1941–1945*, 2nd ed. (Newport, R.I.: Naval War College Press, 2016), 19.

31. 26 February 1942, COMINCH 261630, CINCPAC 280559, February 1942, "Graybook," 1:246, 255, 257.

32. Lundstrom, *Black Shoe*, 85.

33. Parshall and Tully, *Shattered Sword*, 31; Lundstrom, *Black Shoe*, 95; Willmott, *Barrier*, 61; *Secret Information Bulletin No. 1*, 6-1; Vego, *Fleet-versus-Fleet*, 19–20; Bullard, *Japanese Army Operations*, 41; Ugaki, *Fading Victory*, 103.

34. Willmott, *Barrier*, 55–74.

35. Bullard, *Japanese Army Operations*, 66.

36. Bullard, *Japanese Army Operations*, 68.

37. Willmott, *Barrier*, 38; Richard B. Frank, *Guadalcanal: The Definitive Account of the Landmark Battle* (New York: Random House, 1990), 18–25.

38. David C. Evans and Mark R. Peattie, *Kaigun: Strategy, Tactics, and Technology in the Imperial Japanese Navy, 1887–1941* (Annapolis, Md.: Naval Institute Press, 1997), 286–98; Bullard, *Japanese Army Operations*, 3, 69; Willmott, *Barrier*, 39.

39. Bullard, *Japanese Army Operations*, 67–69; Willmott, *Barrier*, 37–43.

40. Ugaki, *Fading Victory*, 92–93; Parshall and Tully, *Shattered Sword*, 30–31; Willmott, *Barrier*, 40–52.

41. Bullard, *Japanese Army Operations*, 3–4, 8, 69–70, 72; Willmott, *Barrier*, 52–54.

42. Ugaki, *Fading Victory*, 86.

43. Ugaki, *Fading Victory*, 75.

44. Parshall and Tully, *Shattered Sword*, 34–36, 43–44.

45. Willmott, *Barrier*, 61.

46. *Commander-in-Chief, United States Pacific Fleet and Pacific Ocean Areas Command History, 7 December 1941–15 August 1945* [hereafter: CCCH] (Historical Section, CINCPACFLT), Appendix A, 16; Joel Ira Holwitt, *"Execute Against Japan": The U.S. Decision to Conduct Unrestricted Submarine Warfare* (College Station, Tex.: Texas A&M University Press, 2009), 159–61.

47. "Organization and Functioning of Naval Staffs," 26 June 1944, *Faculty and Staff Presentations*. Record Group 14 [hereafter: *Presentations*], Naval War College Archives, Newport, R.I., Box 24.

48. CINCPAC 052003, January 1942, *Messages*.

49. CCCH, Appendix A, 16.

50. 27 January 1942, "Graybook," 1:191.

51. "Reorganization, U.S. Pacific Fleet." Commander-in-Chief, United States Pacific Fleet, 23 March 1942.

52. "Reorganization, U.S. Pacific Fleet," 23 March 1942.

53. CINCPAC War Diary, 10 April 1942.

54. CCCH, 46–47.

55. CCCH, 11.

56. Grauer, *Commanding Military Power*, 3, 197–98.

57. Hone, *Learning War*, 335–36.

58. *SRH-012: The Role of Naval Intelligence in the American–Japanese War (August 1941–June 1942)*, 1 September 1942, *Layton Papers*.

59. Andrew Boyd, *The Royal Navy in Eastern Waters: Linchpin of Victory, 1935–1942* (Barnsley, UK: Seaforth, 2017), 231; Elliot Carlson, *Joe Rochefort's War: The Odyssey of the Codebreaker Who Outwitted Yamamoto at Midway* (Annapolis, Md.: Naval Institute Press, 2011), 107–8, 118–23, 202.

60. Carlson, *Joe Rochefort's War*, 120; John Prados, *Combined Fleet Decoded: The Secret History of American Intelligence and the Japanese Navy in World War II* (New York: Random House, 1995), 161–65.

61. Layton et al., *"And I Was There,"* 174; Carlson, *Joe Rochefort's War*, 107–8, 118–23, 202.

62. *SRH-224, Various Reports on Japanese Grand Fleet Maneuvers (August–October 1934), Layton Papers*.

63. COMINCH 122310, January 1942, *Messages*; Layton Notebook, Vol. 1, *Layton Papers*.

64. Layton et al., *"And I Was There,"* 252; Christopher Ford and David Rosenberg, *The Admirals' Advantage: U.S. Navy Operational Intelligence in World War II and the Cold War* (Annapolis, Md.: Naval Institute Press, 2005), 3.

65. Carlson, *Joe Rochefort's War*, 238–39; Layton et al., *"And I Was There,"* 359.

66. 3 March 1942, "Graybook," 1:261; Carlson, *Joe Rochefort's War*, 245–49; Layton et al., *"And I Was There,"* 372–74.

67. Carlson, *Joe Rochefort's War*, 251–53.

68. Morison, *History*, 3:389–90; Craven and Cate, *The Army Air Forces*, 1:438–39.

69. Lundstrom, *Black Shoe*, 102.

70. 25 March 1942, CINCPAC 210147, March 1942, "Graybook," 1:299, 315; Lundstrom, *Black Shoe*, 102–4.

71. Remmelink, *Operations of the Navy*, 571, 601–2; Morison, *History*, 3:382–83; *War with Japan*, 6 vols. (Ministry of Defense (Navy), London: HMSO, 1995), 2:124–25; Angus Britts, *Neglected Skies: The Demise of British Naval Power in the Far East, 1922–42* (Annapolis, Md.: Naval Institute Press, 2017), 18–19.

72. Remmelink, *Operations of the Navy*, 569–70; Morison, *History*, 3:381–82; *War with Japan*, 2:122–24; Britts, *Neglected Skies*, 13–14.

73. Willmott, *Empires*, 445. Fifty years later, the author interviewed a witness to the Japanese strike who was still profoundly impressed by it.

74. Remmelink, *Operations of the Navy*, 646; Morison, *History*, 3:383–85; *War with Japan*, 2:126–31; Britts, *Neglected Skies*, 20–25; Boyd, *Royal Navy*, 387–89; Andrew Boyd, *British Naval Intelligence through the Twentieth Century* (Barnsley, UK: Seaforth, 2020), 470–71.

75. CINCPAC 182359, March 1942, Layton Notebook, Vol. 1, *Layton Papers*; CINCPAC Operation Plan No. 20-42, April 1942, *Plans and Orders*.

76. Morison, *History*, 3:389–98; "Report of Action in connection with the bombing of Tokyo on April 18, 1942," Commander-in-Chief, United States Pacific Fleet, 4 May 1942, *World War II Action and Operational Reports* [hereafter: *Action*], Record Group 38, Records of the Office of the Chief of Naval Operations, National Archives, Washington, D.C.; Craven and Cate, *The Army Air Forces*, 1:441–42; Lundstrom, *First Team*, 147–50.

77. Ugaki, *Fading Victory*, 113; Willmott, *Barrier*, 118; Parshall and Tully, *Shattered Sword*, 43.

78. 27–28 March 1942, COMTASKFOR 17 210833, March 1942, "Graybook," 1:304, 313; Lundstrom, *Black Shoe*, 100–1, 104.

79. 29 March 1942, COMTASKFOR 17 292346, COMINCH 301930, March 1942, "Graybook," 1: 304–5, 322.

80. COMINCH 311455, March 1942, "Graybook," 1:324; Lundstrom, *Black Shoe*, 107.

81. COMINCH 031905, 041850, CINCPAC 051849, April 1942, "Graybook," 1:328–31; "Designation as 'Commander in Chief of the Pacific Ocean Area.'" Commander in Chief, United States Fleet and Chief of Naval Operations, 3 April 1942; "United Nations Operations in the Pacific Theater," The Secretary of the Navy, 20 April 1942, Enclosure B; Frank, *Guadalcanal*, 15.

82. Peter J. Dean, *MacArthur's Coalition: US and Australian Operations in the Southwest Pacific Area, 1942–1945* (Lawrence: Kansas University Press, 2018), 43–44.

83. COM 14 Mailgram 160800, April 1942, *Messages*; "Estimate of the Situation," 22 April 1942, "Graybook," 1:371–407; *SRH-272, Enemy Activities File, April–May 1942*, 22 April 1942, *Layton Papers*.

84. "Estimate of the Situation," 22 April 1942, "Graybook," 1:371–407.

85. "Minutes of Conversations between Cominch and Cincpac, Saturday, April 25," 26 April 1942; "Minutes of Conversations between Cominch and Cincpac, April 26, 1942," 27 April 1942; "Minutes of Conversations between Cominch and Cincpac,

Monday, April 27," 27 April 1942, all *Papers of Fleet Admiral Ernest J. King, USN* [hereafter: *King Papers*], Manuscript Collection 28, Naval History and Heritage Command Operational Archives, Washington, D.C.

86. "Minutes of Conversations between Cominch and Cincpac, Saturday, April 25," 26 April 1942; "Minutes of Conversations between Cominch and Cincpac, April 26, 1942," 27 April 1942; "Minutes of Conversations between Cominch and Cincpac, Monday, April 27," 27 April 1942.

87. "Minutes of Conversations between Cominch and Cincpac, Saturday, April 25," 26 April 1942; "Minutes of Conversations between Cominch and Cincpac, April 26, 1942," 27 April 1942; "Minutes of Conversations between Cominch and Cincpac, Monday, April 27," 27 April 1942.

88. "Minutes of Conversations between Cominch and Cincpac, Saturday, April 25," 26 April 1942; "Minutes of Conversations between Cominch and Cincpac, April 26, 1942," 27 April 1942; "Minutes of Conversations between Cominch and Cincpac, Monday, April 27," 27 April 1942.

89. Potter, *Nimitz*, 32; Rear Adm. Joseph C. Wylie Jr., *The Reminiscences of Rear Admiral Joseph C. Wylie Jr.*, interview by Paul Stillwell (Annapolis, Md.: U.S. Naval Institute, 2003), 18.

90. This change is clear in the nature of the messages between COMINCH and CINCPAC, see "Graybook," 1:411–431; Lundstrom, *Black Shoe*, 128.

91. Epstein, *Range*, 18–28.

92. "Annual Report of the Commander-in-Chief, United States Fleet for the Period 1 July, 1933 to 30 June, 1934," 11, *World War II Command File* [hereafter: *WWII*], Naval History and Heritage Command Operational Archives, Washington, D.C.

93. These assessments come from Ellis Zacharias and Joseph Rochefort and are quoted in Carlson, *Joe Rochefort's War*, 124–25.

## CHAPTER 3. TAKING RISKS

1. Quoted in Osinga, *Science, Strategy, and War*, 101.

2. "Letter of Instructions," Commander-in-Chief, United States Pacific Fleet, 28 May 1942, *Plans and Orders*.

3. For a thorough treatment of the nature of chance and uncertainty in war, see Anders Engberg-Pedersen, *Empire of Chance: The Napoleonic Wars and the Disorder of Things* (Cambridge, Mass.: Harvard University Press, 2015), 37–68.

4. Keegan, *Mask of Command*, 318; "Nimitz Diary," 31 May 1941, *Nimitz Papers*.

5. COMSUBPAC 141830, May 1942, *Messages*.

6. "Organization and Functioning of Naval Staffs," 26 June 1944, *Presentations*. I am indebted to Marc Burgauer for the idea that organizational structure emerges from relationships.

7. Mustin, *Reminiscences*, 1:191, 2:1192–93.

8. Edmondson, *Fearless Organization*, 175–77.

9. CINCPAC Operation Plan No. 23-42, 29 April 1942, *Plans and Orders*; 18 April 1942, "Graybook," 1:365, emphasis in original.

10. Bullard, *Japanese Army Operations*, 42, 49–53; Parshall and Tully, *Shattered Sword*, 58.

11. Bullard, *Japanese Army Operations*, 55–58; Lundstrom, *Black Shoe*, 137–40.
12. 3–4 May 1942, "Graybook," 1:434; Lundstrom, *Black Shoe*, 132–37.
13. Bullard, *Japanese Army Operations*, 61–62; Lundstrom, *Black Shoe*, 144–50.
14. "Cruiser Attack on Japanese Siberian Fisheries," 28 April 1942, "Graybook," 1:417–20; CINCPAC Operation Plan 24-42, 2 May 1942, *Plans and Orders*.
15. Lundstrom, *Black Shoe*, 152–69, 180.
16. 7 May 1942, CINCPAC 102347, May 1942, "Graybook," 1:443, 463.
17. COMINCH 301916, April 1942, 011736, 142100, May 1942, CINCPAC 200359, May 1942, "Estimate of the Situation, Attack on Hawaiian and Alaskan Bases," 26 May 1942, "Graybook," I:425–26, 460, 487, 506–21.
18. Peter J. Dean explained the challenges with MacArthur's approach in detail; see Dean, *MacArthur's Coalition*, 91–101, 116, 187, 232–33, 241, 294–98, 300–3, 311–20; *Reports of General MacArthur*, vol. 1, *The Campaigns of MacArthur in the Pacific* (Washington, D.C.: United States Army Center for Military History, reprint 1994), 1:31–34.
19. CINCPAC 050133, COMINCH 121245, May 1942, "Graybook," 1:440, 456; COM14 060105, May 1942, *Messages*.
20. *SRH-272*, 6–8 May 1942; *SRH-278*, 11 May 1942; COM14 Mailgram, "CINCPAC only," 11 May 1942, *Messages*.
21. *SRH-272*, 14 May 1942; *SRH-278*, 14 May 1942; Carlson, *Joe Rochefort's War*, 308; Layton et al., *"And I Was There,"* 412.
22. Lundstrom, *Black Shoe*, 210.
23. Nimitz, "Thesis on Tactics," 28 April 1923.
24. CINCPAC 140639, May 1942, "Graybook," 1:465–67.
25. 14 May 1942, CINCPAC 160307, May 1942, "Graybook," 1:469, 480; Lundstrom, *Black Shoe*, 211.
26. CINCPAC 160325, May 1942, "Graybook," 1:471.
27. COMINCH 152130, May 1942, "Graybook," 1:468. Part 1 of this message is in the "Graybook." I obtained Part 2 in personal correspondence with Mr. John Lundstrom.
28. Lundstrom, *Black Shoe*, 211–12.
29. *SRH-278*, 16 May 1942; CINCPAC 170407, May 1942, "Graybook," 1:490.
30. CINCPAC 170407, May 1942, "Graybook," 1:490.
31. COMINCH 172220, 172221, May 1942, "Graybook," 1:489–90.
32. Layton et al., *"And I Was There,"* 421–22; Carlson, *Joe Rochefort's War*, 334–36.
33. Bullard, *Japanese Army Operations*, 68.
34. "2nd K Operation," Rear Adm. Edwin T. Layton, USN (Ret.), provided by Jon Parshall; Remmelink, *Operations of the Navy*, 653.
35. Parshall and Tully, *Shattered Sword*, 37, 44–45.
36. "2nd K Operation," Rear Adm. Edwin T. Layton, USN (Ret.); Parshall and Tully, *Shattered Sword*, 48–52, 58–59, 63–67; Lundstrom, *Black Shoe*, 218–22.
37. Ugaki, *Fading Victory*, 118–20; Parshall and Tully, *Shattered Sword*, 61–63.
38. "2nd K Operation," Rear Adm. Edwin T. Layton, USN (Ret.).
39. "Estimate of the Situation Attack on Hawaiian and Alaskan Bases," "Graybook," 1:506–21.

40. "Estimate of the Situation Attack on Hawaiian and Alaskan Bases."

41. "Estimate of the Situation Attack on Hawaiian and Alaskan Bases"; CINCPAC Operation Plan No. 29-42, 27 May 1942, *Plans and Orders*; Richard W. Bates, *The Battle of Midway, Including the Aleutian Phase: June 3 to June 14, 1942, Strategical and Tactical Analysis* (Naval War College, Newport, R.I.: Bureau of Naval Personnel, 1948), 40; Morison, *History*, 4:86; Parshall and Tully, *Shattered Sword*, 96.

42. "Estimate of the Situation Attack on Hawaiian and Alaskan Bases"; Bates, *Midway*, 67; Morison, *History*, 4:92.

43. "Estimate of the Situation Attack on Hawaiian and Alaskan Bases."

44. "Estimate of the Situation Attack on Hawaiian and Alaskan Bases."

45. See, for example: Lundstrom, *Black Shoe*, 228; Layton et al., *"And I Was There,"* 432; Potter, *Nimitz*, 87; Morison, *History*, 4:84.

46. CINCPAC 160325, May 1942, "Graybook," 1:471; "Letter of Instructions," Commander-in-Chief, United States Pacific Fleet, 28 May 1942, *Plans and Orders*; Hone, *Learning War*, 138–45. The idea that it was not an obvious choice comes from a personal conversation between the author and Cdr. Dale C. Rielage, USN.

47. Hughes, *Halsey*, 173; Lundstrom, *Black Shoe*, 223–24; Thomas B. Buell, *The Quiet Warrior: A Biography of Admiral Raymond A. Spruance* (Annapolis, Md.: Naval Institute Press, 1987), 132–36.

48. CINCPAC Operation Plan No. 29-42, 27 May 1942, *Plans and Orders*; 27 May 1942, "Graybook," 1:544–45; Lundstrom, *Black Shoe*, 223.

49. CINCPAC Mailgram 292049, May 1942, *Messages*; Lundstrom, *Black Shoe*, 222; Parshall and Tully, *Shattered Sword*, 94.

50. CTF 7 Mailgram 292300, May 1942, *Messages*; CINCPAC Operation Plan No. 29-42, 27 May 1942; "Employment of Aircraft in Connection with Enemy Attack on Midway." Commander Patrol Wing Two, 23 May 1942.

51. Parshall and Tully, *Shattered Sword*, 69, 97–99; Lundstrom, *Black Shoe*, 221; Morison, *History*, 4:85, 94; CTF 9 Mailgram 280306, May 1942, *Messages*.

52. Ugaki, *Fading Victory*, 131, 135; Parshall and Tully, *Shattered Sword*, 102–4; "Mobile Force Commander's Estimate of the Situation," in *The Battle of Midway: The Naval Institute's Guide to the U.S. Navy's Greatest Victory*, ed. Thomas C. Hone (Annapolis, Md.: Naval Institute Press, 2013), 44.

53. CINCPAC 310357, May 1942, 022319, June 1942, "Graybook," 1:533, 550; COM14 282009, May 1942, *Messages*; Lundstrom, *Black Shoe*, 232–35.

54. CINCPAC 030325, June 1942, *Messages*; CINCPAC Operation Plan No. 29-42, 27 May 1942; Craig L. Symonds, "Mitscher and the Mystery of Midway" in Hone, *Midway*, 259–66; Parshall and Tully, *Shattered Sword*, 134; Lundstrom, *Black Shoe*, 235–36; Buell, *Quiet Warrior*, 143.

55. "Change No. 1 to Operation Plan 28-42," Commander-in-Chief, U.S. Pacific Fleet, 22 May 1942, *Plans and Orders*; Morison, *History*, 4:166; Bates, *Midway*, 40.

56. COMALSEC 032200, June 1942, *Messages*; 1 June 1942, "Graybook," 1:568; Morison, *History*, 4:166–67.

57. COM Flight 0 031917, NAS Kodiak 041159, June 1942, *Messages*; Morison, *History*, 4:175–77.

58. CTG 8.1 031615, COMNWSEAFRON 050533, June 1942, *Messages*; TF 1 Operation Plan No. 1-42, 30 May 1942, *Plans and Orders*; Bates, *Midway*, 167–68; Lundstrom, *Black Shoe*, 288; Morison, *History*, 4:177; *The Aleutians Campaign, June 1942–August 1943*, Combat Narratives (Office of Naval Intelligence, United States Navy, 1945), 7.

59. COMNWSEAFRON 051855, CTF8 052040, June 1942, *Messages*.

60. Potter, *Nimitz*, 70; Layton et al., *"And I Was There,"* 434.

61. Midway 032135, CINCPAC 032135, 032201, 040245, June 1942, *Messages*; Layton et al., *"And I Was There,"* 436.

62. CINCPAC 040801, June 1942, *Messages*; 3 June 1942, "Graybook," 1:569–70; Lundstrom, *Black Shoe*, 239.

63. Midway 041804, 041806, CINCPAC 041823, CTF7 041837, June 1942, *Messages*; "Battle of Midway Island, June 4–6, 1942—Report of," *U.S.S. Enterprise*, 8 June 1942, *Action*; Layton et al., *"And I Was There,"* 438.

64. "Battle of Midway Island, June 4–6, 1942—Report of," *U.S.S. Enterprise*, 8 June 1942; "Battle of Midway; forwarding of reports," Commander Task Force Sixteen, 16 June 1942, *Action*; Buell, *Quiet Warrior*, 145; Parshall and Tully, *Shattered Sword*, 135.

65. "Battle of Midway," Commander-in-Chief, United States Pacific Fleet, 28 June 1942, *Action*; Parshall and Tully, *Shattered Sword*, 128–33, 149–84; Lundstrom, *Black Shoe*, 251–52.

66. Parshall and Tully, *Shattered Sword*, 132–33, 146–84; Lundstrom, *Black Shoe*, 252–55.

67. "Battle of Midway," Commander-in-Chief, United States Pacific Fleet, 28 June 1942; "Report of Action—4–6 June 1942," *U.S.S. Hornet*, 13 June 1942, *Action*; Parshall and Tully, *Shattered Sword*, 190–210; Lundstrom, *Black Shoe*, 248, 258–59; Symonds "Mitscher and the Mystery of Midway" in Hone, *Midway*, 259–66.

68. Parshall and Tully, *Shattered Sword*, 210–19; Lundstrom, *Black Shoe*, 259–61.

69. Parshall and Tully, *Shattered Sword*, 232–43; Lundstrom, *Black Shoe*, 261–62.

70. CINCPAC 042259, CTU 7.1.6 050510, June 1942, *Messages*; "Battle of Midway," Commander-in-Chief, United States Pacific Fleet, 28 June 1942; Parshall and Tully, *Shattered Sword*, 262–71, 302–3.

71. Unknown 050014, CTF17 05001, June 1942, *Messages*; "Report of Action for June 4, 1942 and June 6, 1942," The Commanding Officer, *U.S.S. Yorktown*, 18 June 1942; Lundstrom, *Black Shoe*, 257.

72. "Battle of Midway," Commander-in-Chief, United States Pacific Fleet, 28 June 1942; "Battle of Midway," Commander Cruisers, Pacific Fleet, 14 June 1942; "Report of Action for June 4, 1942 and June 6, 1942," The Commanding Officer, *U.S.S. Yorktown*, 18 June 1942; Parshall and Tully, *Shattered Sword*, 262, 293–97, 310–18; Lundstrom, *Black Shoe*, 264–70; Morison, *History*, 4:141.

73. Parshall and Tully, *Shattered Sword*, 320.

74. CTF16 050204, CTF17 050315, Midway 050621, CINCPAC 050443, June 1942, *Messages*; Parshall and Tully, *Shattered Sword*, 308, 323–29; Lundstrom, *Black Shoe*, 270–73, 279.

75. CINCPAC 051225, 060831, June 1942, "Graybook," 1:552, 554; CINCPAC 050915, 050543, June 1942, *Messages*.

76. CTF16 050912, June 1942, *Messages*; Ugaki, *Fading Victory*, 150–51; Parshall and Tully, *Shattered Sword*, 330–44.

77. CINCPAC 051345, June 1942, *Messages*; "Battle of Midway," Commander-in-Chief, United States Pacific Fleet, 28 June 1942; Parshall and Tully, *Shattered Sword*, 344–46; Lundstrom, *Black Shoe*, 282–83.

78. CTF7 050325, 050629, June 1942, *Messages*; "Battle of Midway," Commander-in-Chief, United States Pacific Fleet, 28 June 1942; "Battle of Midway, Second Supplementary Report," Commander-in-Chief, United States Pacific Fleet, 8 August 1942, *Action*; Bates, *Midway*, 165–66; Parshall and Tully, *Shattered Sword*, 361–63; Lundstrom, *Black Shoe*, 282, 287.

79. Parshall and Tully, *Shattered Sword*, 362–72, 375–80; Lundstrom, *Black Shoe*, 288–91.

80. 6 June 1942, CINCPAC 060831, 070803, 0708829, June 1942, "Graybook," 1:554–55, 572; Lundstrom, *Black Shoe*, 287.

81. CINCPAC 080429, June 1942, "Graybook," 1:556–57; COMNWSEAFRON 071611, COMINCH 071954, COMALSEC 092010, June 1942, *Messages*.

82. CINCPAC 110929, COMINCH 111645, June 1942, "Graybook," 1:575.

83. Layton et al., *"And I Was There,"* 357.

84. Edmondson, *Fearless Organization*, 188.

85. Osinga, *Science, Strategy, and War*, 194.

86. Quoted in Osinga, *Science, Strategy, and War*, 101.

87. "Extract from personal letter written by Comdr. Murphy, War Plans Officer, Staff, Commander in Chief, U.S. Pacific Fleet," *Papers of Adm. Chester W. Nimitz, USN*, Manuscript Collection 334, Naval War College Archives, Newport, R.I.

**CHAPTER 4. SEIZING THE INITIATIVE**

1. "Nimitz Diary," 10 August 1942, *Nimitz Papers*.

2. Woods, "The Theory of Graceful Extensibility," 4.

3. CINCPAC 260012, April 1942, *Messages*; Hone, *Learning War*, 122–62.

4. CINCPAC 200359, May 1942, "Graybook," 1:486–87; Bates, *Midway*, 90.

5. "Battle of Midway," Commander-in-Chief, United States Pacific Fleet, 28 June 1942; Lundstrom, *First Team*, 190, 330.

6. CINCPAC 152201, June 1942, "Graybook," 1:582–83.

7. CCCH, 49; Jeffrey M. Moore, *Spies for Nimitz: Joint Military Intelligence in the Pacific War* (Annapolis, Md.: Naval Institute Press, 2004), 8.

8. Potter, *Nimitz*, 176; Buell, *Quiet Warrior*, 167–75; CCCH, 47; Cdr. H. Arthur Lamar, USN (Ret.), *I Saw Stars* (Fredericksburg, Tex.: The Admiral Nimitz Foundation, 1985), 3.

9. Potter, *Nimitz*, 221–27; Miller, "Fleet Admiral," 71–75; Capt. Michael A. Lilly, USN (Ret.), *Nimitz at Ease* (Apache Junction, Ariz.: Stairway Press, 2019), 45.

10. CINCPAC 172033, June 1942, "Graybook," 1:585.

11. Morison, *History*, 4:180–81.

12. CINCPAC 072145, June 1942, "Graybook," 1:558; COMPATWING 4 110401, 120650, CINCPAC 110727, 110829, June 1942, *Messages*; Morison, *History*, 4:183;

Brian Garfield, *The Thousand-Mile War: World War II in Alaska and the Aleutians* (Fairbanks, Alas.: University of Alaska Press, 1995), 104–16.

13. 21 May 1942, 20, 21 June 1942, "Graybook," 1:538, 598–99; Morison, *History*, 4:164–65; Garfield, *Thousand-Mile War*, 18.

14. COMINCH 160132, 291810, COMALSEC 300215, CINCPAC 290409, 302359, June 1942, "Graybook," 1:601, 674–77.

15. COMTASKFOR8 291920, July 1942, CINCPAC 012355, COMTASKGROUP8.6 090553, August 1942, "Graybook," 1:629, 632, 798; Morison, *History*, 7:9–12.

16. COMINCH 252000, July 1942, COMINCH 050003, COMTASKFOR8 050105, 050520, COMALSEC 051237, August 1942, "Graybook," 1:633–36, 761.

17. CTF8 050105, 050520, CINCPAC 052213, CTF8 150340, August 1942, "Graybook," 1:634–36, 638, 803.

18. COMWESSEAFRON 182340, 202248, COMINCH 181420, CTF8 292340, August 1942, "Graybook," 1:654, 663, 806–7; Garfield, *Thousand-Mile War*, 176–82.

19. COMSOPAC 080731, 080733, 080735, June 1942, "Graybook," 1:557–58.

20. 22 June 1942, "Graybook," 1:599.

21. COMINCH 242303, 242306, 251840, CINCPAC 270251, June 1942, "Graybook," 1:602–4.

22. COMINCH 100046, 231255, June 1942, COMINCH 301601, July 1942, Admiralty 101418, August 1942, "Graybook," 1:600–601, 628, 643; Frank, *Guadalcanal*, 35; Peter C. Smith, *Pedestal: The Convoy that Saved Malta*, 4th ed. (Manchester, UK: Crecy Publishing, 1999), 25–37.

23. Morison, *History*, 4:259–60; Frank, *Guadalcanal*, 33–34.

24. COMINCH 022100, July 1942, "Graybook," 1:605.

25. COMINCH 022145, 022150, 032254, Marshall 042205, July 1942, "Graybook," 1:605–6, 682.

26. Bix, *Hirohito*, 449–50; Parshall and Tully, *Shattered Sword*, 385; Bullard, *Japanese Army Operations*, 66–93.

27. "Estimate of the Situation," 22 April 1942, "Graybook," 1:376; Thomas Wildenberg, *Gray Steel and Black Oil: Fast Tankers and Replenishment at Sea in the U.S. Navy, 1912–1992* (Annapolis, Md.: Naval Institute Press, 1996), 169–75; David C. Fuquea, "Advantage Japan: The Imperial Japanese Navy's Superior High Seas Refueling Capability," *Journal of Military History* 84, no. 1 (January 2020): 213–35.

28. Wildenberg, *Gray Steel*, 168–80; Peter V. Nash, *The Development of Mobile Logistic Support in Anglo-American Naval Policy, 1900–1953* (Gainesville, Fla.: University Press of Florida, 2009), 29. The preliminary target storage capacity at Bora Bora was 200,000 barrels, but only 120,000 could be stored by June 1942. See COMINCH 070015, January 1942, "Graybook," 1:141 and Morison, *History*, 4:263n22.

29. "Joint Logistic Plan for the Support of United States Bases in the South Pacific Area," 15 July 1942.

30. Duncan S. Ballantine, *U.S. Naval Logistics in the Second World War* (Princeton: Princeton University Press, 1949), 50–55.

31. "Advanced Bases, South Pacific, Inspection Report of," Senior Member, South Pacific Advanced Base Inspection Board, Rear Adm. Richard E. Byrd, 15 Aug 1942; 16 June

1942, COMSOPAC 130333, June 1942, "Graybook," 1:579, 595; Richard M. Leighton and Robert W. Coakley, *The War Department*, vol. 5, *Global Logistics and Strategy, 1940–1943*, The United States Army in World War II (Washington, D.C.: United States Army Center for Military History, 1955), 185; Morison, *History*, 4:263n22.

32. Potter, *Nimitz*, 110–11.

33. "Conversations between Cominch and Cincpac 4 July," 5 July 1942, *King Papers*; CINCPAC 160131, June 1942, "Graybook," 1:583.

34. Turner officially assumed command 15 July. See CINCPAC 150237, 15 July 1942, "Graybook," 1:749.

35. "Limited Amphibious Offensive in South and Southwest Pacific," 3 July 1942, *Strategic Plans Division Records* [hereafter: *Strategic*], Record Group 38, Records of the Office of the Chief of Naval Operations, National Archives, Washington, D.C.; "Conversations between Cominch and Cincpac 4 July," 5 July 1942, *King Papers*; "Estimate: An Offensive for the Capture and Occupation of Tulagi and Vicinity," 6 July 1942, "Graybook," 1:709–43; Dean, *MacArthur's Coalition*, 111.

36. "Estimate of the Most Effective Employment of Battleship Type in the Near Future," n.d., *King Papers*; "Conversations between Cominch and Cincpac 4 July," 5 July 1942, *King Papers*; Bullard, *Japanese Army Operations*, 3.

37. Operation Plan No. 37–42, CINCPAC, 25 July 1942, *Plans and Orders*; "Notes for the Commander in Chief for Conference with CINCPAC," 29 June 1942, "Graybook," 1:697–703; CINCPAC 172101, May 1942, CINCPAC 090339, 312145, July 1942, CTG7.15 200830, August 1942, "Graybook," 1:489, 613, 629, 766; Morison, *History*, 4:235–41.

38. "Conversations between Cominch and Cincpac 4 July," 5 July 1942, *King Papers*; Frank, *Guadalcanal*, 35–36; Potter, *Nimitz*, 115.

39. 5–8 July 1942, "Estimate: An Offensive for the Capture and Occupation of Tulagi and Vicinity," 6 July 1942, CINCPAC 062229, 070125, July 1942, "Graybook," 1:609–10, 707–44.

40. "Estimate: An Offensive for the Capture and Occupation of Tulagi and Vicinity," 6 July 1942, "Graybook," 1:709–43; Staff officer Lt. Col. Tsuji Masanobu's instructions. Quoted in Bullard, *Japanese Army Operations*, 101.

41. COMSOWESPACFOR 081012, 081014, 081015, 081017, 081020, 081021, July 1942, "Graybook," 1:610–13.

42. 17–18 July 1942, COMINCH 102100, COMSOPAC 112000, CINCPAC 090633, 120105, Marshall 130035Z, July 1942, "Graybook," 1:613–17, 748, 772–73.

43. COMSOPAC 050730, 050750, 5 August 1942, "Supply of reinforcements to continue campaign in South Pacific," 17 July 1942, Commander in Chief, United States Pacific Fleet, "Graybook," 1:637–38, 774–75, emphasis mine.

44. Letter from Vice Admiral Robert L. Ghormley to Admiral Chester W. Nimitz, 29 July 1942, *Nimitz Papers*.

45. Letter from Vice Admiral Robert L. Ghormley to Admiral Chester W. Nimitz, 29 July 1942.

46. Letter from Vice Admiral Robert L. Ghormley to Admiral Chester W. Nimitz, 2 August 1942, *Nimitz Papers*; Pratt, *Fleet Against Japan*, 41.

47. COMSOPAC 160612, 170602, 170615, July 1942, "Graybook," 1:620–21.

48. Frank, *Guadalcanal*, 54–55.

49. "An Estimate of Enemy Intentions, Month of August–1942," 1 August 1942, COMSOPAC 272211, 281440, CTF61 280201, COMINCH 281830, July 1942, "Graybook," 1:627, 784–91.

50. CINCPAC 081955, CTG61.2 071030, August 1942, "Graybook," 1:638–39; Bix, *Hirohito*, 455–56; John B. Lundstrom, *The First Team and the Guadalcanal Campaign* (Annapolis, Md.: Naval Institute Press, 1994), 78.

51. Fletcher 090315, COMSOPAC 090830, COMINCH 101830, August 1942, "Graybook," 1:639, 641, 643; Letter from Vice Admiral Robert L. Ghormley to Admiral Chester W. Nimitz, 11 August 1942, *Nimitz Papers*.

52. CINCPAC 102147, COMSOPAC 090750, 090950, 110206, CTF62 110650, August 1942, "Graybook," 1:640, 644–45.

53. 13 August 1942, CINCPAC 112209, August 1942, "Graybook," 1:646, 825.

54. 12 August 1942, COMINCH 112030, 121750, CINCPAC 122337, August 1942, "Graybook," 1:646–48, 824.

55. 25 August 1942, COMINCH 151951, CINCPAC 132135, 302123, August 1942, "Graybook," 1:649, 651, 667, 834.

56. 19 August 1942, CINCPAC 172047, 200041, COMSOPAC 120216, August 1942, "Graybook," 1:646, 654, 656, 829; Frank, *Guadalcanal*, 139–40; Robert Sherrod, *History of Marine Corps Aviation in World War II* (Baltimore, Md.: The Nautical & Aviation Publishing Co. of America, 1987), 78.

57. COMSOPAC Op Order 2–42, 180916, 220910, August 1942, "Graybook," 1:655, 808.

58. Frank, *Guadalcanal*, 167–72.

59. Lundstrom, *Black Shoe*, 455–56; Morison, *History*, 5:104–5.

60. CINCPAC 252241, Forrestal 301010, COMINCH 271320, August 1942, COMSOPAC 120544, September 1942, "Graybook," 1:658, 661, 664, 877.

61. CINCPAC 252205, August 1942, "Graybook," 1:660.

62. CTF62 011237, September 1942, "Graybook," 2:863. Although his message was addressed to Ghormley, Turner violated protocol by including Nimitz and King in what should have been a deliberation between COMSOPAC and his subordinates.

63. 4 August 1942, COMSOPAC 010305, September 1942, "Graybook," 1:818, 2:862.

64. 27, 29 August 1942, *Fomalhaut* 260307, COMSOPAC 140640, 261336, August 1942, "Graybook," 1:801, 810, 836–38; Morison, *History*, 5:81, 109–10.

65. Morison, *History*, 5:110–13.

66. CINCPAC 052005, September 1942, Memorandum, Nimitz to McCormick, 10 August 1942, "Estimate of Enemy Intentions," 1 September 1942, "Graybook," 1:844, 856–61, 2:867.

67. CINCPAC 012331, COMSOPAC 020300, September 1942, "Graybook," 2:863.

68. C.G. CACTUS 012313, 1 September 1942, "Graybook," 2:864.

69. COMSOPAC Op Plan 3–42, COMINCH 011315, COMSOPAC 070452, September 1942, "Graybook," 2:868, 872; "Notes on Conference Between COMINCH and CINCPAC," 10 September 1942, *King Papers*.

70. William F. Trimble, *Admiral John S. McCain and the Triumph of Naval Air Power* (Annapolis, Md.: Naval Institute Press, 2019), 93.

71. COMAMPHORSOPAC 120530, September 1942, "Graybook," 2:876; Col. Joseph H. Alexander USMC (Ret.), *Edson's Raiders: The 1st Marine Raider Battalion in World War II* (Annapolis, Md.: Naval Institute Press, 2001), 164–97.

72. Miller, *War Plan Orange*; John T. Kuehn, *Agents of Innovation: The General Board and the Design of the Fleet that Defeated the Japanese Navy* (Annapolis, Md.: Naval Institute Press, 2008).

## CHAPTER 5. ADJUSTING THE SYSTEM

1. *Sound Military Decision* (Annapolis, Md.: Naval Institute Press, 1942), 198.

2. "Nimitz Diary," 17 October 1942, *Nimitz Papers*.

3. "Notes on Conference Between COMINCH and CINCPAC," 10 September 1942, *King Papers*; CINCPAC 072305, September 1942, "Graybook," 2:869.

4. "Notes on Conference Between COMINCH and CINCPAC," 10 September 1942, *King Papers*.

5. 14 September 1942, 27 October 1942, "Graybook," 2:1036, 1106; "Notes on Conference Between COMINCH and CINCPAC," 10 September 1942, *King Papers*; Potter, *Nimitz*, 186–87.

6. 6 September 1942, CTF8 061950, September 1942, "Graybook," 2:868, 1013; "Notes on Conference Between COMINCH and CINCPAC," 10 September 1942, *King Papers*; Potter, *Nimitz*, 187.

7. "Notes on Conference Between COMINCH and CINCPAC," 10 September 1942, *King Papers*; Potter, *Nimitz*, 188; 7 September 1942, "Graybook," 2:1013.

8. COMSOPAC 110516, COMAMPHFORSOPAC 092300, September 1942, "Graybook," 2:874–75; Official Letter from Vice Admiral Robert L. Ghormley to Admiral Chester W. Nimitz, 7 September 1942, *Nimitz Papers*.

9. Personal Letter from Vice Admiral Robert L. Ghormley to Admiral Chester W. Nimitz, 7 September 1942, *Nimitz Papers*; Official Letter from Vice Admiral Robert L. Ghormley to Admiral Chester W. Nimitz, 7 September 1942, *Nimitz Papers*.

10. 13 September 1942, COMAMPHFORSOPAC 120530, COMSOPAC 130540, September 1942, "Graybook," 2:876–77, 1035; Lundstrom, *Guadalcanal Campaign*, 202, 220–22.

11. COMINCH 202147, September, "Graybook," 2:883; Lundstrom, *Guadalcanal Campaign*, 231.

12. COMINCH 182200, CINCPAC 200145, MacArthur 270800, September 1942, "Graybook," 2:881–82, 887.

13. 16, 18 September 1942, "Graybook," 2:1038, 1040; Potter, *Nimitz*, 190.

14. Potter, *Nimitz*, 190; Frank, *Guadalcanal*, 276.

15. "CINCPAC Visit to South Pacific Area, 24 September–5 October 1942," 6 October 1942, *Nimitz Papers*.

16. "Notes on Conference at Palmyra–September 25, 1942," Letter from Nimitz to King, 8 October 1942, *Nimitz Papers*; "CINCPAC Visit to South Pacific Area, 24 September–5 October 1942," 6 October 1942, *Nimitz Papers*.

17. 22 September 1942, "Graybook," 2:1042. Staff attendees included Rear Admiral Callaghan, Ghormley's chief of staff, Brig. Gen. DeWitt Peck, USMC, Ghormley's head of war plans, Colonel Pfeiffer, and Captain Ofstie.

18. "Notes on Conference Held aboard U.S.S. Argonne at Noumea–September 28, 1942," Letter from Nimitz to King, 8 October 1942, *Nimitz Papers*.
19. "Notes on Conference Held aboard U.S.S. Argonne at Noumea–September 28, 1942"; Dean, *MacArthur's Coalition*, 143–44.
20. 5 September 1942, "Graybook," 2:1012; Nimitz to Ghormley, 8 October 1942, *Nimitz Papers*.
21. John Prados, *Islands of Destiny: The Solomons Campaign and the Eclipse of the Rising Sun* (New York: NAL Caliber, 2012), 102–3; Potter, *Nimitz*, 192; Eric Hammel, *Guadalcanal: Starvation Island* (New York: Crown, 1987), 271.
22. "Notes on Conference Held aboard U.S.S. Argonne at Noumea–September 28, 1942," Letter from Nimitz to King, 8 October 1942, *Nimitz Papers*.
23. "Notes on Conference Held aboard U.S.S. Argonne at Noumea–September 28, 1942."
24. "CINCPAC Visit to South Pacific Area, 24 September–5 October 1942," 6 October 1942, *Nimitz Papers*; Potter, *Nimitz*, 192–93; Hammel, *Starvation Island*, 271–73; Prados, *Islands of Destiny*, 103–4.
25. "Notes on Conference Held aboard U.S.S. Argonne at Noumea at 1300, October 2, 1942," Letter from Nimitz to King, 8 October 1942, *Nimitz Papers*.
26. "Notes on Conference Held aboard U.S.S. Argonne at Noumea at 1300, October 2, 1942."
27. "Notes on Conference Held aboard U.S.S. Argonne at Noumea at 1300, October 2, 1942"; Potter, *Nimitz*, 195; James D. Hornfischer, *Neptune's Inferno: The U.S. Navy at Guadalcanal* (New York: Random House, 2011), 154–55; Prados, *Islands of Destiny*, 104.
28. Nimitz to Ghormley, 8 October 1942, *Nimitz Papers*.
29. COMSOPAC 011302, COMAIRSOPAC 020050, 030244, October 1942, "Graybook," 2:888–89; "Report of Air Raid on Buin-Faisi-Tonolei, Bougainville Island," Commander Task Force Seventeen, 14 October 1942; Lundstrom, *Guadalcanal Campaign*, 277–83.
30. Nimitz to Ghormley, 8 October 1942, *Nimitz Papers*; 6 October 1942, "Graybook," 2:1080; "Report of Air Raid on Buin-Faisi-Tonolei, Bougainville Island," Commander Task Force Seventeen, 14 October 1942.
31. Entry 25 September 1942, Entry 1 October 1942, "Combat Intelligence, Fourteenth Naval District," 28 September 1942; "Estimate of Enemy Capabilities," 1 October 1942, "Graybook," 2:1044, 1050–78.
32. "Report of night action 11–12 October, 1942," Commander Task Group 64.2, 22 October 1942, *Action*; 11 October 1942, "Graybook," 2:1088.
33. Ugaki, *Fading Victory*, 232; Herbert Laing Merillat, *The Island: A History of the First Marine Division on Guadalcanal* (Boston: Houghton Mifflin, 1944), 140.
34. 13, 14 October 1942, "Graybook," 2:1090–92; Morison, *History*, 5:172–77; Lundstrom, *Guadalcanal Campaign*, 301–9; Frank, *Guadalcanal*, 320–28.
35. 14, 15 October 1942, COMSOPAC 160440, 16 October 1942, "Graybook," 2:950, 1091–93; Lundstrom, *Guadalcanal Campaign*, 309–10.
36. "Nimitz Diary," 17 October 1942, *Nimitz Papers*; Hammel, *Starvation Island*, 333–34.

37. CINCPAC 160937, COMINCH 160245, October 1942, "Graybook," 2:895.
38. "Guadalcanal," *New York Times*, 16 October 1942, 18; Frank, *Guadalcanal*, 332–33; Sherrod, *Marine Corps Aviation*, 105.
39. 21 October 1942, "Graybook," 2:1099.
40. Hammel, *Starvation Island*, 335–36.
41. 17 October 1942, 18 October 1942, "Graybook," 2:1095–96; Lundstrom, *Guadalcanal Campaign*, 329–30.
42. Personal letter, Halsey to Nimitz, 31 October 1942, *Nimitz Papers*; 22 October 1942, "Graybook," 2:1100–1101.
43. Ugaki, *Fading Victory*, 245.
44. 24 October 1942, "Graybook," 2:1102; Hornfischer, *Neptune's Inferno*, 222.
45. Personal letter, Halsey to Nimitz, 31 October 1942, *Nimitz Papers*; CINCPAC 270251, October 1942, "Graybook," 2:898.
46. 28 October 1942, CINCPAC 282225, COMSOPAC 290130, October 1942, "Graybook," 2:965, 1108; Personal letter, Halsey to Nimitz, 31 October 1942, *Nimitz Papers*.
47. 2–6 November 1942, "Combat Intelligence Fourteenth Naval District," 2 November 1942, "Estimate of Enemy Capabilities," 1 November 1942, "Graybook," 2:1113–56.
48. Hughes, *Halsey*, 205.
49. CINCPAC 092107, November 1942, "Graybook," 2:902–3; "Solomons Islands Campaign–Battle of the Solomons, 11–15 November 1942," 18 February 1942, Commander in Chief, U.S. Pacific Fleet, *Action*.
50. "Solomons Islands Campaign–Battle of the Solomons, 11–15 November 1942."
51. Hone, *Learning War*.
52. 12 November 1942, COMSOPAC 141020, November 1942, "Graybook," 2:981, 1163–64.
53. COMSOPAC 131730, November 1942, "Graybook," 2:981.
54. 14 November 1942, "Graybook," 2:1166.
55. 16, 23 November 1942, COMSOPAC 230612, November 1942, "Graybook," 2:995, 1169, 1174.
56. COMINCH 301915, November 1942, CINCPAC 010931, December 1942, "Graybook," 2:908.
57. COMSOPAC 020637, December 1942, "Graybook," 2:1180–81.
58. 1 December 1942, COMSOPAC 090502, 9 December 1942, "Graybook," 2:1182, 1212; Frank, *Guadalcanal*, 518.
59. 24 November 1942, 3–5 December 1942, "Graybook," 2:1174, 1214–15; Ugaki was promoted to Vice Admiral on 1 November 1942. Ugaki, *Fading Victory*, 256, 295, 317.
60. "Estimate of the Situation," 7 December 1942, "Future Operations in the Solomons Sea Area," Commander-in-Chief, U.S. Pacific Fleet, 8 December 1942, "Graybook," 2:1217–40.
61. 25 September 1942, "Amphibious Training of Army Troops for Operations in Kiska Area," Commander in Chief, United States Pacific Fleet, 24 September 1942, "Graybook," 2:1044–45.
62. 18 October 1942, "Proposed Reduction of Northern Force," 11 October 1942, "Suggested Changes in Air Strength–Alaska"; R. A. Ofstie, 10 October 1942, CINCPAC

162221, 130139, CTF8 140230; October 1943, "Graybook," 2:892–93, 946, 953, 1083–86, 1097.

63. *SRH-278*, 25 October 1942; Garfield, *Thousand-Mile War*, 193.

64. 17 November 1942, 8 December 1942, CTF8 020600, December 1942, "Estimate of the Situation," 7 December 1942, "Review of the Aleutian Situation," Commander in Chief, U.S. Pacific Fleet, 8 December 1942, "Graybook," 2:1170, 1192–93, 1217–33, 1241–43, 1245; Garfield, *Thousand-Mile War*, 194.

65. "Future Operations in the Solomons Sea Area," Commander-in-Chief, U.S. Pacific Fleet, 8 December 1942, "Graybook," 2:1234–40.

66. "Review of the Aleutian Situation," Commander in Chief, U.S. Pacific Fleet, 8 December 1942, "Graybook," 2:1241–43.

67. "Conference Notes, December 11," 14 December 1942; "Conference Notes, December 12," 12 December 1942; "Conference Notes December 13," undated, all *King Papers*.

68. "Conference Notes, December 11," 14 December 1942; "Conference Notes, December 12," 12 December 1942; "Conference Notes December 13"; Moore, *Spies for Nimitz*, xiii, 9–15.

69. "Conference Notes, December 11," 14 December 1942; "Conference Notes, December 12," 12 December 1942; "Conference Notes December 13."

70. "Conference Notes, December 11," 14 December 1942; "Conference Notes, December 12," 12 December 1942; "Conference Notes December 13."

71. "Personnel Matters," 11 December 1942, *King Papers*.

72. COMINCH 311405, December 1942, CINCPAC 020217, January 1943, "Graybook," 3:1376–77.

73. 6 December 1942, "Graybook," 2:1216; Gerald E. Wheeler, *Kinkaid of the Seventh Fleet: A Biography of Admiral Thomas C. Kinkaid, U.S. Navy* (Annapolis, Md.: Naval Institute Press, 1996), 295–97.

74. 14, 29 December 1942, 2 January 1943, COMINCH 181315, CINCPAC 182321, 151959, December 1942, "Graybook," 2:1184–85, 1249, 1260, 1265; Garfield, *Thousand-Mile War*, 210–11; Morison, *History*, 7:17–18.

75. CINCPAC 182345, 190215, COM12 190320, 190324, December 1942, "Graybook," 2:1185–87.

76. CTF8 210830, CINCPAC 220557, 232215, DeWitt 230016, December 1942, "Graybook," 2:1188, 1203–4.

77. 29 December 1942, CINCPAC 230407, CTF8 240225, COMGEN WESTDEFCOM-MAND 252050, December 1942, "Graybook," 2:1189, 1204–5, 1261; Buell, *Master of Sea Power*, 300.

78. 12, 21 January 1943, "Graybook," 3:1274, 1341; Garfield, *Thousand-Mile War*, 214.

79. Morison, *History*, 7:17; Wheeler, *Kinkaid*, 299–342; Garfield, *Thousand-Mile War*, 209.

## CHAPTER 6. COILING THE SPRING

1. "Notes on Conference Held aboard U.S.S. Argonne at Noumea–September 28, 1942," Letter from Nimitz to King, 8 October 1942, *Nimitz Papers*.

2. "Pacific Fleet Tactical Bulletin No. 4TB-42, Commander-in-Chief, Pacific Fleet," 26 November 1942, *WWII*; Timothy S. Wolters, *Information at Sea: Shipboard*

*Command and Control in the U.S. Navy, from Mobile Bay to Okinawa* (Baltimore, Md.: Johns Hopkins University Press, 2013), 206; Hone, *Learning War*, 208–49.

3. 31 January 1943, 27 February 1943, "Graybook," 3:1356, 1414; Layton, et al., *"And I Was There,"* 471–72.

4. Lockwood had become COMSUBPAC after Rear Admiral English died in a plane crash in January 1943; "Conference Notes," 22 February 1943, *King Papers*; Anthony Newpower, *Iron Men and Tin Fish: The Race to Build a Better Torpedo During World War II* (Annapolis, Md.: Naval Institute Press, 2006), 102–11, 131–58; Layton et al., *"And I Was There,"* 472.

5. 29 September 1943, COMINCH 122204, March 1943, "Graybook," 3:1484, 4:1665; Newpower, *Iron Men*, 163–81.

6. COMINCH 192150, February 1943, COMINCH 111819, April 1943, "Graybook," 3:1424–25, 1557.

7. *PAC-10, Current Tactical Orders and Doctrine, U.S. Pacific Fleet,* Commander-in-Chief, U.S. Pacific Fleet, June 1943, v, *U.S. Navy and Related Operational, Tactical, and Instructional Publications* [hereafter: *OpPub*], Entry 337, Record Group 38, Records of the Office of the Chief of Naval Operations, National Archives, Washington, D.C.; Hone, *Learning War*, 250–99; "Revision of Pacific Fleet Cruising Instructions, Pacific Board to Revise Cruising Instructions," 18 May 1943, *Plans and Orders*. The board included Rear Adm. Robert M. Griffin, Capt. Roscoe F. Good, Capt. E. M. Crouch, and Capt. Apollo Soucek.

8. COMSOPAC 270437, October 1942, COMINCH 051524, November 1942, COMSOPAC 061929, December 1942, "Graybook," 2:902, 962, 1195; Letter from Halsey to Nimitz, 20 December 1942, *Nimitz Papers*; Personal letter from Nimitz to Halsey, 18 December 1942, *Nimitz Papers*; "Conference Notes, December 12," 12 December 1942, *King Papers*; "Personnel Matters," 11 December 1942, *King Papers*; "Conference Notes," 23 February 1943, *King Papers*; Jobie Turner, *Feeding Victory: Innovative Military Logistics from Lake George to Khe Sahn* (Lawrence: University Press of Kansas, 2020), 135.

9. "Conference Notes, December 12," 12 December 1942, *King Papers*; Leighton and Coakley, *1940–1943*, 398–404; Richard M. Leighton and Robert W. Coakley, *The War Department*, vol. 6, *Global Logistics and Strategy, 1943–1945*, The United States Army in World War II (Washington, D.C.: United States Army Center for Military History, 1968), 442.

10. Quoted in Ballantine, *U.S. Naval Logistics*, 107.

11. "Basic Logistics Plan for Theatre Involving Joint Army and Navy Operations," undated; "Basic Logistical plan for Command Areas Involving Joint Army and Navy Operations," 8 March 1943, COMINCH & CNO; "Conference Notes," 22 February 1943, *King Papers*; "Conference Notes," 23 February 1943, *King Papers*; Ballantine, *U.S. Naval Logistics*, 128.

12. "Basic Logistical Plan for Command Areas Involving Joint Army and Navy Operations–Establishment of in Central Pacific Area," 6 April 1943, Commander in Chief, U.S. Pacific Fleet.

13. "The Fleet Service Forces and the Logistics Organization in Command Areas," 2 February 1944, *Presentations*.

14. Official Letter from Vice Admiral Robert L. Ghormley to Admiral Chester W. Nimitz, 7 September 1942, *Nimitz Papers*; Ballantine, *U.S. Naval Logistics*, 58, 113.

15. Ballantine, *U.S. Naval Logistics*, 113–14.

16. Marshall 090053, COMSOWESPAC 131131, 131145, 131148, 131150, 131159, COMSOPAC 191022, January 1943, "Estimate of the Situation, Solomon Islands," 15 January 1943, "Brief Estimate on Task 2," 15 January 1942, "CINCPAC Evaluation, Setting Sun Campaign," 15 January 1943, "Graybook," 3:1277–1318, 1371, 1380–83.

17. 20 February 1943, "Notes on the Conference held at Noumea, 1520 to 1700, January 23, 1943," "Graybook," 3:1343–48, 1410.

18. 24–30 January 1943, 7–9 February 1943, COMSOPAC 271145, January 1943, "Graybook," 3:1373–74, 1349–54, 1390–91; "Solomon Islands Campaign–Fall of Guadalcanal, period 25 January to 10 February, 1943," Commander in Chief, U.S. Pacific Fleet, 17 April 1943, *Action*.

19. "Conference Notes," 22 February 1943, *King Papers*; Adams, *Witness to Power*, 203–4; Leighton and Coakley, *1943–1945*, 6.

20. COMINCH 092200, 131250, COMSOPAC 110421, 170617, CINCPAC 112237, 142357, 150113, February 1943, "Graybook," 3:1432, 1434–38; "Conduct of the War in the Pacific Theater in 1943," Memorandum by Joint U.S. Chiefs of Staff, 22 January 1943, C.C.S. 168, *Casablanca Conference, January 1943, Papers and Meeting Minutes* (Office of the Combined Chiefs of Staff, 1943).

21. "CINCPAC Evaluation, Setting Sun Campaign," 15 January 1943, "Graybook," 3:1310–1318; "Estimated Forces for Gilbert Islands Plan and Logistics Therefor," 9 February 1943, F. A. Hart, *Strategic*; "Memo for 16," 17 February 1943, "Graybook," 3:1398–1406; "Memorandum for Secret Files: Courses of Action Open to Us in a Pacific Campaign," undated, *Strategic*; "Brief Plan for the Control of the Marshall Islands," 12 February 1943, *Strategic*; "Conference Notes," 22 February 1943, *King Papers*; "Items from Conference on West Coast," 26 February 1943, *King Papers*.

22. 5, 7 March 1943, COMSOPAC 130247, March 1943, "Graybook," 3:1442–43, 1482; John Miller Jr., *The War in the Pacific*, vol. 5, *Cartwheel: The Reduction of Rabaul*, The United States Army in World War II (Washington, D.C.: United States Army Center for Military History, 1959), 13.

23. Dean, *MacArthur's Coalition*, 220; Adams, *Witness to Power*, 208–9.

24. "Memorandum from Joint Chiefs of Staff to MacArthur, Nimitz, Halsey," 29 March 1943, "Graybook," 3:1473–74; Miller, *Cartwheel*, 14; Leighton and Coakley, *1943–1945*, 7; Adams, *Witness to Power*, 209.

25. 13 April 1943, CINCPAC 230059, COMINCH 231632, 291558; April 1943 "Graybook," 3:1509, 1516, 1525, 1553.

26. 6, 8, 14 April 1943, "Graybook," 3:1504, 1506, 1509; Layton et al., *"And I Was There,"* 474–76; Jeremy A. Yellen, *The Greater East Asia Co-Prosperity Sphere: When Total Empire Met Total War* (Ithaca, N.Y.: Cornell University Press, 2019), 143; Ugaki, *Fading Victory*, 354.

27. CINCPAC 202217, COMSOPAC 210654, COMINCH 011810, 211336, April 1943, COMINCH 081329, COMSOPAC 090501, 160420, May 1943, "Graybook," 3:1513, 1521, 1524, 1555, 1557; Morison, *History*, 6:97; Miller, *Cartwheel*, 25; Hughes, *Halsey*, 264. Note that there does not appear to have been an official Elkton II.

28. 21 March 1943, COMGENWESTDEFCOMMAND 080220, CINCPAC 090342, January 1943, JCS 221939, CTF8 030405, 070103, COMINCH 111221, CINCPAC 130125, 130151, 182011, 230425, March 1943, "Graybook," 3: 1366–67, 1378, 1452, 1477, 1478, 1481–82, 1489, 1491; Lt. Col. Henry G. Morgan Jr., *Planning the Defeat of Japan: A Study of Total War Strategy* (Washington, D.C.: Office of the Chief of Military History, 1961), 88; Morison, *History*, 7:21.

29. COMNORPAC 270805, March 1942, "Graybook," 3:1470–1; Morison, *History*, 7:22–36.

30. 31 March 1943, CTF16 190300, CINCPAC 182011, 182333, March 1943, "Graybook," 3:1457, 1488–89.

31. Wheeler, *Kinkaid*, 309–12.

32. CINCPAC 142135, March 1943, "Graybook," 3:1483–84.

33. CTF51 160602, COMNORPAC 160400, 161013, May 1943, "Graybook," 3:1547, 1558; COMNORPACFOR 150233, Quoted in Wheeler, *Kinkaid*, 325; Wheeler, *Kinkaid*, 326–28.

34. "Conference Notes–May 28, 1943," *King Papers*; "Conference Notes," 29 May 1943, *King Papers*; Maurice Matloff, *The War Department*, vol. 4, *Strategic Planning for Coalition Warfare: 1943–1944*, The United States Army in World War II (Washington, D.C.: United States Army Center for Military History, 1959), 82.

35. 26 April 1943, 7 June 1943, COMINCH 270001, May 1943, "Graybook," 3:1515, 1561, 1567; "Conference Notes," 4 June 1943, *King Papers*; "Brief Plan for the Control of the Marshall Islands," 12 February 1943, *Strategic*.

36. "Memorandum for Admiral King," Horne, 26 May 1943, *King Papers*; "Conference Notes–May 31, 1943," *King Papers*; "Conference Notes," 4 June 1943, *King Papers*; 4 May 1943, "Graybook," 3:1529; Matloff, *1943–1944*, 81.

37. "Conference Notes," 29 May 1943, *King Papers*.

38. Personal letter from Nimitz to Halsey, 18 December 1942, *Nimitz Papers*; "Conference Notes," 29 May 1943, *King Papers*; Hughes, *Halsey*, 244–47; 288–89.

39. "Conference Notes," 29 May 1943; Buell, *Quiet Warrior*, 183.

40. 31 May 1943, 12 September 1943, "Graybook," 3:1541,1655; "Conference Notes," 29 May 1943, *King Papers*; "Conference Notes," 4 June 1943, *King Papers*; Morison, *History*, 7:339.

41. "Conference Notes," 4 June 1943.

42. "Conference Notes–May 28, 1943," *King Papers*; "Conference Notes," 4 June 1943, *King Papers*; 1, 7 June 1943, "Graybook," 3:1565, 1567.

43. 10, 18–19 June 1943, CINCPAC 160226, Funafuti 281628, June 1943 "Graybook," 3:1569, 1574, 1605, 1612; Potter, *Nimitz*, 242; Morison, *History*, 6:147–51.

44. COMSOPAC 031116, COM3RDFLEET 010630, 090502, 090600, July 1943, "Graybook," 4:1710–13, 1718, 1765; Morison, *History*, 6:155–59; 175–80.

45. COM3RDFLEET 060645, 070626, July 1943, "Graybook," 4:1715; Morison, *History*, 6:160–75, 180–91; Hone, *Learning War*, 215–22.

46. 6 August 1943, COM3RDFLEET 140406, 310630, July 1942, "Graybook," 4:1633, 1731, 1767; Morison, *History*, 6:212–22; Hone, *Learning War*, 225–28.

47. 5 August 1943, COM3RDFLEET 260558, 270622, July 1943, "Graybook," 4:1632, 1729; "Further Items in Connection with Visit to CINCPAC," undated, *King Papers*; Morison, *History*, 6:198–206.

48. 7 September 1943, COMSOPAC 110421, July 1943, COMSOPAC 100112, August 1943, "Graybook," 4:1651, 1766, 1788.
49. COMGENWDC 272330, CINCPAC, COMGENWDC 292248, May 1943, CINCPAC 232359, June 1943, "Graybook," 3:1563–64, 1608.
50. CINCPAC 260315, COMINCH 271613, June 1943, CINCPAC 052047, 060655, COMNORPAC 060350, 110911, July 1943, "Graybook," 4:1611–12, 1719, 1764; Garfield, *Thousand-Mile War*, 348–55.
51. COMNORPAC 120929, 210055, July 1943, "Graybook," 4:1721, 1726.
52. *Secret Information Bulletin No. 12*; Fern Chandonnet, ed., *Alaska at War: 1941–1945, The Forgotten War Remembered* (Fairbanks, Alas.: University of Alaska Press, 2008), 31–32; Garfield, *Thousand-Mile War*, 364–72; Morison, *History*, 7:56–61.
53. 6 June 1943, "Graybook," 3:1567; Morgan, *Planning the Defeat of Japan*, 89.
54. CCCH, 85; CCS 242/6, "Final Report to the President and Prime Minister," 25 May 1943, *Trident Conference, May 1943: Papers and Minutes of Meetings* (Office of the Combined Chiefs of Staff, 1943), 170; Leighton and Coakley, *1943–1945*, 391.
55. JCS 151655, 15 June 1943, "Graybook," 3:1604–5; Morgan, *Planning the Defeat of Japan*, 102–3.
56. War Dept. 220200Z, WTO 260210, July 1943, "Graybook," 4:1774.
57. 4 September 1943, "Graybook," 4:1648; Dean, *MacArthur's Coalition*, 146–48, 315.
58. 14, 20 July, 19 August 1943, COMINCH 152220, June 1943, CINCPAC 030021, JCS 202204, July 1943, "Graybook," 4:1606, 1620, 1623, 1640, 1762, 1769, 1771–72.
59. COMINCH 241558, July 1943, *King Papers*.
60. "Conference–1 August, 1943," *King Papers*; "Action Items Resulting from West Coast Conference, July 30–August 1, 1943," *King Papers*; COMINCH 111902, August 1943, "Graybook," 4:1734.
61. "Conference–31 July, 1943," *King Papers*; "Conference–1 August, 1943," *King Papers*.
62. "Conference Notes–May 31, 1943," *King Papers*; "Conference–30 July, 1943," *King Papers*; "Conference–1 August, 1943," *King Papers*; "Further Items in Connection with Visit to CINCPAC," undated, *King Papers*.
63. "Conference–1 August, 1943," *King Papers*; COMINCH 210820, CINCPAC 250215, August 1943, "Graybook," 4:1794, 1798.
64. "Conference–31 July, 1943," *King Papers*.
65. "Further Items in Connection with Visit to CINCPAC," undated, *King Papers*.
66. COMINCH 021437, July 1943, "Graybook," 4:1762.
67. Letter, Leavey to Somervell, 29 July 1943, quoted in Leighton and Coakley, *1943–1945*, 446.
68. "Conference–1 August, 1943," "Conference–31 July, 1943," *King Papers*; No. 6138, No. C-4369, and No. W-6285, July/August 1943, "Graybook," 4:1779–80; CCCH, 47; Dean, *MacArthur's Coalition*, 295.
69. Buell, *Quiet Warrior*, 189.
70. CCCH, 142.
71. VCNO 062025, 062031, September 1943, "Graybook," 4:1739; CCCH, 143.
72. "Tentative Agenda," undated, *King Papers*; "Conference–1 August, 1943," *King Papers*.

73. "Command Relationships and Staff of Commander in Chief, Pacific Ocean Areas and U.S. Pacific Fleet–Reorganization of," 9 September 1943, Commander in Chief, U.S. Pacific Ocean Areas and U.S. Pacific Fleet; CINCPAC Staff Memorandum No. 13–43, "Establishment of Joint Staff," 6 September 1943; CCCH, 53, 55.
74. CCCH, 84.
75. Vice Admiral E. P. Forrestel, USN (Ret.), *Admiral Raymond A. Spruance, USN: A Study in Command* (Washington, D.C.: Government Printing Office, 1966), 66, 77.
76. "Organization Chart, Headquarters of CINCPAC/CINCPOA, 6 September 1943," "Graybook," 4:1650; "Conference–1 August, 1943," *King Papers*; "Conference–31 July, 1943," *King Papers*; CCCH, 56–57; "Establishment of Joint Staff," 6 September 1943, C.W. Nimitz.
77. CINCPAC 140305, September 1943, "Graybook," 4:1743; "Establishment of Joint Staff," 6 September 1943, C.W. Nimitz; Ballantine, *U.S. Naval Logistics*, 159; Leighton and Coakley, *1943–1945*, 447–48.
78. 19 August 1943, "Graybook," 4:1640; CCCH, 86.
79. CCCH, 86–87.
80. "Joint Staff Study: Hotfoot," Commander-in-Chief Pacific Ocean Areas, 5 October 1944, *Strategic*; Forrestel, *Spruance*, 72.
81. Moore, *Spies for Nimitz*, 11–15.

## CHAPTER 7. UNLEASHING THE CAMPAIGN

1. "Nimitz Diary," 29 November 1943, *Nimitz Papers*.
2. Ugaki, *Fading Victory*, 363.
3. Gen. Stanley McChrystal et al., *Team of Teams: New Rules of Engagement for a Complex World* (New York: Penguin, 2015), 223–25.
4. CINCPAC 020205, 2 July 1943, "Graybook," 4:1710.
5. CINCPAC Operation Plan No. 12–43, 16 August 1943, *Plans and Orders*; 2 September 1943, "Graybook," 4:1647; *Operational Experience of Fast Carrier Task Forces in World War II*, Weapons Systems Evaluation Group, WSEG Staff Study No. 4 (Washington, D.C.: Office of the Secretary of Defense, 15 August 1951), 17.
6. "Dater-Duckworth Memorandum," quoted in Clark G. Reynolds, *The Fast Carriers: The Forging of an Air Navy* (Annapolis, Md.: Naval Institute Press, 1992), 87–88.
7. 14 September 1943, "Graybook," 4:1657.
8. 7, 21, 26 October 1943, "Graybook," 4:1670, 1675, 1677.
9. COMINCH 111715, 161451, CINCPAC 090043, 140325, August 1943, COMINCH 081925, September 1943, "Graybook," 4:1733, 1789, 1790, 1792, 1805.
10. Morgan, *Defeat of Japan*, 111–12; CCS 301/3, "Specific Operations in the Pacific and Far East, 1943–44," 27 August 1943, *Quadrant Conference, August 1943: Papers and Minutes of Meetings* (Office of the Combined Chiefs of Staff, 1943), 63–70.
11. CCS 301/3, "Specific Operations in the Pacific and Far East, 1943–44"; Morison, *History*, 8:6; Adams, *Witness to Power*, 220.
12. CCS 313, "Appreciation and Plan for the Defeat of Japan," 18 August 1943, *Quadrant Conference*, 153–70; CCS 323, "Air Plan for the Defeat of Japan, 20 August 1943," *Quadrant Conference*, 288–300; Morgan, *Defeat of Japan*, 116–19.

13. JCS 012115, September 1943, "Graybook," 4:1803–4.
14. "Minutes of Conference," 25 September 1943, *King Papers*; COMINCH 271805, CINCPAC 260439, September 1943, CINCPAC 061801, October 1943, "Graybook," 4:1813–14, 1817; Forrestel, *Spruance*, 71.
15. "Minutes of Conference, Second Day," 26 September 1943, *King Papers*.
16. CINCPAC 160137, CINCSOWESTPAC 160310, COMSOPAC 150635, 220426, September 1943, "Graybook," 4:1809–11; "Minutes of Conference, Second Day," 26 September 1943; "Action Items Resulting from Pearl Harbor Conference," undated, *King Papers*.
17. "Minutes of Conference, Second Day," 26 September 1943.
18. "Minutes of Conference, Second Day," 26 September 1943; COMINCH 161830, October 1943, "Graybook," 4:1749.
19. "Minutes of Conference, 25 September, 1943, Personnel," *King Papers*; "Minutes of Conference, Second Day–26 September, Personnel (Cont'd)," *King Papers*.
20. "Minutes of Conference 26 September, 1943, Personnel (Cont'd.)"; "Action Items Resulting from Pearl Harbor Conference," *King Papers*.
21. Potter, *Nimitz*, 253; Forrestel, *Spruance*, 72.
22. CINCPAC Operation Plan No. 13-43, 5 October 1943, *Plans and Orders*; CINCPOA 050249, October 1943, "Graybook," 4:1815; Morison, *History*, 8:106.
23. Wildenberg, *Gray Steel*, 180–83; Forrestel, *Spruance*, 78.
24. Commander Task Force 54, Operation Plan No. A2-43, 23 October 1943, *Plans and Orders*; Central Pacific Force Operation Plan No. 1-43, 25 October 1943, *Plans and Orders*; Morison, *History*, 7:116–18, 338–40.
25. "Galvanic Operation–General Instructions For," 29 October 1943, R. A. Spruance, *Strategic*; Central Pacific Force Operation Plan 3-43, 24 October 1943, *Plans and Orders*; CINCPAC 182347, September 1943, "Graybook," 4:1811; "Post Galvanic Carrier Strike on Marshalls," 31 October 1943, R. A. Spruance, *Plans and Orders*.
26. CINCPAC Operation Plan No. ___-43, 6 October 1943, *Plans and Orders*; CINCPAC Operation Plan No. 16-43, 12 October 1943, *Plans and Orders*.
27. Morison, *History*, 8:6–7.
28. 24 October, 8 November 1943, COMINCH 221319, CINCPAC 260519, October 1943, "Graybook," 4: 1676, 1682, 1819.
29. JCS 021832, October 1943, "Graybook," 4:1816.
30. Louis Morton, *The War in the Pacific*, vol. 1, *Strategy and Command: The First Two Years*, The United States Army in World War II (Washington, D.C.: United States Army Center for Military History, 1962), "Appendix W, Reno III, Outline Plans Plan for Operations of the SWPA, 1944," 686–92; COMSOPAC 120452, 250815, October 1943, COMSOPAC 010057, November 1943, "Graybook," 4:1818–19, 1822.
31. 2–3 November 1943, COMSOPAC 030100, CINCPAC 030915, November 1943, "Graybook," 4:1679, 1680, 1822, 1824.
32. 5–8 November 1943, CINCPAC 052111, November 1943, "Graybook," 4:1681–82, 1824; Potter, *Nimitz*, 255.
33. CTG50.3 120321, November, "Graybook," 4:1755; Morison, *History*, 6:336.
34. 17–24 December 1943, "Graybook," 4:1701–6.

35. Col. Joseph H. Alexander, USMC (Ret.), *Storm Landings: Epic Amphibious Battles in the Central Pacific* (Annapolis, Md.: Naval Institute Press, 1997), 44.

36. Potter, *Nimitz*, 256.

37. 20 November 1943, "Graybook," 4:1688; Morison, *History*, 7:132–35; Forrestel, *Spruance*, 90.

38. 28 November 1943, "Graybook," 4:1692; Morison, *History*, 7:167; Potter, *Nimitz*, 257.

39. Potter, *Nimitz*, 257; 20–22 November 1943, "Graybook," 4:1688–89.

40. CINCPAC 212225, November 1943, "Graybook," 4:1755; Reynolds, *Towers*, 448; Potter, *Nimitz*, 259.

41. Morgan, *Defeat of Japan*, 93.

42. 25–26 November 1943, "Graybook," 4:1691.

43. CINCPAC 250357, November 1943, "Graybook," 4:1828.

44. "Preliminary Draft of Campaign Plan–Granite II," CINCPOA, 6 May 1944, *Plans and Orders*.

45. Morgan, *Defeat of Japan*, 131–32.

46. CPS 86/7, "Overall Plan for the Defeat of Japan," 30 November 1943, quoted in Morgan, *Defeat of Japan*, 124–25; CCS 397, "Specific Operations for the Defeat of Japan, 1944," 3 December 1943, *Sextant Conference, November-December 1943, Papers and Meeting Minutes* (Office of the Combined Chiefs of Staff, 1943), 65–72; CCS 417, "Over-all Plan for the Defeat of Japan," 2 December 1943, *Sextant Conference*, 253–68; Morgan, *Defeat of Japan*, 124–32.

47. CCCH, 58; "CINCPAC and CINCPOA Staff and Telephone Numbers," 1 October 1944; "Organization and Functioning of Naval Staffs," 18 January 1945, *Presentations*, Box 34.

48. CCCH, 90.

49. CINCPAC 090240, COMINCH 042125, 101609, November 1943, COMINCH 031835, December 1943, "Graybook," 4:1758, 1824–25, 1828; CINCPAC Operation Plan No. 16-43 (Revised), 14 December 1943, *Plans and Orders*; "Catchpole–Outline Plan," and "Catchpole–Detail Plan," 29 November 1943, *Strategic*.

50. 27 November 1943, "Graybook," 4:1692.

51. "Designation of objectives under CINCPAC & POA Operation Plan No. 16-43," 14 December 1943, *Plans and Orders*; "Outline Campaign Plan–Granite," CINCPOA, 13 January 1944, *Plans and Orders*; "Catchpole–Outline Plan," 29 November 1943, *Strategic*; Potter, *Nimitz*, 265.

52. CINCPAC 210221, December 1943, "Graybook," 4:1758; Moore, *Spies for Nimitz*, 71; Potter, *Nimitz*, 265; Layton et al., *"And I Was There,"* 480; Morison, *History*, 7:206; Forrestel, *Spruance*, 60.

53. COMINCH 151525, December 1943, "Graybook," 4:1829; "Preliminary Draft of Campaign Plan–Granite II," CINCPOA, 6 May 1944, *Plans and Orders*; Reynolds, *Towers*, 455.

54. CINCPAC 262130, December 1943, "Graybook," 4:1830; Morton, *Strategy and Command*, "Appendix W, Reno III, Outline Plans plan for Operations of the SWPA, 1944," 686–92.

55. "Preliminary Draft of Campaign–Granite," CINCPOA, 27 December 1943, *Plans and Orders*; Forrestel, *Spruance*, 65.

56. 14 November 1943, "Graybook," 4:1685.
57. "Preliminary Draft of Campaign–Granite," CINCPOA, 27 December 1943; "Strategic Areas: The Mandate Islands and the Guam-Bonin Line," Naval War College, 1936, *Strategic*.
58. "Preliminary Draft of Campaign–Granite," CINCPOA, 27 December 1943; Roadmaker Joint Staff Study, Commander-in-Chief, Pacific Ocean Areas, 26 February 1944, *Strategic*.
59. "Catchpole–Outline Plan," 29 November 1943, *Strategic*, emphasis in original; CINCPAC 262130, December 1943, "Graybook," 4:1830.
60. "Second Day, 4 January, 1944, III Future Operations," *King Papers*; Hailstone Joint Staff Study, Commander-in-Chief, Pacific Ocean Areas, 18 January 1944, *Strategic*; 29 September 1943, CINCPAC 262130, December 1943, "Graybook," 4:1665, 1830.
61. "Second Day, 4 January, 1944, III Future Operations."
62. "Minutes of Personnel Conference, 3 January 1944," *King Papers*; "Agenda for January Conference," no date, *King Papers*; Reynolds, *Towers*, 450–53.
63. "Outline Campaign Plan–Granite," CINCPOA, 13 January 1944, *Plans and Orders*.
64. "Outline Campaign Plan–Granite," CINCPOA, 13 January 1944; Moore, *Spies for Nimitz*, 102.
65. MacArthur 061127, CINCPAC 070521, JCS 231510, 231515, 231520, January 1944, "Graybook," 5:2304–6; Morgan, *Defeat of Japan*, 134; Reynolds, *Towers*, 461–62; Matloff, *1943–1944*, 455–56.
66. CINCPAC 120505, February 1944, "Graybook," 5:2310.
67. Matloff, *1943–1944*, 456; Morison, *History*, 8:8; Morgan, *Defeat of Japan*, 134–36; Reynolds, *Towers*, 462; Potter, *Nimitz*, 283.
68. "Memorandum for Admiral King," 10 February 1944, in Larry I. Bland and Sharon Ritenour Stevens, ed., *The Papers of George Catlett Marshall*, vol. 4, *"Aggressive and Determined Leadership," June 1, 1943-December 31, 1944* (Baltimore and London: The Johns Hopkins University Press, 1996), 4:280–81; Morgan, *Defeat of Japan*, 134–36.
69. Central Pacific Force Operation Plan No. 1-44, 6 January 1944, *Plans and Orders*; V Amphibious Force Operation Plan No. A6-43, 3 January 1944, *Plans and Orders*.
70. "Preliminary Draft of Campaign–Granite," CINCPOA, 27 December 1943, *Plans and Orders*.
71. 31 January 1944, "Graybook," 5:1847.
72. 1, 2 February 1944, "Graybook," 5:1847–48; Morison, *History*, 7:236–50.
73. 4 February 1944, "Graybook," 5:1849; Morison, *History*, 7:251, 257–72.
74. 16, 31 January, 3 February 1944, "Graybook," 5:1839, 1847, 1849.
75. 10, 18–22 February 1944, "Graybook," 5:1853, 1858–61; Moore, *Spies for Nimitz*, 83–87; Morison, *History*, 7:282–304.
76. 29 September 1943, 4, 5, 16 February 1944, CINCPAC 262130, January 1944, COMAIRSOPAC 050623, February 1944, "Graybook," 5: 1665, 1850, 1856, 2306, 2310; Morison, *History*, 7:319–29.
77. Morison, *History*, 7:320–25.
78. 15–18 February 1944, "Graybook," 5:1856–58.
79. "Report of action against Tinian and Saipan conducted by Task Group Fifty-Eight Point Two, 21–23 February 1944," Commander Task Group Fifty-Eight Point Two,

25 February 1944, *Action*; "Report of the Carrier Air Strike on the Saipan-Tinian area 22 February 1944," Commander Task Group Fifty-Eight Point Three, 3 March 1944, *Action*; Operation Plan 3–44, CTF 58, 19 February 1944, *Plans and Orders*; 14, 19, 24 February 1944, "Graybook," 5:1855, 1859, 1862–63; Theodore Taylor, *The Magnificent Mitscher* (Annapolis, Md.: Naval Institute Press, 1991), 186; Morison, *History*, 8:154–55.

80. Bix, *Hirohito*, 472; Ugaki, *Fading Victory*, 332–34.
81. 18 February 1944, "Graybook," 5:1858; Dean, *MacArthur's Coalition*, 323–25; Edward J. Drea, *MacArthur's Ultra: Codebreaking and the War Against Japan, 1942–1945* (Lawrence: Kansas University Press, 1992), 92.
82. 29 February 1944, COM7THFLEET 050623, April 1944, "Graybook," 5:1865, 2198; Drea, *MacArthur's Ultra*, 98–102; Morison, *History*, 6:435.
83. JCS 022941, March 1944, "Graybook," 5:2310; "Reno IV: Outline Pan for Operations in the Southwest Pacific Area," General Headquarters, Southwest Pacific Area, 6 March 1944; Adams, *Witness to Power*, 240; Matloff, *1943–1944*, 458; Morgan, *Defeat of Japan*, 137; Drea, *MacArthur's Ultra*, 105, 117.
84. "1500–March 1944," *King Papers*; Matloff, *1943–1944*, 458; Philip A. Crowl, *The War in the Pacific*, vol. 7, *Campaign in the Marianas*, The United States Army in World War II (Washington, D.C.: United States Army Center for Military History, 1960), 18–19.
85. "1500–March 1944"; Morison, *History*, 8:7–8.
86. JCS 122319, March 1944, "Graybook," 5:2312–14.
87. JCS 122319, March 1944; Adams, *Witness to Power*, 240.
88. COMSOPAC 150538, CINCSWPA 131107, March 1944, "Graybook," 5:2315–16; Morison, *History*, 6:423–24.
89. CINCPAC Op. Plan No. 1-44, 18 March 1944, *Plans and Orders*; CINCPOA 140144, 150306, March 1944, "Graybook," 5:2315, 2316.
90. 23 March 1944, CINCSOWESPAC 140941, CINCSWPA 160614, JCS 170809, March 1944, "Graybook," 5:1881, 2315–17; Drea, *MacArthur's Ultra*, 110.
91. Desecrate Joint Staff Study, Commander-in-Chief Pacific Ocean Areas, 15 March 1944, *Strategic*.
92. Morison, *History*, 7:31–32, 8:12–13; Ugaki, *Fading Victory*, 336.
93. 1 April 1944, "Graybook," 5:1888; Morison, *History*, 8:31–34; Ugaki, *Fading Victory*, 342–43.
94. Ugaki, *Fading Victory*, 342–43, 348.
95. "Operation Plan No. 5-44," Task Force Fifty-Eight, 9 April 1944, *Plans and Orders*; Morison, *History*, 8:158.
96. 23, 24, 27 April 1944, "Graybook," 5:1905, 1906, 1909.
97. Uhl-Bien et al., "Complexity Leadership Theory."
98. Ugaki, *Fading Victory*, 363–68.
99. Ugaki, *Fading Victory*, 368.

### CHAPTER 8. MAINTAINING TEMPO

1. "Outline Campaign Plan–Granite, " CINCPOA, 13 January 1944, *Plans and Orders*.
2. Morgan, *Defeat of Japan*, 138–39.

3. Bix, *Hirohito*, 467–70; Edward J. Drea, *Japan's Imperial Army: Its Rise and Fall, 1853–1945* (Lawrence: Kansas University Press, 2009), 232–33.

4. "Minutes of Conference," 1000, 6 March 1944; "Agenda for Pacific Conference (May 1944)"; "Pacific Conference Minutes, First Day, Friday 5 May, 1944"; "Pacific Conference Minutes, Second Day, Saturday, 6 May, 1944," all *King Papers*.

5. "Agenda for Pacific Conference (May 1944)"; "Pacific Conference Minutes, Second Day, Saturday, 6 May, 1944"; "Preliminary Draft of Campaign Plan–Granite II," CINCPOA, 6 May 1944, *Plans and Orders*.

6. CINCPAC 220356, March 1944, "Graybook," 5:2318; "Preliminary Draft of Campaign Plan–Granite II," CINCPOA, 6 May 1944; "Pacific Conference Minutes, Second Day, Saturday, 6 May, 1944."

7. "Pacific Conference Minutes, Second Day, Saturday, 6 May, 1944"; Memorandum for Rear Admiral D. C. Ramsey, USN, United States Fleet, Headquarters of the Commander in Chief, 21 September 1943, *Strategic*.

8. "Preliminary Draft of Campaign Plan–Granite II," CINCPOA, 6 May 1944.

9. "Pacific Conference Minutes, Second Day, Saturday, 6 May, 1944"; "Preliminary Draft of Campaign Plan–Granite II," CINCPOA, 6 May 1944.

10. "Pacific Conference Minutes, Second Day, Saturday, 6 May, 1944"; "Preliminary Draft of Campaign Plan–Granite II," CINCPOA, 6 May 1944.

11. COMINCH 051300, June 1944, 292206, May 1944, "Graybook," 5:2203–4, 2202.

12. 1 August 1944, Marshall 242030, Richardson 280842, May 1944, Marshall 062045, June 1944, "Graybook," 5:2025, 2320–22, 2324.

13. Kuehn, *Agents of Innovation*, 125–43.

14. "History of Commander Service Force, U.S. Pacific Fleet," 307, Quoted in *Operational Experience of Fast Carrier Task Forces in World War II*, 28; Rear Adm. Worrall Reed Carter, USN (Ret.), *Beans, Bullets, and Black Oil* (Washington, D.C.: Department of the Navy, 1953), 95.

15. "Outline Campaign Plan–Granite II," CINCPOA, 3 June 1944, *Plans and Orders*.

16. "Outline Campaign Plan–Granite II," CINCPOA, 3 June 1944.

17. "Outline Campaign Plan–Granite II," CINCPOA, 3 June 1944; JCS 131545, June 1944, "Graybook," 5:2326.

18. CINCSOWESTPAC 180935, June 1944, "Graybook," 5:2326–27.

19. Morgan, *Defeat of Japan*, 140–41.

20. Forager Joint Staff Study, Commander-in-Chief, Pacific Ocean Areas, 20 March 1944, *Strategic*; CINCPOA Operation Plan No. 3-44, 23 April 1944, *Plans and Orders*.

21. Many other troops did not. Navy submarines killed more than 97,000 Japanese military personnel in attacks on transports and other ships, the vast majority in 1944. See Richard B. Frank, "Slaughter at Sea," *World War II Magazine* 35, no. 6 (April 2021): 28–37.

22. Forager Joint Staff Study; Moore, *Spies for Nimitz*, 105; Crowl, *Campaign in the Marianas*, 60, 65.

23. COMINCH 251859, May 1944, "Graybook," 5:2321; Fifth Fleet Operation Plan No. 12-44, 11 May 1944, *Plans and Orders*.

24. CINCPAC 272136, May 1944, "Graybook," 5:2323; Fast Carrier Task Forces, Pacific, Operation Plan No. 5-44, 9 April 1944, *Plans and Orders*.

25. Drea, *MacArthur's Ultra*, 126–31, 135, 139; Craven and Cate, *The Army Air Forces*, 4:616; Morison, *History*, 8:114.
26. "Combined Fleet Ultrasecret Order 76," *The Campaigns of the Pacific War*, United States Strategic Bombing Survey (Pacific), Naval Analysis Division (Washington, D.C.: United States Government Printing Office, 1946), 226–31; *The "A-Go" Operations: May–Jun. 1944*, Japanese Monograph No. 90, 10 October 1947 (General Headquarters, Far East Command, Military Intelligence Section, General Staff); Vego, *Fleet-versus-Fleet*, 237; Ugaki, *Fading Victory*, 362–79; Morison, *History*, 8:118.
27. 25 May, 4, 5, 9 June 1944, "Graybook," 5:1934, 1945–51; Morison, *History*, 8:120–30; Vego, *Fleet-versus-Fleet*, 229–32.
28. 11–13 June 1944, COM5THFLT 140526, June 1944, "Graybook," 5:1952–56, 2208; Vego, *Fleet-versus-Fleet*, 245–51; Morison, *History*, 8:133.
29. "Operations in Support of the Capture of the Marianas–Action Report of," Commander, Task Force Fifty-Eight, 11 September 1944, *Action*; Fast Carrier Task Force, Pacific, Operation Plan No. 7-44, 24 May 1944, *Plans and Orders*; Fifth Fleet Operation Plan No. 10-44, 12 May 1944, *Plans and Orders*; Fifth Fleet Operation Plan No. 12-44, 11 May 1944, *Plans and Orders*.
30. 14 June 1944, "Graybook," 5:1957–58; Moore, *Spies for Nimitz*, 106.
31. 14 June 1944, "Graybook," 5:1958, 1962; Vego, *Fleet-versus-Fleet*, 258.
32. Buell, *Quiet Warrior*, 285; 15, 17 June 1944, "Graybook," 5:1959–60, 1964.
33. "Operations in Support of the Capture of the Marianas–Action Report of," Commander, Task Force Fifty-Eight, 11 September 1944; E. B. Potter, *Admiral Arleigh Burke* (Annapolis, Md.: Naval Institute Press, 1990), 146–47.
34. "Operations in Support of the Capture of the Marianas–Action Report of," Commander, Task Force Fifty-Eight, 11 September 1944; "Initial Report on the Operation to Capture the Marianas Islands," Commander, Fifth Fleet, 13 July 1944, *Action*; Potter, *Burke*, 147; Forrestel, *Spruance*, 136.
35. 16, 17 June 1944, "Graybook," 5:1962, 1964; Morison, *History*, 8:241–43; Vego, *Fleet-versus-Fleet*, 262–66.
36. "Operations in Support of the Capture of the Marianas–Action Report of," Commander, Task Force Fifty-Eight, 11 September 1944; "Initial Report on the Operation to Capture the Marianas Islands," Commander, Fifth Fleet, 13 July 1944; Buell, *Quiet Warrior*, 286.
37. "Operations in Support of the Capture of the Marianas–Action Report of," Commander, Task Force Fifty-Eight, 11 September 1944; Potter, *Burke*, 148.
38. "Initial Report on the Operation to Capture the Marianas Islands," Commander, Fifth Fleet, 13 July 1944; Potter, *Nimitz*, 299–300. Spruance may have been less concerned about the risk because he was aware that Operation Hotfoot anticipated the carriers would have to fight off one thousand enemy planes.
39. "Operations in Support of the Capture of the Marianas–Action Report of," Commander, Task Force Fifty-Eight, 11 September 1944; Potter, *Burke*, 149.
40. "Initial Report on the Operation to Capture the Marianas Islands," Commander, Fifth Fleet, 13 July 1944; Morison, *History*, 8:252; Buell, *Quiet Warrior*, 295–96.
41. 18, 21, 23 June 1944, "Graybook," 5:1965, 1969, 1971–72; Vego, *Fleet-versus-Fleet*, 277–82, 289.

42. 18 June 1944, "Graybook," 5:1965; Morison, *History*, 8:278–82.
43. "Initial Report on the Operation to Capture the Marianas Islands," Commander, Fifth Fleet, 13 July 1944; Morison, *History*, 8:252.
44. 18 June 1944, "Graybook," 5:1965; Morison, *History*, 8:282–87; Vego, *Fleet-versus-Fleet*, 287–88.
45. "Operations in Support of the Capture of the Marianas–Action Report of," Commander, Task Force Fifty-Eight, 11 September 1944.
46. "Operations in Support of the Capture of the Marianas–Action Report of," Commander, Task Force Fifty-Eight, 11 September 1944.
47. Forrestel, *Spruance*, 146.
48. "Operations in Pacific Ocean Areas–June 1944," Commander in Chief, U.S. Pacific Fleet and Pacific Ocean Areas, 7 November 1944, *Action*; Hughes and Girrier, *Fleet Tactics*, 90–91; Taylor, *Mitscher*, 239–40; Reynolds, *Towers*, 476.
49. Nolan, *The Allure of Battle*, 4; Morison, *History*, 8:342.
50. Operation Plan No. 6-44, Commander-in-Chief, Pacific Ocean Areas, 21 July 1944, *Plans and Orders*.
51. Northern Troops and Landing Force Op Ord No. 9-44, 21 June 1944; "Conduct of operations by 2nd Bn 105th Inf in the Nafutan Point Area," Commanding General, Northern Troops and Landing Force, 27 June 1944; "Summary of events leading up to the relief from command of Major General Ralph C. Smith, USA," Commander Fifth Fleet, 29 June 1944; "Authority to relieve Army officers from command," The Commanding General, Expeditionary Troops, 24 June 1944; "Summary of events leading up to the relief from command of Major General Ralph C. Smith, USA," The Commanding General, Northern Troops and Landing Force, 27 June 1944, all *Nimitz Papers*.
52. "Articles in Time Magazine 18 September 1944, and Life Magazine 28 August 1944," Robert C. Richardson, 14 October 1944; "Articles in Time Magazine 12 September 1944, and Life Magazine 28 August 1944," Commander in Chief, U.S. Pacific Fleet and Pacific Ocean Areas, 27 October 1944; "Memorandum for Admiral King," Marshall, 22 November 1944; "Article in Time Magazine, 12 September 1944," E. J. King, 23 November 1944, all *Nimitz Papers*; "Minutes of Pacific Conference, 24–26 November, 1944," undated, *King Papers*.
53. COMGENCENTPAC 180900, CINCPOA 240514, 240929, COMINCH 271845, June 1944, "Graybook," 5:2325, 2329, 2215.
54. COM5THFLT 030601, July 1944, "Graybook," 5:2331.
55. CINCPAC 032109, COM5THFLT 051425, CINCPOA 060236, July 1944, "Graybook," 5:2331–33; Morison, *History*, 8:379, Buell, *Quiet Warrior*, 312–13.
56. Forrestel, *Spruance*, 152; Alexander, *Storm Landings*, 84.
57. Bix, *Hirohito*, 475–80; Drea, *Japan's Imperial Army*, 239–40.
58. "Stalemate II Joint Staff Study," Commander-in-Chief, Pacific Ocean Areas, 14 July 1944, *Strategic*; CINCPOA 040400, July 1944, "Graybook," 5:2331–32.
59. COMINCH 061840, July 1944, "Graybook," 5:2333; "Minutes of Pacific Conference, Headquarters, Commander in Chief, Pacific Ocean Areas, 13–22 July, 1944," *King Papers*.

60. "Minutes of Pacific Conference, Headquarters, Commander in Chief, Pacific Ocean Areas, 13–22 July, 1944."

61. "Minutes of Pacific Conference, Headquarters, Commander in Chief, Pacific Ocean Areas, 13–22 July, 1944."

62. "Agenda for Conference with Admiral Nimitz," 10 July 1944, *King Papers*; "Minutes of Pacific Conference, Headquarters, Commander in Chief, Pacific Ocean Areas, 13–22 July, 1944," *King Papers*; Furer, *Administration*, 281.

63. "Agenda for Conference with Admiral Nimitz," 10 July 1944, *King Papers*; "Minutes of Pacific Conference, Headquarters, Commander in Chief, Pacific Ocean Areas, 13–22 July, 1944," *King Papers*.

64. "Minutes of Pacific Conference, Headquarters, Commander in Chief, Pacific Ocean Areas, First Day–Thursday, 13 July, 1944," *King Papers*.

65. Buell, *King*, 441; Forrestel, *Spruance*, 163–64.

66. Phillips Payson O'Brien, *The Second Most Powerful Man in the World: The Life of Admiral William D. Leahy, Roosevelt's Chief of Staff* (New York: Dutton, 2019), 289; Adams, *Witness to Power*, 248–49.

67. O'Brien, *Leahy*, 288–89; Adams, *Witness to Power*, 253–54.

68. Adams, *Witness to Power*, 254–57; Morgan, *Defeat of Japan*, 141; Richard B. Frank, *MacArthur* (New York: Palgrave Macmillan, 2007), 104.

69. 24, 30, 31 July, 6 August 1944, "Graybook," 5:2021, 2023–24, 2032.

70. GHQ SWPA 210801, July 1944, "Graybook," 5: 2218; Drea, *MacArthur's Ultra*, 153.

71. MacArthur 180849, 190733, CINCPAC 210816, August 1944, "Graybook," 5:2343–45.

72. CTG38.4 031229, September 1944, "Graybook," 5:2226.

73. COMINCH 021631, July 1944, "Graybook," 5:2334.

74. CINCPOA 240957, July 1944, "Graybook," 5:2334–35.

75. Sherman 270245, July 1944, "Graybook," 5:2335; Craven and Cate, *The Army Air Forces*, 5:282.

76. Joint Staff Planners 271956, July 1944, "Graybook," 5:2336.

77. CINCPOA 100133, Richardson 050457, August 1944, "Graybook," 5:2337, 2339; Robert Ross Smith, "Luzon Versus Formosa," in *Command Decisions*, ed. Kent Roberts Greenfield (Washington, D.C.: United States Army Center for Military History, 1990), 470; Rana Mitter, *Forgotten Ally: China's World War II, 1937–1945* (New York: Mariner Books, 2014), 318–19, 335–44; Nolan, *The Allure of Battle*, 535; Drea, *Japan's Imperial Army*, 244.

78. CINCPOA 070116, August 1944, "Graybook," 5:2338.

79. JCS 152100, CINCPOA 180437, August 1944, "Graybook," 5:2341–42.

80. CINCPOA 232108, August 1944, 050314, September 1944, "Graybook," 5:2347; Smith, "Luzon Versus Formosa," 472.

81. JCS 09314, September 1944, "Graybook," 5:2350; Matloff, *1943-1944*, 485–87. Causeway was short some ten thousand service troops at the time.

82. 22 August 1944, CINCPOA 100125, August 1944, "Graybook," 5:2045, 2339; "Letter of Instructions," Commander-in-Chief, Pacific Ocean Areas, 18 August 1944, *Plans and Orders*; Hughes, *Halsey*, 336.

83. CINCPOA 150355, August 1944, "Graybook," 5:2341; Stalemate II Joint Staff Study, Commander-in-Chief, Pacific Ocean Areas, 14 July 1944, *Strategic*; CINCPOA

Operation Plan No. 6-44, 21 July 1944, *Plans and Orders*; "Establishment of Earthenware Base, Plan for," CINCPAC-CINCPOA, 8 July 1944, *Plans and Orders*; "Base Development Plan–Domestic," CINCPAC-CINCPOA, 7 August 1944, *Plans and Orders*; Commander Third Fleet Operation Plan No. 1-44, 1 August 1944, *Plans and Orders*.

84. CINCPOA Operation Plan No. 6-44, 21 July 1944, *Plans and Orders*; Commander Third Fleet Operation Plan No. 14-44, 1 August 1944, *Plans and Orders*, emphasis in original.

85. Halsey letter to Nimitz, 9 September 1944, *Nimitz Papers*.

86. CTF38 070336, 071245, September 1944, "Graybook," 5:2227.

87. COM3RDFLT 091830, CINCPOA 101955, September 1944, "Graybook," 5:2351; Alexander, *Storm Landings*, 105.

88. CINCSOWESTPAC 111637, CINCPOA 130131, September 1944, "Graybook," 5:2352.

89. COM3RDFLT 130230, 130300, 140800, September 1944, "Graybook," 5:2229–30, 2353.

90. CINCPOA 130813, GHQSWPA 140316, CINCPAC 140835, September 1944, "Graybook," 5:2353–55; Morgan, *Defeat of Japan*, 143–44.

91. CINCPOA 132100, 140101, September 1944, "Graybook," 5:2356.

92. COMINCH 141325, September 1944, "Graybook," 5:2356; Morgan, *Defeat of Japan*, 144; Drea, *MacArthur's Ultra*, 158; Adams, *Witness to Power*, 259.

93. MacArthur 142359, CINCSWPAC 150707, 150419, CINCPOA 152044, 160346, COM3RDFLT 170135, September 1944, "Graybook," 5:2356–60.

94. 14–19 September 1944, "Graybook," 5:2066–74; Bobby C. Blair and John Peter DeCioccio, *Victory at Peleliu: The 81st Infantry Division's Pacific Campaign* (Norman, Okla.: University of Oklahoma Press, 2011), 19–20, 200–44; Moore, *Spies for Nimitz*, 167.

95. Blair and DeCioccio, *Victory at Peleliu*, 200–244; E. B. Sledge, *With the Old Breed: At Peleliu and Okinawa* (New York: Presidio Press, 2007), 147; Maj. Frank O. Hough, USMCR, *The Assault on Peleliu* (Historical Division, Headquarters, U.S. Marine Corps, 1950), 1; 16–19 September 1944, "Graybook," 5:2070–74.

96. CINCPOA 140101, September 1944, "Graybook," 5:2356; Maj. John L. Medeiros, USMC, "Strategic and Operational Importance of Peleliu During the Pacific War," Master's thesis (United States Marine Corps Command and Staff College, Quantico, Va., March 2010), 21; Moore, *Spies for Nimitz*, 163–65, 170–71; "Joint Staff Study, Induction," Commander in Chief Pacific Ocean Areas, 19 October 1944, *Strategic*; Morison, *History*, 12:41 and map 12:126; Craven and Cate, *The Army Air Forces*, 4:693.

97. MacArthur 211042, September 1944, "Graybook," 5:2362–63.

98. Nimitz letter to Halsey, 24 September 1944, *Nimitz Papers*.

99. Buell, *Master of Sea Power*, 441; Forrestel, *Spruance*, 163–64; Morgan, *Defeat of Japan*, 142–45. An additional factor was the recognition that Germany would not be defeated before the end of 1944. That would delay the transfer of U.S. Army forces from Europe to the Pacific.

100. "Agenda–Pacific Conference–September 1944," *King Papers*; "Minutes of Pacific Conference, San Francisco, California, 29 September–1 October 1944," *King Papers*;

Coakley and Leighton, *1943–1945*, 414–15; Peter Mansoor, "Luzon versus Formosa: A Decision Revisited," paper presented at the Annual Meeting of the Society for Military History, Norfolk, Va., 22 May 2021.

101. "Minutes of Pacific Conference, San Francisco, California, 29 September–1 October 1944."
102. "Minutes of Pacific Conference, San Francisco, California, 29 September–1 October 1944."
103. "Minutes of Pacific Conference, San Francisco, California, 29 September–1 October 1944."
104. "Minutes of Pacific Conference, San Francisco, California, 29 September–1 October 1944."
105. "Minutes of Pacific Conference, San Francisco, California, 29 September–1 October 1944."
106. JCS 032255, October 1944, "Graybook," 5:2378; Smith, "Luzon Versus Formosa," 474–77.
107. "Organization and Functioning of Naval Staffs," 18 January 1945, *Presentations*; CCCH, 62; Pratt, *Fleet Against Japan*, 56.
108. CCCH, 61, 93; Reynolds, *Towers*, 467, 478.
109. Milan Vego, *The Battle for Leyte, 1944: Allied and Japanese Plans, Preparation, and Execution* (Annapolis, Md.: Naval Institute Press, 2006), 19.

## CHAPTER 9. SEEKING DECISION

1. Operation Plan No. 6-44, Commander-in-Chief, Pacific Ocean Areas, 21 July 1944, *Plans and Orders*.
2. Quoted in Hughes, *Halsey*, 86.
3. Operation Plan No. 6-44, Commander-in-Chief, Pacific Ocean Areas, 21 July 1944, *Plans and Orders*.
4. "Joint Staff Study: Hotfoot," Commander-in-Chief Pacific Ocean Areas, 5 October 1944, *Strategic*.
5. "Joint Staff Study, Induction," Commander-in-Chief Pacific Ocean Areas, 19 October 1944, *Strategic*.
6. CINCPOA Joint Staff Study, Detachment, 7 October 1944, *Strategic*; "Joint Staff Study: Iceberg," Commander-in-Chief Pacific Ocean Areas, 25 October 1944, *Strategic*.
7. CINCPOA Joint Staff Study, Detachment, 7 October 1944, *Strategic*; Vego, *Leyte*, 49.
8. Vego, *Leyte*, 54.
9. COM3RDFLT 230424, September 1944, CINCPOA 071125, COM3RDFLT 120127, October 1944, "Graybook," 5:2367, 2377, 2381.
10. Halsey letter to Nimitz, 28 September 1944, *Nimitz Papers*; COM3RDFLT 230424, September 1944, "Graybook," 5:2367.
11. Nimitz letter to Halsey, 8 October 1944, *Nimitz Papers*; CINCPOA 262316, September 1944, "Graybook," 5:2370.

12. CINCSOWESPAC 160125, MacArthur 301127, September 1944, MacArthur 041340, October 1944, "Graybook," 5:2239, 2357, 2374; Richard W. Bates, *The Battle for Leyte Gulf, October 1944, Strategical and Tactical Analysis*, vol. 3, *Operations from 0000 October 20th (D-Day) until 1042 October 23rd* (Naval War College, Newport, R.I.: Bureau of Naval Personnel, 1957), 3:341.

13. GHQSWPA 250715, GHQSWPA 220220, September 1944, "Graybook," 5:2234, 2364.

14. Vego, *Leyte*, 161–63; Morison, *History*, 12:91.

15. Quoted in Morison, *History*, 12:93.

16. 13 October 1944, "Graybook," 5:2098.

17. COM3RDFLT 130955, 150149, 150252, CINCPAC 142219, October 1944, "Graybook," 5:2240, 2383–84; Morison, *History*, 12:94.

18. CINCPOA 150932, 150651, CINCPAC 150301, 151230, COMNAVGROUP China 151755, 160953, DEPCOMAF20 150736, October 1944, "Graybook," 5:2384–85.

19. 19 October 1944, "Graybook," 5:2103.

20. Bates, *Leyte*, 3:98–101; Vego, *Leyte*, 211.

21. COM3RDFLT 240314, CTF77 241100, October 1944, "Graybook," 5:2242–43.

22. COM3RDFLT 210645, October 1944, "Graybook," 5:2389; Commander Third Fleet Operation Plan No. 1-44, 1 August 1944; Bates, *Leyte*, 3:337.

23. CINCPAC 211852, MacArthur 212240, COMINCH 211535, COM3RDFLT 210454, 220344, October 1944, "Graybook," 5:2389–90; Bates, *Leyte*, 3:255, 341, 563–64, 573.

24. COM3RDFLT 240314, October 1944, "Graybook," 5:2242; Bates, *Leyte*, 3:772–75.

25. Bates, *Leyte*, 3:729–33.

26. Battle Plan No. 1-44, Commander Western Pacific Task Forces, 9 September 1944, *Plans and Orders*.

27. COM3RDFLT 240612, 241124, October 1944, "Graybook," 5:2242–43; Morison, *History*, 12:195–96; Reynolds, *Fast Carriers*, 270; Potter, *Burke*, 206–7; Vego, *Leyte*, 280.

28. Vego, *Leyte*, 20, 290–91; Trent Hone, "Halsey's Decision," in *The Battle of Leyte Gulf at 75: A Retrospective*, ed. Thomas J. Cutler (Annapolis, Md.: Naval Institute Press, 2019), 81–101.

29. CINCPAC 250044, COM3RDFLT 250215, CTF77 242207, 242225, 242239, 242329, CTU77.4.3 242235, October 1944, "Graybook," 5:2246, 2250; "Memorandum for Fleet Admiral Nimitz (Personal)," 2 December 1947, *Nimitz Papers*; Vego, *Leyte*, 283.

30. COM3RDFLT 251317, October 1944, "Graybook," 5:2392–93; Nimitz to King, 28 October 1944, *Nimitz Papers*; 27 October 1944, "Graybook," 5:2115; United States Pacific Fleet and Pacific Ocean Areas Communique No. 168, "Graybook," 5:2275–78.

31. 28 October, 1, 5, 12 November 1944, Sherman 031241, November 1944, "Graybook," 5:2117, 2122, 2127, 2135, 2400; Drea, *MacArthur's Ultra*, 163.

32. 1–2 November 1944, "Graybook," 5:2122–24; Drea, *MacArthur's Ultra*, 168.

33. COM3RDFLT 110249, CINCPAC 120411, 120905, 130901, 132107, November 1944, "Graybook," 5:2284, 2403–4, 2406–7.

34. CINCSWPA 160101, CINCPOA 170200, 170240, 180935, COMINCH 171835, November 1944, "Graybook," 5:2412, 2414–17.

35. Nimitz letter to Halsey, 18 November 1944, *Nimitz Papers*.

36. Halsey 200720, CINCPOA 210935, November 1944, "Graybook," 5:2418–21.
37. COM3RDFLT 240354, 260700, CINCPOA 250015, COMINCH 251935, November 1944, "Graybook," 5:2424–26, 2433; "Minutes of Pacific Conference, 24–26 November, 1944," undated, *King Papers*.
38. 22, 25 November 1944, COM3RDFLT 260700, November 1944, "Graybook," 5:2147, 2151, 2433.
39. 23–24 November 1944, "Graybook," 5:2148–50.
40. Leighton and Coakley, *1943–1945*, 444, 448–49.
41. Leighton and Coakley, *1943–1945*, 450–51.
42. "Minutes of Pacific Conference, 24–26 November, 1944," undated, *King Papers*; Leighton and Coakley, *1943–1945*, 435–41, 460–70.
43. JCS 100345, December 1944, "Graybook," 5:2448–49; Leighton and Coakley, *1943–1945*, 556–62.
44. "Report of Conferees as to Logistic Support in the Philippine Islands for Pacific Ocean Areas Forces," 4 November 1944, *Plans and Orders*.
45. CINCSWPA 070610, HQSWPA 160017, CINCPOA 200113, November 1944, War Department 051521, December 1944, "Graybook," 5:2409–10, 2413, 2418, 2442; Leighton and Coakley, *1943–1945*, 566–67.
46. "Establishment of a Combat Logistic Support Squadron," Commander Service Force, Pacific Fleet, 20 October 1944, *Plans and Orders*, emphasis in original; "Establishment of a Combat Logistic Support Squadron," Commander Fifth Fleet, 20 October 1944, *Plans and Orders*; "Minutes of Pacific Conference, 24–26 November, 1944," undated, *King Papers*.
47. Nash, *Mobile Logistic Support*, 32.
48. "Establishment of a Combat Logistic Support Squadron," Commander Service Force, Pacific Fleet, 20 October 1944.
49. CTF77 270235, GHQSOWESPAC 271312, November 1944, "Graybook," 5:2426, 2429–30.
50. CINCPOA Operation Plan No. 9-44, 21 November 1944, *Plans and Orders*; COM3RDFLT 290400, GHQSWPA 270831, November 1944, "Graybook," 5:2431, 2433–34.
51. CINCPOA 292349, GHQSOWESPAC 301311, November 1944, "Graybook," 5:2431–32, 2435.
52. CINCPOA 030215, COMINCH 052032, December 1944, "Graybook," 5:2438–39, 2441.
53. COM3RDFLT 132305, CINCPOA 070638, CINCPAC 130650, December 1944, "Graybook," 5:2443, 2451–52; Nimitz to King, 13 December 1944, *Nimitz Papers*.
54. COM3RDFLT 150215, December 1944, "Graybook," 5:2453.
55. CINCSWPA 171101, COM3RDFLT 190222, December 1944, "Graybook," 5:2460, 2462.
56. Morison, *History*, 13:83.
57. "Lessons of Damage in Typhoon," 14CL-45, 13 February 1945, quoted in Morison, *History*, 13:86.
58. 25–26 December 1944, "Graybook," 5:2181–82.

59. CINCPAC 281408, COM3RDFLT 282150, 290045, December 1944, "Graybook," 5:2479, 2481–83, emphasis in original.
60. CTF77.2 060614, 061210, CTF77 060934, 061824, January 1945, "Graybook," 6:2943–46.
61. COM3RDFLT 052203, January 1945, "Graybook," 6:2943–45.
62. 9 January 1945, COM3RDFLT 071044, CINCSWPA 071207, CINCPOA 070312, 072207, January 1945, "Graybook," 6: 2505, 2946–49.
63. 11 January 1945, "Graybook," 6:2508.
64. CTF77 090852, COMINCH 121241, CINCPOA 121606, January 1945, "Graybook," 6:2737–38, 2958, 2960.
65. 21–26 January 1945, CINCPAC 161836, COMINCH 162220, CINCPOA 162359, COM3RDFLT 160211, 170243, 182308, 190438, January 1945, "Graybook," 6: 2522–23, 2971–72, 2974, 2985, 2987.
66. Waldo Heinrichs and Marc Gallicchio, *Implacable Foes: War in the Pacific, 1944–1945* (New York: Oxford University Press, 2017), 313–14; Drea, *MacArthur's Ultra*, 186–87.
67. Marshall 152315, December 1944, Marshall 112206, CINCSWPA 081321, CINCPOA 052306, 181814, COMGEN10THARMY 262113, January 1945, COM5THFLT 200349, CINCPAC 2105114, COMGENPOA 202209, February 1945, Richardson 031022, March 1945, "Graybook," 5:2458, 6:2779, 2955, 2959, 2984–85, 2993, 3019, 3021–22.
68. McMorris to Nimitz, 24 November 1944, *Nimitz Papers*; Richardson 230355, November 1944, CINCPOA 180736, February 1945, CINCPOA 300243, March 1945, "Graybook," 5:2422, 6:3014, 3062.
69. CINCPOA 110216, 130850, CINCPAC 161836, MacArthur 121252, 131431, 171229, COMINCH 162220, January 1945, "Graybook," 6:2956, 2963, 2965–66, 2971–72, 2981.
70. COM3RDFLT 190910, CINCPOA 181812, January 1945, CTF 77 010308, February 1945, "Graybook," 6:2744, 2983–84, 2987.
71. 27 January 1944, CINCPOA 090400, August 1944, "Graybook," 6:2339, 2525.
72. CCCH, 64–65; Reynolds, *Towers*, 497; Moore, *Spies for Nimitz*, 177.
73. CCCH, 143.
74. CINCEF 270603, July 1944, "Graybook," 5:2335; "Notes on Conference Held aboard U.S.S. Argonne at Noumea at 1300 October 2, 1942."
75. "Report to the President and Prime Minister of the Agreed Summary of Conclusions Reached by the Combined Chiefs of Staff at the 'Octagon' Conference," 16 September 1944, Octagon Conference, September 1944, *Papers and Meeting Minutes* (Office of the Combined Chiefs of Staff, 1944), 137.
76. First Sea Lord 121904, November 1944, "Graybook," 5:2405; Nimitz to King, 13 December 1944, *Nimitz Papers*; "Minutes of Pacific Conference, 24–26 November, 1944," undated, *King Papers*.
77. "Memorandum Record of Understandings Reached in Conference 17–19 December 1944 Concerning the Employment of the British Pacific Fleet," 20 December 1944, *Plans and Orders*.
78. COMINCH 131253, 131654, CINCEI 221139, December 1944, CINCBPF 152201, COMINCH 311825, CINCPAC 300615, January 1945, "Graybook," 5:2452, 2470, 6:2973, 2995–96.

79. CINCPAC 012254, COMINCH 072020, CINCBPF 120251, February 1945, "Graybook," 6:3001, 3006, 3011.
80. COMINCH 211635, CINCPAC 110045, CINCSWPA 211328, 211730, CINCPOA 270824, February 1945, "Graybook," 6:2746, 2758–59, 3022, 3027.
81. CINCPAC 192306, CINCBPF 190725, COMINCH 211635, 211650, February 1945, CINCBPF 141205, CTF113 150611, March 1945, "Graybook," 6:3016, 3022–23, 3050–51.
82. CINCPOA Operation Plan No. 11-44, 25 November 1944, *Plans and Orders*.
83. Forrestel, *Spruance*, 166; Morison, *History*, 14:16–17.
84. 21 February 1945, "Graybook," 6:2548; Moore, *Spies for Nimitz*, 176–79, 184, 188.
85. 28 January 1945, COM5THFLT 252041, January 1945, "Graybook," 6:2526, 2993.
86. "Detachment–Operations in Support of," Commander Fifth Fleet, 11 November 1944, *Plans and Orders*; 19 February 1945, COM5THFLT 182215, CINCPOA 190823, February 1945, "Graybook," 6:2544, 2751, 2753.
87. 17, 19 February 1945, CTF51 191320, February 1945, "Graybook," 6:2542, 2545, 3017–18.
88. 23–24 February 1945, CTG52.2 211238, February 1945, "Graybook," 6:2551, 2553, 3022; Morison, *History*, 14:48.
89. CINCPAC 220116, COM5THFLT 220801, February 1945, "Graybook," 6:3023.
90. CINCPAC 192308, COM5THFLT 190129, 200847, February 1945, "Graybook," 6:3015, 3018–19.
91. 26 February, 16 March 1945, CINCPAC 051246, March 1945, "Graybook," 6:2555, 2574, 2783; Heinrichs and Gallicchio, *Implacable Foes*, 281; quoted in Morison, *History*, 14:48.
92. Hughes, *Halsey*, 346–47.

## CHAPTER 10. ACHIEVING VICTORY

1. CINCPAC 250517, 25 May 1945, "Graybook," 6:3232.
2. CCS 417/8, "Operations for the Defeat of Japan 1944–45," 9 September 1944, *Octagon Conference*, 34.
3. Nimitz to King, 28 October 1944 and King to Nimitz, 8 November 1944, *Nimitz Papers*.
4. "Possible Landing in China," Commander Fifth Fleet, 18 November 1944, *Plans and Orders*.
5. "Future Operations," Commander in Chief, Pacific Ocean Areas, 21 November 1944, *Plans and Orders*.
6. "Longtom Concept," *Plans and Orders*.
7. "Minutes of Pacific Conference, 24–26 November, 1944," undated, *King Papers*.
8. "Future Operations," Commander in Chief, Pacific Ocean Areas, 24 January 1945, *Plans and Orders*.
9. JCS 062231, January 1945, "Graybook," 6:2961–62.
10. CINCPOA 031151, JCS 170349, January 1945, "Graybook," 6:2941, 2980.
11. CINCPOA 012240, February 1945, "Graybook," 6:2997.
12. "Tentative Employment of Forces, Pacific Ocean Areas," Commander in Chief Pacific Ocean Areas, 28 February 1945, *Plans and Orders*.
13. Potter, *Nimitz*, 365.

14. Richard B. Frank, *Downfall: The End of the Imperial Japanese Empire* (New York: Random House, 1999), 53–54.

15. Frank, *Downfall*, 55.

16. Frank, *Downfall*, 58–62; 29 January, 5 February 1945, "Graybook," 6:2527, 2532.

17. 9 March 1945, "Graybook," 6:2567.

18. Frank, *Downfall*, 13–14.

19. Frank, *Downfall*, 18.

20. Frank, *Downfall*, 77.

21. DEPCOMAF20 080500, 21 BOMCOM 080730, 131215, March 1945, "Graybook," 6:3040–41, 3048; Robert C. Duncan, *America's Use of Sea Mines* (Silver Spring, Md.: United States Naval Ordnance Laboratory, 1962), 148; Frank, *Downfall*, 77–79.

22. Duncan, *Sea Mines*, 156–57; Frank, *Downfall*, 77–82.

23. CINCPOA Operation Plan No. 14-44, 31 December 1944, *Plans and Orders*.

24. Commander Fifth Fleet Operation Plan No. 1-45, 3 January 1945, *Plans and Orders*; ComFirstCarTaskForPac Operation Order No. 2-45, 1 March 1945, *Plans and Orders*; COM5THFLT 020359, CTF58 050817, March 1945, "Graybook," 6:3030, 3037.

25. 13–14 February 1945, CINCPOA 280529, February 1945, CINCPOA 020152, March 1945, "Graybook," 6: 2538–39, 3028, 3066.

26. 21BOMCOM 080730, 131215, CINCSWPA 120345, CINCPOA 131621, March 1945, "Graybook," 6:3041, 3046, 3048; Craven and Cate, *The Army Air Forces*, 5:630.

27. "Report of Operations of Task Force Fifty-Eight in Support of Landings at Okinawa, 14 March through 28 May," Commander Task Force Fifty-Eight, 18 June 1945, *Action*; Morison, *History*, 14:94.

28. COM5THFLT 210128, CTF 58 202055, March 1945, "Graybook," 6:2797; "Report of Operations of Task Force Fifty-Eight in Support of Landings at Okinawa, 14 March through 28 May," Commander Task Force Fifty-Eight, 18 June 1945; 19, 22, 31 March 1945, "Graybook," 6:2576, 2578, 2589.

29. "Report of Operations of Task Force Fifty-Eight in Support of Landings at Okinawa, 14 March through 28 May," Commander Task Force Fifty-Eight, 18 June 1945; COM5THFLT 271141, March 1945, "Graybook," 6:2803; Morison, *History*, 14:112–13.

30. 28 March 1945, 1 April 1945, CINCPOA 102325, December 1944, CTG51.1 311231, March 1945, "Graybook," 5:2449, 6: 2585, 2591, 3064.

31. CINCPOA 050837, 050838, COM5THFLT 060701, COMGENFMFPAC 060125, April 1945, "Graybook," 6:3073–74; Potter, *Nimitz*, 372.

32. 8 April 1945, "Graybook," 6:2603; Moore, *Spies for Nimitz*, 207–8, 211–21; Morison, *History*, 14:93, 101.

33. "General Action Report, Capture of Okinawa Gunto, Phases I and II, 17 February to 17 May 1945–Submission of," Commander Amphibious Forces, U.S. Pacific Fleet, 25 July 1945, *Action*; 5, 6 April 1945, CTF51 062025, "Graybook," 6: 2597–98, 2821–22.

34. 7 April 1945, "Graybook," 6:2600–1; "Report of Operations of Task Force Fifty-Eight in Support of Landings at Okinawa, 14 March through 28 May," Commander Task Force Fifty-Eight, 18 June 1945.

35. CINCPAC 121215, COM5THFLT 080512, 100716, CTF58 100025, CINCPOA 090125, April 1945, "Graybook," 6:2831, 3079–80, 3201.

36. CINCPAC 142230, COM5THFLT 150100, 152357, April 1945, "Graybook," 6:2853, 2857; Craven and Cate, *The Army Air Forces*, 5:632.

37. 15, 16 April 1945, COM5THFLT 160847, CINCPAC 150806, April 1945, "Graybook," 6:2615-16, 2856, 2861.

38. CINCPOA 122310, April 1945, "Graybook," 6:3082-84.

39. Frank, *Downfall*, 27-28.

40. C.C.S. 417/8, "Operations for the Defeat of Japan 1944-45," 9 September 1944, *Octagon Conference*, 34-35.

41. Morgan, *Defeat of Japan*, 154.

42. Quoted in D. M. Giangreco, *Hell to Pay: Operation Downfall and the Invasion of Japan, 1945-1947* (Annapolis, Md.: Naval Institute Press, 2009), 200.

43. Adams, *Witness to Power*, 279.

44. JCS 032140, April 1945, "Graybook," 6:3067-68.

45. JCS 032141, CINCPAC 050226, COMINCH 091921, April 1945, "Graybook," 6:3069-70, 3078-79.

46. CINCSWPA 090526, CINCPOA 050228, CINCPAC 132346, 142242, 151406, COMINCH 141633, April 1945, "Graybook," 6:3078, 3203-5.

47. GHQSWPA 181010, CINCPOA 160250, 200344, April 1945, "Graybook," 6:3086, 3089-90, 3094.

48. Marshall 211920, MacArthur 211920, April 1945, "Graybook," 6:3211-13.

49. COMINCH 212240, CINCPOA 280235, April 1945, "Graybook," 6:3214-18.

50. CINCPOA 091155, April 1945, CINCPAC 250519, CINCPOA 170841, 170842, May 1945, "Graybook," 6:3079, 3227-29, 3233.

51. Morgan, *Defeat of Japan*, 163.

52. GHQSWPA 251102, CINCSWPA 240518, CINCPOA 241257, May 1945, "Graybook," 6:3140-42.

53. CINCPOA 250519, 260552, May 1945, "Graybook," 6:3233-34.

54. MacArthur 250538, 261442, April 1945, CINCPOA 270117, JCS 252158, May 1945, "Graybook," 6: 3098, 3101, 3143, 3145; Morgan, *Defeat of Japan*, 164-65.

55. CINCPAC 250517, May 1945, "Graybook," 6:3232.

56. CINCPAC 250517, May 1945; Frank, *Downfall*, 147.

57. DEPCOMAF20 020654, Arnold 061419, March 1945, COMGENTEN 090910, CINCPOA 100044, COM5THFLT 160834, CINPOA 181822, April 1945, "Graybook," 6:2860, 3031, 3038, 3077-80, 3207.

58. CINCPAC 240838, COMINCH 251631, CINCPOA 270423, April 1945, CINCPOA 051249, COM5THFLT 061125, COM5THFLT 061142, May 1945, "Graybook," 6:3097, 3100, 3102, 3222-24; Roy E. Appleman et al., *The War in the Pacific*, vol. 11, *Okinawa: The Last Battle*, The United States Army in World War II (Washington, D.C.: United States Army Center for Military History, 1948), 267.

59. Potter, *Nimitz*, 376.

60. CINCPOA 060821, CTF51 071230, COMGENTEN 071507, COM5THFLT 081322, May 1945, "Graybook," 6: 3110, 3113, 3115.

61. CINCPAC 290900, COMPHIBGRP3 291725, COM3RDFLT 301337, CTF31 301445, CINCPOA Pearl 312010, COMPHIBSPAC 310455, May 1945, COM5THFLT 010112, CINCPOA 011201, 011351, June 1945, "Graybook," 6: 3236-39.

62. CINCPAC 120220, May 1945, "Graybook," 6:3227–28.
63. CINCPOA 280910, COMGEN10 291012, CINCPOA 292258, May 1945, "Graybook," 6:3225–37.
64. Frank, *Downfall*, 71.
65. COMAF20 142330, June 1945, "Graybook," 6:3248.
66. Frank, *Downfall*, 134.
67. Frank, *Downfall*, 137–39.
68. "Minutes of Meeting Held at the White House on Monday, 18 June 1945 at 1530," Harry S. Truman Library, The Decision to Drop the Atomic Bomb Collection; Frank, *Downfall*, 144.
69. "Minutes of Meeting Held at the White House on Monday, 18 June 1945 at 1530"; Walter Millis with E. S. Duffield, *The Forrestal Diaries* (New York: Viking, 1951), 52–53; O'Brien, *Leahy*, 346.
70. Quoted in Frank, *Downfall*, 219, 220.
71. Frank, *Downfall*, 200–203; Moore, *Spies for Nimitz*, 225–26.
72. Frank, *Downfall*, 206–10.
73. CINCPAC 290859, May 1945, CINCPAC 061244, June 1945, "Graybook," 6:3243, 3235.
74. Morison, *History*, 14:308.
75. COM3RDFLT 060611, 140903, 160007, CINCPAC 170715, June 1945, CINCPAC 112335, July 1945, "Graybook," 6:3163, 3177–79, 3488; "Directives Concerning Destruction of Japanese Combatant Surface Ships During Current Carrier Operations," 8 July 1945; *War with Japan*, 6:214–29; Frank, *Downfall*, 157.
76. 14, 18 July 1945, COM3RDFLT 132122, 181033, July 1945, "Graybook," 7:3262, 3267, 3323, 3329.
77. CINCPAC 081520, June 1945, "Graybook," 6:3167.
78. Frank, *Downfall*, 157; Morison, *History*, 14:311–12.
79. 24 July 1945, "Graybook," 7:3274; Morison, *History*, 14:330.
80. 6, 8 August 1945, CINCPAC 300601, June 1945, "Graybook," 6:3193, 7:3290, 3292; Frank, *Downfall*, 254, 257; Tsuyoshi Hasegawa, *Racing the Enemy: Stalin, Truman, and the Surrender of Japan* (Cambridge, Mass.: The Belknap Press of Harvard University Press, 2005), 198–99.
81. OPDWAR 071535, August 1945, "Graybook," 7:3509.
82. CINCAFPAC 090443, August 1945, "Graybook," 7:3508–9.
83. CINCAFPAC 090443, August 1945.
84. Drea, *MacArthur's Ultra*, 223.
85. Frank, *Downfall*, 300.
86. COMINCH 110245, April 1945, "Graybook," 6:3202.
87. Moore, *Spies for Nimitz*, 169, 195, 213–18.
88. Bix, *Hirohito*, 509, 514–15; Hasegawa, *Racing the Enemy*, 210–14.
89. COMINCH 101135, 141916, August 1945, "Graybook," 7:3510, 3518.
90. CINCPAC 150842, August 1945, "Graybook," 7:3352.
91. *Recollections of Fleet Admiral Chester W. Nimitz, USN, as Given by Various Officers Who Served with Him in the U.S. Navy* (Annapolis, Md.: U.S. Naval Institute, 1970), Mustin–11.

92. COM3RDFLT 132145, CINCAFPAC 160249, COMFEAF 171725, COMGENUSASTAF 212250, July 1945, "Graybook," 7:3390, 3393–94, 3401.

## CONCLUSION

1. *Newport Harbor News Press*, 21 February 1966, National Museum of the Pacific War Archives.
2. Nimitz, "Thesis on Tactics" 28 April 1923.
3. Uhl-Bien et al., "Complexity Leadership Theory"; Hone, *Learning War*, 98–100.
4. Wylie, *Reminiscences*, 18–19.
5. Edmondson, *Fearless Organization*, 112.
6. Edmondson, *Fearless Organization*, 158–80.
7. This assessment of Nimitz's performance draws on the work of Edmondson as well as the author's own experience coaching individuals and teams. Edmondson, *Fearless Organization*, 158–80.
8. Max H. Boisot, Ian C. MacMillan, and Kyeong Seok Han, *Explorations in Information Space: Knowledge, Agents, and Organization* (New York: Oxford University Press, 2007), 51.
9. Vincent Davis, *The Admirals Lobby* (Chapel Hill, N.C.: The University of North Carolina Press, 1967), 40–41.
10. Anthony King, *Command: The Twenty-First Century General* (Cambridge: Cambridge University Press, 2019), 73–109.
11. McChrystal et al., *Team of Teams*, 214.
12. Davis, *The Admiral's Lobby*, 40–41.
13. Leslie J. Waguespack, *Thriving Systems Theory and Metaphor-Driven Modeling* (New York: Springer, 2010), 39–45.
14. Bradley A. Fiske, *The Art of Fighting* (New York: The Century Co., 1920), 62.
15. This description of "codification" and "abstraction" follows that in Boisot, MacMillan, and Han, *Explorations*, 87–91.
16. Boisot, MacMillan, and Han, *Explorations*, 97, 152.
17. Epstein, *Range*, 227. David Woods suggests a revision of Ashby's Law of Requisite Variety: "Only the ability to revise past answers to 'what is requisite variety' can produce future requisite variety." https://twitter.com/ddwoods2/status/1398235840 468467714?s=20. This concept is central to Boyd's OODA Loop as well. See Osinga, *Science, Strategy, and War*, 236–43.
18. Hone, *Learning War*, 323–27.
19. Murray, *War, Strategy, and Military Effectiveness*, 44.
20. Tom DeMarco, *Slack: Getting Past Burnout, Busywork, and the Myth of Total Efficiency* (New York: Broadway Books, 2001), 41; Trent Hone and Capt. Dale Rielage, USN (Ret.), "No Time for Victory," U.S. Naval Institute *Proceedings* 146, no. 5 (May 2020).
21. Frank G. Hoffman, *Mars Adapting: Military Change During War* (Annapolis, Md.: Naval Institute Press, 2021), 34, 252–61.
22. Miller, *War Plan Orange*, 86–121.
23. Quoting Peter Allen in *The Evolution of Cognitive Maps: New Paradigms for the*

*Twenty-First Century*, ed. Ervin Laszlo and Ignazio Masulli (Newark, N.J.: Gordon and Breach, 1995), 14.

24. Boisot, MacMillan, and Han, *Explorations*, 69.

25. "Doctrine (Conference), Navy Department, Washington, D.C.," 1 December 1917.

26. Martin van Creveld, *Command in War* (Cambridge, MA: Harvard University Press, 1985), 269.

27. Thomas C. Hone, *Power and Change: The Administrative History of the Office of the Chief of Naval Operations, 1946–1986* (Washington, D.C.: Naval Historical Center, 1989), 6.

28. The Constructal Law, which states that any system must "evolve . . . greater and greater access to the currents that flow through it" in order to persist, is a useful frame for understanding the importance of these flows to Nimitz's command. See Adrian Bejan and Sylvie Lorente, "The Constructal Law of Design and Evolution in Nature," *Philosophical Transactions of the Royal Society B: Biological Sciences* 365 (1545) (May 12, 2010): 1335–47.

29. Sumida, *Mahan*, xiii–xiv.

30. Richard P. Rumelt, *Good Strategy, Bad Strategy: The Difference and Why it Matters* (New York: Crown, 2011), 244–45, emphasis in original.

31. Murray, *War, Strategy, and Military Effectiveness*, 20.

32. Mustin, *Reminiscences*, 2:1192–93.

# Bibliography

Adams, Henry H. *Witness to Power: The Life of Fleet Admiral William D. Leahy*. Annapolis, Md.: Naval Institute Press, 1985.

*The "A-Go" Operations: May–Jun. 1944*. Japanese Monograph No. 90, 10 October 1947, General Headquarters, Far East Command, Military Intelligence Section, General Staff.

*The Aleutians Campaign, June 1942–August 1943*. Combat Narratives, Office of Naval Intelligence, United States Navy, 1945.

Alexander, Col. Joseph H., USMC (Ret.). *Edson's Raiders: The 1st Marine Raider Battalion in World War II*. Annapolis, Md.: Naval Institute Press, 2001.

———. *Storm Landings: Epic Amphibious Battles in the Central Pacific*. Annapolis, Md.: Naval Institute Press, 1997.

Appleman, Roy E., James M. Burns, Russell A. Gugeler, and John Stevens. *The War in the Pacific*. Vol. 11, *Okinawa: The Last Battle*. The United States Army in World War II. Washington, D.C.: United States Army Center for Military History, 1948.

Artigiani, Robert. "Chaos and Constitutionalism: Toward a Post Modern Theory of Social Evolution." *World Futures* 34 (1992): 131–56.

Ballantine, Duncan S. *U.S. Naval Logistics in the Second World War*. Princeton: Princeton University Press, 1949.

Bates, Richard W. *The Battle for Leyte Gulf, October 1944, Strategical and Tactical Analysis*. Vol. 3, *Operations from 0000 October 20th (D-Day) until 1042 October 23rd*. Naval War College, Newport, R.I.: Bureau of Naval Personnel, 1957.

———. *The Battle of Midway, Including the Aleutian Phase: June 3 to June 14, 1942, Strategical and Tactical Analysis*. Naval War College, Newport, R.I.: Bureau of Naval Personnel, 1948.

*Battle Evaluation Group Records*. Record Group 23, Naval War College Archives, Newport, R.I.

Bejan, Adrian, and Sylvie Lorente. "The Constructal Law of Design and Evolution in Nature." *Philosophical Transactions of the Royal Society B: Biological Sciences* 365 (1545) (May 12, 2010): 1335–47.

Bix, Herbert P. *Hirohito and the Making of Modern Japan*. New York: Harper Collins, 2000.

Blair, Bobby C., and John Peter DeCioccio. *Victory at Peleliu: The 81st Infantry Division's Pacific Campaign*. Norman, Okla.: University of Oklahoma Press, 2011.

Bland, Larry I., and Sharon Ritenour Stevens, ed. *The Papers of George Catlett Marshall.* Vol. 4, *"Aggressive and Determined Leadership," June 1, 1943-December 31, 1944.* Baltimore and London: The Johns Hopkins University Press, 1996.

Boisot, Max H., Ian C. MacMillan, and Kyeong Seok Han. *Explorations in Information Space: Knowledge, Agents, and Organization.* New York: Oxford University Press, 2007.

Boyd, Andrew. *British Naval Intelligence through the Twentieth Century.* Barnsley, UK: Seaforth, 2020.

———. *The Royal Navy in Eastern Waters: Linchpin of Victory, 1935–1942.* Barnsley, UK: Seaforth, 2017.

Britts, Angus. *Neglected Skies: The Demise of British Naval Power in the Far East, 1922–42.* Annapolis, Md.: Naval Institute Press, 2017.

Buell, Thomas B. *Master of Sea Power: A Biography of Fleet Admiral Ernest J. King.* Boston: Little, Brown, 1980.

———. *The Quiet Warrior: A Biography of Admiral Raymond A. Spruance.* Annapolis, Md.: Naval Institute Press, 1987.

*Building the Navy's Bases in World War II: History of the Bureau of Yards and Docks and Civil Engineer Corps, 1940–1946.* Washington, D.C.: United States Government Printing Office, 1947.

Bullard, Steven, trans. *Japanese Army Operations in the South Pacific Area: New Britain and Papua Campaigns, 1942–43.* Canberra, Australia: Australian War Memorial, 2007.

*The Campaigns of the Pacific War.* United States Strategic Bombing Survey (Pacific), Naval Analysis Division. Washington, D.C.: United States Government Printing Office, 1946.

Carlson, Elliot. *Joe Rochefort's War: The Odyssey of the Codebreaker Who Outwitted Yamamoto at Midway.* Annapolis, Md.: Naval Institute Press, 2011.

Carter, Rear Adm. Worrall Reed, USN (Ret.). *Beans, Bullets, and Black Oil.* Washington, D.C.: Department of the Navy, 1953.

*Casablanca Conference, January 1943, Papers and Meeting Minutes.* Office of the Combined Chiefs of Staff, 1943.

Chandonnet, Fern, ed. *Alaska at War: 1941–1945, The Forgotten War Remembered.* Fairbanks, Alas.: University of Alaska Press, 2008.

Clausewitz, Carl von. *On War.* Translated and edited by Michael Howard and Peter Paret. Indexed ed. Princeton, N.J.: Princeton University Press, 1984.

Coletta, Paolo E., ed. *American Secretaries of the Navy.* Vol. 1, *1775–1913.* Annapolis, Md.: Naval Institute Press, 1980.

*Commander-in-Chief, Pacific and U.S. Pacific Fleets, Microfilmed Incoming and Outgoing Dispatches and Chronological Message Traffic, 1940–45.* Record Group 313, *Records of Naval Operating Forces,* Entry (A1) 125. National Archives, Washington, D.C.

Commander-in-Chief, United States Fleet. *Current Tactical Orders and Doctrine, U.S. Fleet.* USF-10B. 1 May 1945. Microfilm: NRS 1977–44. National Archives, Washington, D.C.

*Commander-in-Chief, United States Pacific Fleet and Pacific Ocean Areas Command History, 7 December 1941–15 August 1945.* Historical Section, CINCPACFLT, Naval History and Heritage Command Library.

*Command Summary of Fleet Admiral Chester W. Nimitz, USN*, Nimitz "Graybook."

Craven, Wesley Frank, and James Lea Cate. *The Army Air Forces in World War II.* 7 vols. Washington, D.C.: Office of Air Force History, 1983. First published 1958 by University of Chicago Press.

Creveld, Martin van. *Command in War.* Cambridge, MA: Harvard University Press, 1985.

Crowl, Philip A. *The War in the Pacific.* Vol. 7, *Campaign in the Marianas.* The United States Army in World War II. Washington, D.C.: United States Army Center for Military History, 1960.

Davis, Vincent. *The Admirals Lobby.* Chapel Hill, N.C.: The University of North Carolina Press, 1967.

Dean, Peter J. *MacArthur's Coalition: US and Australian Operations in the Southwest Pacific Area, 1942–1945.* Lawrence: Kansas University Press, 2018.

DeMarco, Tom. *Slack: Getting Past Burnout, Busywork, and the Myth of Total Efficiency.* New York: Broadway Books, 2001.

Dod, Karl C. *The Technical Services.* Vol. 2, *The Corps of Engineers: The War Against Japan.* The United States Army in World War II. Washington, D.C.: United States Army Center for Military History, 1966.

Drea, Edward J. *Japan's Imperial Army: Its Rise and Fall, 1853–1945.* Lawrence: Kansas University Press, 2009.

———. *MacArthur's Ultra: Codebreaking and the War Against Japan, 1942–1945.* Lawrence: Kansas University Press, 1992.

Duncan, Robert C. *America's Use of Sea Mines.* Silver Spring, Md.: United States Naval Ordnance Laboratory, 1962.

Edmondson, Amy. *The Fearless Organization: Creating Psychological Safety in the Workplace for Learning, Innovation, and Growth.* Hoboken, N.J.: Wiley, 2019.

———. "Psychological Safety and Learning Behavior in Work Teams." *Administrative Science Quarterly* 44, no. 2 (June 1999): 350–83.

Engberg-Pedersen, Anders. *Empire of Chance: The Napoleonic Wars and the Disorder of Things.* Cambridge, Mass.: Harvard University Press, 2015.

Epstein, David. *Range: Why Generalists Triumph in a Specialized World.* New York: Riverhead Books, 2019.

Evans, David C., and Mark R. Peattie. *Kaigun: Strategy, Tactics, and Technology in the Imperial Japanese Navy, 1887–1941.* Annapolis, Md.: Naval Institute Press, 1997.

*Faculty and Staff Presentations.* Record Group 14, Naval War College Archives, Newport, R.I.

Finkel, Meir. *On Flexibility: Recovery from Technological and Doctrinal Surprise on the Battlefield.* Stanford, Calif.: Stanford Security Studies, 2011.

Fiske, Bradley A. *The Art of Fighting.* New York: The Century Co., 1920.

———. *The Navy as a Fighting Machine.* 2nd ed. Annapolis, Md.: Naval Institute Press, 1988. First published 1918 by Charles Scribner's Sons, New York.

Ford, Christopher, and David Rosenberg. *The Admirals' Advantage: U.S. Navy Operational Intelligence in World War II and the Cold War.* Annapolis, Md.: Naval Institute Press, 2005.

Forrestel, Vice Adm. E. P., USN (Ret.). *Admiral Raymond A. Spruance, USN: A Study in Command.* Washington, D.C.: Government Printing Office, 1966.

Frank, Richard B. *Downfall: The End of the Imperial Japanese Empire.* New York: Random House, 1999.

———. *Guadalcanal: The Definitive Account of the Landmark Battle.* New York: Random House, 1990.

———. *MacArthur.* New York: Palgrave Macmillan, 2007.

———. "Picking Winners." *Naval History Magazine* 25, no. 3 (June 2011): 24–32.

———. "Slaughter at Sea." *World War II Magazine* 35, no. 6 (April 2021): 28–37.

Fuquea, David C. "Advantage Japan: The Imperial Japanese Navy's Superior High Seas Refueling Capability." *Journal of Military History* 84, no. 1 (January 2020): 213–35.

Furer, Rear Adm. Julius Augustus. *Administration of the Navy Department in World War II.* Washington, D.C.: Naval History Division, 1959.

Garfield, Brian. *The Thousand-Mile War: World War II in Alaska and the Aleutians.* Fairbanks, Alas.: University of Alaska Press, 1995.

Giangreco, D. M. *Hell to Pay: Operation Downfall and the Invasion of Japan, 1945–1947.* Annapolis, Md.: Naval Institute Press, 2009.

Grauer, Ryan. *Commanding Military Power.* Cambridge: Cambridge University Press, 2016.

Hammel, Eric. *Guadalcanal: Starvation Island.* New York: Crown, 1987.

Hara, Capt. Tameichi. *Japanese Destroyer Captain: Pearl Harbor, Guadalcanal, Midway—The Great Naval Battles as Seen through Japanese Eyes.* Annapolis, Md.: Naval Institute Press, 2011.

Hasegawa, Tsuyoshi. *Racing the Enemy: Stalin, Truman, and the Surrender of Japan.* Cambridge, Mass.: The Belknap Press of Harvard University Press, 2005.

Heinrichs, Waldo, and Marc Gallicchio. *Implacable Foes: War in the Pacific, 1944–1945.* New York: Oxford University Press, 2017.

Hoffman, Frank G. *Mars Adapting: Military Change During War.* Annapolis, Md.: Naval Institute Press, 2021.

Holwitt, Joel Ira. *"Execute Against Japan": The U.S. Decision to Conduct Unrestricted Submarine Warfare.* College Station, Tex.: Texas A&M University Press, 2009.

Hone, Thomas C., ed. *The Battle of Midway: The Naval Institute's Guide to the U.S. Navy's Greatest Victory.* Annapolis, Md.: Naval Institute Press, 2013.

———. "The Effectiveness of the 'Washington Treaty' Navy." *Naval War College Review* 32, no. 6 (November-December 1979): 35–59.

———. *Power and Change: The Administrative History of the Office of the Chief of Naval Operations, 1946–1986.* Washington, D.C.: Naval Historical Center, 1989.

Hone, Trent. "Building a Doctrine: USN Tactics and Battle Plans in the Interwar Period." *International Journal of Naval History* 1, no. 2 (October 2002).

———. "The Evolution of Fleet Tactical Doctrine in the U.S. Navy, 1922–1941." *Journal of Military History* 67, no. 4 (October 2003): 1107–48.

———. "'Give Them Hell!': The U.S. Navy's Night Combat Doctrine and the Campaign for Guadalcanal." *War in History* 13, no. 2 (April 2006): 171–99.

———. "Halsey's Decision." In *The Battle of Leyte Gulf at 75: A Retrospective*, edited by Thomas J. Cutler, 81–101. Annapolis, Md.: Naval Institute Press, 2019.

———. *Learning War: The Evolution of Fighting Doctrine in the U.S. Navy, 1898–1945.* Annapolis, Md.: Naval Institute Press, 2018.

———. "Triumph of U.S. Navy Night Fighting." *Naval History* 20, no. 5 (October 2006): 54–59.

———. "U.S. Navy Surface Battle Doctrine and Victory in the Pacific." *Naval War College Review* 62, no. 1 (Winter 2009): 67–105.

Hone, Trent, and Capt. Dale Rielage, USN (Ret.). "No Time for Victory." U.S. Naval Institute *Proceedings* 146, no. 5 (May 2020).

Hornfischer, James D. *Neptune's Inferno: The U.S. Navy at Guadalcanal*. New York: Random House, 2011.

Hough, Major Frank O., USMCR. *The Assault on Peleliu*. Historical Division, Headquarters, U.S. Marine Corps, 1950.

Hughes, Thomas Alexander. *Admiral Bill Halsey: A Naval Life*. Cambridge, Mass.: Harvard University Press, 2016.

Hughes, Capt. Wayne P., Jr., USN (Ret.), and Rear Adm. Robert P. Girrier, USN (Ret.). *Fleet Tactics and Naval Operations*. 3rd ed. Annapolis, Md.: Naval Institute Press, 2018.

*Individual Personnel Files*, Naval History and Heritage Command, World War II Command File.

Intelligence and Technical Archives. Record Group 8, Naval War College Archives, Newport, R.I.

Juarrero, Alicia. *Dynamics in Action: Intentional Behavior as a Complex System*. Cambridge, Mass.: MIT Press, 1999.

Judge, Sean M. *The Turn of the Tide in the Pacific War: Strategic Initiative, Intelligence, and Command, 1941–1943*. Lawrence: Kansas University Press, 2018.

Keegan, John. *The Mask of Command*. New York: Penguin Books, 1988.

King, Anthony. *Command: The Twenty-First Century General*. Cambridge: Cambridge University Press, 2019.

Koshiro, Yukiko. *Imperial Eclipse: Japan's Strategic Thinking about Continental Asia before August 1945*. Ithaca and London: Cornell University Press, 2013.

Kuehn, John T. *Agents of Innovation: The General Board and the Design of the Fleet that Defeated the Japanese Navy*. Annapolis, Md.: Naval Institute Press, 2008.

Lamar, Cdr. H. Arthur, USN (Ret.). *I Saw Stars*. Fredericksburg, Tex.: The Admiral Nimitz Foundation, 1985.

Laszlo, Ervin, and Ignazio Masulli, eds. *The Evolution of Cognitive Maps: New Paradigms for the Twenty-First Century*. Newark, N.J.: Gordon and Breach, 1995.

Layton, Rear Adm. Edwin T., USN (Ret.), with Capt. Roger Pineau, USNR (Ret.) and John Costello. *"And I Was There": Pearl Harbor and Midway–Breaking the Secrets*. Annapolis, Md.: Naval Institute Press, 1985.

Leighton, Richard M., and Robert W. Coakley. *The War Department*. Vol. 5, *Global Logistics and Strategy, 1940–1943*. The United States Army in World War II. Washington, D.C.: United States Army Center for Military History, 1955.

———. *The War Department*. Vol. 6, *Global Logistics and Strategy, 1943–1945*. The United States Army in World War II. Washington, D.C.: United States Army Center for Military History, 1968.

Lilly, Capt. Michael A., USN (Ret.). *Nimitz at Ease*. Apache Junction, Ariz.: Stairway Press, 2019.

Lundstrom, John B. *Black Shoe Carrier Admiral.* Annapolis, Md.: Naval Institute Press, 2006.

———. *The First Team: Pacific Naval Air Combat from Pearl Harbor to Midway.* Annapolis, Md.: Naval Institute Press, 1984.

———. *The First Team and the Guadalcanal Campaign.* Annapolis, Md.: Naval Institute Press, 1994.

Mansoor, Peter. "Luzon versus Formosa: A Decision Revisited." Paper presented at the Annual Meeting of the Society for Military History, Norfolk, Va., 22 May 2021.

Marolda, Edward J., ed. *FDR and the U.S. Navy.* New York: St. Martin's Press, 1998.

Matloff, Maurice. *The War Department.* Vol. 4, *Strategic Planning for Coalition Warfare: 1943–1944.* The United States Army in World War II. Washington, D.C.: United States Army Center for Military History, 1959.

Matloff, Maurice, and Edwin M. Snell. *The War Department.* Vol. 3, *Strategic Planning for Coalition Warfare: 1941–1942.* The United States Army in World War II. Washington, D.C.: United States Army Center for Military History, 1953.

McChrystal, Gen. Stanley, with Tantum Collins, David Silverman, and Chris Fussell. *Team of Teams: New Rules of Engagement for a Complex World.* New York: Penguin, 2015.

Medeiros, Maj. John L., USMC. "Strategic and Operational Importance of Peleliu During the Pacific War." Master's thesis, United States Marine Corps Command and Staff College, Quantico, Va., March 2010.

Merillat, Herbert Laing. *The Island: A History of the First Marine Division on Guadalcanal.* Boston: Houghton Mifflin, 1944.

Miller, Adah-Marie R., "Fleet Admiral Chester W. Nimitz, U.S.N., A Speculative Study (A Psycho-Biographical Quest for Qualities of Leadership)." Master's thesis, University of Texas, August 1962, National Museum of the Pacific War Archives.

Miller, Edward S. "Kimmel's Hidden Agenda." *Military History Quarterly* 4, no. 1 (1991): 36–43.

———. *War Plan Orange: The U.S. Strategy to Defeat Japan: 1897–1945.* Annapolis, Md.: Naval Institute Press, 1991.

Miller, John, Jr. *The War in the Pacific.* Vol. 5, *Cartwheel: The Reduction of Rabaul.* The United States Army in World War II. Washington, D.C.: United States Army Center for Military History, 1959.

Millis, Walter, with E. S. Duffield. *The Forrestal Diaries.* New York: Viking, 1951.

Mitter, Rana. *Forgotten Ally: China's World War II, 1937–1945.* New York: Mariner Books, 2014.

Moore, Jeffrey M. *Spies for Nimitz: Joint Military Intelligence in the Pacific War.* Annapolis, Md.: Naval Institute Press, 2004.

Morgan, Lt. Col. Henry G., Jr. *Planning the Defeat of Japan: A Study of Total War Strategy.* Washington, D.C.: Office of the Chief of Military History, 1961.

Morison, Samuel Eliot. *History of the United States Naval Operations in World War II.* 15 vols. Boston: Little, Brown, 1984. First published 1962.

Morton, Louis. *The War in the Pacific.* Vol. 1, *Strategy and Command: The First Two Years.* The United States Army in World War II. Washington, D.C.: United States Army Center for Military History, 1962.

Mossio, Matteo, Leonardo Bich, and Alvaro Moreno. "Emergence, Closure and Inter-Level Causation in Biological Systems." *Erkenntnis* 78 (2013): 153–78.

Murray, Williamson. *War, Strategy, and Military Effectiveness*. New York: Cambridge University Press, 2011.

Mustin, Vice Adm. Lloyd M. *The Reminiscences of Vice Admiral Lloyd M. Mustin*. Interviewed by John T. Mason Jr. 2 vols. Annapolis, Md.: U.S. Naval Institute, 2003.

Nash, Peter V. *The Development of Mobile Logistic Support in Anglo-American Naval Policy, 1900–1953*. Gainesville, Fla.: University Press of Florida, 2009.

Newpower, Anthony. *Iron Men and Tin Fish: The Race to Build a Better Torpedo During World War II*. Annapolis, Md.: Naval Institute Press, 2006.

Nolan, Cathal J. *The Allure of Battle: A History of How Wars Have Been Won and Lost*. New York: Oxford University Press, 2017.

O'Brien, Phillips Payson. *The Second Most Powerful Man in the World: The Life of Admiral William D. Leahy, Roosevelt's Chief of Staff*. New York: Dutton, 2019.

*Octagon Conference, September 1944, Papers and Meeting Minutes*. Office of the Combined Chiefs of Staff, 1944.

*Operational Experience of Fast Carrier Task Forces in World War II*. Weapons Systems Evaluation Group, WSEG Staff Study No. 4. Washington, D.C.: Office of the Secretary of Defense, 15 August 1951.

Osinga, Frans P. B. *Science, Strategy, and War: The Strategic Theory of John Boyd*. New York: Routledge, 2007.

*Outline of Operations of the Navy's South Seas Force*. Japanese Monograph No. 139, July 1949, Japanese Research Division, Military History Section, Headquarters, United States Army Forces, Far East.

*Papers of Adm. Chester W. Nimitz, USN*. Manuscript Collection 334, Naval War College Archives, Newport, R.I.

*Papers of Fleet Admiral Chester W. Nimitz, USN*. Manuscript Collection 505, Naval History and Heritage Command Operational Archives, Washington, D.C.

*Papers of Fleet Admiral Ernest J. King, USN*. Manuscript Collection 28, Naval History and Heritage Command Operational Archives, Washington, D.C.

*Papers of Rear Adm. Edwin T. Layton, USN*. Manuscript Collection 69, Naval War College Archives, Newport, R.I.

*Papers of Rear Adm. Henry E. Eccles, USN*. Manuscript Collection 52, Naval War College Archives, Newport, R.I.

Parshall, Jonathan, and Anthony Tully. *Shattered Sword: The Untold Story of the Battle of Midway*. Washington, D.C.: Potomac Books, 2005.

Peattie, Mark R. *Sunburst: The Rise of Japanese Naval Air Power, 1909–1941*. Annapolis, Md.: Naval Institute Press, 2001.

Potter, E. B. *Admiral Arleigh Burke*. Annapolis, Md.: Naval Institute Press, 1990.

———. *Nimitz*. Annapolis, Md.: Naval Institute Press, 1976.

Prados, John. *Combined Fleet Decoded: The Secret History of American Intelligence and the Japanese Navy in World War II*. New York: Random House, 1995.

———. *Islands of Destiny: The Solomons Campaign and the Eclipse of the Rising Sun*. New York: NAL Caliber, 2012.

Pratt, Fletcher. *Fleet Against Japan*. New York: Harper & Brothers, 1946.

Pye, W. S. *The Service of Information and Security*. Washington, D.C.: Government Printing Office, 1916.

*Quadrant Conference, August 1943: Papers and Minutes of Meetings*. Office of the Combined Chiefs of Staff, 1943.

*Recollections of Fleet Admiral Chester W. Nimitz as Given by Admirals Drake, Fife & Layton and Captain Lamar*. Annapolis, Md.: U.S. Naval Institute, 1970.

*Recollections of Fleet Admiral Chester W. Nimitz, USN, as Given by Various Officers Who Served with Him in the U.S. Navy*. Annapolis, Md.: U.S. Naval Institute, 1970.

*Records of the CNO Headquarters*. Records of the Office of the Chief of Naval Operations, Record Group 38, National Archives, Washington, D.C.

Remmelink, Willem, trans. and ed. *The Operations of the Navy in the Dutch East Indies and the Bay of Bengal*. Leiden: Leiden University Press, 2018.

*Reports of General MacArthur*. Vol. 1, *The Campaigns of MacArthur in the Pacific*. Washington, D.C.: United States Army Center for Military History, reprint 1994.

"Research on Striking Force Tactics, Yokosuka Naval Air Group." 20 May 1943. CINCPAC-CINCPOA Item No. 9718, JICPOA Lithographic Dept. Copy provided to author by David Dickson.

Reynolds, Clark G. *Admiral John H. Towers: The Struggle for Naval Air Supremacy*. Annapolis, Md.: Naval Institute Press, 1991.

———. *The Fast Carriers: The Forging of an Air Navy*. Annapolis, Md.: Naval Institute Press, 1992.

Rumelt, Richard P. *Good Strategy, Bad Strategy: The Difference and Why It Matters*. New York: Crown, 2011.

Sawyer, Keith. *Group Genius: The Creative Power of Collaboration*. Rev. ed. New York: Basic Books, 2017.

Schlesinger, Arthur Meier. *The Cycles of American History*. Boston: Houghton Mifflin, 1986.

*Secret Information Bulletin No. 1: Battle Experience from Pearl Harbor to Midway, December 1941 to June 1942, Including Makin Island Raid 17–18 August*. United States Fleet, Headquarters of the Commander in Chief, 15 February 1943.

*Secret Information Bulletin No. 12: Battle Experience Solomon Islands and Alaskan Areas, July–October 1943*. United States Fleet, Headquarters of the Commander in Chief, 12 February 1944.

*Sextant Conference, November-December 1943, Papers and Meeting Minutes*. Office of the Combined Chiefs of Staff, 1943.

Sherrod, Robert. *History of Marine Corps Aviation in World War II*. Baltimore, Md.: The Nautical & Aviation Publishing Co. of America, 1987.

Simpson, B. Mitchell, III. *Admiral Harold R. Stark: Architect of Victory*. Columbia: University of South Carolina Press, 1989.

Sledge, E. B. *With the Old Breed: At Peleliu and Okinawa*. New York: Presidio Press, 2007.

Smith, Peter C. *Pedestal: The Convoy that Saved Malta*. 4th ed. Manchester, UK: Crecy Publishing, 1999.

Smith, Robert Ross. "Luzon Versus Formosa." In *Command Decisions*, ed. by Kent Roberts Greenfield, 461–77. Washington, D.C.: United States Army Center for Military History, 1990.

———. *The War in the Pacific*. Vol. 8, *The Approach to the Philippines*. The United States Army in World War II. Washington, D.C.: United States Army Center for Military History, reprint 1996.

Snowden, David J., and Mary E. Boone. "A Leader's Framework for Decision Making." *Harvard Business Review*, November 2007.

*Sound Military Decision*. Annapolis, Md.: Naval Institute Press, 1942.

*Sound Military Decision, including the Estimate of the Situation and the Formulation of Directives*. Newport, R.I.: Naval War College, 1938.

*Strategic Plans Division Records*. Record Group 38, Records of the Office of the Chief of Naval Operations, National Archives, Washington, D.C.

*Student Papers*. Record Group 13, Naval War College Archives, Newport, R.I.

Sumida, Jon Tetsuro. *Decoding Clausewitz: A New Approach to* On War. Lawrence: University Press of Kansas, 2008.

———. *Inventing Grand Strategy and Teaching Command: The Classic Works of Alfred Thayer Mahan Reconsidered*. Washington, D.C.: Woodrow Wilson Center Press, 1997.

Taylor, Theodore. *The Magnificent Mitscher*. Annapolis, Md.: Naval Institute Press, 1991.

*Trident Conference, May 1943: Papers and Minutes of Meetings*. Office of the Combined Chiefs of Staff, 1943.

Trimble, William F. *Admiral John S. McCain and the Triumph of Naval Air Power*. Annapolis, Md.: Naval Institute Press, 2019.

Turner, Jobie. *Feeding Victory: Innovative Military Logistics from Lake George to Khe Sahn*. Lawrence: University Press of Kansas, 2020.

Ugaki, Matome. *Fading Victory: The Diary of Admiral Matome Ugaki, 1941–1945*. Edited by Donald M. Goldstein and Katherine V. Dillon, translated by Masataka Chihaya. Annapolis, Md.: Naval Institute Press, 2008.

Uhl-Bien, Mary, Russ Marion, and Bill McKelvey. "Complexity Leadership Theory: Shifting Leadership from the Industrial Age to the Modern Era." *The Leadership Quarterly* 18 (2007): 298–318.

Urwin, Gregory J. W. *Facing Fearful Odds: The Siege of Wake Island*. Lincoln: University of Nebraska Press, 1997.

*U.S. Navy and Related Operational, Tactical, and Instructional Publications*. Entry 337, Record Group 38, Records of the Office of the Chief of Naval Operations. National Archives, Washington, D.C.

*U.S. Navy Technical Publications*. Entry 336A, Record Group 38, Records of the Office of the Chief of Naval Operations. National Archives, Washington, D.C.

Vego, Milan. *The Battle for Leyte, 1944: Allied and Japanese Plans, Preparation, and Execution*. Annapolis, Md.: Naval Institute Press, 2006.

———. *Major Fleet-versus-Fleet Operations in the Pacific War, 1941–1945*. 2nd ed. Newport, R.I.: Naval War College Press, 2016.

Waguespack, Leslie J. *Thriving Systems Theory and Metaphor-Driven Modeling*. New York: Springer, 2010.

*War with Japan*. 6 vols. Ministry of Defense (Navy). London: HMSO, 1995.

Wheeler, Gerald E. *Kinkaid of the Seventh Fleet: A Biography of Admiral Thomas C. Kinkaid, U.S. Navy*. Annapolis, Md.: Naval Institute Press, 1996.

Wildenberg, Thomas. *Gray Steel and Black Oil: Fast Tankers and Replenishment at Sea in the U.S. Navy, 1912–1992.* Annapolis, Md.: Naval Institute Press, 1996.

Willmott, H. P. *The Barrier and the Javelin: Japanese and Allied Pacific Strategies February to June 1942.* Annapolis, Md.: Naval Institute Press, 1983.

———. *Empires in the Balance: Japanese and Allied Pacific Strategies to April 1942.* Annapolis, Md.: Naval Institute Press, 1982.

Wolters, Timothy S. *Information at Sea: Shipboard Command and Control in the U.S. Navy, from Mobile Bay to Okinawa.* Baltimore, Md.: Johns Hopkins University Press, 2013.

Woods, David D. "Four Concepts for Resilience and the Implications for the Future of Resilience Engineering." *Reliability Engineering and System Safety* 141 (2015): 5–9. http://dx.doi.org/10.1016/j.ress.2015.03.018.

———. "The Theory of Graceful Extensibility: Basic Rules that Govern Adaptive Systems." *Environment Systems and Decisions* (2018). http://doi.org/10.1007/s10669-018-9708-3.

Woolley, Anita Williams, Ishani Aggarwal, and Thomas W. Malone. "Collective Intelligence and Group Performance." *Current Directions in Psychological Science* 24 (6): 420–24.

Woolley, Anita Williams, Christopher F. Chabris, Alex Pentland, Nada Hashmi, and Thomas W. Malone. "Evidence for a Collective Intelligence Factor in the Performance of Human Groups." *Science* 330 (29 October 2010): 686–88.

*World War II Action and Operational Reports.* Record Group 38, Records of the Office of the Chief of Naval Operations. National Archives, Washington, D.C.

*World War II Bates-Leyte Collection.* Record Group 38, Records of the Office of the Chief of Naval Operations. National Archives, Washington, D.C.

*World War II Command File.* Naval History and Heritage Command Operational Archives, Washington, D.C.

*World War II Plans, Orders, and Related Documents.* Record Group 38, Records of the Office of the Chief of Naval Operations. National Archives, Washington, D.C.

*World War II War Diaries.* Record Group 38, Records of the Office of the Chief of Naval Operations. National Archives, Washington, D.C.

Wylie, Rear Adm. Joseph C. *Military Strategy: A General Theory of Power Control.* Annapolis, Md.: Naval Institute Press, 1989. First published 1967 by Rutgers University Press, New Brunswick, N.J.

———. *The Reminiscences of Rear Admiral Joseph C. Wylie Jr.* Interview by Paul Stillwell. Annapolis, Md.: U.S. Naval Institute, 2003.

Yellen, Jeremy A. *The Greater East Asia Co-Prosperity Sphere: When Total Empire Met Total War.* Ithaca, N.Y.: Cornell University Press, 2019.

# Index

# About the Author

**Trent Hone** is an authority on the U.S. Navy of the early twentieth century and a leader in the application of complexity science to organizational design. He studied religion and archaeology at Carleton College in Northfield, Minnesota, and works as a consultant helping a variety of organizations improve their processes and techniques. Hone regularly writes and speaks about leadership, sensemaking, organizational learning, and complexity. His talents are uniquely suited to integrate the history of the Navy with modern management theories, generating new insights relevant to both disciplines.

The **Naval Institute Press** is the book-publishing arm of the U.S. Naval Institute, a private, nonprofit, membership society for sea service professionals and others who share an interest in naval and maritime affairs. Established in 1873 at the U.S. Naval Academy in Annapolis, Maryland, where its offices remain today, the Naval Institute has members worldwide.

Members of the Naval Institute support the education programs of the society and receive the influential monthly magazine *Proceedings* or the colorful bimonthly magazine *Naval History* and discounts on fine nautical prints and on ship and aircraft photos. They also have access to the transcripts of the Institute's Oral History Program and get discounted admission to any of the Institute-sponsored seminars offered around the country.

The Naval Institute's book-publishing program, begun in 1898 with basic guides to naval practices, has broadened its scope to include books of more general interest. Now the Naval Institute Press publishes about seventy titles each year, ranging from how-to books on boating and navigation to battle histories, biographies, ship and aircraft guides, and novels. Institute members receive significant discounts on the Press' more than eight hundred books in print.

Full-time students are eligible for special half-price membership rates. Life memberships are also available.

For more information about Naval Institute Press books that are currently available, visit www.usni.org/press/books. To learn about joining the U.S. Naval Institute, please write to:

Member Services
**U.S. Naval Institute**
291 Wood Road
Annapolis, MD 21402-5034
Telephone: (800) 233-8764
Fax: (410) 571-1703
Web address: www.usni.org